THE COMPLEAT MOZART

The Mozart Family. Painting by Johann Nepomuk della Croce, Winter, 1780–81.

Mozart, age 24, is shown playing four-hands at the fortepiano with his sister, Maria Anna (Nannerl), age 29, while their father Leopold exhibits his violin and bow, his quill and ink pots, signifying his importance as a performer on, composer for, and teacher of that instrument. On the wall, center, hangs a portrait of Mozart's mother, Maria Anna née Pertl, who had died two years earlier in Paris. In the niche on the right a classical statue of Apollo, god of music and poetry playing his lyre, presides over the family.

THE COMPLEAT
MOZART

A Guide to the Musical Works of Wolfgang Amadeus Mozart

Edited by NEAL ZASLAW

with WILLIAM COWDERY

Mozart Bicentennial at Lincoln Center

AND

W · W · Norton & Company / New York · London

Printed in the United States of America.
The text of this book is composed in 10.5/12 Bembo Linotron 202,
with the display set in Snell Roundhand and Bembo.
Composition and manufacturing by The Maple-Vail Book Manufacturing Group.
Book design by Margaret M. Wagner

Library of Congress Cataloging in Publication Data
Zaslaw, Neal Alexander, 1939–
The compleat Mozart : a guide to the musical works of Wolfgang
Amadeus Mozart / edited by Neal Zaslaw with William Cowdery.
p. cm.
1. Mozart, Wolfgang Amadeus, 1756–1791—Criticism and
interpretation. I. Cowdery, William. II. Title.
MT145.M7Z4 1990
780'.92—dc20 90-30833

ISBN 0-393-02886-0

W. W. Norton & Company, Inc.
500 Fifth Avenue, New York, N.Y. 10110
W. W. Norton & Company, Ltd.
10 Coptic Street, London WC1A 1PU

4 5 6 7 8 9 0

Contents

Introduction

In assembling and editing this collection of essays, my hope was to share with a broad audience some of the enjoyment and sense of discovery I have experienced in studying, teaching, writing about, and performing Mozart's music. In particular, I will regard this book a success if it encourages performers and listeners to explore some of the riches to be discovered when one ventures off the straight-and-narrow path represented by Mozart's works (fewer than a hundred) found in the regular concert and opera repertory.

There are, for instance, dozens of pieces from Mozart's last decade that are seldom heard. And hundreds of others from the 1770s also await proper recognition; for example, the Salzburg divertimentos and serenades, the operas, and the church music, are often undervalued. In a previous generation, when eighteenth-century music was represented by a handful of "masterpieces" by Bach, Handel, Haydn, and Mozart, this undervaluation may have been inevitable. Nowadays, however, when one can hear convincing performances of most of the music of those four famous men as well as music by dozens of their contemporaries, the means for understanding, appreciating, and reveling in "all" of Mozart's music are finally at hand.

A few words about the genesis of this "compleat" Mozart guide: in the winter of 1988 Nathan Leventhal, President of Lincoln Center for the Performing Arts, Inc., Joseph Polisi, President of The Juilliard School, Albert K. Webster, Executive Vice President and Managing Director of the New York Philharmonic, and William W. Lockwood, Jr., Executive Producer, Programming, for Lincoln Center for the Performing Arts, Inc., met to discuss how Lincoln Center's constituent organizations (The Metropolitan Opera, New York Philharmonic, The Juilliard School, New York City Ballet, New York City Opera, The Film Society of Lincoln Center, The Chamber Music Society of Lincoln Center, Lincoln Center Theater, School of American Ballet, The New York Public Library at Lincoln Center, and Lincoln Center for the Performing Arts, Inc.) might commemorate the 200th anniversary of Mozart's death. I was among the Mozarteans invited to that meeting to make comments and suggestions. One of the ideas that was eventually adopted was to perform all of Mozart's music during the bicentennial year. Subsequently, the heads of all of Lincoln Center's constituent organizations joined the project, and I was asked to serve as consultant and musicological adviser.

The first problem was to define *all* in the phrase "all of Mozart's music," for in addition to the large number of unquestionably genuine works by Mozart, there are many others whose status remains uncertain. The latter category includes works lacking authentic sources whose attribution to Mozart may be questioned; works that Mozart never completed; additional versions of works that exist in two or more authentic versions; recently discovered works whose provenance has yet to be clarified; and works of other composers arranged by Mozart. To deal with these and other germane matters, I worked with Fiona Morgan Fein, who had been appointed to coordinate the Mozart Bicentennial at Lincoln Center.

The result of our efforts was the "Mozart Bicentennial at Lincoln Center for the Performing Arts: Repertoire Database," which, because it drew on the latest research, is more complete, accurate, and up-to-date than comparable lists found in such standard references as the sixth edition of the Köchel Catalogue, the *New Grove Dictionary of Music and Musicians,* and the new complete works edition *(Neue Mozart-Ausgabe).*

The trickiest aspect of creating the "Mozart Database" was deciding which pieces to include. After considerable discussion and some trial and error, the following guidelines were established: in addition to the unquestionably genuine works we would include (1) incomplete works with completed movements (for instance, the unfinished opera *L'oca del Cairo,* K. 422, with its seven completed numbers); (2) fragmentary works completed soon after Mozart's death by former pupils or other members of his immediate circle (which meant that we did not have to exclude the Requiem!); (3) recently discovered works of uncertain status (the Symphony in A minor, K. 16a, was eliminated as probably spurious, but the wind octet arrangement of *Die Entführung aus dem Serail* was included on grounds that a shrewd case had been made for the possibility of its genuineness); (4) second and third versions of Mozart's works made by Mozart himself.

Excluded from the canon were questionable and spurious works and Mozart's arrangements of other composers' works (including such items as his reorchestration of Handel's *Messiah*). The only exceptions to the last category were the seven early pastiche concertos for keyboard and chamber ensemble, K. 37, 39, 40, 41, and 107, based on movements of keyboard sonatas from the 1760s by J. C. Bach and others; these were included on the grounds that they are not merely mechanical arrangements or orchestrations, but new compositions in a genre different from their models. The total number of Mozart's compositions according to this way of reckoning (but not counting authentic second versions) proves to be more than 800.

As Lincoln Center's plan to perform "all" of Mozart developed, a committee was formed to discuss what sorts of publications would prove useful in support of this sprawling effort. In addition to the predictable programs, calendars, posters, and the like, I suggested a collection of historical essays for "all" of Mozart's music (as defined above). This would be a solid but accessible reference book for the music lover who wants to be able to look up any piece by Mozart before or after listening to it and to find an accurate, up-to-the-minute description of the work and what is known about it. Thus, a brief, readable essay about each work listed in the "Mozart Database" will be found in the current volume, prefaced by a headnote containing the information that would most interest Mozart lovers.

As this volume had to be assembled expeditiously if it was to be ready for 1991, I asked my former student, the musicologist-harpsichordist William Cowdery, to assist me in locating and editing suitable materials and in organizing the book, all of which he did with great efficiency.

The essays themselves have been chosen for their pertinency, their readability, and their avoidance of both technical jargon and that main curse of writings about music for non-professionals: purple prose. The majority of the essays were originally written to accompany recordings, but others come from books, articles, or concert programs (and several have been written specially for this collection by William Cowdery or the undersigned). All of them have been edited to suit their new context.

The editors would like to thank Claire Brook and Juli Goldfein of W. W. Norton & Company for their efficiency and professionalism in seeing this volume through the press, Fiona Morgan Fein of the Mozart Bicentennial at Lincoln Center and Lauren Cowdery for invaluable editorial suggestions and proofreading, and Jane Marsh Dieckmann for making the index.

NEAL ZASLAW
Ithaca, New York
January 1990

Acknowledgments

Unless otherwise indicated, all notes are reproduced by permission of their authors.

All notes by Rudolf Angermüller are from *Mozart's Operas* by Rudolf Angermüller, published in 1988 by Rizzoli, New York.

All notes by Alfred Beaujean and Graham Dixon are reprinted courtesy of Philips Classics Productions, a division of PolyGram International Music B.V.

All notes by Charles Cudworth are reprinted by kind permission of Mrs. F. H. Cudworth.

All notes by Sibylle Dahms are reprinted courtesy of the Internationale Stiftung Mozarteum.

All notes by Karl Gustav Fellerer are reprinted by kind permission of his daughters, Inamaria Richartz and Gisemar Corsten.

The note by Marius Flothuis on Köchel number 439b is reprinted courtesy of Bärenreiter-Verlag and Foreign Music Distributors, Sole U.S. Agent.

The notes by Marius Flothuis on the eighteen violin sonatas are reprinted courtesy of The Decca Record Company Limited.

All notes by Sir William Glock are reprinted courtesy of Sony Classical USA, a unit of CBS Records Inc.

The note by Harry Halbreich is reprinted courtesy of Vox-Turnabout, The Moss Music Group Division of Essex Entertainment.

Notes by H. C. Robbins Landon on Köchel numbers 174, 406, 423, 424, 515, 516, 593, and 614 are reprinted courtesy of Time-Life Music, a division of Time-Life Books, Inc.

All notes by Ernst Fritz Schmid are reprinted by kind permission of Deutsche Grammophon Gesellschaft / Archiv Produktion.

The Introduction and all notes by Neal Zaslaw on the ten concertos and concerto movements for strings are reprinted courtesy of Time-Life Music, a division of Time-Life Books, Inc.

All notes by the following authors are reprinted courtesy of Time-Life Music, a division of Time-Life Books, Inc.: David Hamilton, Roger Hellyer, Alan M, Kriegsman, William S. Mann, Christopher Porterfield, Andrew Raeburn, Christopher Raeburn, Denis Stevens, and Charles Suttoni.

Terms and Abbreviations

Köchel Numbers

See Appendix A for a description of the Köchel Catalogue and its system of assigning numbers.

Whenever possible, *The Compleat Mozart* cites a given composition of Mozart by the chronological number it received in the original edition of the Köchel Catalogue (K^1). If the composition bears a different number in K^6 (the most recent edition of the Köchel Catalogue), the number is given in parentheses following the title of the composition. For example,

K. 165 ***Exsultate, jubilate, in F major (K⁶ 158a)***
K. 492 ***Le nozze di Figaro***

If the composition has ever borne a different number in any intermediate edition of the Köchel Catalogue, that number is also given in parentheses. For example,

K. 139 ***Missa solemnis in C minor, "Waisenhaus" (K^3 114a, K^6 47a)***

If the composition did not appear in K^1, or if it appeared only in the Appendix of the Köchel Catalogue (the *Anhang,* commonly abbreviated *Anh*) where numbers do not follow chronology, it is cited in *The Compleat Mozart* by the first chronological number it received in later editions. For example,

K^3 45a ***Symphony in G major, "Lambach" (K^1 Anh 221)***

In the course of the text, however, the "Lambach" Symphony may be referred to simply as K. 45a, without the special prefix K^3.

- K^1 L. von Köchel, *Chronologisch-thematisches Verzeichnis der Werke W. A. Mozarts* (Leipzig, 1862).
- K^2 L. von Köchel, *Chronologisch-thematisches Verzeichnis der Werke W. A. Mozarts,* 2nd edn. by P. von Waldersee (Leipzig, 1905).
- K^3 L. von Köchel, *Chronologisch-thematisches Verzeichnis der Werke W. A. Mozarts,* 3rd edn. by A. Einstein (Leipzig, 1937).
- K^{3a} L. von Köchel, *Chronologisch-thematisches Verzeichnis der Werke W. A. Mozarts,* repr. of 3rd edn. with supplement by A. Einstein (Ann Arbor, 1947).
- K^6 L. von Köchel, *Chronologisch-thematisches Verzeichnis sämtlicher Tonwerke Wolfgang Amadé Mozarts*

nebst Angabe der verlorengegangenen, angefangenen, von fremder Hand bearbeiteten, zweifelhaften und unterschobenen Kompositionen, 6th edn. by F. Giegling, A. Weinmann, and G. Sievers (Wiesbaden, 1964).

K. deest This indicates a work by (or attributed to) Mozart that does not appear in any edition of the Köchel Catalogue. It is a form of the Latin verb *deesse,* which means "to be not present."

* (asterisk) In *The Compleat Mozart,* this symbol indicates that Mozart derived the work in question from an earlier composition, and that the derived work has no independent number in the Köchel Catalogue. For example, Mozart derived the Symphony in D major, numbered K. *135 in *The Compleat Mozart,* from the Overture to the opera *Lucio Silla,* K. 135. Similarly, Mozart derived both a Symphony in D major and a Sinfonia concertante in G major, both here numbered K. *320 from the "Post Horn" Serenade, K. 320.

basso The Italian word for "bass," it can mean a low man's voice, an instrument that plays in the bass register (the cello, for instance), or the lowest sounding line of a musical composition. In the last sense, it is sometimes also a shortened version of the more or less synonymous *basso continuo* (literally "continuous bass" or, in English, thoroughbass). Mozart nearly always labeled the lowest sounding line of his scores either *basso* in Italian or *Bass* in German. These terms designated not a particular instrument or instruments, but the harmonic-structural bottom line of a musical composition. Which instruments realized that line depended to a great extent on the genre of the music in question. It could be just a cello (as in much chamber music); or just a double bass (as in many divertimentos and perhaps some orchestral music as well); or a cello plus a double bass (as in *Eine kleine Nachtmusik,* K. 525); or a cello, a double bass, and a bassoon (or several of each of these) with or without a keyboard instrument playing along and adding chords (as in much orchestral music and opera); or an organ alone or with a double bass (as in some church music), as well as various other configurations. It is sometimes possible to ascertain what Mozart had in mind for a particular work, but other times not. In *The Compleat Mozart,* therefore, *basso* has been left untranslated in the enumerations of instrumentation.

continuo (or basso continuo) This indicates that the keyboard instrument in question (organ, harpsichord, or piano) functions as a component of the *basso* part: the performer plays the *basso* notes as written and improvises harmonies above them. Mozart uses keyboard continuo in his church compositions, his operatic recitatives, and a few of his songs and early chamber works. Its use is implied in certain other types of music, such as the tutti sections of piano concertos where no solo part is written out.

doubling This indicates that a player of the instrument in question is expected to play a different instrument in part of the composition. For example, the Symphony No. 24 in B-flat major, K. 182, calls for *2 oboes (doubling flutes),* indicating that both oboists must play flutes in part of the work.

SATB soprano, alto, tenor, and bass voices used chorally; similarly ATB (in the Miserere, K. 85), TTB (in the Masonic works, K. 429, 471, 483, 484), etc.

S/A/T/B (used with the word *soli*) soprano, alto, tenor, and bass voices used soloistically within a choral work; similarly S/T (in the Dixit et Magnificat, K. 193), S/S/T/B (in the Mass, K. 427), etc.

strings 2 violins, viola, and *basso*—the standard orchestral string complement in Mozart's time.

ONE
VOCAL MUSIC AND RELATED WORKS

Das Hochambt in St. Stephans Thombkirchen.
9. Cardinal Piazza Nuntius
10. Der Venetian. Bottschaffter Zane
25. die Abgeordnete von Viertern
Standt 26. die Kay. Hoff Music

1

Music for the Catholic Church

BACKGROUND AND OVERVIEW

As long as Mozart lived in Salzburg, he was involved with music for the Catholic church. As the Prince-Archbishop's title reveals, the ruler of Salzburg had both temporal and sacred powers, and he was responsible neither to the Austrian emperor nor the Holy Roman Emperor but directly to Rome. The prince-archbishops of Salzburg took their church music seriously. According to the "Report of the Present State of the Musical Establishment at the Court of His Serene Highness the Archbishop of Salzburg in the Year 1757" published by Leopold Mozart when his son was an infant, the prince-archbishop employed ninety-nine musicians to provide daily music in the cathedral, at court, and for a variety of other social and ceremonial occasions.

So from his earliest musical consciousness Mozart was surrounded by composers deeply involved in composing and performing music for the Mass, Vespers, and other liturgical occasions, in both the modern concerted style and the *stile antico* (old church style). These men included Mozart's father (some of whose church music was, until recently, attributed to his son), Johann Ernst Eberlin, Giuseppe Francesco Lolli, Anton Cajetan Adlgasser, Franz Ignaz Lipp, and, after his arrival in Salzburg in 1763, Michael Haydn.

Mozart's most frequent contributions to satisfying the continual demand for new, locally composed church music were settings of the cycle of five "ordinary" texts of the Mass: the Kyrie, Gloria, Credo, Sanctus, and Agnus Dei. Fifteen complete Mass cycles come down to us from Mozart's Salzburg years. Writing

---

OPPOSITE. The interior of Saint Stephen's Cathedral, Vienna, during a Solemn High Mass, November 8, 1712. Engraving by Johann Andreas Pfeffel and Christian Engelbrecht after Johann Cyriak Hackhofer.

The engraving portrays the oath of allegiance to the crown taken by the nobility for the new Emperor, Charles VI, after the death of Joseph I. Trumpets can be seen in the musicians' gallery at the left.

to his mentor in Bologna, Padre Giovanni Battista Martini, Mozart explained a constraint that the archbishop of Salzburg placed on his court composers in their Masses:

Our church music is very different from that of Italy, and what is more, a Mass with all its parts—The Kyrie, the Gloria, the Credo, the Epistle sonata, the Offertory or motet, the Sanctus, and the Agnus Dei—must not last longer than three-quarters of an hour. This applies even to the most solemn Mass said by the Archbishop himself.

Mozart is describing a *Missa brevis*. Performances of Mozart's music for a *Missa brevis,* an Epistle (or church) sonata, and an Offertory total about thirty minutes of music. Thus in the remaining fifteen minutes the priest leading the service and the choir of monks singing Gregorian chant would have had to make their way through the Introit, Collect, church sonata, Alleluia, Gospel, Preface, Canon, Communion, Post-Communion, and Ite missa est, which would have been just barely possible, assuming a brisk and unrelenting pace.

But some of Mozart's Masses are headed *"Missa longa,"* and, as their name suggests, cannot be accommodated to the forty-five-minute ruling. These must have been intended for days of special importance and solemnity during the Church calendar—All Saints' Day, Christmas, Easter, and the like—or for one of the other ecclesiastical establishments in or near Salzburg for which Mozart worked and which, unlike the cathedral and parish churches, were not under the direct administrative control of the prince-archbishop. These institutions included the University of Salzburg and its Collegiate Church, run by the Benedictines, churches and monasteries run by the Franciscans, a church and convent run by the Ursulines, the pilgrimage church of Maria Plain, and others.

The three other principal categories into which Mozart's Salzburg church music falls are Vespers (Evensong), Litanies, and motets. Vespers is a sunset service performed daily. The Litanies are a form of liturgical prayer consisting of a series of invocations or supplications with responses, repeated a number of times. Motets are a catch-all category for settings of other liturgical texts useful only at certain times of year and not others. Mozart's Offertories, for instance, are motets to be sung at the mid-point of the Mass, when the priest receives bread and wine to be consecrated at the altar.

After he left Salzburg in 1781, Mozart had little to do with church music. His greatest works, the C-minor Mass and the Requiem, remained torsos. The splendid Kyrie in D minor, K. 341, speculatively redated to c. 1788, is apparently all that was completed from a flurry of church-music activity around 1787–89, when the Viennese theaters were closed down and Mozart was seeking a position at St. Stephen's Cathedral. And there is the isolated, gemlike motet, "Ave verum corpus," from Mozart's last year.

In 1904 Pope Pius XII issued the encyclical *Mediator Dei,* by which he "defrocked" the church music of the classical period, that is, deemed it unsuited for Catholic liturgical use, on the grounds that its character was too worldly (i.e., operatic). But Haydn, Mozart, Beethoven, Schubert, and other composers of the eighteenth and early-nineteenth centuries (and the priests and congregations with whom they associated) must have thought their church music sufficiently spiritual and entirely appropriate, or they would not have composed it as they did. In any case, Austrian Catholics were so upset by the Pope's encyclical that a special dispensation was made for Austria, and even today one may hear Masses by the masters of Viennese classicism performed in the cathedrals in Vienna and Salzburg. The long-standing dispute over the liturgical appropriateness of this repertory became moot, however, when in the early 1960s the Second Vatican Council virtually abandoned Latin as the Church's language of worship. N.Z.

MASSES, KYRIES, AND REQUIEM

K. 33 *Kyrie in F major*
Origin: Paris, June 12, 1766
Scoring: SATB, strings

Perhaps Mozart wished to write a mass for Salzburg before his departure from Paris in 1766. In any case, only the Kyrie for four voices and strings in F major, K. 33, is known. Dated in Paris on June 12, 1766, the ten-year-old boy's composition is not uninfluenced by the impressions of French church music. The manuscript shows the editorial hand of his father.

K.F.

K. 139 *Missa solemnis in C minor, "Waisenhaus" (K³ 114a, K⁶ 47a)*
Origin: Vienna, autumn 1768
Scoring: SATB, S / A / T / B soli, 2 oboes, 4 trumpets and timpani, 3 trombones, strings with organ continuo

". . . The entire music sung by the Waisenchor [orphanage chorus] for the High Mass, which met with universal approval and admiration, was completely newly composed for this ceremony by Wolfgang Mozart, who is well-known because of his special talents and is the twelve-year-old son of Mr. Leopold Mozart, who serves at the court in Salzburg as kapellmeister; it was performed with the greatest accuracy. In addition, motets were also sung. . . ."

So reads a report in a Viennese newspaper about the opening ceremonies for the newly-built Waisenhaus Church in Vienna on December 7, 1768, at which Empress Maria Theresa and her children were present. For years there was a discussion in the studies about Mozart of whether this "music sung by the Waisenchor" referred to the Mass in C minor, K. 139. The highly artistic quality of this broadly dimensioned work appeared to speak against its having been composed by a twelve-year-old, even one named Mozart. On the other hand, the large orchestra required to perform the Mass, which would not have been available in Salzburg, suggests a highly festive occasion in Vienna. The German musicologist Karl Pfannhauser put an end to these discussions for the time being when he showed in 1954, with the help of new evidence, that the traditional appellation of the "Waisenhaus" Mass is in all likelihood justified. Mozart's father, who added the thoroughbass figures to his son's autograph, undoubtedly supervised the boy's work.

A concerted *Missa solemnis* was bound by conventions which brought it occasionally into conflict with the contents of the Latin Ordinary of the Mass. The Kyrie may serve as an example of this: it is modeled on a French overture with a pompous, slow first section, followed by

OPPOSITE. The interior of Salzburg Cathedral (Saint Peter's) during a Solemn High Mass. Engraving by Melchoir Küssel, c. 1680.

In Mozart's time the Cathedral remained as it had been in the previous century. Leopold Mozart described the musicians' placement as follows: "In the rear over the entrance to the church, the archiepiscopal cathedral has a great organ, in the front near the choir four side-organs [in the four musicians' galleries], and below the choir near the hymn-singers is a small choir-organ. In large-scale concerted music the great organ is used only to improvise preludes; during the concerted music itself, however, one of the four side-organs is constantly played, namely, the one next to the altar on the right-hand side, where the solo singers and the bass instruments are. Opposite by the left side-organ are the violinists, etc., and by both the other side-organs are the two choirs of trumpets and kettledrums [for fanfares]. The lower choir-organ and double-bass play along only in the tutti passages."

a joyful Allegro, which does not particularly suit the text, "Lord, have mercy upon us." In addition, the supplication for peace, the concluding "Dona nobis pacem," was often composed as a gay final Allegro, a tradition which was naturally not ignored by Mozart. The solo movements of the Gloria and Credo, which are broadly dimensioned and similar to a cantata in form, with the exception of the highly ornamented soprano aria "Quoniam tu solus," tend to be lyrical and melodious rather than virtuoso operatic music. The Sanctus and Benedictus are composed more succinctly; only the Benedictus incorporates a solo voice, the soprano.

In reference to Mozart's early C-minor Mass, Karl Gustav Fellerer has suggested that the young composer wanted "with childlike naiveté to dedicate everything which his talents could offer to his Lord." It would be difficult to say this more beautifully. A.B.

K. 49 *Missa brevis in G major (K⁶ 47d)*
Origin: Vienna, October or November 1768
Scoring: SATB, S/A/T/B soli, [3 trombones], strings with organ continuo

Nothing is known about the circumstances which led to the composition of this *Missa brevis,* except that it seems to have been written in Vienna. The basically straightforward idiom, allied to the traditional ecclesiastical style, suggests that it cannot be associated with any festive occasion. It is interesting to note that Mozart takes a few liberties with the liturgical texts: in the Kyrie, for instance, the phrases "Kyrie eleison" and "Christe eleison" are intermingled. G.D.

K. 65 *Missa brevis in D minor (K⁶ 61a)*
Origin: Salzburg, January 14, 1769
Scoring: SATB, S/A/T/B soli, strings, organ

Mozart was about to turn thirteen when he completed this *Missa brevis.* It dates from the months in which the Mozart family returned to Salzburg after fifteen months in Vienna, where Wolfgang had composed his opera *La finta semplice.* It received its first performance in the Collegiate Church in Salzburg on February 5 for the initiation of the Forty Hours Devotion on Quinquagesima Sunday. The ceremony marked the beginning of a particular form of eucharistic devotion in which the consecrated host was exhibited on the altar for a period of forty hours, during which time people prayed before it and special services were held.

The chromatic setting of the Benedictus has been singled out for praise. The manuscript of the Mass reveals two earlier, rejected attempts to set this text, before Mozart penned this third version which he may even have added some years later. The Mass conforms to the standard model of the *Missa brevis,* in which some phrases of the Credo text are "telescoped"; this means that various sections of the text are superimposed on others in the interest of brevity. G.D.

K. 66 *Missa in C major, "Dominicus"*
Origin: Salzburg, October 1769
Scoring: SATB, S/A/T/B soli, 2 oboes, 2 horns, 2 [+2] trumpets and timpani, [3 trombones], strings with organ continuo

The "Dominicus" Mass can be connected with a specific celebration, the first mass celebrated by Cajetan Hagenauer, a longtime friend of the composer, who assumed the name "Dominicus" on his ordination.

After the initial performance in Salzburg, the Mass was heard on subsequent occasions: in August 1773 Leopold Mozart wrote to his wife from Vienna, "A Mass by Wolfgang was performed at the Jesuit church . . . on the octave of the feast of St. Ignatius, namely the "Dominicus" Mass; I directed the performance, and the Mass gave remarkable pleasure."

Even though Mozart designated the work simply as "Missa," it can certainly be regarded as a *Missa solemnis:* with its additional wind parts, the scoring is more lavish than that of K. 49 and 65. The broader canvas allows for more contrast, and this brings with it a wider variety of textures; more extended solos and duets provide a foil to the full passages. G.D.

K. 140 *Missa brevis in G major (K^3 Anh 235d, K^6 Anh C 1.12)*

Origin: Salzburg? 1773?
Scoring: SATB, S/A/T/B soli, 2 violins, basso, organ

Many authorities suggest that the *Missa brevis,* K. 140, is not the work of Mozart himself, and it is included among the doubtful works in the most recent edition of Ludwig von Köchel's catalogue. The Mass seems to date from the early 1770s, and the manuscript has clearly been corrected and paginated in Mozart's own hand. In the preface to K. 140 in the *Neue Mozart-Ausgabe,* the editor Walter Senn argues in favor of Mozart's authorship: he believes that the composer would not have taken such great care to amend and correct the manuscript had it not been his own original composition. Nonetheless, Senn finds no parallels for this piece among Mozart's other masses, and he is forced to look further afield to the composer's other works to discern common stylistic traits. G.D.

K. 167 *Missa in C major, "Holy Trinity"*

Origin: Salzburg, June 1773 (except the Kyrie, which is older)
Scoring: SATB, 2 oboes, 4 trumpets and timpani, [3 trombones], 2 violins, basso, organ

By June 1773, when he wrote the "Missa in honorem SS^mae^ Trinitatis" (Mass in honor of the Holy Trinity), Mozart had returned to Salzburg from his period of travel in Italy. The scoring of the work is unusual, since there are no soloists, and the orchestra includes parts for four trumpets. It could well have been intended for a special occasion such as the feast of the Holy Trinity which fell on Sunday, June 6, in that year. The Mass could have been first performed at the Collegiate Church, or at the church dedicated to the Trinity itself; it seems probable that it was not intended for the Salzburg Cathedral.

In the year prior to its composition, Hieronymus Colloredo had been appointed archbishop of Salzburg, and his liturgical reforms included keeping a tight rein on musical style. The lack of soloists may well be in response to his demands, which Mozart was bound to accept in his capacity as concertmaster to the archiepiscopal court. A few years afterward he complained that he was forced to make the music for an entire celebration of the Mass (including epistle sonata and motet) last no longer than three-quarters of an hour. G.D.

K. 192 *Missa brevis in F major, "Little Credo" (K^6 186f)*

Origin: Salzburg, June 24, 1774
Scoring: SATB, S/A/T/B soli, [3 trombones], 2 violins, basso, organ (2 trumpets added later)

Mozart's *Missa brevis* in F major, K. 192, is an utterly concentrated work, in which only the Kyrie and Agnus Dei begin with a short instrumental prelude. In spite of its modest scale (the orchestra of the original version consists of strings only, without violas), it impresses us as being a more convincing and heartfelt piece than the preceding Mass, K. 167. It is also more deliberately vocal in spirit, and introduces a quartet of soloists. Its melodic curves are flexible, graceful, and tender, notwithstanding the drastic concision of each motive and the flashing speed of the choral declamation. Concise as this work is, however, Mozart never superimposes different parts of the text. The most remarkable parts of the Mass are in the Credo, in which the famous four-tone motive culminating in the Finale of the Jupiter Symphony, K. 551, appears (it is also to be found in Haydn's early Symphony No. 13 in D major) to stress the words "Credo, Credo." At the end, the piece builds up to a masterly fugato on "Amen, Amen." The grave and moving beauty of the Agnus Dei, in D minor, leads into the merry "Dona nobis pacem," whose airy lightness recalls the finale of a fine Italian symphony. H.H.

K. 194 *Missa brevis in D major (K⁶ 186h)*
Origin: Salzburg, August 8, 1774
Scoring: SATB, S/A/T/B soli, [3 trombones], 2 violins, basso, organ

The *Missa brevis* in D major, K. 194, was intended for ordinary daily use—this can be seen from the sparse instrumental scoring with a "church trio" (two violins, bass, organ) and trombones doubling the voices. It quickly became one of the most popular settings of the Mass by Mozart, who later had it performed in Munich in 1775.

Not only the conciseness but also the prominent role of counterpoint are traditional features: thus the final portions of the Gloria and Credo are styled as fugues, and the "Et incarnatus" is set apart, occupying a musical sphere of its own. The strongly triadic Kyrie undergoes contrapuntal development and, like the following movement, favors a full choral sound, while the Benedictus is reserved in customary manner for solo voices, which this Mass employs only occasionally. The concluding Agnus Dei, on the other hand, has an almost *concertante* character, featuring tutti passages that occur at intervals in the manner of ritornellos. W.K.

K. 262 *Missa longa in C major (K⁶ 246a)*
Origin: Salzburg? June or July 1775?
Scoring: SATB, S/A/T/B soli, 2 oboes, 2 horns, 2 trumpets, (timpani added later) [3 trombones], 2 violins, basso, organ

The Mass in C major, K. 262, is one of the most extensive of Mozart's liturgical works, as indicated in the manuscript itself by the description *"Missa longa."* Recent studies of the manuscript's watermarks have tentatively dated the work to mid-1775. The archbishop of Salzburg suffered such lengthy masses to be performed only on very special occasions; such an occasion in mid-1775 has yet to come to light.

On November 17, 1776, however, Count Ignaz Joseph Spaur, the coadjutant of the bishopric of Brixen, and a longstanding acquaintance of the Mozart family, was ordained as titular Bishop of Chrysopel at a ceremony in Salzburg Cathedral. In a letter of May 28, 1778, Leopold Mozart mentions a certain mass that his son composed for Count Spaur; this could conceivably refer to a mass for the ordination. On stylistic grounds, K. 262 would seem to be the most likely candidate; but the evidence of the watermarks argues against the hypothesis that Mozart composed it originally for that purpose. (See also the note for the *Missa brevis* in C major, K. 258, below.)

With its overriding pathos and grand dimensions, K. 262 stands in complete contrast to Mozart's succinct and intense *Missae breves* of about the same period. This applies not so much to the role of the *soli*—which remain episodical and never actually engage in aria-type parts as we know them in Mozart's later masses—but refers rather to that of the orchestra. Not only does Mozart, in addition to the "church trio," use oboes, trumpets, and horns, as well as timpani and trombones—he also writes extensive orchestral preludes to the beginning of the Kyrie and by way of an introduction to the "Et in spiritum sanctum." And finally, in accordance with the representative nature of the work, there is the grandiose style of the great fugues. Even more extensive and complex than the "Cum sancto spiritu" in the Gloria is the final fugue of the Credo, "Et vitam venturi"—more than 120 measures rich in coloratura. However, there is much more to Mozart's composition than mere ostentatious wallowing in sound and polyphonic complexity; there are (for instance in the drama and grief of the "Qui tollis," the emotion and peacefulness of the "Benedictus," the chromaticism and despair of the "Miserere nobis") moments of deeply subjective intensity of expression which raise this Mass far above most contemporary South German and Austrian church music. W.K.

K. 220 *Missa brevis in C major, "Sparrow" (K⁶ 196b)*

Origin: Salzburg? 1775 or early 1776?
Scoring: SATB, S/A/T/B soli, 2 trumpets and timpani, [3 trombones], 2 violins, basso, organ

The Mass in C major, K. 220, is an extreme example of Mozart's submission to Archbishop Colloredo's rigorous regulations about the length of the music in Salzburg Cathedral. The popular title "Spatzenmesse" (Sparrow Mass), conferred on the work in Germany in the nineteenth century, is leveled at the stereotyped accompanying figure of the violins in the Sanctus. This may not be one of Mozart's greatest church compositions, but the sovereignty with which he combines formal conciseness with festive effect remains worthy of admiration. A.B.

K. 258 *Missa brevis in C major, "Piccolomini"*

Origin: Salzburg, December 1775
Scoring: SATB, S/A/T/B soli, [2 oboes added later], 2 trumpets and timpani, [3 trombones], 2 violins, basso, organ

K. 258 is the first of three Masses, K. 258, 259, and 257, whose original manuscripts have been preserved as a group. The manuscripts are dated November 1776 (for K. 257) and December 1776 (for K. 258 and 259). Recent analysis of the handwriting has shown that these dates were tampered with and may not be authentic. Analysis of the manuscripts' watermarks has also helped to establish a new tentative dating for the three Masses as indicated here.

K. 258 is entitled *"Missa brevis et solemnis"*: that is to say, concise in the form of the movements and short in duration, but with a more extensive orchestration. The character of the *Missa brevis* is shown particularly in the two inner movements of the Ordinary with their full texts: in the Gloria Mozart manages to do without every traditional insertion, contrapuntal detail, and repetition of text; the "Et incarnatus" is included in the Credo as merely a trio. The expressively lyrical Adagio with its opening tenor solo, nevertheless, certainly ranks among the finest moments in Mozart's liturgical compositions of the Salzburg period. With the Sanctus once again concise and contained, the Benedictus overflowing with rich melody, and the Agnus Dei, with its chromatically intoned plea for peace, woven with restless violin figuration, this is an expressive work of depth, despite its brevity of form.

K. 258 has occasionally been called the "Spaur" Mass because the date written on the manuscript corresponds approximately to the date of the ordination of Bishop Spaur, an occasion for which Mozart may have composed a mass (see the note for the *Missa longa* in C major, K. 262, above); however, the recent manuscript redating weakens this attribution. The nickname "Piccolomini" is somewhat more obscure; it probably does not refer to the great Sienese family of that name; perhaps it is a bowdlerization of *piccolo* (little), referring to the brevity of the Mass. W.K.

K. 259 *Missa brevis in C major, "Organ Solo"*

Origin: Salzburg, December 1775 or December 1776

Scoring: SATB, S/A/T/B soli, 2 trumpets and timpani, 2 violins, basso, organ

This work is in the "Colloredo tradition" of the short mass with economic scoring. To distinguish it from its companions, most of which are in the standard church key of C major (standard for solemn masses, that is), K. 259 is known as the "Organ Solo" Mass. The solo occurs in the Benedictus and thus follows a tradition well known in Austria: Haydn's *Missa brevis S. Joannis de Deo,* composed about a year earlier, has a similar, though more elaborate, organ solo. The whole of Mozart's Mass is very Austrian, even to the delightful Agnus Dei, with its songful first violin (later vocal) part and its mischievous pizzicato bass part—as innocently Baroque and worldly as many an altar in southern Germany and Austria. H.C.R.L.

K. 257 *Missa in C major, "Credo"*

Origin: Salzburg, late 1776 or early 1777

Scoring: SATB, S/A/T/B soli, 2 oboes, 2 trumpets and timpani, [3 trombones], 2 violins, basso, organ

Like K. 258 and 259, this is a short Mass, according to the wishes of Archbishop Colloredo of Salzburg. Here Mozart forgoes polyphonic development, and even the traditional closing fugues of the Gloria and Credo are avoided. It later gained the nickname "Credo" Mass because of the frequent repetition of the word *Credo,* although this, too, is part of the Baroque tradition. The work is remarkable for the songlike, almost popular character of its melodies and a warmth and geniality of expression which had not previously been much in evidence in Mozart's church composition. The requisite formal conciseness did not exclude an abundance of invention; indeed the great structural intensity achieved seems to illustrate a passage from a letter written by Mozart to Padre Martini earlier that year. In it Mozart refers to the "special study" required, without considering that what is needed is not "study" but genius.

A.B.

K. 275 *Missa brevis in B-flat major (K⁶ 272b)*
Origin: Salzburg, late 1777
Scoring: SATB, S/A/T/B soli, 2 violins, basso, organ

The *Missa brevis* in B-flat major, K. 275, uses the same sparse instrumental scoring of a "church trio" that one finds in K. 140, 192, and 194. However, its plan is much less tradition-bound: the customary fugues are missing and the contrapuntal treatment of individual sections is eschewed; only the Sanctus is complex in structure, while elsewhere homophonic choral writing predominates. The solo parts are vocally more demanding. Mozart departs most from tradition in the concluding Agnus Dei. Whereas the mood in this section is normally pastoral and festive, the present movement is dramatically tense, almost grimly determined in places. W.K.

K. 317 *Missa in C major, "Coronation"*
Origin: Salzburg, March 23, 1779
Scoring: SATB, S/A/T/B soli, 2 oboes, 2 horns, 2 trumpets and timpani, 3 trombones, 2 violins, basso, organ

The Mass in C major, K. 317, has become widely popular. The claim that it was written for the anniversary of the coronation of the miracle-working image of the Virgin in the pilgrimage church of Maria Plain near Salzburg is questioned by recent Mozart scholarship, even though the work bears the title "Coronation" Mass. The extensive scoring assigns the work to the Salzburg Cathedral, where it was probably heard on Easter 1779. In festive verve, in richness of contrasts, in the variety of musical ideas developed within the narrowest confines, and in melodic strength, the "Coronation" Mass surpasses all the other Salzburg masses. Behind the apparent problem-free flow of the work lies very deliberate delicacy of detail. The Credo, for example, is conceived in rondo form, the heart of which is formed by the "Et incarnatus." The *concertante* juxtaposition of solo quartet and chorus takes various forms, and the soprano solo of the Agnus Dei appears as a precursor of the aria "Dove sono" from *Le nozze di Figaro*. In the work's concentration, symphonic traits are discernable, so that it bursts the accepted bounds of the *Missa brevis* and anticipates the late high masses of Haydn, even though it does not employ the art of fugue taken up again by the older composer. A.B.

K. 337 *Missa solemnis in C major*
Origin: Salzburg, March 1780
Scoring: SATB, S/A/T/B soli, 2 oboes, 2 bassoons, 2 trumpets and timpani, [3 trombones], 2 violins, basso, organ

In March 1780 Mozart composed his last mass for Salzburg, the *Missa solemnis* in C major, K. 337. His only later mass is the magnificent torso constituting the Mass in C minor, K. 427. The designation *Missa solemnis* refers less to the duration of the work than to its rich scoring—so the work was presumably composed for a festive occasion. The tendency toward homophony that was already incipient some years earlier is encountered here again: the contrast of different vocal and instrumental sonorities takes precedence over contrapuntal artistry. This aspect has caused purists to reproach the work for certain "operatic effects," which include the sudden switch to *a cappella* style on the words "Jesu Christe" in the Gloria and the *concertante* woodwind instruments in the soprano solo of the

Agnus Dei. Criticism of this kind is misplaced, however, for it fails to acknowledge the stylistic unity of music in the eighteenth century and attempts to assign church music to an imperfectly understood *stile antico*. Mozart has abandoned tradition here in other respects as well: the Benedictus, usually a graceful section, is made severely contrapuntal—and adopts the astringent A-minor tonality that we know from the piano sonata K. 310. And the "Dona nobis pacem" closes not in a jubilant mood but softly, almost diffidently. With this independent-minded piece Mozart concluded his duties as a composer of church music for the Salzburg court. W.K.

K. 427 *Missa in C minor (K⁶ 417a)*

Origin: Vienna, c. July 1782 to May 1783
Scoring: SATB (double chorus), S/S/T/B soli, 2 oboes (one doubling flute), 2 bassoons, 2 horns, 2 trumpets and timpani, 3 trombones, strings with organ continuo

The powerful fragment that is the C-minor Mass, K. 427, has an isolated position in Mozart's output. It throws up a whole series of questions that to this day cannot be resolved with certainty. Mozart, whose departure in May 1781 from the service of the archbishop of Salzburg freed him from any further obligation to write church music, began in the summer of 1782 without any known external motivation to compose a large-scale mass, and this circumstance is not entirely explained in terms of the fulfillment of a much-quoted vow. Mozart wrote to his father on January 4, 1783, saying he had "promised to his heart" that if he succeeded in bringing Constanze to Salzburg as his wife he would perform a new mass there, and he mentioned "as proof that I really made the promise . . . the score of half a Mass for which I still have high hopes." But as these "high hopes" remained only hopes, the vow was obviously not binding. Is it possible that so private a problem as the struggle for Constanze's hand could have given rise to the composition of a Mass which in its formal arrangement and stylistic diversity stands apart from the rest of Mozart's church music?

We do not know what made Mozart choose a form which was no longer "modern," the cantata-like mass of Baroque tradition; the most powerful example was found in J. S. Bach's B-minor Mass (to which Mozart might have been introduced by Baron van Swieten in Vienna). About a decade before K. 427 this form was taken up again by Joseph Haydn in his *St. Cecilia Mass,* his last use of it before he finally developed, in his late, mature high masses, the classical type of symphonic mass in which each movement is a continuous whole.

A more powerful factor in the composition of Mozart's Mass than the marriage problem and the vow may have been the crisis that arose when Mozart came into contact with the work of Bach. Other works inspired by Bach also came from these years, including the Fugue in C minor for two pianos (K. 426) which became better known in its later string version. We do not know why Mozart put the unfinished Mass aside. His hurried transcription for an academy (as concerts were then called) in 1785 of the Kyrie and Gloria, with two added arias, into an Italian occasional cantata *Davidde penitente* (K. 469), fixes the ending of work on the projected Mass at this time at the latest: the creative Bach crisis was over.

For a long time August 25, 1783, was accepted as the date of the first performance. The Austrian conductor Bernhard Paumgartner, however, was able to fix the date as October 23 of that year. It is not known how Mozart set about supplying the missing sections necessary for a liturgical performance in St. Peter's Church, Salzburg. Attempts to complete the work by using sections of earlier Mozart masses have also been made since then, but modern performances are almost always restricted to the original parts.

Mozart composed the Kyrie, the Gloria, the Credo as far as the "Et incarnatus," the Sanctus, and the Benedictus. The missing sections are therefore the second part of the Credo from the "Crucifixus" onwards, and the entire Agnus Dei. In the "Et incarnatus" Mozart wrote out only the vocal part, the three obbligato woodwind parts, and the figured bass, while the "Hosanna" from the Sanctus lacks the second chorus which has to be reconstructed from the orchestral parts. This task was carried out at the turn of the present century by the German musician Alois Schmitt, who was responsible for retrieving the work from the oblivion into which it had sunk. The orchestration follows the Salzburg norm: besides strings there are a pair each of oboes, bassoons, horns, and trumpets, together with timpani. An organ continuo was taken for granted.

Mozart, in his work on this Mass, was little concerned with unity of style, and he has often been criticized for this. Bach's inspiration would seem particularly apparent in the grandiose double-choruses—the "Qui tollis" in G minor, a Largo of great expressive weight which is indeed the spiritual climax of the work, and the Sanctus together with the "Hosanna," the latter being a rich and florid double fugue. But the other choral movements also far exceed the expressive range of earlier Mozart masses: the grave, freely contrapuntal Kyrie, a spirited Gloria reminiscent of Handel's ceremonial manner (both these being in four voices), and especially the "Gratias agimus tibi," which, with its five-part harmony spiced with suspensions and its emotional tension, is second only to the "Qui tollis" as the most expressive chorus of the work. A brilliant double fugue in *alla breve* time with two sharply contrasting themes forms the "Cum sancto spiritu" which ends the Gloria.

Nevertheless, not only Bach but also the eighteenth-century Italian tradition went into the composition of this Mass. This is apparent in the solo sections, whose "operatic" character has often been a stumbling block. They include the slightly stiff coloratura aria for mezzo-soprano in the "Laudamus te," and in particular the "Et incarnatus" which stands completely outside the liturgical framework. This virtuoso coloratura aria for soprano, with obbligato parts for three *concertante* wind instruments and a long bravura cadenza, reminded one modern English Mozart specialist more of the Mad Scene from Gaetano Donizetti's *Lucia di Lammermoor* than of a religious service. However, one is reminded equally strongly, with musicologist Alfred Einstein, of the naiveté of Italian Christmas music.

More than any other religious work for voices, Mozart's great C-minor Mass sums up the entire eighteenth century. It is indeed a summing-up that bears the stamp of the highest creative power and originality, even if this is gained at the expense of compactness and unity of style.

A.B.

K. 341 *Kyrie in D minor (K^6 368a)*
Origin: Vienna, 1788 to 1791?
Scoring: SATB, 2 flutes, 2 oboes, 2 clarinets, 2 bassoons, 4 horns, 2 trumpets and timpani, strings with organ continuo

This Kyrie's very full scoring of double woodwind, four horns, two trumpets, and timpani led German scholar Otto Jahn to assign it to the period of *Idomeneo* in Munich: November 1780 to March 1781. Mozart specialist Alan Tyson, however, on examining sketches for several Kyries on paper datable around 1788, suggested that Mozart may well have been at work then on a Mass, with a view to obtaining an ecclesiastical position, and that the present Kyrie, which is not datable as the autograph is lost, may have been from this period too. A date just prior to *Don Giovanni,* with its central key of D minor, is not unthinkable. It is an intense work with a remarkable scoring that includes four horns, and a style arguably belonging to Mozart's works of the late 1780s. E.S.

K. 626 *Requiem in D minor*
Origin: Vienna, late 1791
Scoring: SATB, S/A/T/B soli, 2 bassett horns, 2 bassoons, 2 trumpets and timpani, 3 trombones, strings with organ continuo

On December 14, 1793, Count Franz Walsegg-Stuppach, an Austrian aristocrat and musical dilettante, directed the performance of a Requiem Mass in memory of his wife. The score, written in his own hand, was headed with the legend "composed by Count Walsegg." The extent of the count's "composition," however, was his copying of a score written in the hand of Wolfgang Amadeus Mozart and his pupil and amanuensis Franz Xaver Süssmayr. The music played and sung that day in the Cistercian monastery of Neukloster in the Wiener Neustadt was the work we know as Mozart's Requiem.

Count Walsegg was a liar, but not a thief: he would commission composers to write music for him, which he would then recopy and pass off as his own. The composers were well paid, his own vanity was satisfied, and if the members of his court knew about the deception they must have reflected that they were probably better off listening to the music of professionals than to that of the amateur Count himself.

It may be that Walsegg had solicited advice about the commission from his wealthy friend Michael Puchberg, a merchant who was also a friend and benefactor of Mozart. At all events, one day in the summer of 1791, a tall, lean, and unsmiling man appeared at Mozart's lodgings in Vienna. Without disclosing his name, he asked the composer to write a setting of the Requiem Mass. He produced fifty ducats, already a generous fee, promising to pay a further fifty when the work was finished. Mozart, desperate for money, accepted the commission, telling the mysterious stranger that he would have the score ready in four weeks. It seems that Mozart soon became obsessed with the idea that his visitor was an emissary from another world, bidding him write Mozart's own Requiem.

The grim man was in fact an agent of Count Walsegg, one Franz Anton Leitgeb, owner or manager of a gypsum plant situated near the Walsegg estate. It is little wonder that Mozart, whose health was failing, should have felt bound to accept the commission. Not only were his debts piling up, but he had recently been appointed deputy (unpaid) kapellmeister of St. Stephen's Cathedral, and may have wanted to prove himself with a new piece of church music.

He began work on the Requiem at once, but was soon interrupted by a commission for a new opera to be given at Prague for the coronation of Emperor Leopold II. He left Vienna, accompanied by Süssmayr, on August 25 or 26, and wrote most of *La clemenza di Tito* in the incredibly short space of about eight weeks.

The Magic Flute had been largely finished in July, but there were final touches yet to be made and the premiere to be prepared. Mozart conducted the premiere himself on September 30. But he continued to work on the Requiem until the middle of October, when Constanze returned from taking the curative waters at Baden, and found him so weak and mentally disturbed that she took the score away from him. It seems from others' accounts that Mozart was now convinced that he had been poisoned. By November 15 Constanze thought her husband well enough to work, however, and returned the score. His last illness forced him to bed five days later, but he continued composing.

On December 4 Mozart was desperately weak, and a constant stream of friends visited him. In the early afternoon three singers from the theater sang through with him the completed movements of the Requiem, Mozart himself taking the alto line. When they reached the "Lacrimosa," of which he had finished only the first eight measures, he wept and put the music aside. The same evening his temperature rose alarmingly, and when the doctor arrived he had cold compresses put on Mozart's head. The shock was so great that the feverish composer lost consciousness. Just before one o'clock the following morning he died. The swollen body was buried in a common grave on December 6 in the churchyard of St. Mark's, Vienna, together with the corpses of some dozen other unfortunates who had happened to die the same day.

Constanze was determined to have the Requiem completed and a score delivered to the strange client who had commissioned the work. First she went to Joseph Eybler, a young composer who had helped nurse Mozart during his last weeks. But Eybler, overawed by the task, gave up after sketching a few measures. Constanze then went to Süssmayr, and it was his version that was finally handed to Leitgeb.

How much of the finished Requiem is actually Süssmayr's original work is a matter of some doubt; it was thought until recently that he was entirely responsible for the Sanctus, Benedictus, and Agnus Dei, for the completion of the "Lacrimosa" after Mozart's first eight measures, and for the instrumentation of the entire Dies Irae and Offertorium. But this theory was challenged in 1962 when a sheet of sketches for the Requiem in Mozart's hand was found. It is now argued that this sheet is, in all likelihood, but one of several that the composer had made and that Constanze gave to Süssmayr. She often said later that Süssmayr had only done "what anyone could have done." The implication is that he had only to fill in the details of Mozart's existing sketches; but it can also be argued that the widow's loyalty had distorted her memory. Ultimately it does not matter who wrote what. The Requiem, despite occasional inadequacies probably attributable to Süssmayr, is a powerful work of genius. A.R.

LITANIES AND VESPERS SETTINGS

The interior of the Cathedral of Frankfurt, October 9, 1790, during the coronation of Leopold II as Holy Roman Emperor. Engraving by F. L. N.

On this occasion Mozart had gone to Frankfurt at his own expense, pawning the family's silverware to raise the necessary funds, in hope of finding patronage and earning money by giving concerts for the assembled dignitaries.

K. 109 *Litaniae Lauretanae BVM, in B-flat major (K^6 74e)*
Origin: Salzburg, May 1771
Scoring: SATB, S/A/T/B soli, [3 trombones], 2 violins, basso, organ

Litanies were a favorite form of worship in the eighteenth century. The *Litaniae Lauretanae* (Lorettan Litany, invoking the Virgin Mary) and the *Litaniae de venerabili altaris sacramento* (Litany of the sacrament of the venerable altar) were the most important. The text of the Lorettan Litany was established by approbation (by Pope Sixtus V, 1587) while that of the sacramental litany follows local tradition. Litanies were used particularly in monasteries and pilgrimage churches. In Vienna, litanies composed by Johan Fux, Antonio Caldara, and others enjoyed popularity; in Salzburg, those of Leopold Mozart, Michael Haydn, and others found widespread use in parish services. W. A. Mozart wrote altogether four litanies for church festivals in the Salzburg Cathedral or in the chapel of the Mirabell Palace.

Mozart made two settings of the popular Lorettan Litany, which took its name from Loreto, a place of pilgrimage. This, the first of them, has the customary five sections (Kyrie, Sancta Maria, Salus infirmorum, Regina angelorum, Agnus Dei) and employs the usual forces found in Mozart's Salzburg church music. The extremely concise form matches the requirements of the Salzburg liturgy, which was musically rather restrained; the careful consideration of the words of the text may be attributable to the tuition of Padre Martini in Bologna, who was particularly helpful in this respect. The work's popular tone and strong vein of sweetness were entirely in keeping with the current taste in church music, while its thematic homogeneity, making the separate sections seem like variants on one main idea, demonstrates Mozart's feeling for cyclical unity over and above the obligations imposed by the words of the text. W.K.

K. 125 *Litaniae de venerabili altaris sacramento, in B-flat major*

Origin: Salzburg, March 1772
Scoring: SATB, S/A/T/B soli, 2 oboes (doubling flutes), 2 horns, 2 trumpets, [3 trombones], strings with organ continuo

Unlike the Lorettan litanies, which tend to be sweetly serene, the invocation of the Blessed Sacrament requires a tone of high seriousness. This work is formally arranged on the traditional Salzburg pattern favored by the likes of Anton Adlgasser and Johann Ernst Eberlin, and draws on a litany by Leopold Mozart in a number of details. But tonally and stylistically it incorporates what Mozart had learned of the Neapolitan manner, which was then the height of modernity; South German and Italian characteristics are intermingled. The large forces in themselves indicate the work's standing. Of the nine movements (Kyrie, Panis vivus, Verbum caro factum, Hostia sancta, Tremendum, Panis omnipotentia, Viaticum, Pignus, Agnus Dei), the most compelling are the slow movements, conspicuous for their bold, somber harmonies and much more palpably individual in style than the somewhat long-winded fugue of the Pignus—which indeed was later shortened by the composer. The affinity with symphony and opera is equally unmistakable; the Kyrie is not so much the introduction to a piece of church music as an independent symphonic movement with added choir, and the Panis vivus aria, studded with coloratura, might just as well be part of an Italian opera. Yet at a time when in practice the stylistic divisions among church music, opera, and chamber works (including the symphony) were progressively disappearing, this is not so much an aesthetic deficiency as a sign that the composition was up-to-date. W.K.

K. 195 *Litaniae Lauretanae BVM, in D major (K[6] 186d)*

Origin: Salzburg, May 1774
Scoring: SATB, S/A/T/B soli, 2 oboes, 2 horns, [3 trombones], strings with organ continuo

Whereas the Lorettan Litany in B-flat, K. 109, stays within the Salzburg tradition, the D-major Litany of 1774 shows touches of independence, even though the formal design reflects Eberlin's model and the relatively narrow limitations of the Salzburg court are observed in the instrumentation. The cycle of five movements (as in K. 109) testifies to the mixture of styles that was normal at the time. The Kyrie takes the shape of a sonata movement with slow introduction, while the Salus infirmorum and Agnus Dei are slow polyphonic choral movements of which the latter, introduced by a strongly expressive soprano solo, is one of the jewels of Mozart's Salzburg church music. The two intervening movements are evidently influenced by the Italian operatic tradition; here there are extended virtuoso solo sections, which in character and in the technical demands they make on the voice could just as well belong to an *opera seria* of the period. W.K.

K. 193 ***Dixit et Magnificat, in C major (K⁶ 186g)***
Origin: Salzburg, July 1774
Scoring: SATB, S/T soli, 2 trumpets and timpani, 3 trombones, 2 violins, basso, organ

These are the opening and closing sections of a vesper setting which usually had six parts; when K. 193 was performed the central sections employed may well have been by other composers or sung in Gregorian chant. Stylistically the two somewhat succinct movements keep to older models, though Mozart expands the tonal spectrum with two trumpets and timpani, which particularly make their presence felt in the closing Magnificat. What raises these pieces above the everyday output of his contemporaries is, on the one hand, the careful declamation of the text and, on the other, the free elaboration of the doxology at the end of each movement. W.K.

K. 243 ***Litaniae de venerabili altaris sacramento, in E-flat major***
Origin: Salzburg, March 1776
Scoring: SATB, S/A/T/B soli, 2 oboes (doubling flutes), 2 bassoons, 2 horns, 3 trombones, strings with organ continuo

This Litany of the Sacrament was performed not only in Salzburg Cathedral but also with great success in Augsburg and other towns, as Mozart's correspondence with his father attests. Here too, following the principle of contrast within the nine movements, strict polyphonic choral writing (in the Kyrie, Verbum caro factum, Tremendum, and Pignus) alternates with operatic solo configurations (tenor solo in the Panis vivus, soprano in the Dulcissimum convivium and the Agnus Dei). The seventh movement, the Viaticum, demonstrates the bonds of tradition particularly well; here Mozart uses the Gregorian Corpus Christi hymn "Pange lingua" as a *cantus firmus* in the choral soprano line (the other choral parts have rests), which allows one to guess the circumstances of the work's performance—probably in the context of a great Corpus Christi procession.

W.K.

K. 321 ***Vesperae de Dominica, in C major***
Origin: Salzburg, 1779
Scoring: SATB, S/A/T/B soli, [bassoon], 2 trumpets and timpani, [3 trombones], 2 violins, basso, organ

This vesper setting is in six movements: Dixit, Confitebor, Beatus vir, Laudate pueri, Laudate Dominum, and Magnificat. Stylistically it already stands close to the composition of the mature masses, even though formally and in its scoring it follows the line of the South German and Austrian tradition. Mozart himself had a very high opinion of this work; as late as 1783 he had it sent to Vienna by his father so as to be able to show it to Baron Gottfried van Swieten. This music lover, who had made Mozart aware of Johann Sebastian Bach and George Frideric Handel, would surely have been the first to notice the strict part-writing (the perpetual canon in the Laudate pueri, for instance). Yet Mozart does not persist in rigid counterpoint. He fashions individual movements homophonically (Dixit), or even in an operatic manner, saturated with coloratura (Laudate Dominum), and he obtains a particularly charming effect by always composing a fresh version of the closing Gloria Patri (the doxology) at the end of each of the six psalms. W.K.

K. 339 *Vesperae solennes de confessore, in C major*

Origin: Salzburg, 1780

Scoring: SATB, S/A/T/B soli, [bassoon], 2 trumpets and timpani, [3 trombones], 2 violins, basso, organ

While the *Vesperae de Dominica,* K. 321, were intended for ordinary Sunday use, the *Vesperae solennes de confessore,* K. 339, were written for a saint's day. We do not know which saint is being celebrated as we have no information on the immediate circumstances surrounding the work's composition. Mozart is concerned here again with the formal conciseness which suited Archbishop Colloredo's requirements. The five psalms and the Magnificat are not divided up, following the Neapolitan model, verse by verse into separate arias, ensembles, and choruses but composed in each case as continuous movements. A performance scarcely takes longer than the simple Gregorian chant of the vespers. Little scope is given for soloistic display except in the famous "Laudate Dominum," in which the *cantabile* soprano line over a choral foundation is one of the most magical passages in all Mozart's vocal music. In the first three psalms and the final Magnificat, choir and soloists engage in a lively dialogue in the most spirited and festive manner. The fourth psalm, the "Laudate pueri," an elaborate and methodical fugue in *alla breve* time, has an archaic flavor; in particular the fugal subject, with a diminished seventh, belongs to the traditional vocabulary of Baroque polyphony (and returns at the end of Mozart's life in the Kyrie of the Requiem, K. 626). In spite of the concise form, Mozart displays an abundance of musical ideas and great diversity of timbre and compositional technique. A.B.

SHORT LITURGICAL SETTINGS AND MOTETS

An Austrian church service. Engraving by J. E. Mansfeld, 1784.

The polemical book from which this engraving is taken rails against the theatrical ambience of some Austrian church services. Here the female singer in the nearest of the two musicians' galleries is a fashionable opera star, and the populace is ogling her rather than worshipping.

K. 20 ***God Is Our Refuge*****, in G minor**
Origin: London, July 1765
Scoring: SATB

In key and thematic construction, this short anthem shows similarities to a setting of the same psalm by the English composer Jonathan Battishill (1738–1801), composed in 1765. Mozart perhaps became acquainted with this setting in London and was prompted by it to compose his own setting. The ten-year-old Mozart's composition of twenty-three measures imitates the style of sixteenth-century English polyphony, a style that he must have heard in England. K.G.F.

K. 34 *Scande coeli limina, in C major*
Origin: Seeon Monastery, Bavaria? early 1767?
Scoring: SATB, soprano solo, 2 trumpets and timpani, 2 violins, basso, organ

This is a setting of the offertory for the feast of Saint Benedict. Instead of the liturgical offertory text, it uses a rhymed text, which, in its typical Baroque style, was probably composed by a Benedictine poet. According to an unsubstantiated nineteenth-century tradition that goes back to the Altötting chapel organist Max Keller, Mozart wrote this offertory for the Benedictine monastery of Seeon on the return trip from the grand tour to London, Paris, and the Low Countries. The Mozart family visited this cloister on many occasions. Mozart sets the text with cheerful abandon, though with occasional technical mistakes. K.G.F.

K. 47 *Veni Sancte Spiritus, in C major*
Origin: Vienna, autumn 1768
Scoring: SATB, S/A/T/B soli, 2 oboes, 2 horns, 2 trumpets and timpani, strings with organ continuo

While Mozart's settings of psalms and canticles reflect Baroque sacred ideals and demands, his antiphons are written in the spirit of *Empfindsamkeit,* the new sentimental trend in music of the time. K. 47 gives the orchestra considerable attention both in the dimensions of the instrumental passages and in the richness of scoring. The setting juxtaposes contrasting themes that reflect Mozart's attempt to match music with words. The text is suitable for Pentecost (Whitsunday).
K.G.F.

K. 117 *Benedictus sit Deus, in C major (K⁶ 66a)*
Origin: Salzburg, 1769
Scoring: SATB, soprano solo, 2 flutes, 2 horns, 2 trumpets and timpani, strings with organ continuo

This offertory on "Benedictus sit Deus," with the following psalm verse "Introibo domum tuam," is divided into three movements, like a symphony: Allegro (chorus)—Andante (solo)—Allegro (chorus). The first chorus follows a sonata form, which Mozart also uses in the Kyrie and Agnus Dei of the Mass K. 139. The middle section, "Introibo," is a free-form two-part aria with rich coloratura in the solo voice, similar to the "Quoniam" and "Et in spiritum" of the Mass K. 66. The final chorus uses the eighth psalm tone four times in a row, descending stepwise through soprano, tenor, bass, and alto; it is accompanied by instrumental runs in a style typical of the church music of Salzburg and Vienna. The text is one that may be used at any time in the liturgical year.

Despite what has sometimes been asserted, K. 117 is not the same work as the lost offertory, K. 47b, which Mozart composed for the consecration of the Waisenhaus Church in Vienna in December 1768. K.G.F.

K. 141 *Te Deum, in C major (K⁶ 66b)*
Origin: Salzburg, end of 1769
Scoring: SATB, 4 trumpets [and timpani], 2 violins, bass, organ

The authenticity of this Te Deum was long disputed. No autograph has survived, and the striking resemblance, often traceable bar by bar, to a Te Deum, also in C major, composed in 1760 by Michael Haydn in Grosswardein, caused many scholars to assume that this work, too, derived from the younger Haydn. Some years ago, however, performing parts with annotations in Leopold Mozart's hand were discovered in Salzburg, so that few doubts now remain as to the authenticity of this early work. And it is hardly surprising that, particularly with forms which had to be handled strictly, a young composer (Mozart was thirteen in 1769) finds his way by following models. In many respects this piece manages to be completely convincing, and even the rigorous musicologist Alfred Einstein describes the work as "sure in construction, thrilling in its choral declamation, and having a certain rustic South-German grandeur, even in the closing double fugue: a good finish to Mozart's activities as a composer of church music before he set out on his Italian journeys." W.K.

K. 143 *Ergo interest . . . Quaere superna, in G major (K⁶ 73a)*
Origin: Salzburg, late 1773
Scoring: soprano solo, strings with organ continuo

This brief motet is cast in the form of a recitative and aria—an example of the affinity between church music and operatic music. Certainly Mozart uses some of his favorite dramatic devices in the aria. It is an Andante in triple meter, not without hints of resemblances to other, more familiar works (like the slow movement of the Bassoon Concerto, K. 191, or the ultimately poignant treatment of the opening motif, "Porgi amor," in *Figaro*). The aria is in a typical sonata-form pattern. At the end the singer has the opportunity to supply a brief cadenza. S.S.

K. 85 *Miserere, in A minor (K⁶ 73s)*
Origin: Bologna, July or August 1770
Scoring: ATB, basso continuo

In this setting of Psalm 50 for the office, composed in the strict style of Padre Giovanni Battista Martini albeit with certain technical liberties, Mozart adopted the most externally strict sacred practice. Carrying on the Renaissance polyphonic tradition, Mozart intends an *alternatim* performance: only the odd verses are composed, since the even verses would have been performed as simple Gregorian chant. The original manuscript (entirely in Leopold Mozart's hand) contains only verses one, three, five, seven, nine, eleven, thirteen, and fifteen; verses seventeen, nineteen, and twenty-one were added later, possibly from a composition by Martini, possibly composed by Johann André. K.G.F.

K. 86 *Quaerite primum regnum Dei, in D minor (K⁶ 73v)*
Origin: Bologna, October 9, 1770
Scoring: SATB

During their first trip to Italy, Mozart and his father spent the summer of 1770 at Count Pallavicini's house, near Bologna. Before leaving Bologna Mozart underwent and passed tests for admittance to membership of the ancient and esteemed Accademia Filarmonica; the surviving manuscripts of his test piece, a twenty-two measure antiphon on a *cantus firmus* (K. 86) with annotations by Padre Martini, and his clean copy of the reworking, suggest that he had help. The work follows the Academy's strict rules for the *stile osservato* (style to be observed), that is, the Renaissance style of church music as it survived in the seventeenth and eighteenth centuries. K.G.F.

K. 108 *Regina coeli, in C major (K^6 74d)*
Origin: Salzburg, May 1771
Scoring: SATB, soprano solo, 2 oboes (doubling flutes), 2 horns, 2 trumpets and timpani, strings with organ continuo

This is a full-dress, ceremonial piece, set in the key customary for such works. There are four movements. This first is akin to a concerto allegro, with a ritornello; notable here are the *rauschenden Violinen* (rushing violins) so beloved of Austrian ecclesiastical composers of the eighteenth century. The second movement, Tempo moderato, follows the same formal scheme, although here the vocal contribution is assigned mainly to a solo soprano; the "operatic" manner is evident in the florid passages and the wide leaps. A still slower movement follows: an Adagio un poco andante for solo voice and strings, in A minor; the throbbing string accompaniment and the rising sequences of florid phrases carry the expressive sense. The final "Alleluia" is like a miniature symphony finale; there are two episodes for the solo voice, but the message is chiefly sustained in the choral reiteration of "alleluia," the vigorous string writing, and the confident brass assertions of the celebratory C major. S.S.

K. 72 *Internatos mulierum, in G major (K^6 74f)*
Origin: Salzburg? May or June 1771?
Scoring: SATB, 2 violins, basso, organ

In this Offertory Mozart shows more mature powers of textual interpretation than in earlier proper settings. In its unified structure, the Offertory rises above works written before the first visit to Italy. A large instrumental prelude introduces the main choral section, rich in contrasting ideas; earlier works begin with the chorus immediately. The orchestra is subordinate to the voices, although the individual handling of instruments is more developed than in earlier sacred works. K.G.F.

K. 127 *Regina coeli, in B-flat major*
Origin: Salzburg, May 1772
Scoring: SATB, soprano solo, 2 oboes (doubling flutes), 2 horns, strings with organ continuo

Like K. 108, this motet in three sections has for its text the Marian antiphon, "Queen of Heaven," which many composers had set. Both the richness of the instrumental scoring and the prominent role given to the solo soprano illustrate the accomplishments in the operatic style which Mozart had acquired in Italy. The light choral setting, rather sparing in its use of imitation, and the independent instrumental writing demonstrate this, as do the solos, which are laid out like arias. For the soprano part Mozart seems to have had in mind as soloist the wife of his Salzburg colleague Michael Haydn, as we learn from a letter of Leopold's dated April 12, 1778: "Ceccarelli will sing the 'Salve' from the 'Regina coeli,' which Wolfgang did for Haydn's wife." The letter shows that Mozart still thought the work worth performing even in later years. W.K.

K. 142 *Tantum ergo, in B-flat major (K^3 Anh 186d, K^6 Anh C 3.04)*
Origin: Salzburg? begun 1772?
Scoring: SATB, soprano solo, 2 trumpets, strings with organ continuo

The two settings of the sacramental motet text "Tantum ergo," K. 142 and 197, are in a simple folksong style. The authenticity of each is doubtful, though upheld by the *Neue Mozart-Ausgabe*. K.G.F.

K. 165 *Exsultate, jubilate, in F major (K⁶ 158a)*

Origin: Milan, January 1773
Scoring: soprano solo, 2 oboes, 2 horns, strings with organ continuo

It was for the famous castrato Venanzio Rauzzini that Mozart wrote "Exsultate, jubilate," an unbelievably advanced work for a boy not yet seventeen. Rauzzini sang the first performance on January 17, 1773, at the Church of the Theatines in Milan. Rauzzini must have had a voice of great agility to have negotiated the fast runs and wide leaps that Mozart demanded of him. The motet is in three movements, with the addition of a short recitative preceding the central Andante. No "learned" or archaic hints give a special ecclesiastical flavor; the motet is a straightforward operatic anthem of cheerful praise.

There is a substantial introduction before the entry of the voice in the Allegro first movement. The simple but carefully composed recitative is supported by organ alone, while the central Andante is scored for voice with strings and organ; this movement is the longest and most substantial. The second and third movements are linked by a two-measure modulating passage. After a short phrase of introduction, the oboes and horns now rejoining the strings, the first "Alleluia" rings out. The movement continues as a dazzling concerto for voice and orchestra, ending in a paean of joy. A.R.

K. 197 *Tantum ergo, in D major (K³ Anh 186e, K⁶ Anh C 3.05)*

Origin: Salzburg? 1774?
Scoring: SATB, 2 trumpets and timpani, strings with organ continuo

See the note for the Tantum ergo, K. 142, above.

K. 198 *Sub tuum presidium, in F major (K³ 158b, K⁶ Anh C 3.08)*

Origin: Salzburg? 1774?
Scoring: soprano and tenor soli, strings with organ continuo

The text is an antiphon to the Nunc dimittis in the Marian office, used as an offertory. Mozart's composition appears to have a stylistic similarity to the Missa brevis, K. 192. It achieves a certain expressivity through its gentle sonority. Its authenticity is widely doubted, though upheld by the *Neue Mozart-Ausgabe.*

K.G.F.

K. 222 *Misericordias Domini, in D minor (K⁶ 205a)*

Origin: Munich, early 1775
Scoring: SATB, 2 violins, basso, organ

Mozart wrote this offertory in Munich, where he was performing his *opera buffa, La finta giardiniera,* for Elector Maximilian III Joseph of Bavaria, who had expressed a desire "de sentir qualche mia musica in contrapunto" (to hear some contrapuntal music by me), as Mozart later explained in a letter to Padre Martini in Bologna. Mozart, finding himself challenged to demonstrate his skill in polyphony, dealt with the pattern of responses in this liturgical text on the Sacrificial Act not by the traditional division between soloists and choir, but by alternating eleven times between homophony (Misericordias Domini) and polyphony (Cantabo in aeternam) in the choral writing. The work's avoidance of repetition and its attention to the emotional content of the text make it a masterpiece of counterpoint. W.K.

K. 260 *Venite populi in D major (K⁶ 248a)*
Origin: Salzburg, mid-1776
Scoring: SATB (double chorus), 2 violins ad libitum, basso, organ

Mozart composed this "Offertorium de venerabili sacramento" for an Ascension Day service. Here he uses two four-part choirs in chordal antiphony as well as in strict eight-part polyphony. The work has three sections—"Venite populi" (allegro), "O sors cunctis" (adagio), and "Eja ergo epulemur" (allegro)—and, like the earlier "Misericordias Domini," displays profound contrapuntal development within its narrow confines. This work had a great admirer in Johannes Brahms, who performed it in Vienna in 1872.
W.K.

K. 277 *Alma Dei creatoris, in F major (K⁶ 272a)*
Origin: Salzburg? 1777?
Scoring: SATB, S/A/T soli, 2 violins, basso, organ

In this "Offertorium de B. V. Maria" Mozart writes an antiphonal sequence of responds, alternating verse by verse between a soprano solo in *concertante* style and the largely homophonic four-part choir. The brief, relatively simple and unpretentious offertory provides a good idea of the everyday practice of florid liturgical music in the Salzburg of Mozart's time.
W.K.

K. 273 *Sancta Maria, Mater Dei, in F major*
Origin: Salzburg, September 9, 1777
Scoring: SATB, strings with organ continuo

Mozart wrote this "Graduale ad festum" to the Virgin for unknown reasons shortly before setting out on his journey to Mannheim; perhaps it may be regarded as a sort of votive offering on his part. This impression is strengthened by the fact that, with its ternary structure derived from sonata form, its singing melodies, and its homophonic vocal lines dominating the orchestra, the motet does not conform to the Salzburg tradition of church music and may perhaps be seen as a precursor of the late "Ave verum corpus," K. 618.
W.K.

K. 146 *Kommet her, ihr frechen Sünder, in B-flat major (K⁶ 317b)*
Origin: Salzburg? March or April 1779?
Scoring: soprano solo, strings with organ continuo

This three-verse German passion aria shows the development of Mozart's expressive abilities since composing the early German sacred cantata, *Die Schuldigkeit der ersten Gebots*. It may have been intended as an insertion aria in a passion oratorio, or as a vernacular motet for a passiontide service.
K.G.F.

K. 276 *Regina coeli, in C major (K⁶ 321b)*
Origin: Salzburg? 1779?
Scoring: SATB, S/A/T/B soli, 2 oboes, 2 trumpets and timpani, 2 violins, basso *with organ continuo*

Since no autograph has survived, the affinity between this Marian antiphon and the Vesperae de Dominica, K. 321, has meant that its date has been set at 1779, at the time of Mozart's return from France; but Mozart's Salzburg church music is so consistent in style that this estimate is not necessarily correct. The orchestration itself emphasizes the festive character of the work, which could have been composed in connection with Mozart's promotion to the post of Salzburg court organist.
W.K.

K. 343 *Two German Hymns (K^6 336c): "O Gottes Lamm" in F major, and "Als aus Ägypten" in C major*
Origin: Prague or Vienna, early? 1787
Scoring: soprano solo, basso continuo

These two works, the second of which has a text based on Psalm 114, adhere to the simple hymn style of the day, the best examples of which come from Michael Haydn. At the end of May 1787, Mozart wrote to Gottfried von Jacquin that he was forwarding a hymn. Perhaps the composition of hymns was occasioned by the reforms of Archbishop Hieronymus Colloredo, who in his pastoral letter of June 15, 1782, refers to a new hymnbook with *basso continuo* accompaniments. K.G.F.

K. 618 *Ave verum corpus, in D major*
Origin: Baden, June 17, 1791
Scoring: SATB, strings with organ continuo

The last year of Mozart's life was fraught with hardship. Out of favor at the court of the new Austrian emperor, Leopold II, he had to live from hand to mouth by teaching a few pupils, earning whatever he could from his compositions, and borrowing from friends. He was seriously in debt, his wife Constanze was in ill health and pregnant for the sixth time, and his surviving son, Karl, had to be educated and cared for.

On June 4, 1791, Constanze went with young Karl to Baden, the spa near Vienna, to take the waters. Wolfgang visited as often as he could, otherwise keeping in touch with affectionate letters full of jokes, gossip, and medical advice. His own problems he thoughtfully hid from her. On the 15th he left Vienna for a short stay in Baden, and a day or two later wrote the "Ave verum corpus."

It was a gift for Anton Stoll, organist and choirmaster of the Baden parish church. Stoll was both admirer and friend, often performing Mozart's music with his choir, and keeping an eye out for Constanze on her rather frequent medical visits. His choir and orchestra must have been reasonably proficient; they had performed the "Coronation" Mass, K. 317, the previous year, and in July of 1791 were to give the *Missa brevis* in B flat, K. 275.

"Ave verum corpus" was the first church music to come from Mozart's pen since the unfinished C-minor Mass, K. 427, written some eight years earlier, excepting perhaps the Kyrie, K. 341. It was, it seems, intended for the celebration of the Feast of Corpus Christi on June 23. It is a piece of wonderful simplicity, a pure distillation of heartfelt devotion. A.R.

OPPOSITE. The young women of the Pietà, an orphanage in Venice, performing a sacred work for instruments and voices. Museo Correr, Venice.

Placed in the organ gallery, the young women are also behind a screen for modesty's sake. In Protestant churches in which elaborate music was cultivated (for instance, in Bach's Lutheran services), cantatas or oratorios on sacred texts were usually part of the worship service. In the Catholic countries of southern Germany, Austria, and northern Italy, however, they were more likely to be separate productions, sometimes in churches but more often in halls or theaters as a kind of substitute for opera, which was proscribed on various holy days.

2

Cantatas and Oratorios

BACKGROUND AND OVERVIEW

Operas are plays set to music from beginning to end, and oratorios are operas with sacred subjects—and some other differences. Oratorios were usually not meant to be acted, but performed in concert form. Like eighteenth-century opera, eighteenth-century oratorio has recitatives, arias, and ensembles. Not all opera reserves a major role for the choir, but most oratorio does. The choruses of oratorios are often fugal and there is frequently a (singing) narrator. Oratorio texts are sometimes scriptural, sometimes newly written poetry, and sometimes a mixture of the two. These texts usually contain a great deal more didactic, meditative, and philosophical content than would be workable in the more psychological and action-oriented opera librettos. Oratorios were most often commissioned to be performed during Lent and on other holy days of the church calendar, when theaters and opera houses were closed. They were sometimes performed by church musicians and sometimes by opera musicians, but more often than not in a hall or theater rather than a church. They were almost never a formal part of a church service.

A cantata is a work in the style of an oratorio but much briefer. Cantatas exhibit an extremely wide range of functions, styles, and subject matter, and the genre is therefore difficult to define. There were also cantatas on secular subjects, but Mozart's secular cantatas are usually called *serenatas.* Some of his Masonic works could also be considered cantatas, and their poems are quasi-religious. N.Z.

K. 35 *Die Schuldigkeit des ersten Gebots, Part 1*

Origin: Salzburg, early 1767
Author: Ignaz Anton Weiser
Scoring: 3 sopranos, 2 tenors, 2 flutes, 2 oboes, 2 bassoons, 2 horns, trombone, strings

---

Throughout the seventeenth and eighteenth centuries the prince-archbishops of Salzburg showed a particular predilection for the theater. Grand operatic spectacles, organized by the personnel of their own court chapel, were presented on festive occasions at court. Of special significance for Salzburg's musical life was a genre of school drama whose aims were chiefly pedagogic and moral. The librettists, who were principally Benedictine instructors, took the subject matter for their texts from the Bible, from the lives of saints, and from church history. Mythological and historical themes were also a popular choice for these plays. Initially music played only a modest part in school dramas. Relatively brief choruses were soon followed by dance interludes; and, finally, arias and entire music-dramatic complexes found their way into the genre.

Structurally a sacred *Singspiel* differs little from a school opera. Its subject matter is sacred, and its main accent is placed on allegorical figures. Performances of such works are known to have taken place in Salzburg in St. Peter's, in the cathedral, in the church or monastery on the Nonnberg, and in the archbishop's palace.

It was customary in Salzburg for a sacred *Singspiel* to be divided among a number of composers. There were, accordingly, three local composers entrusted with the task of setting *Die Schuldigkeit des ersten und fürnehmsten Gebots* (The obligation of the first and most emminent commandment: referring to St. Mark 12:30, "And thou shalt love the Lord thy God with all thy heart, and with all thy soul, and with all thy mind, and with all thy strength: this is the first commandment"). The three composers were Mozart, Michael Haydn, and Anton Adlgasser. The whereabouts of the music to the second and third parts remain unknown.

The text was by Ignaz Anton Weiser, an eminent member of the local middle classes and a textile merchant. The aim and purport of the poem is made clear in the preface to the printed text, a piece written in ornate language typical of the time: "That there is no more perilous spiritual state than lukewarmness in the pursuance of our soul's salvation is most assuredly confirmed for us by that same divine truth that is expressed in the words of the sacred Revelation of St. John 3:14, 16: 'I know thy works, that thou art neither cold nor hot: I would thou wert cold or hot. So then, because thou art lukewarm, and neither cold nor hot, I will spue thee out of my mouth.' "

Die Schuldigkeit des ersten Gebots is a multilayered work musically, which took the eleven-year-old Mozart 201 pages of musical manuscript to complete. Almost without exception the text of the recitatives was copied into the manuscript by Leopold Mozart, who also took it upon himself to touch up some of the arias and to add dynamic markings in the full score. The records of the Salzburg treasury for March, 18, 1767, record: "To little Mozartl for composing the music of an oratorio a 12 ducat gold medallion . . . 60 florins." In writing *Die Schuldigkeit des ersten Gebots* Mozart not only enriched the Salzburg sacred Singspiel repertory, he also showed that he could assimilate local traditions and adapt them to suit his own stylistic ends. R.A.

K. 42 *Grabmusik (K⁶ 35a)*
Origin: Salzburg, 1767, revised mid-1770s
Author: anonymous
Scoring: soprano, bass, [2 oboes], 2 horns, strings (SATB added later)

The performance in church of a passion oratorio on Good Friday is a custom that survives in southern Germany to this day. The Emperor Leopold II himself, together with his court musicians, composed such *sepolcri* (passion oratorios) for Vienna. During Holy Week the court staged these *sepolcri* in front of the sacred tomb in the palace chapel. These scenic performances first took place with music by Italian composers such as Antonio Draghi and Antonio Caldara. The era of the *Empfindsamkeit* saw a heightened emotional level in the texts of the passion oratorios, which sometimes gave rise to a kind of sentimentalism in the texts and music that offends modern sensibilities.

Mozart composed his "Cantata on Christ's Grave," K. 42, for Holy Week 1767, under extraordinary circumstances. The archbishop of Salzburg "not crediting that such masterly compositions were really those of a child, shut him up for a week, during which he was not permitted to see any one, and was left only with music paper, and the words of an oratorio. During this short time he composed a very capital oratorio, which was most highly approved of upon being performed."

The text given Mozart is a dialogue between a Soul (bass) and an Angel (soprano); it was probably written by a local Salzburg poet. Textually the work has the form of a short cantata for two voices. The work is a notable achievement for the eleven-year-old composer, so firmly is it grounded in fashionable traditionalisms. Mozart had already made considerable strides in formal and expressive developments. The use of G minor, which had become the key of grief among the Italians, the sentimental thrust of melody and harmony, and the clarity with which the form reflects the text all place this passion cantata on the level of *Die Schuldigkeit des ersten Gebots*.

In about 1775 the work was revived. Mozart wrote for it a new, simple choral conclusion, "Jesu wahrer Gottes Sohn," and a preceding recitative, "O lobenswerter Sinn." K.F.

K. 118 *La Betulia liberata (K[6] 74c)*
Origin: Italy and Salzburg, March to July 1771
Author: Pietro Metastasio
Scoring: SATB, S/S/S/S/T/B soli, 2 oboes (doubling flutes), 2 bassoons, 4 horns, 2 trumpets, strings

Whereas *opera seria* took its subject matter from classical history and mythology, the *azione sacra* or oratorio drew repeatedly on the Holy Scriptures. The source of *La Betulia liberata* is the apocryphal Book of Judith, formerly included in the Old Testament.

We have only sketchy information concerning the genesis of *La Betulia liberata*. Leopold Mozart and his son are known to have left Venice for their first visit to Italy and to have arrived in Padua on March 13, 1771. The same day Mozart received a commission or *scrittura* to write an oratorio for Padua. On the 14th Leopold wrote from Vicenza to inform his wife that Mozart had been given "work" and that he "had to write an oratorio for Padua, which can be done as and when he likes." A good four months later, on July 19, 1771, we find Leopold writing from Salzburg to Count Gian Luca Pallavicini in Bologna, revealing that the oratorio had been commissioned by the Padua music lover Don Giuseppe Ximenes de Principi d'Aragona. Ximenes used to hold musical gatherings in his palazzo (as a rule it was oratorios and cantatas that were performed), and he was an important figure in Padua's musical life. Ximenes would no doubt have preferred it if Mozart had completed the work by Holy Week 1771. But the composer is unlikely to have made any progress on it during his return journey from Padua to Salzburg, which lasted from March 14 to 28, 1771. We can probably conclude from this that *La Betulia liberata* was written in Salzburg after the Mozarts' return there in the summer of 1771. We do not know whether Mozart sent the manuscript to Padua. Contemporary sources maintain an equally impenetrable silence on the question of a performance of the work. What is certain is that a *Betulia liberata* by the local composer Giuseppe Calegari was performed in Padua in 1771, and it may well be that Calegari's composition replaced Mozart's, either because the latter's setting was in some way unacceptable or because it arrived too late.

It was standard practice in Italy until around 1770 to replace operas with oratorios during the period of Lent. By about 1770 the oratorio had become a kind of *opera seria* without costumes and scenery. Indeed, oratorio had grown so like *opera seria* that a distinction can be sought only in its subject matter and dramaturgical conception.

Mozart's *La Betulia liberata* is written in the style of *opera seria,* well suited to the heroic subject matter of the piece, which demanded musical forms similar to those of *opera seria*. In consequence, what we find in Mozart's score is a tripartite overture, da capo and bravura arias, and accompanied and unaccompanied recitatives. Particular attention has been devoted to the instrumental writing, and Mozart also involves the chorus in the action, as Christoph Willibald Gluck did, giving its members an independent life and setting them off from the background. The arias are richly scored, with the winds in particular being integrated into the structure. The extravagant coloratura of individual arias points the way to Mozart's Italian masterpieces. The recitatives also reveal particular care on the composer's part.

The four-fold melody of the final chorus (No. 16) is not by Mozart, but has been taken over from Michael Haydn's Latin school-opera *Pietas christiana*. The melody is derived from a Gregorian psalm tone on the words "In exitu Israel de Aegypto."

In his *La Betulia liberata* Mozart pulled out all the stops, so to speak, and painted a lively picture using a highly colorful palette in order to show that he could effortlessly adapt his style to suit oratorio and complete his commissioned work without any difficulty. R.A.

K. 469 *Davidde penitente*
Origin: Vienna, early March 1785
Author: Lorenzo da Ponte?
Scoring: SATB, S/S/T soli, 2 flutes, 2 oboes, 2 clarinets, 2 bassoons, 2 horns, 3 trombones, timpani, strings

In 1783, Mozart petitioned the Viennese Tonkünstler-Sozietät, a musicians' benevolent organization, for membership. There ensued a lengthy correspondence between the composer and the organization, with Mozart repeatedly inquiring after the status of his application and the Sozietät repeatedly requesting his birth certificate, which he apparently never furnished. Mozart was never granted admission but for several years, probably in an attempt to curry their favor, he allowed the Sozietät to perform his music at benefits.

In January 1785 the Sozietät commissioned Mozart to write a new piece for their Lenten pension fund concert to benefit musicians' widows. He accepted the assignment but perhaps came to feel that the fee offered did not justify writing an entire original composition. In February Mozart wrote the Sozietät to say that he was unable to complete the psalm setting he had promised them and offered to substitute a previously written psalm which had never been heard in Vienna. This idea was evidently rejected, for by March, Mozart had arrived at a different solution: he fashioned an oratorio by recycling his incomplete Mass in C minor, K. 427, and supplementing it with two freshly composed arias whose manuscripts are dated March 6 and 11.

Mozart must have understood the worth of his unfinished Mass and must have been glad to afford the music another hearing, albeit in disguised form. To create *Davidde penitente,* he lifted the Kyrie and Gloria wholesale; he did not use the two movements of the Credo. The newly written Italian text, comprising paraphrases of sections of David's penitential and laudatory psalms, has often been attributed, on circumstantial evidence, to Lorenzo da Ponte, who would soon provide the librettos for Mozart's three greatest Italian operas.

For all the music's undiminished splendor, *Davidde penitente* exhibits infelicities of prosody rarely encountered elsewhere in Mozart's canon. For instance, in the Terzetto, No. 9, a lowly article, "Le," is sung by all three soloists in their high registers, beginning on a strong beat and lasting a full measure; and in No. 3, the aria for soprano II, the preposition "da" takes off on a cheeky four-measure flight of melisma and high notes, landing on a trill. The overall effect is rather like watching a great dancer leap gracefully about in ill-fitting, second-hand clothes.

The oratorio's two original numbers were tailor-made for its first soloists, both friends and frequent collaborators of

Mozart. For Johann Valentin Adamberger, Mozart supplied "A te, fra tanti affanni" (No. 6), a tenor tour de force beginning with a supplicatory Andante and closing with a hardy, florid Allegro. Mozart obliged Caterina Cavalieri with the soprano aria, "Fra l'oscure ombre funeste" (No. 8); though it opens with an ominous, chromatic Andante, this wastes little time in giving way to an extended, brilliant Allegro with much coloratura and wide intervallic leaps.

In announcing its performances of *Davidde penitente,* the Tonkünstler-Sozietät gingerly skirted the issue of Mozart's self-piracy: "A new cantata adapted to this occasion by Sig Amadeo Mozart, for 3 voices with choruses, performed by Sig^ra^ Cavallieri [sic], Sig^ra^ Distler, and Sig Adamberger." *Davidde penitente* served as the second half of a program that began with a new Joseph Haydn symphony. The premiere performance, at Vienna's Burgtheater on March 13, 1785, boasts the curious distinction of having been perhaps the most poorly attended and financially unsuccessful concert ever given by the Sozietät. It pulled in only a few hundred people, and the receipts were a mere 733 florins, thirteen kroner (of which nearly one-third had been donated by the emperor). A second performance the following week netted about one-fourth that amount. May posterity hold *Davidde penitente* in higher esteem. C.E.

3

Masonic Music

Frontispiece of the libretto of Mozart's and Emanuel Schikaneder's Singspiel *Die Zauberflöte* (The Magic Flute). Engraving by Ignaz Alberti.

The premiere took place at the Freihaus Theater in a Viennese suburb on September 30, 1791, slightly more than two months before Mozart's death. The Masonic nature of The Magic Flute *is made plain by the symbols shown in this engraving.*

BACKGROUND AND OVERVIEW

The fraternal secret society known as the Freemasons may well owe its name and origin to a Medieval craftsmen's guild of master builders, but the organization's clandestine nature precludes accurate knowledge of its early stages. In the eighteenth century, at least, Freemasonry became associated with the humanitarian ideals of the Enlightenment in Western Europe. Though not antireligious, Masonry was persistently opposed by the Catholic church, and usually regarded with suspicion or worse by reactionary governments—perhaps rightly, for its numbers included many apostles of freer speech and more liberal government. (George Washington and other Founding Fathers of the American republic were Masons.)

In the Austrian Empire, Freemasonry had been banned by Empress Maria Theresa in 1764. During the 1780s, Emperor Joseph II, a more liberal ruler, tolerated the movement, but from 1790 his successor, Emperor Leopold II, returned to suppression. Mozart became a Mason during the calmer years of the 1780s. On December 14, 1784, he was admitted as an Apprentice to the Viennese lodge known as Beneficence (Loge zur Wohlthätigkeit). The city's most prominent and aristocratic lodge was the True Concord (Loge zur wahren Eintracht), which Mozart frequently visited and where, on January 7, 1785, he was raised to the second degree, that of Journeyman.

That spring, Mozart's father visited Vienna, and was also admitted as an Apprentice to the Beneficence lodge. Probably because of his age and professional standing, Leopold quickly passed the next degrees, reaching that of Master Mason on April 22, before he returned to Salzburg. Although the surviving records are vague about Wolfgang's progress, it seems that he did not become a Master Mason until the following year.

At the end of 1785, the emperor decreed that the eight Viennese lodges should be combined into two or three—no doubt to make it easier to keep an eye on this potentially subversive movement. Mozart's lodge was joined with two others to form the Crowned Hope lodge (Loge zur gekrönten Hoffnung), which opened on January 14, 1786.

The most renowned expression of Mozart's Freemasonry is, of course, the opera *The Magic Flute* (1791), which celebrates the Masonic ideals of truth, brotherhood, and love, and incorporates a good deal of Masonic symbolism in its action and stagecraft. Mozart also wrote a number of pieces specifically for the ceremonies of the lodges in the early years of his membership, and again at the end of his life. D.H.

K. 148 *Lobgesang auf die feierliche Johannisloge, "O heiliges Band der Freundschaft treuer Brüder" (K[1] Anh 276, K[6] 125h)*

Origin: Salzburg? 1775–76?
Author: Ludwig Friedrich Lenz
Scoring: voice, basso continuo

On the basis of its text and an inscription on the manuscript ("Song of Praise—solemnly, for the St. John Lodge"), this simple song, with only a figured-bass part as accompaniment, has often been ascribed to Mozart's Masonic period, 1784 or later. However, the evidence of the musical style, the paper, and the handwriting point to an origin in Salzburg in the 1770s (see also p. 92). D.H.

K. 429 ***Dir, Seele des Weltalls (K^3 420a, K^6 468a)***

Origin: Vienna, 1785?
Author: L. L. Haschka
Scoring: TTB, tenor solo, flute, 2 oboes, clarinet, bassoon, 2 horns, strings

Mozart finished two movements of this cantata, and broke off a third movement after seventeen measures—for what reason we do not know. After Mozart's death his friend the Abbé Maximilian Stadler made two performing versions of the completed movements; his orchestration is the basis of many present-day performances. The key of the opening chorus, E-flat (also the principal key of *The Magic Flute*), was regarded as particularly Masonic—its three flats had special significance in the rituals of the lodges. D.H.

K. 468 ***Lied zur Gesellenreise, "Die ihr einem neuen Grade"***

Origin: Vienna, March 26, 1785
author: Franz Joseph Ratschky
Scoring: voice, organ or piano

This graceful song celebrates promotion to *Geselle* (Journeyman), the second degree of Masonry. Since Mozart's father was elevated to that grade on April 16, at a ceremony in the True Concord lodge, it is likely that it was sung on that occasion. The frequent pairs of tied notes sung to a single syllable are another Masonic musical symbol, representing brotherhood.

D.H.

K. 471 ***Die Maurerfreude, "Sehen, wie dem starren Forscherauge die Natur"***

Origin: Vienna, April 20, 1785
Author: Franz Petran
Scoring: TTB, tenor solo, 2 oboes, clarinet, 2 horns, strings

On April 24, 1785, the True Concord lodge held a celebration in honor of its master, the distinguished naturalist Ignaz von Born, who that day had been made a Knight of the Realm for his discovery of a new and more economical method of smelting. Mozart and his father were both present, and a new cantata by Wolfgang was sung, *Die Maurerfreude* (The Mason's Joy), with words by the lodge's resident poet. The tenor soloist was Johann Valentin Adamberger, who had been the first Belmonte in *Die Entführung aus dem Serail*. Also in E-flat major, this cantata is principally for tenor solo, the chorus entering only near the end to clinch the final message, the praise of the emperor. D.H.

K. deest ***Meistermusik, "Replevit me amaritudinibus"***

Origin: Vienna, July 1785
Scoring: unison men's voices, 2 oboes, clarinet, basset horn, 2 horns, strings

This is the recently reconstructed first version of the work better known as *Maurerische Trauermusik* (Masonic Funeral Music, K. 477). Mozart composed it for a ceremony at the True Concord lodge on August 12, 1785, on the occasion of the elevation of a visiting brother, Carl von König, to the rank of Master. It differs from the more familiar version by the inclusion of men's voices that intone, in octaves with the oboes and clarinets, the twenty-bar *cantus firmus* in the central section.

The *cantus firmus* is based on the psalm tone for the singing of the Miserere and the Lamentations of Jeremiah during Holy Week. The verses that fit Mozart's scansion are Lamentations 3, v. 15 and 54:

He filled me with bitter herbs, and made me drunk with wormwood.
Waters flooded over my head; I said, I am lost.

The first of these verses may allude to the Masonic trial by earth, the second to the trial by water. The music is astonishing in its somber intensity, effected through low orchestral timbres, dramatic changes of dynamics, and a sweeping violin descant above the static chant intonation.

W.C.

K. 477 ***Maurerische Trauermusik (K^6 479a)***
Origin: Vienna, November 1785
Scoring: 2 oboes, clarinet, basset horn, 2 horns, strings (2 more basset horns, contrabassoon added later)

In November 1785, when Mozart was probably busy composing *Figaro,* two important Masons died: on the 6th, Georg August, Duke of Mecklenburg-Strelitz, and on the next day, Count Franz "Quin-quin" Esterházy of Galántha. On the 17th, a memorial service was held at the Crowned Hope lodge, for which Mozart arranged the Masonic Funeral Music from his *Meistermusik* of a few months earlier (see the preceding entry). On this occasion, Mozart dispensed with voices for the *cantus firmus.*

A second performance of this arrangement probably took place on December 9. For this occasion Mozart added a part for contrabassoon, and then two more basset horn parts—evidently because two well-known players of the instrument, fellow Masons, were in Vienna (and in somewhat indigent condition, as they were given a benefit concert by one of the lodges).

D.H.

K. 483 ***Zerfliesset heut', geliebte Brüder***
Origin: Vienna, late 1785
Author: Augustin Veith Edler von Schittlersberg
Scoring: TTB, tenor solo, organ or piano

The songs K. 483 and 484, each with two verses for the soloist and a refrain for the chorus, are evidently related to the consolidation of the Viennese lodges. The words of "Zerfliesset heut' " contain clear references to this event; headed "For the opening of the lodge," the song presumably served for the inauguration of the Crowned Hope lodge in January 1786.

D.H.

K. 484 ***Ihr unsre neuen Leiter***
Origin: Vienna, late 1785
Author: Augustin Veith Edler von Schittlersberg
Scoring: TTB, tenor solo, organ or piano

Just as K. 483 was intended for the opening of a new lodge, K. 484 was for the closing of an old one, the Benificence lodge.

D.H.

K. 619 ***Die ihr des unermesslichen Weltalls Schöpfer ehrt***
Origin: Vienna, July 1791
Author: Frank Heinrich Ziegenhagen
Scoring: tenor, piano

In the summer of 1791, F. H. Ziegenhagen, a merchant from Hamburg who belonged to a lodge in Regensburg, commissioned this setting, for solo voice and piano, of his own text. The six movements of the "little German cantata" are brief and continuous, mixing arioso and recitative, and passing through a variety of moods. The style both of this work and of K. 623 shares the clarity, directness, and euphony of *The Magic Flute.*

D.H.

K. 623 ***Laut verkünde unsre Freude***
Origin: Vienna, November 15, 1791
Author: Emanuel Schikaneder
Scoring: 2 tenors, bass, flute, 2 oboes, 2 horns, strings

The final entry in Mozart's catalogue of his own works is this "little Masonic cantata," finished and dated on November 15, during a brief period of remission in his final illness. Three days later, Mozart was well enough to conduct the new piece at the opening of the new temple of Crowned Hope, but on the 20th he took to his bed again, and died on December 5. The cantata was published the following year, with the title *Kleine Freimaurer-Kantate,* to raise money for "his distressed widow and orphans." The opening and closing choruses of this work are identical. D.H.

4

Theater Music

A Venetian theater during an opera performance. Anonymous engraving, from Zaccaria Seriman, *I viaggi d'Enrico Wanton* (Venice, ca. 1749)

The prima donna *and* primo uomo *sing a duet accompanied by a typically situated eighteenth-century opera orchestra: two rows of musicians, half facing the stage, half the audience. Two horn players, their bells in the air, can be seen at the extreme right of the orchestra. It is carnival season, so the audience is masked.*

BACKGROUND AND OVERVIEW

Mozart was a man of the theater. At almost every moment in his career he was either searching for a good libretto to set, seeking a commission to write an opera, actually composing an opera, or rehearsing a production. He went to hear plays, operas, and ballets whenever opportunities presented themselves. He knew that the greatest prestige and money and best performing forces that his society could offer were to be found in the opera houses supported by almost every large and small European city and court. The urgency with which he pursued opera can be sensed almost palpably in many of his letters. "I have looked through at least a hundred libretti and more, but I have hardly found a single one with which I am satisfied," he wrote to his father in desperation in May 1783.

Mozart's operatic apprenticeship began in London in 1764–65, where his father took him to the opera and set him to composing arias to texts drawn from famous librettos by Pietro Metastasio. Throughout his life, Mozart continued to compose isolated arias and operatic scenes, as concert arias for singers he favored, as insertion arias for other composer's operas, and as trial pieces of one kind or another.

As for operas themselves, Mozart wrote in the three genres cultivated in Italy and central Europe: serious, all-sung Italian opera *(opera seria);* comic, all-sung Italian opera *(opera buffa);* and *Singspiel,* which was German-language operetta with spoken dialogue liberally spiced by arias, ensembles, dances, and the like. If one includes those works that Mozart did not complete (but for which he composed large amounts of viable music) as well as serenatas (*opera seria* texts intended to be performed in concert rather than staged), the production of his short career is astonishing in this genre alone (see lists below).

Mozart's dramatic gifts have long been celebrated: he not only had a genius for beautiful melody and catchy rhythms, an ability to capture the feel and meaning of words and phrases, and an intense sense of dramatic timing, but he seems also to have been an intuitive psychologist who could "paint" in tones for his listeners the personalities, emotions, and situations of his characters in ways that make them come to life. The characters who people Mozart's operas come from distant times and places, inhabiting strange and quaint landscapes, but as soon as the music starts, we think that we know them, that they resemble our friends and neighbors, and even ourselves. N.Z.

OPERA SERIA

Apollo et Hyacinthus
Mitridate, rè di Ponto
Ascanio in Alba
Il sogno di Scipione
Lucio Silla
Il rè pastore
Idomeneo, rè di Creta
La clemenza di Tito

OPERA BUFFA

La finta semplice
La finta giardiniera
L'oca del Cairo
Lo sposo deluso
Le nozze di Figaro
Don Giovanni
Così fan tutte

SINGSPIEL

Bastien und Bastienne
Zaide
Die Entführung aus dem Serail
Der Schauspieldirektor
Die Zauberflöte

OPERAS AND SINGSPIELS

K. 38 *Apollo et Hyacinthus*
Origin: Salzburg, before May 1767
Author: Rufinus Widl?

Following his success abroad Mozart was invited to demonstrate his abilities in his hometown of Salzburg. *Apollo et Hyacinthus* (Apollo and Hyacinth) was commissioned by the town's university, an institution with which the composer's father Leopold was already on the best of terms. Many of his pupils attended the university high school, where the theater played an important part in the school's activities. The young Mozart had first come into contact with the University theater on September 1 and 3, 1761, when as a five-year-old boy he had appeared as an extra in performances of the Latin school drama *Sigismundus Hungariae Rex* with words by Jakob Anton Wimmer and music by Johann Ernst Eberlin. As a rule school performances were given at the end of the academic year, although the term time itself was by no means unusual.

In 1767 the University arranged for its fourth-year high-school students or "syntaxians" to present a performance "ex voto." (Details of the promise or vow are not known.) The author of the piece was probably Rufinus Widl, a Dominican monk from the monastery of Seeon in Bavaria. Widl wrote the Latin tragedy *Clementia Croesi* for a performance planned for the summer term, interpolating a musical *intermedio* in between the acts of the spoken drama. The task of setting the *intermedio* to music was entrusted to Widl's fellow citizen, the eleven-year-old Wolfgang Mozart, who—it will be remembered—never enrolled at a school or university in his whole life.

Preparations for the performances are known to have been taken in hand by at least April 29, 1767. On May 1 mass was held in the University Church, the platform in the Great Hall being unusable because of the elaborate sets. Stage rehearsals were held on May 10, 11, and 12. The school records for May 13 report, "Wednesday. After the midday meal the syntaxians' play was performed in keeping with our promise; written by their excellent teacher and admirably presented by his pupils, it afforded the liveliest pleasure. I congratulate their excellent teacher on his great acclaim. Moreover, the music by Herr Wolfgang Mozart, an eleven-year-old boy, met with general approbation; in the evening he gave us excellent proof of his musical skills on the keyboard." The performance was a great success, but, apart from this single amateur airing, the work was not heard again during Mozart's lifetime.

Mozart later reused an abbreviated form of the duet, "Natus cadit, atque Deus" (No. 8), in his F-major Symphony, K. 43 (see p. 167). R.A.

The Greek legend as told by Ovid relates that Zephyr and Apollo both loved a youth, Hyacinth, who, however, cared only for Apollo. When out of jealousy Zephyr killed Hyacinth, Apollo gave Hyacinth immortality by turning his blood into the flower that bears his name. This overtly homosexual story was altered for performance by the students of Salzburg University. In the libretto for K. 38 Hyacinth and Zephyr are friends, and both Zephyr and Apollo love Hyacinth's sister Melia. This rivalry is the basis for the action. N.Z.

K. 51 *La finta semplice* (K[6] *46a*)
Origin: Vienna, between April and July 1768
Author: Marco Coltellini, after Carlo Goldoni

Mozart's second stay in Vienna from September 11, 1767, to January 5, 1769, was principally intended to provide him with an opportunity to write an opera for the Imperial and Royal capital of the Austro-Hungarian Dual Monarchy. In a letter dated January 30 to February 3, 1768, and addressed to his landlord in Salzburg, Johann Lorenz Hagenauer, Leopold revealed that Wolfgang was to write an opera for Vienna: "and what sort of an uproar do you suppose has secretly arisen among the composers?—what?—today it is a (Christoph Willibald) Gluck and tomorrow a boy of twelve who is seen sitting at a keyboard and conducting his opera—yes, in spite of all their grudging envy! I have even won over Gluck to our side, so that, although he is not altogether whole-hearted, he dare not show what he really thinks, since our patrons are his too, and in order to secure ourselves with regard to the *acteurs,* who generally cause the composer the greatest annoyance, I have taken up the matter with them myself, and one of them has given me all the suggestions himself. But to tell the truth, the initial idea of getting Wolfgangerl to write an opera came from the Emperor himself, since he twice asked Wolfgangerl if he would like to compose an opera and conduct it himself."

On June 29, however, we find Leopold writing to Hagenauer that "envy has broken forth on every side," and on July 30, he wrote to say that all of Vienna's composers, with Gluck at their head, had left no stone unturned in their efforts "to hinder the progress of this opera. The singers were incited and the orchestra stirred up against us, everything was done to prevent the performances of this opera from going ahead. . . . In the meantime it was being put about by certain persons that the music was not worth a rap, while others were saying that the music did not fit the words or the meter, since the boy did not understand the Italian language sufficiently well."

The hope that *La finta semplice* (The Pretend Simpleton) would finally be performed in Vienna in August proved unfounded, and so, when Leopold was granted an audience with Joseph II on September 21, he handed the emperor a *species facti* or letter of complaint. Above all he complained of intrigues against Wolfgang, and expressed his regret that, in spite of a positive response on the part of the court and various influential individuals, the opera was not to be staged after all.

Two arguments may be adduced in support of the claim that a performance of *La finta semplice* took place in Salzburg in 1769: firstly, the libretto was published in the city in 1769; and, secondly, Mozart's manuscript score contains alterations dating from that year. The singers named in the Salzburg libretto were members of the prince-archbishop's ensemble. There is no direct evidence of any performance material from Salzburg, but that it once existed is clear from passages in letters by Leopold Mozart (December 17, 1769) and Mozart's sister, Nannerl Berchtold von Sonnenburg (March 23, 1800).

It is not known for certain who selected the libretto of *La finta semplice* for Mozart. The text is based on Carlo Goldoni's *dramma giocoso, La finta semplice,* first performed during the 1764 carnival in the Teatro Giustiniani di S. Moisè in Venice with music by Salvatore Perillo. When Mozart composed *La finta semplice* in 1768, he had yet to set foot on Italian soil, which makes it all the more astonishing that the twelve-year-old Austrian had such an excellent grasp of the Italian language, and that he was able to do justice to that supreme law of *opera buffa*—textual intelligibility. R.A.

K. 50 *Bastien und Bastienne* (K⁶ 46b)
Origin: Salzburg? 1767? and Vienna, 1768
Author: Friedrich Wilhelm Weiskern, Johann Heinrich Friedrich Müller, and Johann Andreas Schachtner, after Jean-Jacques Rousseau, and Charles Simon Favart and Marie-Justine-Benoîte Favart, together with Harny de Guerville

In its choice of subject Mozart's *Bastien und Bastienne* is closely bound up with Jean-Jacques Rousseau's operetta *Le Devin du village* (The Village Soothsayer), first performed in Fontainebleau on October 18, 1752. Rousseau's piece was one of the great operatic successes of the Paris Académie Royale de Musique (better known as the Paris Opéra) during the second half of the eighteenth century and first third of the nineteenth century. After *Le Devin du village* had been performed thirty-three times at the Académie Royale de Musique, the Comédiens Italiens Ordinaires du Roi (more commonly known as the Comédie Italienne) presented a parody of Rousseau's piece under the title *Les Amours de Bastien et Bastienne* (The Loves of Bastien and Bastienne). The authors of the parody were Charles Simon Favart and Marie-Justine-Benoîte Favart, together with Harny de Guerville. The version by Favart and de Guerville is an adaptation in which members of the country's rural population appear in a realistic setting, speaking and singing in their dialects.

Les Amours de Bastien et Bastienne was a piece known to Viennese audiences. It was performed in Laxenburg on June 16, 1755 and in Vienna on July 5, 1755. Count Giacomo Durazzo, who had come to Vienna in 1749 as Genoese ambassador to the city following a stay in Paris and was appointed *directeur des spectacles* in 1754, ordered the parody to be performed at the Vienna Burgtheater. His period as director coincided with the appointment there of the actor, translator, and topographer Friedrich Wilhelm Weiskern, and it was presumably on Durazzo's instructions that Weiskern translated *Les Amours de Bastien et Bastienne* in 1764. As Weiskern indicates in his note to the translation, three of the numbers (11, 12, and 13) are by the actor Johann Heinrich Friedrich Müller, whom Durazzo engaged in 1763.

The theory advanced in many biographies of Mozart that *Bastien und Bastienne* was written for the garden theater of the Viennese magnetist and physician Dr. Anton Mesmer is untenable. Mesmer's theater, an open-air stage hewn out of beech hedges, had not been completed by 1768. Or might it perhaps have been the case that, because of the lateness of the season, the performance in October 1768 took place in what Mozart's widow's second husband Georg Nikolaus Nissen called Mesmer's "summer-house," that is, in the rooms of Mesmer's country house? Nissen speaks of a "society theater," in other words an amateur company, not a garden theater or open-air stage. Or was *Bastien und Bastienne* not performed in Vienna at all at that time? Contemporary sources leave us in the dark on all of these questions. But analysis of Leopold Mozart's "List of Everything that this Twelve-Year-Old Boy has Composed Since his Seventh Year" from September 1768 makes it clear that this little operetta originated in Vienna in 1768. R.A.

K. 87 *Mitridate, rè di Ponto* (K^6 *74a*)
Origin: Bologna and Milan, September to December 1770
Author: Vittorio Amadeo Cigna-Santi, after Jean Racine and Giuseppe Parini

On March 12, 1770—during Mozart's first visit to Italy from December 13, 1769, to March 28, 1771—the fourteen-year-old composer received a *scrittura* or operatic commission from Count Carlo di Firmian, Governor General of the Austrian province of Lombardy and nephew of the former Salzburg prince-archbishop, inviting him to write an opera to open the season at Milan's Regio Ducal Teatro. The fee was fixed at 100 gold florins plus free board during his stay in the Lombard capital.

Mozart did not learn what subject he would be setting to music until July 27. This was the day on which he was handed the libretto to *Mitridate, rè di Ponto* (Mithridates, King of Pontus), an existing text that was the work of one of the members of Turin's Accademia dei Trasformatori, Vittorio Amadeo Cigna-Santi. The theme was already an acknowledged success in the literary and musical world. The Italian operatic stage in particular favored themes from Roman history. Mithridates VI Eupator, a tyrannical ruler from pre-Christian Asia Minor who inflicted three wars on the Roman Empire, provided a popular subject with which to glorify the Imperium Romanum. Cigna-Santi's version had already been set by Abbate Quirino Gasparini in 1767 for the Teatro Regio in Turin before Mozart was entrusted with it in 1770.

Mozart was allowed only five months to write his first opera for Italy, so there was no time to be lost if the lengthy score was to be delivered to the performers on time, and the singers needs had to be met above all else. Mozart certainly had problems with his singers while he was working on *Mitridate*. The final distribution of the roles was not known until October. No other opera by Mozart has so many different versions, sketches, fragments, and variants of the individual numbers. The singer entrusted with the role of Aspasia did not trust the maestro but planned instead to create a brilliant impression by interpolating arias from Gasparini's *Mitridate*. Not until she set eyes on Mozart's score and saw the pieces he had written specially for her did she admit to being "beside herself for joy."

Meanwhile, intrigues were being plotted behind the young composer's back: ten days before the first performance it was being suggested that such a young boy—and a German to wit—could not possibly write an Italian opera, since, although regarded as a great virtuoso, he allegedly lacked the *"chiaro ed oscuro* [light and shade] that is necessary in the theater." Mozart taught his would-be critics a lesson: following the orchestral rehearsal in Milan's Sala di Ridotto all disparaging gossip was silenced, and the first performance was a sensational success. Leopold Mozart wrote to his wife in Salzburg on December 29, "God be praised, the first performance of the opera took place on the 26th to general acclaim: and two things which have never before happened in Milan occurred, namely, that (contrary to the usual custom of a first night) an aria by the prima donna was repeated, although normally at a first performance the audience never calls out 'f[u]ora' (Author!), and secondly, after almost all the arias, with the exception of a mere handful *delle ultime Parti* [in the last act], there was the most tremendous applause and cries of 'Viva il Maestro, viva il Maestrino' after the aria concerned."

Mitridate, rè di Ponto is a number opera. It contains twenty-five separate numbers, not including the Overture. The entire opera, moreover, boasts only a single duet (No. 18) and one chorus (No. 25), which is in fact a quintet performed by the soloists at the end of the work.

Opera seria involves a stylistic unity that precludes the possibility of experimentation. Music, words, costumes, sets, gestures, stage, and auditorium are subject to the stylistic principles of all Baroque art. The fourteen-year-old Mozart entered no new compositional territory with *Mitridate, rè di Ponto,* but he accomplished the task brilliantly. Without denying convention or destroying the generic type, he made himself familiar with the genre of *opera seria,* and delivered the goods as requested. Without the need to experiment, Mozart scored an immediate success in the international opera world and in a large opera house of European caliber. R.A.

K. 111 ***Ascanio in Alba***

Origin: Milan, late August to September 1771
Author: Giuseppe Parini

On March 18, 1771, Leopold wrote from Verona to inform his wife (who had remained behind in Salzburg) that he had received a letter from Milan which had arrived the previous day and which had announced that a further missive was on its way to him from Vienna; this second letter, however, would not reach him until after his return to Salzburg from Italy. According to Leopold, it "will not only fill you with amazement, but will bring our son imperishable honor." The letter in question contained a commission from the Empress Maria Theresa for a *serenata teatrale* to be written for the politically important wedding between the seventeen-year-old Archduke Ferdinand of Austria and Princess Maria Beatrice Ricciarda of Modena, of the House of Este. On July 19, 1771, Leopold wrote to Count Gian Luca Pallavicini, who had been in the service of Austria since 1731 and a field marshal since 1754, informing the latter that he and his son Wolfgang were expected in Milan at the beginning of September in order to comply with the conditions of the commission. The oldest of Maria Theresa's *maîtres de musique,* Johann Adolf Hasse, was to compose the festival opera, while her youngest composer was to write the serenata.

The libretto arrived in Milan on Thursday, August 30. As early as September 13 Leopold was able to report back to Salzburg that "With God's help Wolfgang will have completely finished the serenata in twelve days' time, though really it is more of an *azione teatrale* in two parts." The Archduke Ferdinand, Governor and Captain General of Lombardy by profession, arrived in Milan on October 15, and the wedding took place the same day in the city's cathedral. The formal ceremonies began on the 16th with Hasse's final stage work *Il Ruggiero, ovvero L'eroica gratitudine* (Ruggiero, or Heroic Gratitude) to words by Pietro Metastasio, while Mozart's *Ascanio in Alba* was premiered on the 17th in Milan's Regio Ducal Teatro.

Wolfgang's *festa teatrale* was destined to enjoy a considerable success. Further performances were planned for October 19, 24, 27, and 28. Hasse is said to have described Mozart's success to the Abbate Giovanni Maria Ortes, a musical friend and writer, in terms that show a complete want of jealousy: "This boy will mean that we are all forgotten." Even if his words are apocryphal, they may indicate the general enthusiasm that was felt for the young composer. The newlywed couple attended the performance on the 24th and honored Mozart with cries of "bravissimo maestro," while Count Pallavicini sent a letter of congratulation from Bologna. In addition to a respectable fee, the composer received a watch studded with diamonds.

The libretto was the work of Abbate Giuseppe Parini, orator at the University of Milan, resident poet at the Milan Court Theater, and a writer of satires; it was intended, as it were, to congratulate the married couple, to wish them well, and to pay them homage on stage. As an allegory, it paid homage to Maria Theresa in the figure of Venus, while her son Ferdinand is not difficult to recognize in the figure of Ascanio.

Mozart himself regarded *Ascanio in Alba* as immensely attractive and special. After all, the composer had not yet had the opportunity in any of his previous stage works to write a grandiose pastoral play with choral and ballet sections, and with arias of a predominantly pastoral character. The strong preference for the chorus may well be a concession to Viennese tradition. Certainly the combination of singing and dancing was far from everyday practice for Milanese audiences. *Ascanio in Alba* should not be regarded as merely an occasional composition in Mozart's dramatic oeuvre, since the *festa teatrale* reveals Mozart's development as a man of the theater. R.A.

K. 126 *Il sogno di Scipione*

Origin: Salzburg, probably between April and August 1771
Author: Pietro Metastasio

The names of two of Salzburg's prince-archbishops, Count Sigismund von Schrattenbach and Count Hieronymus Colloredo, are closely bound up with the *azione teatrale, Il sogno di Scipione* (Scipio's Dream). When Mozart returned to Salzburg from his second Italian expedition on December 15, 1771, Schrattenbach was already dying. Philological investigations have revealed that the composer had originally intended *Il sogno di Scipione* to mark the fiftieth anniversary of Schrattenbach's ordination, which was due to fall on January 10, 1772. The prince-archbishop's sudden death on December 16, 1771 prevented the *azione teatrale* from being performed at court. Mozart revised the work for the installation of Schrattenbach's successor, Hieronymus Colloredo, on April 29, 1772, and altered the dedication from "Sigismondo" to "Girolamo" (Hieronymus).

The libretto by Pietro Metastasio had been written in 1735 for the birthday celebrations of Emperor Karl VI. It consists of one act comprising twelve numbers. The text presents the allegorical story of the Roman general Scipio, who in a dream chose the goddess Costanza (constancy) over Fortuna (luck) as a guide in mortal life. R.A.

K. 135 *Lucio Silla*

Origin: Salzburg and Milan, autumn 1771
Author: Giovanni de Gamerra

Following the successful first performance of Mozart's *Mitridate, rè di Ponto,* the *associati* (sponsors) of Milan's Regio Ducal Teatro decided on March 4, 1771, to commission a second opera from the young Salzburg composer, this time for the 1772–73 carnival season.

The text of *Lucio Silla,* the last of Mozart's operas written for Italy, is by Giovanni de Gamerra. Mozart had already begun work on the recitatives in Salzburg in October 1772, but he was later obliged to change these passages, and in some cases to rewrite them completely, after Gamerra had sent his libretto to the imperial and royal court poet Pietro Metastasio in Vienna. Metastasio improved and altered Gamerra's text, and added an entirely new scene in the second act.

Lucius Cornelius Sulla—the classical pronunciation of the name was later changed to Süll a and then to Sylla, or Silla in Italian—is an enigmatic and somewhat shady character from pre-Christian Roman history. In 83 B.C., after numerous victories over enemies both outside and inside the Empire, Sulla had himself elected dictator for life and invested with unlimited power. He was utterly vindictive in dealing with his enemies, and a sense of humanity was totally alien to him. Then, in 79 B.C. he renounced his dictatorship, and restored to the common people the right to elect its consuls. Indeed, he did not even apply for the office of consul, but wandered round the marketplace like any ordinary citizen. He offered to requite all who called him to account.

Accompanied by his father, Mozart set off for Milan on October 24, arriving in the Lombardy capital about midday on November 4. The premiere of *Lucio Silla* took place on the second day after Christmas.

Leopold gives an account of the premiere in a letter to his wife of January 2, 1773, which reads in part: "The opera passed off successfully, although on the first evening a number of very annoying incidents took place. The first such incident was that the opera, which generally starts one hour after the bells have rung for vespers, started three hours late on this occasion, in other words, about 8 o'clock by German time, and it did not end until 2 in the morning. The singers are always very nervous the first evening at having to perform before such a distinguished audience. But the terrified singers, together with the orchestra and the whole of the audience, many of them standing, had to wait impatiently in the heat for three hours for the opera to begin. Secondly, the tenor has never acted on such a distinguished stage before. In her first aria (No. 4), the prima donna Anna de Amicis should expect him to show her a gesture of anger, but he performed this angry gesture in such an exaggerated way that it looked as though he was about to box her ears and knock off her nose with his fist, which made the audience laugh. She did not sing well for the rest of the evening, because she was also jealous that the *primo uomo* [leading man, Venanzio Rauzzini] was applauded by the archduchess the moment he came on stage. This was a typical trick of the kind that castratos play, since he had arranged for the archduchess to be told that, such was his fear, he would be unable to sing, his intention being to ensure that the court would encourage and applaud him. In order to console her, Signora de Amicis was summoned to court at around noon the next day, and she had an audience with Their Royal Highnesses which lasted for a whole hour; only then did the opera begin to go well."

The Milanese audience appears to have liked Mozart's opera. On January 23 Leopold wrote to tell his wife that *Lucio Silla* had now been given twenty-six times: "The theater is astonishingly full every day."

Mozart appears not to have given his complete approval to Gamerra's libretto, since he came closer to the essential drama of the theme than the poet had done, and expressed more, in terms of his music, than the text demanded. Mozart's view of music and drama in *Lucio Silla* has been described by Mozart's biographers

Theodore de Wyzewa and Georges Saint-Foix as a "grande crise romantique." But attempts have also been made to attribute the work to a *Sturm und Drang* phase in the composer's output. What is striking about *Lucio Silla* are the subjective moods that reflect the darker sides of the individual's emotional life, and the full-scale vocal numbers that are given to secondary characters, both of which diverge from *opera seria* practice and give greater emphasis to the protagonists.

Lucio Silla is the first of Mozart's operas in which the composer devoted his particular attention to the *recitativo accompagnato* and (as far as we know) the last in which the overture was written before the rest of the work. In comparison to his first Italian opera, *Mitridate,* the orchestration in *Lucio Silla* is much more ambitious. Events on stage are accompanied and interpreted instrumentally, as it were. Many numbers give the impression of being symphonic compositions with obbligato vocal accompaniment. Mozart also created a ballet for *Lucio Silla,* which was entitled *Le gelosie del Serraglio* (Jealousy in the Harem) (K. 135a), and choreographed by the great dancer Jean-Georges Noverre, with whom Mozart would work again in Paris in 1778. Unfortunately, the completed version of Mozart's ballet music is lost, and only sketches survive.

With *Lucio Silla* Mozart bade farewell not only to Italy but also to his youth. In completing his commission, he broke the chain of convention. It is difficult to understand how Mozart's music could have entranced the Milanese public while eliciting no further commission for an opera from him. How much he himself wanted such a commission is clear from a letter that he wrote from Mannheim on February 4, 1778, in which he begged his father, "Please do your utmost to arrange for us (Wolfgang and Aloysia Weber) to come to Italy. You know my greatest desire is to write operas." R.A.

K. 196 *La finta giardiniera*

Origin: begun Salzburg, September 1774

Author: Giuseppe Petrosellini? after Raniero de Calzabigi; revised by Marco Coltellini; German version by Johann Franz Joseph Stierle

A three-act *dramma giocoso* by Pasquale Anfossi, *La finta giardiniera* (The Pretended Gardener) was first performed at Rome's Teatro delle Dame on December 26(?), 1773. The libretto was probably by the prolific Roman poet Giuseppe Petrosellini and based on a text by Raniero de Calzabigi. With few exceptions—cuts in the recitatives in the second and third acts and the suppression of two arias in the third act—Mozart set the Roman libretto as it stood.

Who obtained the Munich commission for Mozart in the summer or fall of 1774? The editor of the Mozart family's correspondence, Joseph Heinz Eibl, assumes that it was the Bishop of Chiemsee, Count Ferdinand Christoph Waldburg-Zeil, who for many years was in charge of the affairs of the Salzburg archbishopric. He was a lifelong patron of Mozart's. The Bavarian Mozart scholar Robert Münster, on the other hand, argues that Mozart received the *scrittura* from Count Joseph Anton Seeau, the Elector Maximilian III Joseph's Controller of Opera. The two views are not mutually exclusive. It is entirely possible that Count Waldburg-Zeil suggested that the young Salzburg composer should write the new opera; the definitive commission would have come from the appropriate authority, in other words, from the theater intendant Count Seeau himself.

Wolfgang and his father Leopold set off for Munich on December 6, 1774, with parts of the opera—principally the recitatives—already included in their luggage. On December 14 Leopold was able to venture the opinion that the opera would be rehearsed before Christmas and that the first performance would take place on December 29. On the 28th, however, we learn that "It has been postponed until the 5th of January 1775 so that the singers can learn their parts properly and, once they have the music in their heads, act with greater confidence, so that the opera is not ruined in consequence." However, the first performance of *La finta giardiniera* did not take place as planned on January 5. We learn from Leopold's letter to his wife of January 5, "Wolfg.'s opera is not to be performed until the 13th."

Mozart was heavily and decisively involved in the rehearsals for *La finta giardiniera,* although he did not conduct the performances. The Munich orchestra contained about twenty-three musicians and is said to have been in some disarray. Exact details concerning the cast of Mozart's opera are not known.

Mozart himself gives us a graphic account of the premiere of *La finta giardiniera* in a letter to his mother dated January 14, 1775: "Thank God! My opera was performed yesterday, the 13th; and it turned out so well that it is impossible for me to describe the noise to Mamma. In the first place, the theater was packed to the rafters, so that a good many people were turned away. After every aria there was the most frightening noise with clapping and shouts of 'Viva Maestro.' "

A second performance of *La finta giardiniera* took place on February 2, not in the Salvatortheater on this occasion but in the Sala di Ridotto. Leopold reported on the performance in a letter to his wife: "Wolfg.'s opera has been performed again, but it had to be cut because the soprano was ill. I could write a good deal about this woman: she was dreadful." It is not known what cuts were involved, since the performing material in question has not survived. The third and final performance of *La finta giardiniera* took place on March 2 in Munich, when the audience included the Elector Maximilian III Joseph.

Mozart revised the Italian text of *La finta giardiniera* in the fall and winter of 1779–80. It was translated into German, probably by the buffo bass Johann Franz Joseph Stierle, a member of Johann Böhm's traveling company. Mozart made various cuts, especially to parts of the second and third acts. Böhm's company was in Augsburg between March 28 and May 19, 1780, and it was probably here that they performed the German version of *La finta giardiniera* under the title *Die verstellte Gärtnerin* (The Disguised Gardener). Other performances known to have taken place during Mozart's lifetime include German-language productions in Frankfurt and Mainz, both in 1789.

The text that Mozart set marks a new departure in the development of *opera buffa*. It includes *parti serie* and *parti buffe,* both of which demand their own individual characterization. What Mozart has set is basically a *drame bourgeois* in the mold of Denis Diderot, a genre which was intended to offer the spectator a world of feelings both solemn and not-so-solemn. By drawing upon these two emotional spheres, the composer enriched the genre of *opera buffa* both instrumentally and formally, so that it was no longer subject to a single unified scheme. In consequence the way was open for Mozart to write an opera of immense diversity.

La finta giardiniera did not find a place

for itself in the eighteenth-century *buffa* repertory. In Munich it was shelved after only three performances. And in Paris, which Mozart visited from March to September 1778, there was no attempt to stage the work at all, although contemporary *opere buffe* were regularly seen here. In contrast to Anfossi's work, which was performed throughout Europe, *La finta giardiniera* remained a passing attraction. It has been left to present-day productions to reveal Mozart's inventiveness and imaginative power and to recognize the psychological and dramatic depth of his handling of the subject. R.A.

K. 208 *Il rè pastore*
Origin: Salzburg, spring 1775
Author: adapted from Pietro Metastasio

Pietro Metastasio, poet to the Imperial Court in Vienna, completed his libretto to *Il rè pastore* (The Shepherd King) on April 18, 1751. The first performance took place on October 27, 1751, before the Viennese court at Schönbrunn. The music was by Giuseppe Bonno, who was later to become kapellmeister to the Viennese court. What is arguably the poet's finest lyric work had already been set to music by a series of famous contemporary composers before Mozart turned his hand to it in 1775. The list of the earlier composers includes Agricola, Sarti, Hasse, Uttini, Gluck, Galuppi, Lampugnani, Jommelli, and Guglielmi.

Mozart received a new commission for an opera immediately after his return to Salzburg from Munich at the beginning of March 1775. Two dramatic works were to be prepared for a visit that the Archduke Maximilian Franz, the youngest son of the Empress Maria Theresa and future Elector of Cologne, was to pay to the town on the Salzach. The archduke left Vienna on his way to Italy on April 20 and the following day arrived in Salzburg, where he stayed at the prince-archbishop's palace. A serenata for five voices, *Gli orti esperidi,* with words by Metastasio and music by the Neapolitan court kapellmeister in Salzburg, Domenico Fischietti, was performed on April 22, and on the 23rd Mozart's serenata *Il rè pastore* was heard for the first time. It is striking that both works were written for five voices and that both were settings of texts by Metastasio. Are we to imagine that a musical competition was held here between the court kapellmeister and the second concertmeister, as Mozart was at this time in Salzburg?

Metastasio's three-act libretto was compressed into two acts for Salzburg. The most striking feature of the music is the detailed instrumental writing. The overture, written in a single movement, passes straight into the first scene, as was customary in any school drama. The dramaturgy of *Il rè pastore* rests essentially upon the contrast between recitative and aria. That Mozart himself thought highly of *Il rè pastore* emerges from the fact that in October 1777 he sent the work to his "good and true friend" Josef Mysliveček, and that he performed the Overture (converted into a three-movement symphony, K. 208 + 102) at an *accademia* (concert) at the Mannheim home of the composer Christian Cannabich on February 13, 1778. R.A.

K. 344 *Zaide (K^6 336b)*
Origin: Salzburg, 1779–80
Author: Johann Andreas Schachtner, after Franz Josef Sebastiani

In 1779 Mozart, just returned from an abortive trip to Mannheim, Munich, and Paris in search of a kapellmeister's post, was unhappily installed as a rank-and-file court musician at Salzburg. He and his father had observed a new trend: patrons and intellectuals were striving to create German-language musical theater as a nationalistic response to Italian opera. In Salzburg and other small, German-speaking courts visiting theatrical troupes were (for lack of a native repertory) mounting translated Italian comic operas and French operettas transformed into *Singspiels,* while in Vienna and Mannheim original works were being commissioned.

The Mozarts perceived this as an opportunity to advance Wolfgang's career. They acquired a copy of a libretto entitled *Ein musikalisches Singspiel, gennant: Das Serail. Oder: Die unvermuthete Zusammenkunft in der Sclaverey zwischen Vater, Tochter und Sohn* (A Musical Drama Called: The Seraglio, or The Unexpected Reunion of Father, Daughter and Son in Slavery) which, set to music by one (Johann) Joseph Friebert, had been performed in Wels (between Salzburg and Linz) in 1777, but published only in 1779. Plays and operas on "Turkish" (that is, Moslem) subjects were all the rage. This one must have appealed to the Mozarts for they gave it to their close friend, the court trumpeter Johann Andreas Schachtner, who had helped them before with German librettos, and he used it as the basis of a new libretto for Mozart to set.

Mozart was hard at work on this Singspiel when a major commission came for an *opera seria* for Munich—*Idomeneo,* the first of his great operas. So the Singspiel was put aside, even though by then he had completed fifteen numbers constituting perhaps three-quarters of the music. After the triumph of *Idomeneo,* Mozart was ordered to Vienna by the archbishop of Salzburg. There he broke with the archbishop, with Salzburg, and with his father, settling permanently in the imperial capital. Soon thereafter, when he needed a Singspiel for Joseph II's new German Theater, Mozart took out *Zaide* again, but something—most likely the libretto, although the "melodramas" of Nos. 2 and 9 were in an experimental style that Mozart soon abandoned—displeased him. (Perhaps hoping to avoid offending Schachtner, he wrote to his father cryptically, and not too credibly, that the work was "too serious" for the Viennese.) So he put aside this glorious music forever, commissioning another libretto on the same subject: *The Abduction from the Seraglio.*

What remains of the earlier project is a shapely torso, lacking a title, an overture, the spoken dialogue, and an ending. For a title either *Zaide,* as in the first edition of 1838, or *Das Serail,* after the Wels libretto, will serve. Mozart was only twenty-three to twenty-four years old when he composed *Zaide,* but he was already a master, with numerous successful operas, symphonies, concertos, masses, serenades, and chamber-music works to his credit. Everywhere in this work foreshadowings of *The Abduction* and *The Magic Flute* can be heard, bearing witness to one of the most gifted dramatic composers in the history of Western music awaiting his main chance. N.Z.

K. 366 *Idomeneo, rè di Creta*

Origin: Salzburg and Munich, autumn 1780 to January 1781

Author: Gianbattista Varesco, after A. Danchet

At some point during the course of 1780 Mozart received a commission to compose an opera for the 1780–81 carnival season in Munich. Whoever suggested Mozart's name is not known. It is generally assumed that Christian Cannabich, music director at the Mannheim Court and a friend of Mozart's, and Anton Raaff, Court singer and first interpreter of the role of Idomeneo, prevailed upon Countess Josepha von Paumgarten to intercede on Mozart's behalf with the Elector Karl Theodor. The latter would have instructed Count Joseph Anton Seeau, Intendant or Controller of Operatic and Dramatic Performances at the Electoral Court, to convey the *scrittura* to Mozart.

Nor do we know who chose Gianbattista Varesco as librettist, although it was presumably Mozart himself. Varesco was baptized in Trent on November 25, 1735, and from 1753 to 1756 he attended the Jesuit College in the town and took minor orders. In 1766 he obtained an appointment with the Salzburg prince-archbishop Count Sigismund von Schrattenbach. Varesco, in addition to being a priest, was also a musician. His salary was 100 gulden per annum—Mozart earned 150—in return for which Varesco was expected to "make himself available in the Court Chapel."

During the course of 1780 the Munich Court conveyed to Varesco a detailed plan for producing a libretto, *Idomeneo, rè di Creta* (Idomeneus, King of Crete), in return for which he was to be paid the sum of 90 gulden. The text of *Idomeneo* was then translated into German by the Salzburg Court trumpeter, Johann Andreas Schachtner, who was a friend of Mozart and who received 45 gulden for his pains. What Mozart himself received for the work we do not know, but we can assume that it was in the region of 200 gulden, a sum which Wolfgang considered too little. For a "payment such as this one cannot leave one's score behind," his father Leopold commented mockingly. Certainly Mozart did not relinquish his autograph score to the Munich Court, but kept it safe in Vienna.

Mozart left Salzburg on November 5, 1780, and made his way via Wasserburg am Inn to Munich to prepare for the premiere there of *Idomeneo.* When he arrived in the Bavarian capital at around one o'clock on the afternoon of the 6th, the score was far from being sufficiently complete for rehearsals to begin at once. A glance at the correspondence relating to *Idomeneo,* most of which is now preserved in the Library of the Mozarteum in Salzburg, reveals that the composer was involved in a constant round of revisions, alterations, rewriting, and rehearsals. The opera was not ready musically until January 18, 1781, and the premiere took place on the 29th. Almost no contemporary reports have survived describing the premiere of *Idomeneo.*

An amateur performance of *Idomeneo* was given in the private mansion of Prince Johann Adam Auersperg in Vienna on March 13, 1786, a performance for which Mozart made extensive revisions to his score and wrote two new numbers, a duet for soprano and tenor, "Spiegarti non poss'io," K. 489, and a *scena* and rondo for soprano and violin solo, "Non più, tutto ascoltai . . . Non temer, amato bene," K. 490 (see the notes under Concert Arias, p. 81).

Idomeneo occupies a key position in Mozart's oeuvre and is a turning point in his operatic career. In it he bursts asunder the bonds of conventional *opera seria* and invests the genre with individual features, combining Baroque and newer "subjective" stylistic elements, making *opera seria* and its stereotyped characters less rigid, and creating a scenically representative work of artistic freedom and boldness which embraces both dramatic and lyric extremes of expression. The musical vocabulary that is deployed here reveals Italian, French, and German elements, and demonstrates the cosmopolitanism of the twenty-five-year-old composer who had assimilated and synthesized all the various European stylistic characteristics.

The work is conceived for singers trained in the Italian tradition, its basic structure being formed by recitative and aria: the former frequently loses its *secco* character and passes over into the more permissive area of *recitativo accompagnato,* while the arias are predominantly binary in form, seeking to intensify the musical expression and using Italianate melody and coloratura writing to depict psychological processes that reflect the emotional state of the individual character concerned. The tradition of French *tragédie lyrique* that Mozart was able to study in Paris in 1778 is revealed not only by his handling of the chorus, by the scenes involving priests, by the oracular pronouncement, and by the orchestral recitatives, but also by his introduction of marches and processions and by the elaborately structured ballet music both within the work and at the end of the drama. It is to the Electoral Ballet Company that we owe the individual choreographic features of the work and the great closing orchestral suite, K. 367, which is an integral part of the opera (see the note under Ballet and Incidental Music on p. 71). In writing *Idomeneo,* Mozart was not concerned to portray the rationalism of Gluckian characters but rather to create subjective individuals, each with his or her own emotional life and depth of sensitive expression. The chorus—both dynamic and theatrical—functions as a body of extras, as a catalyst in the action, and as a distant choir, but is always bound up with the plot, and has lost its static, decorative aspect.

Idomeneo impresses with its rich and brilliant orchestral fabric. No restrictions were imposed on the composer in Munich in writing for the orchestra, for, unlike in Salzburg, he was dealing with a top-flight international orchestra recently transferred to Munich from Mannheim, creating a sensual tonal impression, accompanying and emphasizing the vocal writing, and devising picturesque details. Thus we find—for the first time in any Mozart opera—a provision for clarinets, while he also writes for four horns, and introduces trombones for the oracular pronouncement and a piccolo for the storm.

Varesco's verbose libretto borrows from French libretti of the time as well as from Pietro Metastasio. The reduction in the number of characters to five is entirely in the spirit of Metastasio. Varesco has worked his humanist and Jesuit background into the piece, and also introduced elements of clasical antiquity and medieval Christianity, elements which Mozart himself was at pains to digest intellectually.

Idomeneo is one of the works that was misunderstood by musicologists and theater directors throughout the nineteenth century and even as recently as the end of the Second World War. It was subjected to numerous revisions, and not until the 1970s did it begin to enter public consciousness in its original form. R.A.

K. 384 *Die Entführung aus dem Serail*
Origin: Vienna, July 30, 1781 to the end of May 1782
Author: (Johann) Gottlieb Stephanie the younger, after Christoph Friedrich Bretzner

---

Operatic composition brought in the best financial return, and Mozart probably counted on the success of *Idomeneo* to bring him more such work. Vienna, long a stronghold of Italian opera, now had a German opera company at the Burgtheater, established at Emperor Joseph II's command. Mozart made the acquaintance of Gottlieb Stephanie, a playwright and producer at the Burgtheater, who, though widely regarded in Vienna as a shady character, was friendly and helpful to the young composer. That unfinished Turkish *Singspiel* of two years earlier (see the note for *Zaide,* p. 51) was not polished enough for Vienna and lacked a comic element that Mozart felt it needed, but Stephanie promised Mozart a new and better libretto.

This was delivered at the end of July 1781, to Mozart's delight. *Die Entführung aus dem Serail* (The Abduction from the Seraglio) was anything but original, and its source in an earlier libretto, by Christoph Friedrich Bretzner, was openly acknowledged. Plots about Europeans held captive by Turkish pashas are found throughout the latter half of the eighteenth century, in fact; less than a hundred years after the Ottoman Turks had been with difficulty repulsed from the gates of Vienna, they had become the stuff of popular entertainment, regarded as exotic and amusing rather than menacing. Sometimes, as in Stephanie's tale, the Turks are presented as superior to Europeans in humanity and magnanimity.

Mozart began composing the music immediately, for there was hope of performances during a projected fall visit by the Grand Duke of Russia. As was the practice of the time, libretto and music were written with consideration for the skills of specific performers. Thus, additional arias were supplied for the role of Osmin, which was to be sung by Karl Ludwig Fischer, who, as Mozart wrote to his father, "certainly has an excellent bass voice. We must take advantage of it, particularly as he has the whole Viennese public on his side." Fischer had a range from a rock-bottom low C to a baritonal high A and could negotiate rapid scales and passagework with the agility of a coloratura soprano.

The role of Osmin was not the only one that benefited from Mozart's genius and the skill of the singers at his disposal. The German opera company also performed Italian works in German translation. For this repertoire, the singers needed full, rich voices, able to encompass the florid Italian technique. Mozart took advantage of these superior singers in writing his opera. Although his music for the plebeian characters in *The Abduction* resembles that of the traditional Singspiel, with regular rhythms, symmetrical phrases, simple forms, and unadorned melodies, he made the patricians speak the musical language of serious Italian opera. (For some reason, the part of the Pasha Selim, originally planned for a singer, ended up as merely a speaking role.)

The first performance of *The Abduction* took place on July 16, 1782. Mozart's letter to his father the next day has unfortunately been lost, but later comments indicate that the premiere was a success. *The Abduction* remained popular, and was probably Mozart's greatest stage success during his lifetime, both in Vienna and elsewhere.

An early biography reports the Emperor's comment when he heard the work: "Very many notes, my dear Mozart!" Later criticism has conceded a grain of truth to the imperial observation; glorious as Mozart's music is, there is sometimes more of it than is good for the forward motion of the plot. The libretto is no masterpiece of proportion; it concentrates too much of Osmin near the beginning, too much of the heroine, Constanze, in the middle of the second act.

Still, even if Mozart overcomposed, and even if he failed to blend the disparate German, Italian, and French musical styles into a convincing whole, he nonetheless gave the German opera a new stature, a new potential for dealing with grander and profounder emotions than the Singspiel had previously known. Beyond that, in the figure of Osmin he created a new and vivid vocal and dramatic type, the German *basso buffo,* who would figure prominently in German opera right up to Richard Strauss's character Baron Ochs in *Der Rosenkavalier* of the twentieth century. D.H.

K. 422 *L'oca del Cairo*

Origin: Salzburg, summer 1783, and Vienna, winter 1783–84

Author: Gianbattista Varesco

Mozart wrote to his father from Vienna on December 21, 1782, to inform Leopold that the Court Theater Intendant Count Franz Xaver Wolf Orsini-Rosenberg had invited him to write an Italian opera. Mozart wanted a good libretto: "I've looked through at least 100 libretti—probably more," he wrote to his father on May 7, 1783, "but I've hardly found a single one that I could be satisfied with. . . . We've a certain Abbot da Ponte here as poet. He has a tremendous amount to do at present, revising pieces for the theater, and—*per obligo*—he has to write an entirely new libretto for Salieri."

Since Abbé Lorenzo da Ponte was working for Salieri, Mozart turned once again to his *Idomeneo* librettist, Gianbattista Varesco, with whom he had already experienced considerable difficulties in 1780–81. His reason for turning to Varesco again was presumably because the latter delivered the goods on time, and because the composer wanted to strike while the iron was still hot by following up *The Abduction from the Seraglio* with a successful *opera buffa*. On May 21, 1783, he asked his father to "keep on" reminding Varesco: "the comic element must be uppermost in importance, for I know the taste of the Viennese." Perhaps Mozart worked on the libretto with Varesco during his visit to Salzburg from the end of July to October 27, 1783. If so, the composition of *L'oca del Cairo* (The Goose of Cairo) may have been begun during this period.

On December 6, 1783, we find Wolfgang writing to his father: "Only three more arias to go, and I'll have finished the first act of my opera. The *buffa* aria ['Siano pronte alle gran nozze'], the quartet ['S'oggi, oh Dei'], and the finale ['Su via, putti, presto'] are cause for the greatest satisfaction, and I'm actually looking forward to them [that is, hearing them performed]. And so I'd be sorry if I'd written such music in vain. . . . I have to say that my only reason for not objecting to this whole goose story was because two people with more insight and judgment than myself could not find anything to object to in it; I mean you and Varesco."

Mozart, then, found fault in Varesco's text and demanded changes to the words and plot. He finally abandoned *L'oca del Cairo* on February 10, 1784: "I've no thought of giving it at present. I've things to write at present that are bringing in money right now, but which won't do so later. The opera will always bring in money; and besides, the more time you take, the better the result. Herr Varesco's verse smacks too much of haste!—I hope that he'll realize this himself in time;—that's why I want to see the opera as a whole (tell him just to jot his ideas down on paper)—only then can we raise fundamental objections;—but for God's sake let's not be hasty!—If you were to hear what, for my own part, I have already written, you'd agree with me that it doesn't deserve to be spoilt!—And it's so easy to do!—and happens so often. The music I've completed is lying on my desk, and sleeping soundly. Among all the operas that may be performed before mine is finished, no one will think up a single idea like mine, I'll bet!" R.A.

K. 430 ***Lo sposo deluso (K^6 424a)***
Origin: Salzburg? and Vienna, second half of 1783
Author: unknown, after Giuseppe Petrosellini

At carnival 1780 the extraordinarily successful and prolific Italian opera composer Domenico Cimarosa (1749–1801) had the premiere of a new comic opera in the Teatro Valle in Rome. This work, entitled *Le donne rivali* (The Rival Women), must have enjoyed some success, because other productions followed in Florence and Venice (autumn 1780), Siena (1782), Montecchio (1783), and in a revised version called *Le due rivali* (The Two Rivals) in St. Petersburg (1789), Moscow (1790–91), Monza (1791), and Ferrara (1801).

In the spring of 1783 a new Italian opera troupe was established in Vienna, which enjoyed great success. Mozart wrote to his father in May 1783 that he had read through more than a hundred Italian librettos looking for a suitable one to compose for the new troupe. A copy of Cimarosa's score, or probably just of the libretto, came into Mozart's hands at about that time. He must have liked this libretto (probably by Giuseppe Petrosellini), for he commissioned someone to make a new version with the title *Lo sposo deluso, ossia La rivalità di tre donne per un solo amante* (The Deluded Bridegroom, or The Rivalry of Three Women over One Lover). Setting to work, Mozart first decided on casting, assigning roles to the leading Viennese singers: Francesco Benucci (later Mozart's Figaro), Ann Selina (Nancy) Storace (later his Susanna), Stefano Mandini (later the Count), Catarina Cavalieri (earlier Constanze), Therese Teyber (earlier Blondchen), and Francesco Bussani (later Don Basilio). Then he started to compose in earnest (probably in the winter of 1783–84), first sketching at least two numbers and then drafting full scores of the overture, an opening quartet based on the overture, an aria for Bussani, another for Storace, and a *terzetto,* all from the first act. Only in the last item did he fill in all of the orchestration, although the other four numbers are complete in concept. Then, for unknown reasons, Mozart put the work aside, perhaps on learning that the opera commission for that season was not to be his, perhaps out of some dissatisfaction with the libretto.

After Mozart's death, one of his pupils or some other member of his circle completed the orchestration of the overture and quartet for Mozart's widow Constanze, who, in a benefit concert given on her behalf in Prague on November 15, 1797, performed the overture, quartet, and *terzetto,* singing in the latter two. (In a letter written three years later, Constanze wrote that the *terzetto* had enjoyed great success.) In the twentieth century the orchestration of the two arias has also been completed and all five numbers have been performed. N.Z.

K. 486 ***Der Schauspieldirektor***
Origin: Vienna, January 18 to February 3, 1786
Author: (Johann) Gottlieb Stephanie the younger

According to Mozart's own entry in his thematic catalogue, *Der Schauspieldirektor* (The Impresario) is "a comedy with music, consisting of an overture, two arias, a trio and vaudeville." The lackluster comedy for which this music was written was a topical satire that quickly lost its currency. Thus Mozart's portion of the work survives as a collection of five pieces in a vaguely dramatic context but without a true libretto—a freestanding and miraculously verdant vine for which the original arbor has long since rotted away.

The occasion for *The Impresario* was a state visit to Vienna, in 1786, by a duke and archduchess who were joint governors-general of the Austrian Netherlands. In their honor Emperor Joseph II planned a "pleasure festival" in the Orangery at his palace in nearby Schönbrunn, which would show off both his German and Italian opera troupes. The Italian work was assigned to the celebrated composer Antonio Salieri and his frequent librettist Giovanni Battista Casti; the German, to Mozart and the veteran Viennese actor-manager Gottlieb Stephanie, Jr., who had collaborated four years earlier on *The Abduction from the Seraglio*. At this time Mozart was hard at work on *The Marriage of Figaro* and probably did not welcome the interruption, but he was scarcely in a position to refuse a commission for an imperial entertainment. He received the text on January 18, 1786. Working quickly, but with no lack of care or inspiration, he finished scoring it a little more than two weeks later, on February 3. The work was premiered at Schönbrunn on February 7, then repeated in three public performances in Vienna later in the month.

Stephanie based his play on the hoary plot of an impresario's backstage tribulations as he struggles to assemble a company and mount a new season. Except for the overture, Mozart's segment comes late in the script, when the impresario turns to the musical elements of his venture and auditions two jealous sopranos. (The more sentimental one was sung by Aloysia Weber Lange, Mozart's first love, whose sister Constanze he had eventually married.) A well-meaning tenor tries to pacify the feuding sopranos, and finally all three are joined by a *buffo* actor-singer for a moralizing vaudeville (in musical parlance, a song with verses sung by different characters in turn).

No sooner had the appeal of Stephanie's local theatrical references faded than efforts to salvage the musical numbers began—attempts have persisted to this day. A line of authors from Goethe to Peter Ustinov have tried to reinvent dramatic underpinnings for Mozart's work, either by drastically revamping Stephanie or by substituting a different comedy altogether. One popular mid-nineteenth-century version was *Mozart and Schikaneder,* by German actor-writer Louis Schneider, which made the composer and his real-life contemporaries characters in the play. None of these adaptations has proved entirely satisfactory for the general repertoire.

The music, meanwhile, brilliantly holds its own. When he composed it, the thirty-year-old Mozart was arriving at the peak of his creative powers, with the Piano Concerto No. 22 and the six quartets dedicated to Haydn just behind him, *Figaro* on the drawing board, and the "Prague" Symphony just ahead. However fleeting its occasion and insubstantial its text, *The Impresario*—with its rich lyricism, penetrating psychology, and consummate craftsmanship—could not help partaking of some of the timeless quality of these more ambitious achievements. C.P.

K. 492 *Le nozze di Figaro*
Origin: Vienna, October 1785 to April 29, 1786
Author: Lorenzo da Ponte

Pierre Augustin Caron de Beaumarchais (1732–99), son of a watchmaker, was one of the eighteenth century's more colorful picaresque figures. He was willing to try his hand at anything: he taught harp to the daughters of Louis XV, speculated in grandiose business schemes, spent several years entangled in one of the age's most complex and scandalous lawsuits, acted as a secret agent for France during an exile in England, published the first complete edition of Voltaire's works, ran guns for the American Revolutionaries in 1776, and founded the French Society of Dramatic Authors. He also wrote plays. Some of them were conventional bourgeois dramas, but two of his comedies attained immortality, both in their own right and in the form of operas that stand at the center of the international repertory.

The first of these comedies, *Le barbier de Séville* (The Barber of Seville), produced in Paris in 1775, ingeniously blends the tradition of Molière and the comedy of intrigue with figures from the classical Italian *commedia dell'arte*. The youthful lover (Count Almaviva) and the miserly old man (Doctor Bartolo) contend for the hand of the beautiful Rosina, and Figaro (the barber of the title), by wit and stratagem, helps the count to win the prize. Set to music by Giovanni Paisiello in 1782, *The Barber* quickly swept the operatic world, though it was eventually superseded by Gioachino Rossini's version, which came along in 1816.

In 1778, tempting the customary fate of sequels, Beaumarchais wrote *The Marriage of Figaro*. Daringly, he made an even more unconventional play, not only revealing that the Almavivas lived something less than happily ever after, but pitting Figaro and his fiancée, Susanna, in a battle of wits against their "superior" the count—a battle that, in the play, they win. The play's implied criticism of the existing social order was enough to ensure it a rocky road in pre-Revolutionary France, and not until 1784 did the censorship allow a public performance, thanks in part to pressure from the aristocrats who had seen and been delighted by a private production. The result was one of the greatest successes of the French theater.

The sensation of Paris was soon the talk of Europe, for printed copies and translations spread quickly. Early in 1785, a Viennese theatrical troupe led by Emanuel Schikaneder (later to be the librettist of Mozart's *The Magic Flute*) put into rehearsal a German version, but the production, announced for February 3, was forbidden by the imperial censor, though he allowed the play to be published. Mozart had been looking for a satisfactory subject for a comic opera since 1782, and now, despite the ban, Beaumarchais's comedy struck him as highly promising.

We know few details about the creation of *Le nozze di Figaro* (The Marriage of Figaro), compared to others of Mozart's operas. Our nearest firsthand source is the famous and entertaining memoirs of Lorenzo da Ponte, the cosmopolitan poet and adventurer from Venice who had already agreed to write a libretto for Mozart.

The first we hear about the new piece in the Mozart family correspondence is a letter from father Leopold to sister Nannerl on November 3, 1785, complaining that he gets no news of his son except by second hand; a journalist has mentioned something about a new opera. On November 11, he reports, "At last I have received a letter of twelve lines from your brother, dated November 2. He begs to be forgiven, as he is up to his eyes in work at his opera *The Marriage of Figaro*. . . ."

During these months his son was playing and composing at a furious rate, According to da Ponte, "As fast as I wrote the words, Mozart set them to music. In six weeks everything was in order." If that is true, the six weeks must have come roughly between October 16, 1785, when Mozart finished the great Quartet in G minor for piano and strings (K. 478), and the beginning of December, for the only other works attributable to that time are two operatic ensembles, K. 479 and 480.

What ensued between composition and first performance is equally vague. The approval of the censors must have taken time, even though da Ponte had toned down the more inflammatory parts of the play. There were doubtless intrigues, such as have always swirled about opera houses and courts, but their nature can now be only dimly discerned through the mists of history. Apparently the Abbé Casti (da Ponte's chief rival), Antonio Salieri (Mozart's chief rival), and the opera manager Count Orsini-Rosenberg himself were involved in trying to prevent the production of *Figaro*.

After a postponement, it premiered at the court theater on May 1, 1786. Mozart conducted from the keyboard. The first night was a considerable, if not a total, success, and enthusiasm grew at the repetitions. So many encores were demanded at the third performance that the Emperor ordered a ban against the repetition of ensemble pieces, to keep the performances from running all night.

A Prague production in December was so great a triumph that Mozart visited the city in January 1787 and conducted a performance himself. To his friend Baron Nicolaus Josef von Jacquin he wrote, "Here they talk about nothing but *Figaro*. Nothing is played, sung or whistled but *Figaro*. No opera is drawing like *Figaro*. Nothing, nothing but *Figaro*." Furthermore, the Prague company commissioned him to write a new opera, which would become *Don Giovanni*, also to a da Ponte libretto.

After Prague, *Figaro* traveled widely. For a Vienna revival in August 1789, Mozart made some revisions, primarily to accommodate a new Susanna, Francesca Adriana Gabrielli, known as Il Ferrarese, who may have been da Ponte's mistress but was evidently not as fine a musician, as charming an actress, or as warm a friend of the composer as Nancy Storace. In any event, the arias Mozart wrote for her—"Un moto di gioia" (K. 579) to replace "Venite inginocchiatevi" in the second act, and "Al desio di chi t'adora" (K. 577) to replace "Deh vieni, non tardar" in the last act—have never been accepted into the standard performing text of the opera (as were, for example, the new arias Mozart composed for the Vienna production of *Don Giovanni*). (See the notes for K. 577 and 579 under Concert Arias, p. 82).

The temptation to ascribe perfection to *Figaro* is great, and has not always been resisted. Much of it is, indeed, close to perfection. Although divided into four acts, *Figaro* moves in two substantial sweeps, climaxing in the elaborate finales of Acts II and IV, with effective but lesser curtains for Acts I and III. There is a falling-off of inspiration only at the start of the fourth act, where an excess of comings and goings is required to accommodate a string of arias—two of them, for minor characters, are not from Mozart's top drawer and are often omitted. But this brief descent from Olympus serves only to remind us that the level of the rest is so extraordinarily high. D.H.

K. 527 *Don Giovanni*

Origin: begun in Vienna, March 1787?; completed in Prague, October 28, 1787
Author: Lorenzo da Ponte

Il dissoluto punito, o sia il Don Giovanni (The Punished Dissolute, or Don Juan) was the second operatic collaboration of Mozart and his librettist Lorenzo da Ponte, who, some fifteen months earlier, had had a great success with their *Le nozze di Figaro*. Their third and last opera together was to be *Così fan tutte*. This triumvirate of masterworks has earned them their current reputation as one of the world's greatest opera-writing teams, rivaled only by Giuseppe Verdi-Arrigo Boito and Richard Strauss-Hugo Hofmannsthal.

Da Ponte and Mozart were first introduced in Vienna in 1783 by Mozart's landlord, Baron Karl Abraham Wetzlar von Plankenstern, and soon afterward Mozart wrote his father that da Ponte had promised to write him a libretto, after completing one for Antonio Salieri, court composer in Vienna. "But who knows whether he will be able to keep his word—or will want to? For, as you are aware, these Italian gentlemen are very civil to your face. Enough, we know them! If he is in league with Salieri, I shall never get anything out of him. But indeed I should dearly love to show what I can do in an Italian opera!"

As it turned out, Mozart got little or nothing from da Ponte for three years. But the triumphant premiere of *Figaro* in Vienna on May 1, 1786, proved that da Ponte had been worth waiting for. The opera was such a raging success at its second production in Prague that Pasquale Bondini, the impresario of the Prague opera, commissioned Mozart to write another opera for the 1787 season. Da Ponte proposed the story of Don Juan and the stone guest.

Da Ponte was born in Ceneda near Venice in 1749 as Emmanuele Conegliano; he was of Jewish stock, but, in 1763, his widowed father turned Christian, and had himself and his three sons baptized by the Bishop of Ceneda. They all assumed the Bishop's surname, da Ponte; Emmanuele was also given his Christian name, Lorenzo.

Da Ponte wrote opera librettos for many other composers besides Mozart. But he was constantly in hot water due to his taste for intrigue of every sort, and after the death of his protector, Emperor Joseph II, he made a precipitous exit from Vienna in 1791, shortly before Mozart's death. After some travels he wound up in New York; there he masterminded the American premiere of *Don Giovanni,* published his racy but unreliable *Memoirs,* and died in 1838, at the age of 89, honored as the founder of Italian Studies at Columbia University.

The legend of Don Giovanni was already old, not to say hackneyed, in 1787. The first dramatic version of the Don Juan story (Giovanni is the Italian and Juan the Spanish equivalent of John) was written by a monk, Gabriel Tellez (1571–1648), who called himself Tirso de Molina and entitled his verse play *El burlador de Sevilla* (The Playboy of Seville); published in 1630, this version of the legend includes much of the content assembled for Mozart's opera by da Ponte. In Italy the story became a favorite theme with the strolling extempore comedians known as the *commedia dell'arte;* Molière, much influenced in his plays by the *commedia dell'arte,* subtitled his own prose version of 1665 *Le Festin de pierre*. His Don Juan is a stiff, cold cynic, has an epigram forever on his lips, and lacks the gaiety and irrepressible bravery that render Tirso de Molina's hero attractive as well as deplorable.

Da Ponte kept both plays on his desk while writing his *Don Giovanni,* and borrowed some of Molière's lines. He also referred to Carlo Goldoni's *Don Giovanni Tenorio* (1736), another sophisticated reshaping of the subject as treated by *commedia dell'arte* troupes. Operatic versions of the legend were rife in Italy during the 1770s and 1780s, and da Ponte was fired in particular by the most successful of them; the music was by Giovanni Gazzaniga, the libretto the work of Giovanni Bertati, a personal and professional *bête noire* of da Ponte's.

Knowing that he could expand Bertati's one-act libretto into two acts with the aid of Tirso, Molière, and Goldoni, da Ponte set to work. Those authors would help him to provide new action for the scenes between Elvira's exit after the quartet "Non ti fidar" and the Cemetery Scene. (Some commentators have complained that the dramatic action remains static throughout that long stretch of new writing, simply duplicating what went before or follows afterward, but da Ponte's filling-in enhances the characterization of the *dramatis personae* and prepares all the more purposefully for the opera's final scenes.)

Mozart's new opera had been commissioned to celebrate the marriage of the Emperor's niece, Archduchess Maria Theresa, with Prince Anton Clemens of Saxony (eventually Emperor Franz II). It was to be another comic opera that should appeal as much to Prague as had *Le nozze di Figaro;* it also had to be suitable for the royal couple, and could not strain the resources of Bondini's available repertory company of three sopranos, a tenor, and three basses.

The first performance was planned for October 14, 1787. Mozart returned to Vienna with the commission on about February 12. As da Ponte completed each scene, or handful of scenes, he passed it on to his composer. His memoirs say he finished the libretto after sixty-three days, perhaps by early May.

Mozart would be expected to send completed portions of the score to Prague in early September for study by the performers. Fortunately Mozart had met most of the *Don Giovanni* cast when he visited Prague to hear them sing *Le nozze di Figaro.* The manuscript score, now in the library of the Paris Conservatoire, shows which numbers were composed in Vienna and which in Prague. He did not send in advance the passages involving the chorus, because he was not sure what choristers would be available; nor was he certain of the stage wind band that he wanted for Don Giovanni's supper, so he left till later all of the second act finale. Mozart also left the composition of the opera's overture, as was his custom, until he had finished all the rest of the music.

During the rehearsals, the Don Giovanni, Luigi Bassi, complained that his part included no major aria; Mozart could have protested that there were already two splendid ones, the brilliant "Fin ch'han dal vino" and the conspiratorial "Metà di voi," which exploited Bassi's admired gift for mimicry. The singer's dissatisfaction encourages belief in a contemporary description of Bassi as "very handsome and very stupid." Nevertheless Mozart added Don Giovanni's serenade "Deh, vieni alla finestra" (and put mandolinists forever in his debt); unlike the other two arias, it would show off Bassi's capacity for honeyed, amorous singing.

Mozart and his wife arrived in Prague on October 4; ten days were evidently considered time enough to learn, rehearse, and mount a difficult full-length new opera. Mozart, however, found that few arrangements had been made for preparation of the work, and that the singers were lazy and the stage staff slow to learn their duties. Three days of each week, moreover, were unavailable for rehearsal because there were opera performances on those nights. Mozart had five days, not ten, in which to prepare *Don Giovanni* for its premiere. This proved impossible, given the opera's many ensembles, unfamiliar music, and elaborate stage action. The premiere was postponed by ten days, and, by the Emperor's command, *Le nozze di Figaro* was substituted for the royal nuptial, Mozart himself conducting.

A few days later one of the singers became indisposed and the first performance was again set back, to October 29. Mozart composed the overture on the night of October 27–28, just in time to have the orchestral parts copied before the final dress rehearsal that day. At the first performance, Mozart, who conducted, was cheered each time he entered or left the orchestra pit; newspaper reports were adulatory, and subsequent performances frequent. Mozart and da Ponte had, indeed, trumped the success of *Figaro* in Prague.

The reports followed the Mozarts back to Vienna. Soon after Mozart's return in mid-November the Emperor appointed him court chamber composer, succeeding Christoph Willibald Gluck, and ordered a production of *Don Giovanni* at the Burgtheater. It took place on May 7, 1788, and required a significant quantity of musical revision, including the composition of Elvira's great recitative and aria "In quali eccessi. . . . Mi tradì quell' alma ingrata" (K. 540c). Francesco Morella, the Vienna Don Ottavio, was not up to the taxing, florid "Il mio tesoro," so "Dalla sua pace" (K. 540a) was inserted into the middle of the first act, suavely lyrical rather than would-be-heroic. Both arias are first-rate and most modern Don Ottavios sing them both. A legend that, in this Vienna production, the opera ended with Giovanni's descent to hell, omitting the final sextet, depended on an annotated libretto of the time; it has since been proved unauthentic, though it encouraged nineteenth century performers to do likewise in the interests of a more "dignified" *Don Giovanni.*

The Vienna production of the opera lapsed from the repertoire after fifteen performances and was not revived until after Mozart's death. But even during his remaining four years of life it was widely and successfully produced in Germany, Austria, and Bohemia, even when disparaged as excessively sophisticated and noisy. With the arrival of nineteenth-century Romanticism, *Don Giovanni* was hailed as a great precursor of Ludwig van Beethoven, Carl Maria von Weber, Heinrich August Marschner, and grand opera in general.

The present century has seen a reexamination of the finest classical qualities of *Don Giovanni,* and of its psychological detail. Thanks to the magnificence, charm, and subtlety—indeed the effective ambivalence—of Mozart's music, *Don Giovanni* has survived many and diverse interpretations and will surely triumph over others yet to come. W.M.

K. 588 *Così fan tutte*
Origin: completed in Vienna, January 1790
Author: Lorenzo da Ponte

Any composer who could present to the operatic world, in successive years, two masterpieces such as *The Marriage of Figaro* and *Don Giovanni* should never again have a moment's worry about making a living or finding employment worthy of his gifts. Or so one might suppose, if artistic merit and worldly rewards went hand in hand. In fact Mozart, who composed *Figaro* in 1786 and *Don Giovanni* in 1787, went for the next two years without another operatic commission, or indeed without a major commission of any kind. At the age of thirty-three, his career seemed becalmed and his financial fortunes slid into disaster.

Emperor Joseph II had appointed Mozart court chamber composer in 1787, but the post carried a meager salary and required him to write nothing more than occasional minuets, waltzes, and country dances for court balls. The fickle Viennese aristocrats, who could not get enough new Mozart piano concertos just a few years earlier, now showed scant interest in the subscriptions he circulated for his concerts. Moreover, jealous rivals such as the composer Antonio Salieri proved far more adept than he at political maneuvering.

Fending off creditors, Mozart moved his family from one lodging to another. During the summer of 1789 a pregnant Constanze fell ill and had to be sent to Baden, a health resort a few miles south of Vienna—a burdensome expense. As he had done so many times before, Mozart abjectly begged a loan from (Johann) Michael Puchberg, a wealthy businessman and fellow Mason. "Oh God," he wrote all too typically to Puchberg on July 12, "I am in a situation that I would not wish on my most wicked enemy; and if you, my best of friends and brothers, forsake me, I am *unhappily* and *innocently* lost with my poor sick wife and my child."

Six weeks after this letter was written, however, deliverance seemed at hand. *Figaro* was revived in Vienna, with enough success to prompt the Emperor to call for a new comic opera by Mozart. The librettist was once again to be Mozart's collaborator on *Figaro* and *Don Giovanni*: that busy, clever Italian émigré and intriguer, Lorenzo da Ponte.

Thus was the way prepared for *Così fan tutte* (All Women Behave Like This), the third of the four great operas of Mozart's maturity (the last, *The Magic Flute,* would follow in 1791, only a few months before his death.) Among the most astonishing things about this astounding work are the harried circumstances under which it was written and the distracted and anxious emotions from which its sublimely genial music flowed.

The first two Mozart-da Ponte efforts, *Figaro* and *Don Giovanni,* had been based on popular plays or librettos. For *Così,* da Ponte invented his own plot (granting that invention was a highly relative concept in the 1700s). The story goes that the Emperor himself proposed the central situation, drawing it from current Viennese gossip about two gallants who disguised themselves in order to test the constancy of their sweethearts. But a strikingly similar tale had been told four years earlier in Giovanni Battista Casti's libretto for *La Grotta di Trifonio,* composed by none other than Salieri; and the general idea has ample precedent in other *opere buffe* and in stage works going back to the *commedia dell'arte* and into antiquity.

The libretto and score took shape over four months, beginning in September 1789. Mozart could give his full attention to the project, since he had few other assignments. His only other compositions from this period are some concert arias, two big sets of dances (K. 585 and 586), and the great clarinet quintet, K. 581, completed on September 29.

Da Ponte's libretto is a marvel of witty, concise, and symmetrical dramatic construction—a standing rebuttal to those who believe that all opera librettos are fustian and second-rate stagecraft. Ever the classicist, da Ponte observed the unities as he had in *Don Giovanni,* laying out the action so that it could be construed, at least symbolically, as taking place within twenty-four hours (the first scene is set in the morning and subsequent scenes are set at later hours of the day, leading to the finale at night). He used only six characters and they fall neatly into three pairs: the two young officers, the two sisters whom they so sentimentally adore, and a final pair consisting of the sisters' maid and the officers' older friend, the worldly bachelor who sets the plot in motion.

The libretto proceeds by symmetrically playing the characters off against one another, subdividing and recombining them in gratifying formations, with plenty of high-spirited, if artificial, comedy along the way. It was only natural that Mozart should reflect this intricate deployment of the characters in his music, and so *Così,* among all his works, is preeminently an opera of ensembles. There are six duets, five trios, a quartet, two quintets, and a sextet, plus two finales that are positive gallimaufries of vocal combinations.

By late December 1789 the work was ready for its first singers' rehearsal, which was held at Mozart's apartment on New Year's Eve, presumably accompanied by the composer at the piano. To this rehearsal Mozart invited two special guests, his benefactor Michael Puchberg and his revered colleague Joseph Haydn—a sign that he took some pride in his score. The production was to be presented at Vienna's Burgtheater by the resident Italian opera company, the same troupe that had just revived *Figaro* and had given the Vienna version of *Don Giovanni*. Mozart knew in advance who his singers would be and tailored the parts to their voices.

In January 1790 the rehearsals moved into the theater. The premiere took place on January 26, probably with Mozart conducting from the keyboard. There were four more performances in January and February; then, after the period of public mourning following the death of Emperor Joseph II, *Così* was performed five more times in the summer.

In the years after Mozart's death, *Così* fell into a curious limbo. The libretto, with its mockery of lovers' sighs and protestations and its exposure of the sisters' fickleness capped by Don Alfonso's motto of "Così fan tutte," came to strike later generations as far less amusing than Mozart's contemporaries found it.

The present age is inclined to grant the work more psychological seriousness, without losing sight of its special iridescence. There, in the music, all the conflicting strains of mockery and tenderness, of sincerity and inconstancy, are fully reconciled. Delicious in its parody, ravishing in its lyricism, *Così* holds laughter and sympathy in a perfect equilibrium that, in critic Joseph Kerman's phrase, celebrates "the mystery of feeling itself."

C.P.

K. 620 *Die Zauberflöte*

Origin: Vienna, begun spring 1791; completed September 28, 1791

Author: Emanuel Schikaneder

Die Zauberflöte (The Magic Flute) was Mozart's first full-scale German opera since *The Abduction from the Seraglio,* composed nearly ten years earlier, in 1782. He did collaborate once more with Gottlieb Stephanie, the librettist of *The Abduction,* on a one-act comedy, *The Impresario,* for an imperial festivity in 1786. But opportunities to perform vernacular opera for the general public were severely curtailed when the Burgtheater—which had been devoted exclusively to the German repertoire since 1776—went back to Italian opera in 1788. Mozart himself became an "Italian" composer again between 1786 and 1790 when he collaborated with the librettist Lorenzo da Ponte on the masterpieces *Figaro, Don Giovanni,* and *Così fan tutte.*

Early in 1790, the liberal emperor Joseph II died. His brother and successor, the reactionary Leopold II, cared little for Mozart's music, which dimmed the composer's chance of ever obtaining a well-paying imperial appointment. By this time, he badly needed a steady income. Though playing, teaching, and composing as much as possible, he still could not make ends meet; his wife Constanze was not well, and there was a five-year-old child, with another to come in July 1791. During 1789 and 1790, Mozart borrowed more than 1,000 florins from Michael Puchberg, a Viennese businessman and music lover, who was also a member of the Masonic lodge to which the composer belonged. (To gauge the scale of this debt, consider that it was more than double the annual salary that Mozart's late father earned as assistant musical director in Salzburg.)

Mozart had become a Freemason at the end of 1784. Though this secret fraternal society had been banned by Empress Maria Theresa in 1764, her son Joseph II tolerated it because it counted many distinguished and intellectual citizens among its members. Another Viennese Freemason was the actor and impresario Emanuel Schikaneder, director of the Theater auf der Wieden. This suburban house, with a thousand seats, played not only classical drama but also works of the Singspiel variety—that is, German opera with spoken dialogue—including a genre known as *Zauberoper* (magic opera) that was enormously popular with less sophisticated audiences because of its spectacular scenic effects. Presumably in early 1789, Schikaneder proposed that Mozart write the music for such a *Zauberoper,* based on a pseudo-Oriental fairy tale, "Lulu, or the Magic Flute" by A. J. Liebeskind.

Mozart had many other obligations in the last year of his life, including commissions to compose a Requiem Mass and an Italian opera. The opera, *La clemenza di Tito,* was designed for the festivities surrounding the coronation in Prague of the Emperor Leopold as King of Bohemia, and Mozart had to travel to Prague to see it through production. He returned to Vienna in time to finish *The Magic Flute* for its premiere on September 30, 1791. The composer conducted, and Schikaneder took the role of the bird catcher Papageno, which he had tailor-made to show off his gifts as a comic actor. Mozart's sister-in-law, Josefa Weber Hofer, sang the dazzling coloratura role of the Queen of the Night. Though coolly received by the critics, the new work immediately captivated the public; by November 6 there had been twenty-four performances. Mozart was enormously proud of his new opera. He loved to attend performances and listen to the audience's reactions; he invited Haydn, Salieri, and other musical connoisseurs to enjoy the opera with him and must have regretted that his father—who had always encouraged him to write more popular and accessible music—had not lived long enough to hear *The Magic Flute* and witness his triumph.

The triumph came none too soon. Late in November Mozart became seriously ill, and he died on December 5; it is said that during his final delirium he followed in imagination that evening's performance of his last opera.

The Magic Flute soon came to occupy a special place in the repertoire, reserved for works that combine the utmost simplicity and directness with the greatest profundity and seriousness of purpose. It was a fortunate moment in the history of music, for the languages of art music and folk melody had then much in common; it was possible to be learned and popular at the same time. Much more successfully than in *The Abduction,* Mozart made the Italian style of the Queen of the Night's arias and the Singspiel idiom of Papageno's songs appear to belong to the same musical language. Indeed, he wrote a duet (No. 7) in which an Italianate soprano and a singing actor with a restricted vocal range (Schikaneder) were perfectly at ease together. As for Sarastro's music, the British playwright and devout Mozartean George Bernard Shaw said his two arias were the only music yet written fit for the mouth of God.

Much has been made of the role of Freemasonry in *The Magic Flute*. There is little doubt that its Masonic authors made the brotherhood of Sarastro's temple a representation of their order. Sarastro himself is an allegorical depiction of one of their number and the Queen of the Night represents Empress Maria Theresa, who sternly opposed the humanitarian and liberal ideals of the Masonic order. Masonic symbols are spread throughout the libretto, scenery, and music (the prevalence of the sacred number three—three introductory chords, three boys, three ladies, even the opera's central key of E flat, which is written with three flats—is but one example). These details need not concern the modern listener unduly, however. The opera's overt message of tolerance and human brotherhood is surely the substance of what Mozart, as man and as Mason, wanted to communicate. D.H.

K. 621 *La clemenza di Tito*

Origin: begun in Vienna, mid-July? 1791; completed in Prague, September 5, 1791
Author: Caterino Mazzolà, after Pietro Metastasio

The Roman Emperor Titus Flavius Sabinus Vespasianus is a rather dubious character from first-century Roman history. His father, Vespasian, had doubts about Titus's suitability as his successor: his son was fond of oriental harem life, he maintained a household of eunuchs and dancers, and he had a Jewish mistress, Bernice. He was seen as a latter-day Nero. These apprehensions were not fulfilled, however. On his father's death he assumed the rule of state and showed self-discipline, clemency, and liberality. During his reign Pompeii and Herculaneum were destroyed when Vesuvius erupted on August 24, 79 A.D., and a major fire and pestilence broke out in Rome in 80 A.D. He offered generous support to all who had suffered, and financed a rebuilding program from his own purse. He showered gifts on the populace, paying for festivities and gladiatorial games. He became popular through his proverbial clemency.

The basic text of Mozart's *La clemenza di Tito* (The Clemency of Titus) is by the imperial court poet Pietro Metastasio and dates from 1734. It was first set by Antonio Caldara and performed on November 4, 1734, in the presence of their "augustissimi sovrani" at the large Vienna Court Theater. It is very much the ideal court opera, the opera of enlightened absolutism. This libretto was set at least forty-five times between 1734 and 1839.

Metastasio's text was revised for Mozart by the Saxon court poet Caterino

Mazzolà, who made various changes, and turned the piece into a *vera opera* by the following artistic means: he cut the text by about a third and removed virtually the whole of Metastasio's second act, since it contained a subplot irrelevant to the main action. Mazzolà tightened up the action, gave the protagonists distinctive characters, and skillfully arranged the order of their appearance. He created two great finales (as was usual at the time), both of which aim at being impressive and spectacular.

La clemenza di Tito was commissioned by the Bohemian Estates to mark the coronation celebrations of Leopold II as king of Bohemia. The theme was tailored to suit the new ruler's qualities: during his twenty-five-year rule of Tuscany, Leopold had created a model state of European enlightenment. He concluded the war with Turkey on August 4, 1791, by signing the Peace of Sistova, and was given the honorary title of "Il Rè Pastore." In speeches and epigrams on Leopold's death there are repeated allusions to the figure of Titus, who had become the symbol of supranational Austrian culture in the eighteenth century.

The contract requiring an effective festival opera to be written for these celebrations was concluded on July 8, 1791, between the theater manager Domenico Guardasoni and the Bohemian Estates. It emerges from the contract that the Estates were chiefly concerned to engage famous singers—the composer was a matter indifference to them—and to ensure a magnificent spectacle. It appears to have been Guardasoni alone who chose Mozart. Mozart did not hear of the definitive cast in Prague until the middle of August, which means that, although Mozart had already been working on the opera for about five weeks, he wrote the greater part of it in the remaining three weeks.

The gala premiere of *La clemenza di Tito* began at seven o'clock on September 6, 1791, attended exclusively by the highest social circles. In the *Krönungsjournal für Prag* we read:

FESTIVITIES OF THE ESTATES.

On the 6th, being coronation day, and in order to celebrate this day for His Majesty, the Estates gave a newly composed opera, the text of which, though based upon Metastasio's Italian, had been adapted by Herr Mazzolà, the theater poet in Dresden. The composition is by the famous Mozart, and does him honor, although he did not have much time to write it and was moreover, afflicted by an illness during which he had to complete the final part of it.

The Estates had spared no expense in performing the same, they had sent their entrepreneur to Italy: from where the latter had brought back with him a prima donna and a leading male singer. The title of the opera itself was *La clemenza di Tito*. Admission was free, and many tickets had been distributed. The house was filled with a large number of people, but one can imagine that on such an occasion the demand for tickets is so great that they finally ran out, so that many local and foreign visitors, including persons of high degree, were turned away, since they had not come . . . with tickets.

Later performances before a local, middle-class audience proved a success for the opera. "All the pieces were applauded," Mozart wrote to his wife in Baden on October 7, 1791.

Mazzolà and Mozart extended *opera seria* to the very limits of its possibilities, and in their ensemble technique are already some distance removed from the prototype of the genre. In his music, too, Mozart has eliminated the ballast of the traditional *opera seria*. The sweeping ritornellos have disappeared, the forms have become more concise, the arias are limited to shortened da capos, and the instrumentation is as transparent as in his symphonic works. Mazzolà and Mozart have overcome the limitations of the Metastasian libretto and created a new form of libretto which give the music more scope.

In the eighteenth century, an *opera seria* was a regular part of coronation celebrations, an element in the arsenal of events that added luster to celebrations in princely houses. It gave the coronation the same outward glamour as official celebratory poems. A decorative element of immense power and colorfulness is one of the essential aspects of *opera seria* and suitable as such for a coronation. The overture is, so to speak, attuned to this mood of high festivity. Mozart brought nuance and shade to *opera seria*. Gluck and his reform opera may have been his model, but the Salzburg composer wrote "more" music, refusing to sacrifice it to the drama.

R.A.

BALLETS AND INCIDENTAL MUSIC

K^3 Anh 207 *Sketches for the Ballet in* Ascanio in Alba? *(K^6 Anh C 27.06)*

Origin: Milan? late 1771
Choreographer: Jean Georges Noverre

These nine untitled pieces are preserved in piano score and are playable on the keyboard. They each consist of sixteen to thirty-two measures of music in simple binary form; thus, they appear to form a suite of dances. The pieces may have originated as ballet music for the opera *Ascanio in Alba*. W.C.

K^3 299b *Ballet,* Les petits riens *(K^1 Anh 10)*

Origin: Paris, May to June 1778
Choreographer: Jean Georges Noverre

Mozart and the great ballet master and theoretician Jean Georges Noverre (1727–1810) were old friends; they had collaborated in Milan in 1772 on the ballet music (*Le gelosie del Serraglio,* K^6 135a [K^2 Anh 109]) for Mozart's opera *Lucio Silla,* which unfortunately survives only as an incomplete draft. in 1778 the young composer often dined with Noverre in Paris, and hoped to obtain through his influence a commission to write a big opera in the French style. The opera never came about, but Mozart did create a ballet for Noverre, though he was not actually paid for it. On the ninth of July, 1778, Mozart gives his father the sad news of his mother's death; he goes on a little later, "about Noverre's ballet I only wrote that he might produce a new one—well, he only needed half a ballet and I wrote the music for it—that is to say, 6 pieces in it would be by others, they consist of a lot of rotten old French airs, the Symphony and Contredanse, 12 pieces in all would be by me. This ballet has already been done 4 times with great applause—but I shall write nothing more now unless I know in advance what I am to get for it—for this was written only to do Noverre a friendly service."

The first performance took place at the Paris Opéra at the conclusion of Niccolò Piccinni's *Le finte gemelle* on June 11. Mozart's name appeared nowhere. The next day the *Journal de Paris* described the contents of the ballet: "It consists of three scenes forming separate and almost detached episodes. The first is purely

Anacreontic: it shows Cupid ensnared and put into a cage, a most agreeable choreography. In it Mlle. Guimard and M. Vestris the Younger employ all the grace and skill the subject allows. The second is a game of blind-man's-bluff; M. d'Auberval, whose talent so pleases the public, plays the principal part here. The third is a mischievous prank of Cupid's, who introduces a shepherdess disguised as a shepherd to two other shepherdesses."

The music thereupon disappeared for a century. The copy which came to light in 1872 contains an overture and twenty pieces. The ballet as it is usually played is grouped by key into three parts, not necessarily corresponding to the three scenes danced in 1778. E.S.

K. 300 ***Gavotte in B-flat major***
Origin: Paris, May or June 1778

An unusual amount of mystery pervades the music composed by Mozart during his 1778 visit to Paris. It seems likely that his Gavotte was intended by Mozart for the Ballet *Les petits riens* and then laid aside for some unknown reason. E.S.

K. 345 ***Incidental Music for* Thamos, König in Ägypten *(K[6] 336a)***
Origin: (2 choruses) Vienna, 1773; (final version) Salzburg, 1776–79?
Author: Baron Tobias Philipp von Gebler

Mozart was an avid fan of the theater, both musical and non-musical, and his letters are laced with lively reports of the many performances he attended. He was, then, undoubtedly pleased when in 1773 the celebrated playwright Baron Tobias Philipp von Gebler, asked him to provide the incidental music for his five-act heroic drama *Thamos, König in Ägypten* (Thamos, King of Egypt), for performances at Vienna's Kärntnerthor Theater in April 1774. Gebler had been displeased with the music written by his original collaborator, Johann Tobias Sattler.

Judging from the surviving autographs, it may be said with certainty that two choruses by Mozart (one for Act I and one for Act IV) were performed at that time. The orchestral numbers were most likely written for a later performance, on January 3, 1776, in Mozart's native Salzburg. The music heard in Vienna in April 1774 was probably a mixture of Mozart's and Sattler's.

The years 1779 and 1780 found Mozart, after unsuccessful travels about Europe in search of a lucrative post, back home in Salzburg serving as court organist to the archbishop. His drudgery was somewhat brightened by the Salzburg seasons of the theatrical troupe directed by Johann Heinrich Böhm, an old Mozart family friend. During its 1779 visit, Mozart revised and expanded the two *Thamos* choruses of 1773, perhaps composed some of its orchestral numbers, and definitely supplied a new choral finale with text by another family friend, Johann Andreas Schachtner. In orchestrating *Thamos,* Mozart pulled out all the stops, using a luxurious orchestral complement.

Thamos proved to be the only incidental theater music Mozart would ever write, and its life span in that form was brief. In a letter to his father written in Vienna on February 15, 1783, Mozart lamented, "I am extremely sorry that I shall not be able to use the music of *Thamos,* but this piece, which failed to please here, is now among the rejected works which are no longer performed. For the sake of the music alone it might possibly be given again, but that is not likely. Certainly it is a pity!" Mozart allowed Böhm to recycle some of the *Thamos* music in a more popular play, *Lanassa,* by Karl Martin

Plümicke. In this incarnation the music did circulate about Germany; Mozart had occasion to attend one of these performances, in September 1790, while in Frankfurt for the emperor's coronation. The *Thamos* choruses also turn up from time to time in church, fitted out with sacred texts.

Thamos represents one of Mozart's first musical brushes with Freemasonry, a movement which was to become increasingly important in both his personal and professional life. At the time of its composition, Mozart could not have fully understood all of the arcane allegory in *Thamos,* for he was not initiated until 1784, but the music he wrote for it clearly demonstrates that the ideas struck him deeply.

Thamos points squarely in the direction of that greatest of Mozart's Masonic works, *Die Zauberflöte.* The trio of C-minor chords in the Entr'acte, No. 2, the majestic, hymn-like choruses, the Egyptian setting, the High Priest's Sarastro-like incantation in the final chorus, and the highly fraught juxtapositions of dark and light all give tantalizing previews of the greatness to come. C.E.

K. 367 *Ballet for* Idomeneo

Origin: Munich, December 1780 to January 1781

Choreographer: Jean-Pierre Le Grand

The composition and production of *Idomeneo* was one of Mozart's happiest times, yet he wrote on December 19, 1780, "One cannot but be happy to be finally freed of such a great, laborious task . . ." and then on December 30, "Afterwards I shall have the honor of writing a *divertissement* for the opera, for there is to be no separate ballet." On January 18, he wrote," 'Till now I've been kept busy with those cursed dances—*Laus Deo*—I have survived it all." The premiere took place on January 29, 1781 in the Elector's new opera house, later to be called the Residenztheater. The ballet-master was Monsieur Jean-Pierre Le Grand. The dances were almost certainly connected with the subject matter of the opera. The theme of the opening Chaconne was taken straight from the Chaconne in Gluck's *Iphigénie en Aulide.* It and the Pas Seul are joined together to form an immense and powerful work, perhaps Mozart's longest instrumental movement. It is also quite varied in its moods, the chief of which is, however, brilliance and pomp. In the score the names of the dancers are indicated though not the nature of the action of the dances. Thus, the entire corps dances at each recurrence of the Chaconne's rondo theme and in the concluding Più allegro; each intervening episode is a "Pas seul de Mad. Falgera," a "Pas de deux de Mad. Hartig et Mr. Antoine," etc. Monsieur Le Grand kept the best and longest spot for himself. The Passepied and Passacaille are finely orchestrated, while the Gavotte is an evergreen melody that occurred to Mozart again when he wrote the Finale of the piano concerto, K. 503, in 1786. E.S.

5

Concert Arias, Duets, Trios, and Quartets

A concert in a stately home. Engraving by Georg Friedrich Schmidt, 1752.

A male singer performs an aria accompanied by two violins, a viola, and a flute, with harpsichord and cello realizing the basso continuo. *The cellist cranes his neck to read from the harpsichordist's music. At the top a Latin motto proclaims that "Performance is the soul of composition."*

BACKGROUND AND OVERVIEW

The fifty-four arias and four ensembles chronicled in this section are loosely but somewhat misleadingly known as "concert arias." Properly speaking, a concert aria is an aria intended not for an opera but for inclusion as one item of a concert otherwise made up of unrelated music. This is confusing in more than one way. Popular arias drawn from operas could be and frequently were used as concert arias, suggesting that the boundaries between concert arias and other arias were vague. Then, hidden in this category are several types of arias: "true" concert arias, often written for Mozart's favorite singers to perform at his or their benefit concerts; insertion arias on newly written texts meant to be added to someone else's opera to extend the role of one of the characters; substitution arias, added to Mozart's or someone else's opera but in place of an already existing aria and often taking over its text; domestic or house-music arias, for use at home with friends; arias for occasions of state *(licenze)*, with texts flattering a rich and powerful patron; and apprentice or practice works, mostly set to aria texts by the reigning librettist of serious opera: Pietro Metastasio.

Some of these arias technically constitute what is called a *scena* or "scene." This does not mean the same thing as a scene in a spoken play, which is usually a self-contained dramatic sub-unit of an act. Rather it refers to a single aria with the recitative that precedes it and "sets the scene" for the aria. It was a convention in eighteenth-century Italian opera that whenever a character entered or exited the stage, a new scene was said to begin. But since it was another convention that a character, after unburdening him- or herself of an aria, would leave the stage (the so-called exit aria), an aria plus its introductory recitative usually constituted a scene. These scenes can immediately be recognized in the following notes because their titles are double, giving the opening words of both the recitative and the aria.

Mozart's best concert arias contain some of his most extraordinary music. Some of them present formidable technical difficulties for their soloists. Nearly all show him grappling with the musical, dramatic, and psychological issues that distinguish his operas from the majority of operas by his contemporaries. Here is a rich vein of precious masterpieces waiting to be mined. N.Z.

CONCERT ARIAS AND SCENES FOR SOPRANO

K. 23 *Conservati fedele*
Origin: The Hague, October 1765
Author: Pietro Metastasio
Scoring: soprano, strings

In September 1765, Mozart, a child of nine, and his sister Nannerl traveled to the Netherlands, where Nannerl nearly died of typhoid. Mozart composed an initial version of this aria in The Hague in October before coming down with typhoid himself. He probably revised it during his convalescence in January 1766. The aria may have been written for Princess Caroline of Nassau-Weilburg, sister of Prince William V of Orange.

The text is from Metastasio's *Artaserse,* a libretto so popular in its day that it was set 107 times. Mozart may have seen the opera during his year-and-a-half sojourn in London in 1764–65. At any rate, he was drawn to Metastasio's text for four of his earliest concert arias (K. 23, 78, 88, and 79). In this aria from the opening of the opera, Mandane expresses the hope that Arbace will remain faithful to her. C.R.

K. 78 *Per pietà, bell'idol mio* (K⁶ *73b*)
Origin: Holland, 1765–66
Author: Pietro Metastasio
Scoring: soprano, 2 oboes, 2 horns, strings

Like K. 23, K. 78 derives its text from Metastasio's *Artaserse*. It is a simple song, without introductory recitative, in which Artaserse protests his love of Semira and his sadness that the course of their love does not run smoothly. C.R.

K. 79 *O temerario Arbace . . . Per quel paterno amplesso* (K⁶ *73d*)
Origin: Holland, 1765–66
Author: Pietro Metastasio
Scoring: soprano, 2 oboes, 2 bassoons, 2 horns, strings

The text for K. 79 is from *Artaserse,* Act II, Scene 11. Arbace has been wrongly imprisoned for crimes actually committed by his father, Artabano, but he refuses to betray the latter. Addressing his father, Arbace nobly accepts his destiny. As sometimes happened in concert versions of operatic scenes, the singer assumes the roles of both characters in the recitative, in order to preserve dramatic continuity. She first delivers Arbace's words in orchestrally accompanied recitative, next sings a few words of response from Artabano in *secco* recitative, and then concludes with Arbace's aria. C.R.

K. 70 *A Bernice . . . Sol nascente* (K⁶ *61c*)
Origin: Salzburg, 1767–69
Author: anonymous
Scoring: soprano, 2 horns, strings

This *scena* was probably composed as a *licenza,* or epilogue of homage, to accompany a performance of Giuseppe Sarti's opera *Vologeso.* Mozart added the *licenza* to honor the sixty-ninth birthday of the prince-archbishop Sigismund von Schrattenbach, which occurred on February 28, 1769. Such pieces were a popular form of musical flattery in the mid-eighteenth century; although coming at the end of a full evening's opera and sung by one of the characters in the opera, they had little or nothing to do with the plot. In this case the text makes a brief transition from the happy outcome of the opera's plot to the happy birthday wishes for Sigismund. C.R.

K. deest *Cara, se le mie pene*
Origin: Salzburg? 1769? or Olomouc, Moravia? 1767?
Author: anonymous
Scoring: soprano, 2 horns, violin, viola, bass

This recently discovered work appears to date from the late 1760s. It is warmly lyrical, with just a touch of pyrotechnical coloratura. It differs from Mozart's other concert arias of this period both in its use of a non-Metastasian text, and in its scoring without a second violin. Its scoring is the same, however, as that of another early aria fragment, "Un dente guasto e gelato" (K⁶ 209a), from 1775.

Leopold Mozart claims, in a letter of May 28, 1768, that Wolfgang composed an aria in Olomouc, in December 1767, for the daughter of a physician, a certain Dr. Wolf. As nothing else exists that can be identified as this aria, perhaps "Cara, se le mie pene" was the work. W.C.

K. 88 *Fra cento affani e cento (K[6] 73c)*
Origin: Milan, February or March 1770
Author: Pietro Metastasio
Scoring: soprano, 2 oboes, 2 horns, 2 trumpets, strings

This is the last of the arias drawn from Metastasio's *Artaserse.* It is also the most ambitious—a full 266 measures long, even though it lacks an opening recitative. In eighteenth-century Italy this sort of grand *opera seria* aria, or *aria monumentale,* was greatly admired by the aristocratic opera lovers of the day. Mozart undoubtedly designed this piece for a virtuoso castrato voice.

The text is the opening aria of the hero Arbace. In the scene leading up to it, his father Artabano has handed him the bloody sword with which Artabano has slain King Serse, the father of Arbace's beloved Mandane. The aria is Arbace's heroic meditation on Mandane's approaching sorrow and Artabano's treachery. C.R.

K. 77 *Misero me . . . Misero pargoletto (K[6] 73e)*
Origin: Milan, March 1770
Author: Pietro Metastasio
Scoring: soprano, 2 oboes, 2 bassoons, 2 horns, strings

This is one of five concert arias (K. 77, 82, 83, 74b, 368) that Mozart drew from Metastasio's music drama *Demofoonte (Demophoön).* The complete text was set by some of the finest masters of the first half of the eighteenth century: Leonardo Leo, Antonio Caldara, Christoph Willibald Gluck, Johann Adolf Hasse, Niccolò Jommelli, Niccolò Piccini, and Giovanni Paisiello.

In the opera's plot, it seems that the hero and heroine, Timante and Dirce, have innocently committed incest. In K. 77 Timante, sung by a soprano, soliloquizes on the horror of discovering he has married a woman he believes to be his sister. The recitative is long and magnificent—Mozart's first great dramatic *recitativo accompagnato.* C.R.

K. 82 *Se ardire, e speranza (K[6] 73o)*
Origin: Rome, April 25, 1770
Author: Pietro Metastasio
Scoring: soprano, 2 flutes, 2 horns, strings

Mozart again used a text from Metastasio's *Demofoonte* in this aria, written for the celebrated castrato Giovanni Manzuoli. As a nine-year-old, Mozart had taken some singing lessons from Manzuoli in London. In 1771 Manzuoli sang the role of Ascanio in the Milan premiere of Mozart's *Ascanio in Alba.* He was a florid singer of formidable powers, but Mozart chose to show off his quiet, legato style in K. 82. In this scene of the opera, Timante has just witnessed his beloved Dirce dragged off to be a sacrificial victim, chosen by the king of Thrace as his yearly sacrifice to Apollo. C.R.

K. 83 *Se tutti i mali miei (K[6] 73p)*
Origin: Rome, April or May 1770
Author: Pietro Metastasio
Scoring: soprano, 2 oboes, 2 horns, strings

K. 83 is the third of Mozart's *Demofoonte* arias, composed possibly for the soprano Anna Lucia de Amicis, who two years later created the role of Giunia in Mozart's *opera seria, Lucio Silla.* In this scene from Act III, Dirce, believing that she is to die a sacrificial death, pours out her grief to

Creusa, her rival for Timante's love. Mozart gives the singer three opportunities to improvise cadenzas in this aria.

C.R.

K[3] 74b ***Non curo l'affetto***

Origin: Milan or Pavia, early 1771
Author: Pietro Metastasio
Scoring: soprano, 2 oboes, 2 horns, strings

On December 26, 1770, Mozart's first large-scale opera, *Mitridate, rè di Ponto,* was performed in Milan. In the aftermath of this performance, Mozart composed his last concert aria before his return to Salzburg. Little is known about the genesis of "Non curo l'affetto." The autograph is lost, but a copyist's manuscript in Prague bears a notation that it was composed for the theater in Pavia, a town some thirty miles south of Milan.

The text is again from Metastasio's *Demofoonte.* In Act I, Scene 7, Timante has incurred the wrath of Princess Creusa by spurning her love. In retaliation, she insists to his brother Cherinto, who is madly in love with her, that he kill Timante if he wishes to enjoy her favors.

C.R.

K. 217 ***Voi avete un cor fedele***

Origin: Salzburg, October 26, 1775
Author: anonymous, after Carlo Goldoni
Scoring: soprano, 2 oboes, 2 horns, strings

In the fall of 1775 an Italian opera troupe visited Salzburg, performing Baldassare Galuppi's *opera buffa, Le nozze di Dorinda* (Dorinda's Wedding). Mozart was apparently called on to provide a new aria for the prima donna. Rapidly becoming a master of the style, he turned out a comic gem that surpasses anything in his own *opera buffa* of ten months earlier, *La finta giardiniera.* "Voi avete un cor fedele" constitutes a watershed in Mozart's creative life.

In Act I, Scene 4, Dorinda addresses her suitor: "You have the faithful heart of an impassioned lover." Her words are filled with ironic overtones; she really finds her interlocutor a dull fellow, and Mozart's music sparkles with a young woman's amused contempt.

C.R.

K. 272 ***Ah, lo previdi . . . Ah, t'invola agl'occhi miei***

Origin: Salzburg, August 1777
Author: Vittorio Amadeo Cigna-Santi
Scoring: soprano, 2 oboes, 2 horns, strings

This is the first of Mozart's great concert arias. According to American musicologist Alfred Einstein, Mozart "almost never wrote anything more ambitious, or containing stronger dramatic feeling, than this aria." The work was an artistic breakthrough for Mozart in the vocal realm comparable to the instrumental breakthroughs in the first G-minor Symphony and the "Jeunehomme" Piano Concerto. The aria was commissioned by the great Prague-born soprano Josephine Duschek in the summer of 1777. She was an oratorio singer and specialist (perhaps the first ever) in vocal music for the concert stage. Beethoven was to write his concert aria "Ah! Perfido" for her in 1796.

The text of "Ah, lo previdi" was drawn from the opera *Andromeda,* originally set by Giovanni Paisiello from a libretto by Cigna-Santi, who also supplied Mozart with the libretto for his first Milan opera, *Mitridate, rè di Ponto.* In Act III, Scene 10, Euristeus, betrothed to Andromeda, tells her that he has met Perseus, her true lover, wandering in a garden, holding an unsheathed sword and bereft of his senses. Andromeda, imagining that Perseus has killed himself, at first turns in rage upon

Euristeus for not having prevented the suicide. Then in the second recitative and the concluding *cavatina,* her passion turns to resignation and she welcomes death so that she can accompany Perseus to "Lethe's other shore." C.R.

K. 294 *Alcandro, lo confesso . . . Non sò d'onde vieni*
Origin: Mannheim, February 24, 1778
Author: Pietro Metastasio
Scoring: soprano, 2 flutes, 2 clarinets, 2 bassoons, 2 horns, strings

This great work is one of the landmarks among Mozart's concert arias. It was the first of eight he wrote for Aloysia Weber. Mozart was closer to her than to any other singer in his life and was, in fact, already deeply in love with her when he completed the work. The aria with its special connection with Aloysia Weber was obviously of enormous importance to Mozart, and he frequently made references to the aria and to her in his letters home during his visit to Mannheim.

The words are from Metastasio's *Olimpiade,* another of his librettos that dozens of composers set to music. In the opera, an attempt is made on the life of King Clisthenes of Sicyon by a young man who is later revealed to be his son, separated from his father since infancy. Clisthenes has just condemned the would-be assassin to death. Deeply troubled by an inexplicable sense that he knows the youth, he asks his confidant, Alcander, what this sudden pounding of his heart, these tender feelings, can mean.

According to his letters, Mozart began to set this scene for the tenor Anton Raaff, but felt compelled to change to the soprano register. Just three days after that, he compensated Raaff with a tailor-made aria, K. 295. Nine years later he set the text again, to entirely new music for a bass voice (see the note for K. 512, p. 86, and also p. 120). C.R.

K^2 486a *Basta vincesti . . . Ah, non lasciarmi, no (K^6 295a)*
Origin: Mannheim, February 27, 1778
Author: Pietro Metastasio
Scoring: soprano, 2 flutes, 2 bassoons, 2 horns, strings

Mozart designed this *scena* from Metastasio's *Didone abbandonata* for Dorothea Wendling of Mannheim, for many years the most celebrated singer of the Palatine stage. Two years later Mozart was to create the role of Ilia in *Idomeneo* for her.

In Metastasio's version of the turbulent love affair of Aeneas and Dido, Dido pretends to agree to a marriage proposal from Jarba, King of the Moors. The jealous Aeneas demands that she retract her written promise, and Dido hands him the paper containing the retraction. But still fearing that she will lose Aeneas, she pleads with him, in tones of quiet, understated intensity, not to abandon her.

C.R.

K. 538 *Ah se in ciel, benigne stelle*
Origin: drafted in Mannheim? 1778?; completed in Vienna, March 4, 1788
Author: Pietro Metastasio
Scoring: soprano, 2 oboes, 2 bassoons, 2 horns, strings

Of all the arias Mozart composed for Aloysia Weber, this is the most brilliant and dazzling. While his other works for her fairly glow with warmth and tenderness, this one is largely a matter of transcendental vocal cords. Mozart rarely wrote more difficult vocal music.

The words are drawn from Metastasio's *L'eroe cinese (The Chinese Hero)*. The hero Sevino, son of the Regent of China, sings them in Act I, when he and his princess Lisinga are in danger of being separated.

The aria exists both in a full score from 1788 and in a *particella,* or continuity draft, containing only the vocal part and the bass line, written ten years earlier during Mozart's first visit to Mannheim. The earlier version would seem to date from about the time Mozart first became fond of Aloysia Weber; the later version was to be his last composition for her. Why Mozart put the work aside remains unexplained. C.R.

K. 316 *Popoli di Tessaglia . . . Io non chiedo, eterni dei (K⁶ 300b)*

Origin: Paris, July 1778; Munich, January 8, 1779

Author: Raniero de Calzabigi

Scoring: soprano, oboe, bassoon, 2 horns, strings

While Mozart was in Paris in the summer of 1778, he set aside time from his busy rounds to begin an ambitious operatic *scena* for Aloysia Weber. He deliberately set himself a challenge in choosing the text from Gluck's opera *Alceste,* which had been a sensational success both in Vienna in 1767 and in Paris in 1776. This was a bold and (some must have thought) arrogant gesture coming from a twenty-three-year-old composer.

The opera tells the story of the Thessalian King Admetus, who is on his deathbed when an oracle of Apollo announces that the king will be spared if one of his subjects volunteers to die in his place. Only his wife, Alcestis, comes forward. Mozart composes Alcestis's entrance scene in the first act, before the oracle has been heard; she addresses the people in dignified, priestess-like tones of lament and resignation. Only in the final section of her long aria does she give way and allow her grief to pour forth. C.R.

K. 368 *Ma che vi fece, o stelle . . . Sperai vicino il lido*

Origin: Salzburg, 1779–80, or Munich, 1780–81

Author: Pietro Metastasio

Scoring: soprano, 2 flutes, 2 bassoons, 2 horns, strings

Mozart turned to Metastasio's *Demofoonte* for the fifth and last time in this work (see K. 77 on p. 75). Musicologist Alfred Einstein believes that the aria was intended for the Munich soprano who created the demanding role of Electra in *Idomeneo,* Elisabeth Wendling. She was a sister-in-law of Dorothea Wendling, the Ilia of the *Idomeneo* premiere and the dedicatee of the concert aria K. 486a.

In Act I, Scene 4, Timante discovers that his supposed father, Demophoön, has promised him in marriage to Creusa. Secretly married to Dirce, Timente laments the sorrows that afflict his wife and himself. C.R.

K. 369 *Misera, dove son! . . . Ah! non son' io che parlo*

Origin: Munich, March 8, 1781

Author: Pietro Metastasio

Scoring: soprano, 2 flutes, 2 horns, strings

This is the last work that Mozart wrote before taking up residence for the rest of his life in Vienna. The aria was written in Munich in the aftermath of the premiere and great success of *Idomeneo.* It was designed for and dedicated to an aristocratic amateur, the Countess Josepha von Paumgarten.

The text comes from another Metastasio libretto, *Ezio,* which was set by dozens of composers. The Roman general Ezio has exchanged vows of love with Fulvia, the daughter of Ezio's false friend, Massimo. Massimo spreads false rumors to poison their love, and has Ezio cast into prison. Fulvia is fully aware of her father's treachery, but filial duty has sealed her lips. Now, with her betrothed flung into prison and threatened with death, she ponders her destiny. C.R.

K. 374 *A questo seno deh vieni . . . Or che il ciel*
Origin: Vienna, April 1781
Author: Giovanni de Gamerra
Scoring: soprano, 2 oboes, 2 horns, strings

In the spring of 1781 Mozart was in Vienna with a fellow Salzburg musician, the male soprano Francesco Ceccarelli. Both were in the retinue of their employer, the archbishop of Salzburg, who was visiting the capital. Mozart composed this vocal rondo for Ceccarelli to perform at a concert given by the archbishop's father, Prince Rudolf Joseph Colloredo, on April 8, 1781.

The text comes from the Paisiello's opera *Sismano nel Mogul,* with words by de Gamerra, the librettist of Mozart's own early opera *Lucio Silla.* In this scene the heroine, Zaïra, gives vent to her relief and joy when her lover returns safely from battle. C.R.

K. 119 *Der Liebe himmlisches Gefühl (K⁶ 382h)*
Origin: Vienna? 1782?
Author: anonymous
Scoring: soprano, [2 oboes, 2 horns, strings]

This aria exists only in an undated nonautograph version for voice and piano. Its original scoring was reported by Ludwig Köchel (in K[1]), who examined a set of orchestral parts that are now lost. Its style seems to suggest Mozart's early Viennese period. Of the various hypothetical origins proposed by historians, the one most commonly accepted places it as a companion piece to K. 383 (see below), which is likewise a German concert aria. Since K. 119 is a bravura aria in fast tempo, it provides a nicely contrasting counterpart to K. 383. Both arias were presumably composed for Aloysia Weber Lange. W.C.

K. 383 *Nehmt meinen Dank, ihr holden Gönner!*
Origin: Vienna, April 10, 1782
Author: anonymous
Scoring: soprano, flute, oboe, bassoon, strings

This delicate little piece is the most exquisite of the handful of concert arias Mozart wrote in his native German tongue. Like the great aria "Ch'io mi scordi di te?" K. 505, it was written for a singer who was leaving Vienna and wanted to take a graceful farewell of her faithful Viennese public. In this case the singer was Mozart's future sister-in-law Aloysia Lange, née Weber, an artist whom Mozart had fallen in love with in Mannheim in 1778. The aria is a simple ballad in two verses, but not without original features, including sudden dropouts or pauses in the vocal line that suggest a certain coquettishness that was apparently very much a part of Aloysia's nature. C.R.

K. 416 *Mia speranza adorata . . . Ah, non sai qual pena*
Origin: Vienna, January 8, 1783
Author: Gaetano Sertor
Scoring: soprano, 2 oboes, 2 bassoons, 2 horns, strings

This aria is perhaps the most distinguished of the series dedicated to Aloysia Weber Lange. She sang it a mere three days after its composition at a concert in a Viennese casino. On March 23 she repeated the aria in more formal surroundings at a mammoth all-Mozart concert in the Burgtheater.

The text comes from Pasquale Anfossi's opera *Zemira,* which had its premiere in Venice in the winter of 1781–82. The hero Gandarte must abandon his fiancée, Zemira, to the Emperor of Mongolia; in the presence of the tearful Zemira and her father, he takes an emotional farewell. C.R.

K. 178 *Ah, spiegarti, oh Dio (K³ 125i, K⁶ 417e)*
Origin: Vienna? June 1783?
Author: anonymous
Scoring: soprano, [orchestra]

This aria exists only in an undated non-autograph version for voice and piano. There is also an undated autograph copy of the vocal part. Since the aria is similar in text and affect (key of A major, slow tempo, duple meter) to K. 418 (see below), historians have suggested that it represents an early attempt at an aria for the same purpose. It differs from K. 418 mainly in that it remains in slow tempo throughout, while K. 418 concludes with an allegro section. W.C.

K. 418 *Vorrei spiegarvi, oh Dio!*
Origin: Vienna, June 20, 1783
Author: anonymous
Scoring: soprano, 2 oboes, 2 bassoons, 2 horns, strings

The circumstances concerning the composition and performance of K. 418 and K. 419 (see below) provide the best possible illustration of the stormy politics surrounding the whole question of interpolating new arias into other composers' operas. Both arias were written to be sung by Aloysia Weber Lange at her Viennese debut with the Italian Opera Company in Anfossi's *Il curioso indiscreto* (The indiscreet snoop). Mozart wrote his father, "My friends were malicious enough to spread the report beforehand that 'Mozart wanted to improve on Anfossi's opera.' I heard of this and sent a message to Count Rosenberg that I would not hand over my arias unless the following statement was printed in the copies of the libretto, both in German and Italian: 'Notice. The two arias on p. 36 and p. 102, have been set to music by Signor maestro Mozart to oblige Signora Lange, those written by Signor maestro Anfossi not being commensurate with her ability, but meant for someone else. This must be notified, so that honor should be accorded where it is due, and this without prejudice to the reputation of the already well-known Neapolitan.' " By insisting that the statement be printed in the libretto, he ensured that the audience would listen with special attention to his two arias.

In the opera's plot, the Marquess Calandrano, in order to test the fidelity of his fiancée, Clorinda, sends his friend, the Count of Ripaverde, to court her. "Vorrei spiegarvi, oh Dio!" occurs toward the end of the first act, when Clorinda nobly sends the count away to find happiness with her rival, Emilia. C.R.

K. 419 *No, no, che non sei capace*
Origin: Vienna, June 1783
Author: anonymous
Scoring: soprano, 2 oboes, 2 horns, 2 trumpets and timpani, strings

This aria occurs later in the action of Anfossi's *Il curioso indiscreto.* His pride wounded by Clorinda's rebuff, the count tells the Marquess that Clorinda was unfaithful. When she discovers this, in Act II, she reacts with a bravura aria, protesting her innocence. C.R.

K. 490 *Non più, tutti ascolti . . . Non temer, amato bene*
Vienna, March 10, 1786
Author: anonymous (Lorenzo da Ponte?)
Scoring: soprano, 2 clarinets, 2 bassoons, violin obbligato, strings

An opportunity arose during the Lenten season of 1786—when the public theaters were closed—for a single private performance of Mozart's opera *Idomeneo* at the palace of Prince Johann Adam Auersperg in Vienna. For this performance Mozart composed two extra numbers with new texts. One of the new pieces is a duet, K. 489, for Ilia and Idamante; the second is a recitative and aria for Idamante.

At the beginning of Act II Ilia, the captive Trojan princess, begs Idamante to forget her in favor of Elettra, the woman his father has chosen for him. In the ensuring aria, Idamante refuses. The aria and much of the recitative are set to the same text Mozart was to use again nine months later in K. 505. C.R.

K. 505 *Ch'io mi scordi di te? . . . Non temer, amato bene*
Origin: Vienna, December 26, 1786
Author: anonymous (Lorenzo da Ponte?)
Scoring: soprano, 2 clarinets, 2 bassoons, 2 horns, piano obbligato, strings

This is arguably the greatest concert aria ever composed. It is of monumental proportions, it has the added delight of being a solo aria and a duet (for it contains an obbligato piano part that is in every sense but the literal one a second voice), and it provides a unique link between Mozart's great piano concertos and his operas. Mozart wrote the work for the English soprano Ann Selina (Nancy) Storace when she was about to leave Vienna, having recently premiered the role of Susanna in Mozart's *Marriage of Figaro*. He designed the piano obbligato for himself, and played it at her farewell concert in the Kärntnerthortheater. Mozart had set the text once before, as the insertion aria K. 490, composed for the private revival of his opera *Idomeneo* in 1786 (See p. 52). C.R.

K. 528 *Bella mia fiamma . . . Resta, o cara*
Origin: Prague, November 3, 1787
Author: D. Michele Scarcone
Scoring: soprano, flute, 2 oboes, 2 bassoons, 2 horns, strings

Don Giovanni opened in Prague on October 29, 1787. Five days later Mozart completed this magnificent concert aria which, like "Ah, lo previdi" (K. 272), was for Josephine Duschek, the Bohemian soprano. At the time he was a guest of Josephine and her husband at their estate outside Prague. Mozart had possibly originally intended this aria for his friend Gottfried von Jacquin, an amateur bass. But it had gone far beyond the abilities of an amateur singer, and apparently the charming Duschek persuaded Mozart to turn it over to her.

The text comes from *Cyrere placata* (Ceres Appeased), composed by Niccolò Jommelli, based on the myth of Proserpina and her mother Ceres. Ceres separates Proserpina from her mortal lover, Titano, who she decrees shall die. Titano expresses his profound anguish at losing not only his life but his beloved Proserpina. C.R.

K[3] 540c *In quali eccessi . . . Mi tradì quell'alma ingrata*
Origin: Vienna, April 30, 1788
Author: Lorenzo da Ponte
Scoring: soprano, flute, 2 clarinets, bassoon, 2 horns, strings

See the note for *Don Giovanni* on p. 61.

K. 577 *Al desio, di chi t'adora*
Origin: Vienna, July 1789
Author: Lorenzo da Ponte?
Scoring: soprano, 2 basset horns, 2 bassoons, 2 horns, strings

The Marriage of Figaro was revived in Vienna in 1789. The original Susanna had been the vivacious English soprano Ann Selina (Nancy) Storace. In the revival the role went to Francesca Adriana Grabrielli, known as "Il Ferrarese," perhaps a finer singer technically than "La Storace," with a greater range and brilliance, but certainly not her equal as a comic actress. Six months later she was to create the demanding role of Fiordiligi in *Così fan tutte*.

This is the first of two replacement arias (K. 577, 579) for Susanna. It was intended to replace the fourth-act aria, "Deh vieni, non tardar." Susanna is teasing Figaro who she knows is eavesdropping, for he suspects that she is about to keep a rendezvous with Count Almaviva. C.R.

K. 578 *Alma grande e nobil core*
Origin: Vienna, August 1789
Author: Giuseppe Palomba
Scoring: soprano, 2 oboes, 2 bassoons, 2 horns, strings

Mozart wrote this aria to be inserted in a revival of Cimarosa's *I due baroni di Rocca Azzura*, performed in Vienna on September 6, 1789, a week after the revival of *Figaro*. He wrote it for the soprano Louise Villeneuve, a popular singer newly arrived in Vienna. Three months later she created the part of Dorabella in the premiere of *Così fan tutte*.

The story involves a clever young man who wins a beautiful and wealthy bride, Donna Laura, by impersonating a suitor, the Baron of Rocca Azzura, whom her father has chosen for her, sight unseen. When the real baron arrives, he is attracted by another woman, Sandra. A quarrel between the two women culminates in Laura's aria, "Alma grande e nobil core," an apostrophe to her highborn ideals and her scorn of the likes of Sandra, who should treat her with more respect. Laura finally vents her rage on the baron.

C.R.

K. 579 *Un moto di gioia*
Origin: Vienna, August 1789
Author: Lorenzo de Ponte
Scoring: soprano, flute, oboe, bassoon, 2 horns, strings

This is the second of two replacement arias (K. 577, 579) for Susanna in the 1789 revival of *The Marriage of Figaro*. It is a little arietta, barely a minute and a half long and as light as thistledown. It is uncertain exactly where it fits into the action of *Figaro*. To make room for it, Mozart dropped Susanna's Act II aria, "Venite inginocchiatevi," sung as she is fitting Cherubino with a mobcap and teaching him a lady's deportment. The replacement cannot compare with the original but is irresistible nonetheless, and since Mozart himself made an elegant piano reduction, it has often been appropriated by lieder singers as a song with piano accompaniment. C.R.

K. 580 *Schon lacht der holde Frühling*
Origin: Vienna, September 17, 1789
Author: anonymous
Scoring: soprano, 2 clarinets, 2 bassoons, 2 horns, strings

This little-known but substantial aria has been neglected because the composer merely sketched the orchestration, although the voice part is complete. Plans were afoot in 1789 to mount a new production in German of Paisiello's enormously popular *Il barbiere di Siviglia* (The Barber of Seville) in Vienna, with Mozart's eldest sister-in-law, Josefa Hofer, starring as Rosina. For some reason the project was shelved, and Mozart simply dropped work on the aria. It was, in all probability, designed to serve as Rosina's singing lesson in the second act. C.R.

K. 582 *Chi sà, chi sà, qual sia*
Origin: Vienna, October 1789
Author: Lorenzo da Ponte?
Scoring: soprano, 2 clarinets, 2 bassoons, 2 horns, strings

K. 582 and K. 583 are two more interpolation arias written, like K. 578, for Louise Villeneuve, this time for a revival of Antonio Soler's *Il burbero di buon cuore* (The Good-Hearted Churl), which was presented at the Vienna Burgtheater on November 9, 1789.

This is the more brilliant of the two arias. The heroine, Madame Lucilla, is puzzled by the churlishness of her suitor, who, unbeknownst to her, is hopelessly in debt. Excitedly and without giving reason, he has forbidden her to mix in his personal affairs. C.R.

K. 583 *Vado, ma dove?*
Origin: Vienna, October 1789
Author: Lorenzo da Ponte?
Scoring: soprano, 2 clarinets, 2 bassoons, 2 horns, strings

This is the other interpolated aria in Antonio Soler's *Il burbero di buon cuore.* The situation is similar: Lucilla is troubled by the bizarre behavior of her suitor. The aria shows her deep and tender feelings, not far removed from those of Countess Almaviva. C.R.

CONCERT ARIAS AND SCENES FOR ALTO

K. 255 *Ombra felice . . . Io ti lascio*
Origin: Salzburg, September 1776
Author: Giovanni de Gamerra
Scoring: alto, 2 oboes, 2 horns, strings

This recitative and aria *en rondeau* was composed for the alto castrato Francesco Fortini. It is one of Mozart's most noble concert arias, but because it is his only one for alto voice it seems to have been unjustly overlooked. Fortini was a *virtuoso da camera* (chamber virtuoso) of the elector of Bavaria and was in Salzburg performing with an Italian troupe that specialized in *opere buffe*. It was most unusual for castrati to sing in comic opera (they were already the subjects of much comic repartee), and Fortini may have appeared only in concert repertory with the company. Mozart may have provided this distinctly *opera seria* aria for such a concert.

The text is traceable to a *dramma per musica* called *Arsace,* with music by Michele Mortellari, which deals with a tragic love affair between Selene, wife of King Medonte, and Arsace, the king's chief of staff. Here, early in the opera, Arsace takes leave of his beloved and wonders if he will ever see her again. C.R.

CONCERT ARIAS AND SCENES FOR TENOR

K. 21 ***Va, dal furor portata (K⁶ 19c)***
Origin: London, 1765
Author: Pietro Metastasio
Scoring: tenor, 2 oboes, 2 bassoons, 2 horns, strings

The occasion for the composition of this aria, Mozart's earliest known vocal work, is uncertain, but its date is attested by a manuscript note in his father's hand. The text comes from Metastasio's *Ezio,* which the Mozarts saw sung in *pasticcio* format (that is, with inserted arias from other sources) in early 1765 in London. It is highly questionable that Wolfgang's aria was ever inserted in this production, however, since Leopold mentions no such occurrence in his correspondence.

The aria is sung by Massimo, who has just made an unsuccessful attempt on the life of the emperor. Suspicion has fallen not on Massimo, but on Ezio, who is beloved of Massimo's daughter Fulvia. When Fulvia expresses contempt for her father's actions, Massimo angrily accuses her of filial treason. W.C.

K. 36 ***Or che il dover . . . Tali e cotanti sono (K⁶ 33i)***
Origin: Salzburg, December 1766
Author: anonymous
Scoring: tenor, 2 oboes, 2 bassoons, 2 horns, 2 trumpets and timpani, strings

This aria is one of Mozart's first works after his return to Salzburg from his grand tour to London and northern Europe. He composed it as a *licenza* (an inserted epilogue of homage) for the intermezzo "Il cavaliere di spirito" (on a text by Carlo Goldoni), which was performed on the occasion of the anniversary of the consecration of Archbishop Sigismund von Schrattenbach in Salzburg on December 21, 1766. The text makes specific reference to this occasion. Mozart composed another *licenza,* K. 70, for a similar occasion in Salzburg; see the note on p. 74.
W.C.

K. 209 ***Si mostra la sorte***
Origin: Salzburg, May 19, 1775
Author: anonymous
Scoring: tenor, 2 flutes, 2 horns, strings

In 1775 and 1776 Mozart appears to have written no fewer than five arias and scenes in connection with a visiting Italian *opera buffa* troupe in Salzburg: these include K. 209, 210, and 256 for tenor, K. 217 for soprano, and K. 255 for alto. The autograph score of the first of these arias bears a date in Leopold Mozart's hand; otherwise nothing has come to light concerning its purpose. Perhaps it served as an insertion aria in the same opera as the contemporaneous aria, K. 210. It is conceivable that Mozart wrote these arias for the use of a local Salzburg singer performing with the Italian troupe. W.C.

K. 210 ***Con ossequio, con rispetto***
Origin: Salzburg, May 1775
Author: anonymous
Scoring: tenor, 2 oboes, 2 horns, strings

Contemporaneous with K. 209, this aria served as an insertion aria in Niccolò Piccinni's opera *L'Astratto, ovvero Il giocatore fortunato* (The Absent-Minded Man, or The Lucky Joker) on a text by Giuseppe Petrosellini. The aria comes in Act II, Scene 20, but departs from Petrosellini's text, which sets the entire scene as recitative. In this scene the devil-may-care Capitano Faccenda, disguised as a doctor, appeals boastfully for the hand of Clarice, the daughter of Don Timoteo,

the wealthy but choleric landowner who sings the present aria. The following year Mozart composed another insertion aria, K. 256, for the same scene (see below).
W.C.

K. 256 ***Clarice cara mia sposa***
Origin: Salzburg, September 1776
Author: anonymous
Scoring: tenor, 2 oboes, 2 horns, strings

Mozart composed this aria specifically for the singer Antonio Palmini. It is an insertion aria for the same opera and scene as K. 210, sung by the character of Capitano Faccenda. Typically for a *buffa* aria of this sort, a second character (Don Timoteo) interrupts with commentary in *recitativo secco*.
W.C.

K. 295 ***Se al labbro mio non credi***
Origin: Mannheim, February 27, 1778
Author: Antonio Salvi
Scoring: tenor, 2 flutes, 2 oboes, 2 bassoons, 2 horns, strings

This is one of the three concert arias (K. 294, 295, and 486a) that Mozart composed within the space of four days during his first stay in Mannheim. He composed the works for three of the principal singers of Mannheim: the sopranos Aloysia Weber [Lange], and Dorothea Wendling, and the tenor Anton Raaff. According to a letter from Mozart to his father, he chose a text of an aria that was already in Raaff's repertory, hoping to make so much the stronger an impression of the celebrated tenor. Raaff was reportedly delighted, but asked Mozart to shorten the composition. Indeed, Mozart's manuscript contains many changes and deletions that would appear to correspond to such a request. Mozart was later to create the title role in his opera *Idomeneo* for Raaff.

Mozart took the text from an aria in Johann Adolf Hasse's *Artaserse* (libretto by Metastasio), an aria that the composer had actually borrowed from his own earlier opera *Arminio* (libretto by Salvi).
W.C.

K. 435 ***Müsst'ich auch durch tausend Drachen (K^6 416b)***
Origin: Vienna? 1783?
Author: anonymous
Scoring: tenor, flute, oboe, clarinet, 2 bassoons, 2 horns, 2 trumpets and timpani, strings

On February 5, 1783, Mozart wrote to his father, "I am now writing myself a German opera—I have picked out a comedy by Goldoni—*Il servitore di Due Padroni*—and the whole first act is already translated—the translator is Baron Binder—but the whole thing is still a secret until it is all finished." It is possible that the tenor aria K. 435 and a bass aria, "Männer suchen stets zu naschen," K. 433, were designed for this opera, which presumably would have gone by the title *Der Diener zweier Herren* (The Servant of Two Masters). No more is known of the projected opera. The present aria, unlike the fragmentary K. 433, survives composed from beginning to end but with the orchestration incomplete.
W.C.

K. 420 ***Per pietà non ricercate***
Origin: Vienna, June 21, 1783
Author: anonymous
Scoring: tenor, 2 clarinets, 2 bassoons, 2 horns, strings

Like the two arias K. 418 and 419 (see the note on p. 80), K. 420 was designed as an insertion aria for Pasquale Anfossi's opera *Il curioso indiscreto*. Mozart composed it specifically for the German Johann Valentin Adamberger, one of the finest tenors of his day, for whom Mozart later created the role of Belmonte in *The Abduction from the Seraglio.*

In Act II, the Count of Ripaverde overhears a conversation between Clorinda and Aurelio, a friend of the Marquess Calandro. Left alone, the count gives vent to his overwhelming envy of Clorinda's love for the Marquess; in desperation he seeks only death. W.C.

K. 431 *Misero! O sogno . . . Aura che intorno spiri (K[6] 425b)*

Origin: Vienna? December 1783?
Author: anonymous
Scoring: tenor, 2 flutes, 2 bassoons, 2 horns, strings

A note on Mozart's manuscript indicates that he composed this scene, like the preceding aria, for Johann Valentin Adamberger, but no other details of the work's origin are certain. It is often equated with a "new rondo" of Mozart's that Adamberger is reported to have sung in a concert of December 22, 1783.

W.C.

K[3] 540a *Dalla sua pace*

Origin: Vienna, April 24, 1788
Author: Lorenzo da Ponte
Scoring: tenor, flute, 2 oboes, 2 bassoons, 2 horns, strings

See the note for *Don Giovanni* on p. 61.

CONCERT ARIAS AND SCENES FOR BASS

K. 432 *Così dunque tradisci . . . Aspri rimorsi atroci (K[6] 421a)*

Origin: Vienna? 1783
Author: Pietro Metastasio
Scoring: bass, 2 flutes, 2 oboes, 2 bassoons, 2 horns, strings

Although from boyhood onward Mozart composed separate soprano or tenor arias to be interpolated in other composers' operas, it was not until 1783 that he began writing concert arias for bass. The inspiration for this new departure was the prodigiously talented *basso profundo* Karl Ludwig Fischer, who created the role of Osmin in Mozart's *Die Entführung aus dem Serail.* He was eager to be recognized as a master of Italian operatic music and asked Mozart for a highly effective solo that he could introduce into a forthcoming Vienna production of the opera *Temistocle,* originally set to music by Andrea Bernasconi. In this aria, Sebaste, a subsidiary character, has been found out in evil-doing, and is filled with remorse. W.S.M.

K. 512 *Alcandro, lo confesso . . . Non sò d'onde vieni*

Origin: Vienna, March 19, 1787
Author: Pietro Metastasio
Scoring: bass, flute, 2 oboes, 2 bassoons, 2 horns, strings

This aria was also composed at the request of Ludwig Fischer. While Mozart was engaged in preliminary work on *Don Giovanni,* Fischer asked for a dramatic solo aria in Italian suitable for the singer's subscription concert on March 21, 1787. Fischer had been dropped from the Vienna Italian Opera Company and he evidently wished to show authority its grave mistake. Again Mozart went back to a Metastasio text; this time he chose words he had already set in 1778 for the soprano Aloysia Weber Lange (see K. 294, p. 77). For Fräulein Weber's aria Mozart had imagined the situation of a mother and her son; for Fischer's aria he restored the true situation, that of a father and son.

W.S.M.

K. 513 ***Mentre ti lascio***
Origin: Vienna, March 23, 1787
Author: Duca Sant' Angioli-Morbilli
Scoring: bass, flute, 2 clarinets, 2 bassoons, 2 horns, strings

Like the aria K. 512, this one was composed during preliminary work on *Don Giovanni.* It was written for Mozart's young friend Gottfried von Jacquin, a good amateur bass singer, for whom Mozart wrote other music. The text comes from Paisiello's opera *La disfatta di Dario,* which was composed in 1777. In this aria, a father is bidding farewell to his daughter.

W.S.M.

K. 539 ***Ein deutsches Kriegslied ("Ich möchte wohl der Kaiser sein")***
Origin: Vienna, March 5, 1788
Author: Johann Wilhelm Ludwig
Scoring: bass, piccolo, 2 oboes, 2 bassoons, 2 horns, percussion, strings

Mozart composed "Ein deutsches Kriegslied" (A German War Song") for a patriotic concert in Vienna at the beginning of the Turkish wars—hence the piccolo, cymbals, and bass drum in the orchestral accompaniment (all three were synonymous with "Turkish" music in Viennese music of Mozart's day). The poem was by J. W. L. Gleim, a noted German writer; Mozart's setting was tailor-made for the limited vocal gifts of the popular Viennese comedian Friedrich Baumann, Jr. This charming trifle came into being while the master was busy preparing *Don Giovanni* for its Vienna premiere.

W.S.M.

K. 541 ***Un bacio di mano***
Origin: Vienna, May 1788
Author: Lorenzo da Ponte?
Scoring: bass, 2 oboes, 2 bassoons, 2 horns, strings

Mozart wrote this aria for Francesco Albertarelli, his first Viennese Don Giovanni. It was to be introduced into Pasquale Anfossi's comic opera *Le gelosie fortunate* (Jealousy Rewarded), produced in Vienna in June of 1788. The text's ironic literary content suggests the hand of da Ponte. The aria is famous chiefly because it includes a melody (at the words "Voi siete un po' tondo") that Mozart was to borrow, three months later, for the first movement of his "Jupiter" Symphony. In this aria Girò, a Frenchman, is giving jocular advice on love to his highly susceptible friend, Pompeo.

W.S.M.

K^{3} **621a** ***Io ti lascio (K**^{1} ***Anh 245)***
Origin: Vienna? 1788?
Author: anonymous
Scoring: bass, strings

The clouds of mystery have not yet completely lifted from this short piece. Mozart's widow insisted in 1799 that it was not her husband's work, but a collaboration between him (the string accompaniment) and his friend Gottfried von Jacquin, who wrote the vocal part as an adieu to Countess Hortense Hatzfeld. Musicologist Alfred Einstein, having examined the extant half of the manuscript score, felt little doubt that "Io ti lascio" is pure and authentic Mozart, accepting the tradition that Mozart jotted down its thirty-nine measures just before leaving Prague after the first production of *La clemenza di Tito* in September 1791.

But the English scholar Alan Tyson has shown that the surviving autograph fragment is of a type of paper that Mozart used primarily in 1788. W.S.M.

K. 584 ***Rivolgete a lui lo sguardo***
Origin: Vienna, December 1789
Author: Lorenzo da Ponte
Scoring: bass, 2 oboes, 2 horns, 2 trumpets and timpani, strings

In 1789 Mozart was composing his third and last Italian comic opera with da Ponte, *Così fan tutte.* In it, two young soldiers dress up in outlandish disguises and woo each other's sweethearts in order to test their fidelity. The bass soldier, Guglielmo, is the first to do the courting on behalf of both of them: da Ponte gave him an unusually long aria text, brilliantly and wittily imagined, and vividly inspiring to Mozart. But the result proved too extended for the balance of the scene in context, and it was replaced, before the first performance, by the shorter and less pretentious aria "Non siate ritrosi."

The disguised Guglielmo begins the aria by addressing his own sweetheart, recommending his tenor friend to her attention; he then asks her sister to admire his own virtues. When his wooing turns out to be unsuccessful, he is delighted: it means that the two young women are (for the time being at least) faithful to their lovers. W.S.M.

K. 612 ***Per questa bella mano***
Origin: Vienna, March 8, 1791
Author: anonymous
Scoring: bass, flute, 2 oboes, 2 bassoons, 2 horns, strings with double bass obbligato

In March 1791, shortly before beginning work on *Die Zauberflöte,* Mozart wrote this unusual aria for Franz Gerl (who was to be the first Sarastro in that opera) and Friedrich Pichelberger, the principal double bass player in the orchestra at Emanuel Schikaneder's theater, where *Die Zauberflöte* was to have its premiere. The occasion was most likely a subscription concert for Gerl or Pichelberger. Mozart treats both soloists as virtuosi, asking the double bassist for plentiful double-stops in thirds, rapid scales, arpeggios, and wide leaps, and the bass singer for comparable feats. W.S.M.

CONCERT DUETS, TRIOS, AND QUARTETS

K. 479 ***Dite almeno in che mancai***
Origin: Vienna, November 5, 1785
Author: Lorenzo da Ponte?
Scoring: soprano, tenor, 2 basses, 2 oboes, 2 clarinets, 2 bassoons, 2 horns, strings

K. 480 ***Mandina amabile***
Origin: Vienna, November 21, 1785
Author: Lorenzo da Ponte?
Scoring: soprano, tenor, bass, 2 flutes, 2 oboes, 2 clarinets, 2 bassoons, 2 horns, strings

Mozart composed these two works as replacement ensembles for the Vienna premiere of Francesco Bianchi's *opera buffa, La villanella rapita* (The Abducted Country Girl), on November 28, 1785. The original opera had premiered the previous year in Bologna. Both of Mozart's ensembles replaced passages of *secco* recitative in Bianchi's original composition; in both cases the texts were altered from Giovanni Bertati's original libretto.

In the opera, the Count is in love with Mandina, a simple peasant girl who is engaged to marry the peasant boy Pippo. Mandina and her father Biagio take the

Count's approaches as innocent indications of his benevolence. In K. 480, the Count attempts to demonstrate the true nature of his favor to Mandina, who is too simple-minded to understand, although Pippo sees through the scheme. Finally the Count decides to abduct Mandina by giving her a sleeping potion. In K. 479, Pippo and Biagio discover Mandina in the Count's palace and, jumping to conclusions, they shower her with abuse and reproaches; the entrance of the Count only adds to the confusion.

Though it happened without his knowledge, K. 480 was Mozart's only vocal composition to be published in full score during his lifetime (Paris, c. 1789–90).

W.C.

K. 489 ***Spiegarti non poss'io***
Origin: Vienna, March 10, 1786
Author: anonymous
Scoring: soprano, tenor, 2 oboes, 2 bassoons, 2 horns, strings

See the note for *Idomeneo* on p. 52.

K^3 540b ***Per queste tue manine***
Origin: Vienna, April 28, 1788
Author: Lorenzo da Ponte
Scoring: soprano, bass, 2 flutes, 2 oboes, 2 bassoons, 2 trumpets, strings

For the Vienna revival of *Don Giovanni* (see p. 63), Mozart added two new arias (K. 540a and 540c) and this duet.

6

Songs and Vocal Ensembles

BACKGROUND AND OVERVIEW

Mozart composed his songs in the manner of bagatelles, *Freundstücke* (offerings to friends), or occasional pieces that owe their existence mainly to the private circumstances of household music-making among friends. Indeed, there was no shortage of such occasions in Mozart's life, and it is entirely possible that there once existed even more of these *Freundstücke* than are attested to by the thirty songs that comprise this relatively small category of Mozart's works. The fact that Mozart attached relatively little weight to his solo songs, that he probably didn't include them among the works that "went forth into the world," is explained by the nature of the genre and its significance in the late eighteenth century. The solo song with piano accompaniment, that finds its complete crystallization in the works of Franz Schubert, attained a firm footing rather late in the Viennese musical consciousness. While the North-, Middle-, and South-German schools of song writing had already gone far in the dissemination and popularization of the German lied by mid-century, the absolute Italian domination of vocal music in Austria, and especially Vienna, stood in the way of similar developments there. The first collection of German lieder by Joseph Anton Steffan appeared, significantly, in 1778, the same year that the opening of the German National Singspiel Theater by Emperor Joseph II countered the influence of Italian opera in Vienna.

Contrary to the case of the German songwriters, the texts selected by Viennese songwriters of the late eighteenth century attest to no particular awareness of literary quality. The texts of choice, drawn from the ephemeral poetry almanacs and paperbacks of the day, are almost without exception the works of fashionable poetic kleinmeisters of the day. They are mostly of Anacreontic character, idealizing the light, entertaining pastoral genre with no particular soul-searching depth. And here, as regards the choice of texts, Mozart the songwriter is no exception. In comparison to Schubert, Mozart's song composition is hardly inspired by the text in the same degree. And yet, many of his songs are brilliant little character pieces, in which the wealth of opera-inspired melodic invention dominates the insubstantial text with ease.

For Mozart, who in his song composition often proves himself a "playwright for the most intimate space" in the words of Ernst August Ballin, editor of the songs for the *Neue Mozart-Ausgabe,* this miniature vocal form served a function in opera composition surprisingly often, in part perhaps as a mere accessory, but also as a compact means of study; motivic correspondences between song tunes and themes in his contemporaneous operas point in this direction. In general the development of Mozart's song composition shows a stylistic similarity to that of

---

OPPOSITE. "Leopold Mozart, father of Marianne Mozart, eleven-year-old virtuosa, and of J. G. Wolfgang Mozart, seven-year-old composer and maestro." Engraving by Jean Baptiste Delafosse (1764) after a watercolor by Louis Carregis de Carmontelle (1763).

During the tours with his children, Leopold Mozart often lied about their ages, making them each a year younger. In 1763 when Carmontelle painted his watercolor, Wolfgang and Nannerl were seven and eleven as stated, but the artist drastically shortened Wolfgang's legs (compared to his sketches) to exaggerate his youth. They are shown here performing a song or aria for soprano with harpsichord and violin accompaniment.

his other vocal works. Although he did not systematically cultivate this "by-product of his muse" (in musicologist Paul Nettl's phrase), nevertheless the process of songwriting served again and again as an important starting point for all other types of vocal composition, often so intensively that whole groups of songs were composed at once. S.D.

SONGS

K. 53 *An die Freude, in F major* (*K^3 43b, K^6 47e*)
Origin: Vienna, autumn 1768
Author: anonymous

K. 147 *Wie unglücklich bin ich nit, in F major* (*K^6 125g*)
Origin: Salzburg, c. 1772?
Author: anonymous

Mozart's early songs, like the contemporaneous products of Viennese song composers, are *basso continuo* songs; these include both a little song *An die Freude* (To Joy), presumably composed in November 1768 at the same time as the Singspiel *Bastien und Bastienne,* and two songs probably composed in the early summer of 1772 in Salzburg: the sentimental love song *Wie unglücklich bin ich nit* (How Unlucky I Am), in which the fifteen-year-old Mozart pointedly depicts the sighs of a slighted lover, and the Masonic song *Lobgesang auf die feierliche Johannisloge* (K. 148), the text of which he took from a Regensburg Masonic songbook of 1772. The occasion and purpose of the latter song are unknown (see p. 36).

Mozart returned again to the technique of *basso continuo* accompaniment that he had used in his early songs for the *Two German Hymns* (K. 343), presumably composed in early 1787, and for "Die Alte" (K. 517) of the same year (see below). S.D.

K. 307 *Oiseaux, si tous les ans, in C major* (*K^6 284d*)
Origin: Mannheim, winter 1777–78
Author: Antoine Ferrand

K. 308 *Dans un bois solitaire, in A-flat major* (*K^6 295b*)
Origin: Mannheim, winter 1777–78
Author: Antoine Houdart de la Motte

The two French ariettas, *Oiseaux, si tous les ans* (Birds, if every year) and *Dans un bois solitaire* (In a lonely wood), were composed during Mozart's Mannheim visit from October 30, 1777, to March 14, 1778, for Augusta Wendling, the charming daughter of the flutist Johann Baptist Wendling and the soprano Dorothea Wendling. She is said to have performed "incomparably" these ariettas, conceived in the spirit of the French *opéra comique,* and containing for the first time in Mozart's songs a fully written out piano part. S.D.

K. 349 *Die Zufriedenheit, in G major* (*K^6 367a*)
Origin: Munich, winter 1780–81
Author: anonymous

K. 351 *Komm, liebe Zither, in C major* (*K^6 367b*)
Origin: Munich, winter 1780–81
Author: anonymous

The two songs with mandolin accompaniment, *Komm, liebe Zither* (Come,

Beloved Harp) and *Die Zufriedenheit* (Contentment), were presumably composed during Mozart's visit to Munich, at the time of *Idomeneo,* for the Munich hornist Martin Lang. S.D.

K. 392 *Verdankt sei es dem Glanz, in F major (K⁶ 340a)*
Origin: Vienna, 1781–82
Author: Johann Timotheus Hermes

K. 391 *Sei du mein Trost, in B-flat major (K⁶ 340b)*
Origin: Vienna, 1781–82
Author: Johann Timotheus Hermes

K. 390 *Ich würd' auf meinem Pfad, in D minor (K⁶ 340c)*
Origin: Vienna, 1781–82
Author: Johann Timotheus Hermes

The three songs, *Verdankt sei es dem Glanz* (It Is Due to the Lustre), *Sei du mein Trost* (Be Thou My Comfort), and *Ich würd' auf meinem Pfad* (I Would Along my Path), were composed during the early Viennese years, 1781 to 1782, in the immediate vicinity of *The Abduction from the Seraglio.* They have curious performing indications: "gleichgültig und zufrieden" (indifferently and contentedly), "traurig, doch gelassen" (sadly yet calmly), and "mäßig gehend" (moving with restraint). Their texts come from J. T. Hermes's novel *Sophiens Reise von Memel nach Sachsen* (*Sophia's Journey from Memel to Saxony*), one of the great sentimental effluences of the day. S.D.

K. 472 *Der Zauberer, in G minor*
Origin: Vienna, May 7, 1785
Author: Christian Felix Weisse

K. 473 *Die Zufriedenheit, in B-flat major*
Origin: Vienna, May 7, 1785
Author: Christian Felix Weisse

K. 474 *Die betrogene Welt, in G major*
Origin: Vienna, May 7, 1785
Author: Christian Felix Weisse

K. 476 *Das Veilchen, in G major*
Origin: Vienna, June 8, 1785
Author: Johann Wolfgang von Goethe

K. 506 *Lied der Freiheit, in F major*
Origin: Vienna, end of 1785?
Author: Johannes Aloys Blumauer

K. 517 *Die Alte, in E minor*
Origin: Vienna, May 18, 1787
Author: Friedrich von Hagedorn

K. 518 *Die Verschweigung, in F major*
Origin: Vienna, May 20, 1787
Author: Christian Felix Weisse

On May 7, 1785, Mozart entered three settings of texts by C. F. Weisse, an especially popular poet among the Viennese songwriters, into his catalogue: *Der Zauberer* (The Enchanter), *Die Zufriedenheit* (Contentment), and *Die betrogene Welt* (The Deceived World)—the text of K. 518, *Die Verschweigung* (The Secret) also comes from Weisse. The texts represent a typically rococo brand of happy shepherds' life, mixed at times with a dryly moralizing stance. Wholly un-Arcadian and grippingly dramatic, however, is Mozart's setting of the flirtatiously playful text of Weisse's *Der Zauberer.* In a few swift strokes the concise introduction and conclusion depict the violent excitement of a young maiden bewitched by love.

On June 8 came the centerpiece among Mozart's songs, *Das Veilchen* (The Violet) in which (for the only time) his name was linked with that of Johann Wolfgang von Goethe. Here Mozart departed in a most willful way from traditional strophic form, and composed each verse independently. The finely shaded textual expression—both in the vocal melody and even more in the piano accompaniment, which is handled with utmost variety—truly outlines a "drama for the most intimate space."

With the *Lied der Freiheit* (Song of Freedom) on a moralizing text by J. A. Blumauer, Mozart returns to the conventional strophic song form. A deliberately anachronistic, intentionally parodic retrogression to the *basso continuo* style appears in his setting of Hagedorn's verse, *Die Alte* (The Old Woman), in which he nostalgically yearns, with tongue in cheek, for the good old days. S.D.

K. 519 *Das Lied der Trennung, in F minor*
Origin: Vienna, May 23, 1787
Author: Klamer Eberhardt Karl Schmidt

K. 520 *Als Luise die Briefe ihres ungetreuen Liebhabers verbrannte, in C minor*
Origin: Vienna, May 26, 1787
Author: Gabriele von Baumberg

K. 523 *Abendempfindung an Laura, in F major*
Origin: Vienna, June 24, 1787
Author: Joachim Heinrich Campe

K. 524 *An Chloe, in E-flat major*
Origin: Vienna, June 24, 1787
Author: Johann Georg Jacobi

K. 529 *Des kleinen Friedrich Geburtstag, in F major*
Origin: Prague, November 6, 1787
Author: Johann Eberhard Friedrich Schall

K. 530 *Das Traumbild, in E-flat major*
Origin: Prague, November 6, 1787
Author: Ludwig Heinrich Christopher Hölty

K. 531 *Die kleine Spinnerin, in C major*
Origin: Vienna, December 11, 1787
Author: anonymous

K. 552 *Beim Auszug in das Feld, in A major*
Origin: Vienna, August 11, 1788
Author: anonymous

The "*Don Giovanni* year," 1787, brings the richest harvest of Mozart songs, with a total of 9 works, in addition to the *Two German Hymns* (K. 343) discussed on p. 28. After *Die Alte* and *Die Verschweigung,* mentioned above, came *Das Lied der Trennung* (The Song of Separation), whose roundly tasteless text, by K. E. K. Schmidt, could have inspired Mozart to such a passionate F-minor setting only on the spur of the moment.

The two songs *Als Luise die Briefe ihres ungetreuen Liebhabers verbrannte* (As Louise Burned the Letters of Her Unfaithful Lover) and *Das Traumbild* (The Dream Scene) have a close connection to Mozart's friend and pupil Gottfried von Jacquin. Mozart frequently emerges as a songwriter within the circle of Jacquin's family and friends, but in such a way that the listener is occasionally left in the dark as to a song's precise authorship; this has given rise to all sorts of mixups and misattributions. For a long time Jacquin was assumed to be the author of these two songs. In fact, Jacquin dedicated the dramatic monologue of the abandoned Louise—in whose piano accompaniment are distilled all the elements of *recitativo accompagnato*—to a certain Fräulein von Altomonte, after having, it seems, jokingly forced his friend Mozart to compose it under lock and key. (This was probably the gifted singer, Katharina von Altomonte, who sang many of the arias in the March 1789 premiere in Vienna of Mozart's reorchestration of Handel's *Messiah.*) The text comes from the Viennese poetess Gabriele von Baumberg, who wrote it out of her own personal experience.

In 1789 at Artaria and Co. in Vienna, under the title of *Zwei deutsche Arien zum Singen beim Clavier* (Two German Arias to Sing at the Piano), Mozart published two songs that are among his most popular today: *Abendempfindung* (Sentiments At Evening) and *An Chloe* (To Chloe), both entered in his catalogue on June 24, 1787. *Abendempfindung* is a deeply felt, through-composed portrait of the soul. Contrastingly, the setting of J. G. Jacobi's text *An Chloe,* which is stamped with the spirit of rococo *galanterie,* approximates a rondo form.

The simple little strophic song, *Des kleinen Friedrich Geburtstag* (Little Frederick's Birthday), was composed in Prague, possibly for a children's magazine. Whether the "little Frederick" of Schall's verse refers to the crown prince Friedrich of Anhalt-Dessau has not been convincingly proven. In another unassuming strophic song, *Die kleine Spinnerin* (The Little Spinner), Mozart set a naive, childlike text by an unknown author.

The author of Mozart's *Beim Auszug in das Feld* (On Going Forth into the Field) is likewise unknown. The eighteen-verse song was first published as a supplement to a handbook, *Angenehme und lehrreiche Beschäftigung für Kinder in ihren Freistunden* (Pleasant and Instructive Pastimes for Children), and has only recently been accepted as an authentic work of Mozart. S.D.

K. 596 *Sehnsucht nach dem Frühlinge, in F major*
Origin: Vienna, January 14, 1791
Author: Christian Adolf Overbeck

K. 597 *Im Frühlingsanfang, in E-flat major*
Origin: Vienna, January 14, 1791
Author: Christian Christoph Sturm

K. 598 *Das Kinderspiel, in A major*
Origin: Vienna, January 14, 1791
Author: Christian Adolf Overbeck

These three songs, on verses by C. A. Overbeck and C. C. Sturm, appeared in early 1791 in the *Liedersammlung für Kinder and Kinderfreunde am Clavier: Frühlingslieder* (Collection of Songs for Children and Those Who Love Children at the Piano: Spring Songs), published by Ignaz Alberti in Vienna. The first of these three children's songs, the "Mayday Song," has particularly enjoyed an almost folkloric popularity. Just a few days before writing down this little strophic song, easily accessible even to children, Mozart lent another dimension to its introductory theme in the rondo of his last piano concerto, in B flat, K. 595. S.D.

VOCAL ENSEMBLES

K³ 43a *Ach, was müssen wir erfahren? (K¹ Anh 24a)*
Origin: Vienna, shortly after October 15, 1767
Author: anonymous
Scoring: 2 sopranos, [keyboard]

This tiny, sorrowful duet ("Ah, what must we suffer?") was probably inspired by the untimely death on October 15, 1767, from smallpox, of the sixteen-year-old Archduchess Maria Josepha, bride-to-be of King Ferdinand of Naples.

N.Z.

K. 441 *Liebes Mandel, wo is's Bandel?*
Origin: Vienna, 1783?
Author: Wolfgang Amadeus Mozart?
Scoring: soprano, tenor, bass, strings

The "Bandel" Trio owes its existence to an amusing incident in Mozart's household, as we may guess from the designations of the vocal parts in the score ("Constantz," "Mozart," and "Jacquin"). Before going for a drive, Mozart and his wife look agitatedly for a new ribbon with which Constanze wants to adorn herself. The friend Gottfried von Jacquin arrives and is drawn into the general commotion. He finds the ribbon and closes the work, together with the Mozarts, with a most hilarious victory song.

The first line of text *(Dearest Almond, where's my hatband?)* indicates the level of nonsense present here. Gottfried von Jacquin was a young Viennese friend and student of Mozart's, for whom the latter composed his Notturnos and Canzonetta for voices and winds (see below). E.F.S.

K. 436 *Notturno, "Ecco quel fiero istante"*
Origin: Vienna, c. 1787
Author: Pietro Metastasio
Scoring: 2 sopranos, bass, 3 basset horns

K. 437 *Notturno, "Mi lagnerò tacendo"*
Origin: Vienna, c. 1787
Author: Pietro Metastasio
Scoring: 2 sopranos, bass, 2 clarinets, basset horn

K. 438 *Notturno, "Se lontan ben mio"*
Origin: Vienna, c. 1787
Author: Pietro Metastasio
Scoring: 2 sopranos, bass, 2 clarinets, basset horn

K. 439 *Notturno, "Due pupille amabile"*
Origin: Vienna, c. 1787
Author: Pietro Metastasio?
Scoring: 2 sopranos, bass, 3 basset horns

K. 346 *Notturno, "Luci care, luci belle" (K^6 439a)*
Origin: Vienna, c. 1787
Author: Pietro Metastasio?
Scoring: 2 sopranos, bass, 3 basset horns

K. 549 *Canzonetta, "Più non si trovano"*
Origin: Vienna, July 16, 1788
Author: Pietro Metastasio
Scoring: 2 sopranos, bass, 3 basset horns

Mozart's composition of these works was sparked by his friendship with the family of the famous botanist Nicolaus Josef von Jacquin (1727–1817) whose son Gottfried (1767–92) and daughter Franziska (1769–1857) were very musical. She was one of Mozart's best piano students and it is said that he composed his well-known Trio for Piano, Clarinet, and Viola in E flat, K. 498, for her. Mozart was fond of Gottfried, who was gifted musically and known as such, which may explain why Mozart's five Notturni were later ascribed to Gottfried von Jacquin. Mozart's widow Constanze supposed that Jacquin and Mozart collaborated on the Notturni, but Mozart's authorship is generally accepted.

K. 436, 437, and 438 are based on texts by Pietro Metastasio, the most important librettist of the eighteenth century; the texts were taken from the *Canzonette,* the *opera seria Siroe,* and the *Strofe per musica* (Verses for Music), respectively. Sources for the texts of K. 439 and 346 have not yet been discovered. K. 549 is based on lines taken from Metastasio's often-composed opera *Olimpiade.* All the Notturni are short, simple love songs, comprising between sixteen and seventy measures each. The style of K. 437 approaches that of an operatic terzetto.

A most interesting aspect is the employment of the basset horn for the accompaniments. Mozart had previously used this instrument, an alto member of the clarinet family, only in the Serenade, K. 361, and Constanze's G minor aria in *The Abduction from the Seraglio* (Act II, No. 10). In the Notturni—as well as the five Divertimentos for three basset horns, K. 439b, which were presumably also intended for the musical activities of the Jacquin family—the basset horns, emancipated from the full orchestra, come into their own. The technical prowess of the brothers Anton and Johann Stadler, two fine Viennese clarinetists who presumably participated in the sessions held in the home of the Jacquins, stimulated Mozart to experiment with the instrument. These endeavors were to climax in Mozart's last works, *The Magic Flute, La clemenza di Tito,* and the Requiem. J.B.

7

Canons

A puzzle canon from Giovanni Battista Martini's *Storia della musica*, 3 vols. (Bologna, 1757, 1770, 1781).

Mozart studied counterpoint with Padre Martini in Bologna in 1770, receiving a copy of Volume 2 of his Storia della musica *from him as it came off the press. In the next few years Mozart copied out many of the dozens of puzzle canons that decorate Martini's first two volumes and worked out their resolutions. This double canon is the opening vignette of Chapter 1, Volume 1. Its text, "Sing unto the Lord, all the earth," is the first verse of Psalm 96 (in the new numbering, but 95 in the old). The legend over the top canon reads "Canon: [enter] after one tempus [double whole-note]," the legend over the bottom one reads "6th, 7th, and 8th parts, if desired," revealing that the top five-part canon can be sung simultaneously with the bottom three-part one. Mozart's solution of this canon is found in the Köchel Catalogue as K. 73x, No. 4.*

BACKGROUND AND OVERVIEW

The canon is at once the simplest and strictest of all compositional procedures. It is the earliest technique to be grasped by children, in the singing of rounds; and yet it has furnished a point of departure for the most sophisticated counterpoint, from polyphonic masses of the mid-Renaissance masters to the late instrumental works of J. S. Bach.

Although by Mozart's time the canon had waned in importance in concert and church music, it remained very much alive both in the popular singing of rounds and as a pedagogical subject in the teaching of composition. Mozart's canons reflect both of these uses. On one hand there are large groups of pedagogical or study-canons dating both from the period of his Italian tutelage in the early 1770s and from the time he taught composition in Vienna in the mid-1780s. On the other hand there is a cornucopia of popular canons and rounds of all types; very few of these can be precisely dated, but they are usually presumed to have originated mainly as a byproduct of his convivial social life in Viennese musical circles of the 1780s. The fact that Mozart intended his canons for strictly personal use is suggested by his having recorded none of them in his catalogue of compositions, except for an apparently retrospective group of ten in 1788. Given the ephemeral nature of Mozart's canons, it is fortunate that a large number of them have been preserved.

In discussing Mozart's canons, one may distinguish between relatively complex canons and simpler rounds, the latter consisting of a series of voice entries always at the same pitch, and always at regular intervals of time. An "interval canon" is one in which each new voice begins at a given pitch-interval above or below the previous voice. Mozart often penned his canons in "abbreviated" notation, that is, in only one voice, with the entries for the other voices being indicated by signs or verbal directions. (This is, in fact, the origin of the term *canon,* meaning the "rule" or "directions" for singing a piece in abbreviated notation.)

It deserves mention that Mozart also composed a fair number of canonic passages as sections of larger works. Like Joseph Haydn, Mozart occasionally turned his minuet trios into canons, especially in the Salzburg serenades. (Beethoven later followed this lead in his piano sonatas opuses 101 and 106.) There are occasional canons in vocal works as well, notably in the Act II finale of *Così fan tutte,* and the "Rex tremendae majestatis" and "Recordare" of the Requiem. Thus Mozart's interest in canonic procedures is attested in many periods and avenues of his career.

W.C.

K^2 89a I ***Canon in A major, 4 or 5 voices in 1 (K^6 73i)***
Origin: Rome? April 1770?

K. 89 ***Kyrie in G major (K^6 73k)***
Origin: Rome? May 1770?

K^2 89a II ***4 Riddle Canons (K^6 73r):***
"Incipe Menalios," 3 voices in 1
"Cantate Domino," 9 voices in 1
"Confitebor tibi Domini," 2 voices in 1, +3rd voice
"Thebana bella cantus," 6 voices in 2
Origin: Bologna? July or August 1770?

K^6 73x Canonic Studies (K^3 Anh 109d)
Origin: Italy or Salzburg? Summer 1770 or later?

K. deest *Canon in A Minor, 8 voices in 1*
Origin: Italy or Salzburg? Summer 1700 or later?

These various canons and canon groups are preserved among manuscripts that contain a large number of studies, fragments, and sketches; they appear to date from about the time of Mozart's first Italian tour, or perhaps slightly later in Salzburg. In the most recent Köchel catalogue (K^6), most of these items are included among the entries 73h to 73x. It is possible that the manuscripts all belonged to a notebook or series of notebooks that Mozart carried with him on his journey.

The earliest canon appears to be K. 89a I, a textless round. Mozart notated the canon as a single line of fifteen measures, with indications for the entrance of each new voice at measures 4, 7, and 10. It may be reasonably assumed that a fifth voice should enter at measure 13, for otherwise certain triadic harmonies are left incomplete as the canon repeats itself. In recent times, the jovial tune has been underlaid with various lyrics, including "Hei, wenn die Gläser klingen . . ." (Hey, when glasses clink) and "Hei, wenn Musik erklinget . . ." (Hey, when music sounds).

The Kyrie, K. 89, is a much more substantial work; it is, in fact, a full-fledged composition suitable for practical luturgical use. It is generally believed that Mozart composed this work under the influence of the Florence court composer, the Marquis de Ligniville, who was known for his expertise in strict counterpoint. Mozart met and studied with Ligniville in April 1770, and copied parts of the latter's canonic setting of the *Stabat Mater* in his notebooks. K. 89 consists of a series of three canons on the texts "Kyrie eleison," "Christe eleison," and "Kyrie eleison." The three canons are tailored to lead into each other without a pause, and there is a cadential coda at the end. The ethereal work is notable for its skillful modulation through several tonal centers.

The four Riddle (or Puzzle) Canons, K. 89a II, are closely modeled on works of another Italian composer, Padre Giovanni Battista Martini, with whom Mozart studied in Bologna in March and October 1770. At the beginning and end of each chapter of Martini's *Storia della Musica* (History of Music, 3 vols., 1757–81), the author placed beautifully engraved vignettes, each one containing a canon. (One of the vignettes is reprinted as the introductory illustration to the present essay.) They must have struck Mozart's fancy, for not only did he write out solutions to several of the canons, he also composed four of his own using the same texts and similar canonic structures. The "riddles" consist of terse Latin epigrams that give a clue to the solution of each canon. For example, Mozart's riddle for the first canon is ,"Sit trium series una" (Let there be one series of three [parts]).

The Canonic Studies, K^6 73x, include several more solutions to Martini's riddle canons, together with a few canons that may be original compositions. In K^6 (p. 113) these are the studies no. 1 for twelve voices, no. 2 for twelve voices, the retrograde canon no. 6, and no. 7 for six voices; K^3 (p. 832) mentions another canon for 4 voices, which is edited by G. Wolters in *Mozart-Kanons im Urtext* (Wölfenbüttel: Möseler, 1956). The occasion for these various studies is unknown.

With these last canons may be grouped an eight-voice round in A minor (K *deest*). It is preserved on a recently discovered leaf of studies, one of which is a solution of a Martini canon. It is published in the *Mozart Jahrbuch* of 1971–72, p. 431.

W.C.

K. 229 *Canon in C minor, 3 voices in 1 (K⁶ 382a)*
K. 230 *Canon in C minor, 2 voices in 1 (K⁶ 382b)*
K. 231 *Canon in B-flat major, 6 voices in 1, "Leck mich im Arsch" (K⁶ 382c)*
K. 233 *Canon in B-flat major, 3 voices in 1, "Leck mir den Arsch fein recht schön sauber" (K⁶ 382d)*
K. 234 *Canon in G major, 3 voices in 1, "Bei der hitz im Sommer ess ich" (K⁶ 382e)*
K. 347 *Canon in D major, 6 voices in 1 (K⁶ 382f)*
K. 348 *Canon in G major, 12 voices in 4, "V'amo di core teneramente" (K⁶ 382g)*
Origin (of all the above): Vienna? c. 1782?

These seven canons are known mainly in posthumous editions: for the first five there is no trace of an autograph, and for the last the autograph is lost. The hypothetical date of c. 1782 was proposed for all of them by musicologist Alfred Einstein in K³, because the texts of K. 231, 233, and 234 would seem to owe their existence to the "bright social life" of Mozart's early Viennese years. Ludwig Köchel (in K¹) had previously dated them somewhat earlier, since their occasionally obscene lyrics find a counterpart in Mozart's correspondence from his Salzburg years. However, the presence of similarly obscene lyrics in certain later Viennese canons, especially K. 559 through 561, might argue just as well for an origin in the middle or late 1780s. (In fact, K. 232, which has the same history of dissemination as K. 229–234, can be reasonably dated in 1787; see the note below).

K. 229 and 230 differ from the others in that they are not merely simple rounds, but extended essays in canonic counterpoint. They are, in fact, serenely beautiful little works, comparable in poignancy to the canonic Adagio for winds, K. 410 (see the note on p. 247). K. 229 is notable especially for its chromaticism, and K. 230 for the unusual entry of the answer on an offbeat. Breitkopf & Härtel published the works with underlaid poetic texts by L. H. C. Hölty (1748–76), the first as "Sie ist dahin, die Sängerin" (Gone is She, the Singer) from *Auf den Tod einer Nachtigall* (On the Death of a Nightingale), the second as "Selig alle sie, die im Herrn entschliefen" (Blessed [are] all who die in the Lord) from *Elegie beim Grab meines Vaters* (Elegy on My Father's Grave).

K. 231, 233, and 234 were published with new words added: K. 231 as *Lass froh uns sein* (Let's be joyous), K. 233 as *Nichts labt mich mehr als Wein* (Nothing pleases me more than wine), and K. 234 as *Essen, trinken, das erhält den Leib* (Eating, drinking support love). Tantalizingly, for each canon the edition cites only the first line of Mozart's original texts; they were presumably written by Mozart and are somewhat off-color: "Kiss me on the ass," "Kiss my ever so nice clean fine ass," and "In the heat of summer I eat." With or without Mozart's texts, however, the music of these canons holds its own. K. 231 is an essay in progressive "series" counterpoint: the first answer is syncopated, the second is in half-note values, the third in quartered note values, and the fourth and fifth use mixed values, including eighths. K. 233 and 234 are examples of "fugue-canons": each answer begins with a rest followed by a quasi-imitation of the previous voice, thus producing a stretto effect each time the cycle beings. K. 234, especially, is rich in further imitative devices among the voices.

K. 347 appeared in print similarly with an unauthentic text, *Wo der perlende Wein im Glase blinkt* (Where the effervescent wine sparkles in the glasses). The autograph is textless. The music has its own charm: Mozart sustains interest through the first five voice-entries by never resolving the harmonic progression. Only with the final entry does a full cadence occur.

K. 348 is a remarkable canon for three four-part choirs, each one entering as a unit. The work's authenticity has been clouded by a letter of Mozart's widow to the publisher Johann Anton André. In response to the latter's doubts, Constanze claimed that "the *V'amo* looked like a fragment, but it is not, according to [Maximilian Stadler], who added to it just what he claims Mozart would have added—and he claims he could not possibly have added anything else—thereby making it a complete composition." The music is perhaps not unworthy of Mozart, however. Though the harmonies are simple, the texture is enlivened by the deft use of hocketing (dovetailing sounds and silences through a staggered arrangement in two or more voices) and quasi-imitation from choir to choir. It is even possible to sing the canon with a fourth choral entry, at the second half of measure 4. W.C.

K. 507 ***Canon in F major, 3 voices in 1***
Origin: Vienna, between June 3 and August 1786

K. 508 ***Canon in F major, 3 voices in 1***
Origin: Vienna, between June 3 and August 1786

K[6] 508A ***Canon in C major, 3 voices in 1***
Origin: Vienna, after June 3, 1786

K[3] 508a and deest ***2 Canons in F major, 3 voices in 1***
14 Interval Canons in F major, 2 voices in 1
Origin: Vienna, between June 3 and August 1786

K. deest ***Canon in F major, 4 voices in 1***
Origin: Vienna, August 1786 or earlier

K. 228 ***Canon in F major, 4 voices in 2 (K[6] 515b)***
Origin: Vienna, August 1786 or earlier

It seems likely that Mozart penned these short canons primarily for purposes of study or pedagogy. There is no known practical occasion for any of them, although copies of most of them turn up in the notebooks kept by Thomas Attwood, who studied composition with Mozart from the autumn of 1785 until August 1786. This fixes the latest possible date of origin for all but two of the canons (K. 508A and 508a/2). Two facts suggest that all of these canons are interrelated in their origin: (1) all but one (K. 508A) are in F major, and (2) they all fall into groups of progressive interval canons, with the intervals following a more or less clear-cut arithmetical pattern.

K. 507, 508, and 508A appear together on a single manuscript page, where they follow a sketch for an early version of a movement of the piano quartet in E-flat major, K. 493. Mozart dated the quartet June 3, 1786, the earliest possible date for the canons. K. 508A appears only as a sketch, but a viable final version can be reasonably ascertained. The three works are a series of apparently related three-voice interval canons, the first having answers both at the unison, the next having answers at the 2nd above and 6th below (= 3rd above), and the last having answers at the 3rd above and 9th (= 2nd) below. The first two of these canons were originally published with underlaid words by Gottfried Christoph Härtel, to which they are still often sung: "Heiterkeit und leichtes Blut" (Cheerfulness and high spirits) and "Auf das Wohl aller Freunde" (To the health of all our friends).

The eight canons of K. 508a appear, curiously, on a similar manuscript page that contains a sketch of the *final* version of the same movement of K. 493. The first two are three-voice interval canons: in 508a/1 the answering voices enter at 4th and 7th (= 4th above the 4th) above the first voice, in 508a/2 at the octave and the 11th (= 4th above the octave). The remaining are two-voice interval canons at the 2nd, 3rd, 4th, 5th, 6th, and 7th, each time with the answer entering lower than the first voice.

Attwood's notebook (vol. 3, pp. 112–18) contains a copy of the six interval canons, K. 508a/3–8, together with a continuation of the series (K. *deest*). This includes six more canons at the same intervals as K. 508a/3–8, but with the answer entering *higher* than the first voice. To complete the scheme, there are also two canons at the unison, for a total of fourteen interval canons in all. (The Köchel catalogue does not assign numbers to the eight additional canons.)

Following the fourteen two-voice canons in Attwood's notebook come copies of three three-voice canons, K. 507, K. 508, and K. 508a/1. Finally come two four-voice canons. The first of these (K. *deest*) is a simple round. The second, K. 228, is a double interval canon, the upper voice being answered at the 4th above (= 5th below) and the lower at the 5th below (= 4th above). Mozart was apparently fond of this last canon, for on April 24, 1787 he inserted it as a personal memento in the album of his friend Josef Franz von Jacquin, brother of Mozart's close companion and student, Gottfried von Jacquin. He inscribed the canon with a sentiment, curiously, in substandard English, "Don't never forget your true and faithfull friend Wolfgang Amadè Mozart mp." He wrote out the canon in abbreviated form but, again curiously, used an incorrect double clef for the upper voice. Perhaps to correct this error he recopied the canon in full score on a separate page of Jacquin's book.

It should be added that an extant sketch for another four-voice interval canon in F major seems possibly to be related to this group of canons; the piece was later reworked into K^6 562c (see below on p. 105). W.C.

K. 232 *Canon in G major, 4 voices in 1, Lieber Freistädtler, lieber Gaulimauli (K^6 509a)*

Origin: Vienna, after July 4 (and before October?), 1787

This comical canon pokes fun at one of Mozart's students, Franz Jakob Freystädtler, whom he nicknamed "Gaulimauli" (horse-mouth), "Stachelschwein" (porcupine), and "Herr Lilienfeld" (Mr. Lilyfield). The text borrows words and phrases from Mozart's farcical dramatic sketch, *Der Salzburger Lump in Wien* (The Salzburg Scoundrel in Vienna), penned at about the same time, in which the character of Freystädtler plays a role. The names Finto and Scultetti refer to other mutual acquaintances (the name Kitscha has not been identified); the canon has been dated on the basis of these personal references. W.C.

K. 553 ***Canon in C major, 3 voices in 1, Alleluia***

K. 554 ***Canon in F major, 4 voices in 1, Ave Maria***

K. 555 ***Canon in A minor, 4 voices in 1, Lacrimoso son'io***

K. 556 ***Canon in G major, 4 voices in 1, Grechtelt's enk, wir gehn im Prater***

K. 557 ***Canon in F minor, 4 voices in 1, Nascoso è il mio sol***

K. 558 ***Canon in B-flat major, 4 voices in 1, Gehn wir im Prater, gehn wir in d'Hetz***

K. 559 ***Canon in F major, 3 voices in 1, Difficile lectu mihi Mars***

K. 560 ***Canon in F major, 4 voices in 1, O du eselhafter Peierl! (K^{3} 560a, K^{6} 559a)***

K. 561 ***Canon in A major, 4 voices in 1, Bona nox! bist a rechta Ox***

K. 562 ***Canon in A major, 3 voices in 1, Caro bell' idol mio***

Origin (of all the above): Vienna? on or before September 2, 1788

Mozart entered this eclectic group of ten short rounds in his personal catalogue of compositions with the date of September 2, 1788. This fact is unusual for two reasons: (1) they are the only canons he entered into his catalogue, and (2) some extant sketches for K. 553 and 557 appear to date from at least as early as February 1787 (along with a sketch of K. 228 above). A possible explanation is that Mozart collected the canons together on that date for performance or dissemination. Indeed, several of the canons are preserved on slips of paper that appear to have been cut from a large autograph manuscript; moreover, the numbering of the canons on these slips of paper is congruent with their order in the catalogue. No occasion for such a collection has yet come to light.

K. 553 and 554 use simple sacred texts of two words each: "Alleluia, Amen," and "Ave Maria." The first uses a Gregorian *cantus firmus*, the *incipit* of the Alleluia for Holy Saturday, for its first line. The second is perhaps Mozart's finest example of a "fugue-canon," like K. 233 and 234.

K. 555, 557, and 562 use Italian texts taken from canons of the older Viennese court composer Antonio Caldara. The same three texts were also set as canons by Leopold Mozart and other composers; none other than Franz Schubert was later to make two more canonic settings of the text of K. 557. All of Mozart's settings have a florid *bel canto* cast that is strikingly reminiscent of his operatic compositions. K. 555 is notable for its melismatic style, K. 557 for its use of chromatic and suspended harmonies, K. 562 for its thematic indebtedness—presumably intentional—to Caldara's original setting.

K. 556 and 558 are textually related both in their use of pungent Viennese dialect and in their specific reference to the Prater, the large central park and fairground in Vienna. Though the lyrics (presumably by Mozart) of both canons are nonsense, they both appear to portray the same scene: an argumentative dialogue over whether or not to go on an outing to the park. Musically, both pieces make clever use of imitation and hocketing within each canonic cycle.

K. 559 and 560 both arose as jokes aimed at Johann Nepomuk Peyerl, a Bavarian tenor who entered Mozart's circle around the end of 1785, and who was reportedly much teased about his dialect. The text of K. 559 is nonsense Latin, but the words "lectu mihi Mars" presumably became "leck du mich im Arsch" (kiss my ass) in Peyerl's pronunciation; K. 560 continues this verbal motif in explicit German. Both texts are presumably by Mozart. As in several of the canons already mentioned, the music makes brilliant use of imitative and hocket-like devices. K. 560a, especially, possesses the clockworklike vocal interplay of a well-wrought *opera buffa* ensemble. (It also exists in a slightly revised later version, K. 560b [K^6 560], using the name "Martin" instead of "Peyerl.")

K. 561 is a fitting conclusion to Mozart's comic canons. The text, presumably by Mozart, says "good night" with an insult in five languages, then ends with a memorable sentiment in Viennese dialect, "sleep tight, and stick your ass to your mouth." Its terse but intricate musical setting is of a piece with the other comic canons; the final words are set to a cadential formula that is appropriately assertive. W.C.

K^3 562a ***Canon in B-flat major, 4 voices in 1***

Origin: Vienna? 1780s?

This tiny canon has no known text, but the presence of a group of unbeamed eighth-notes (consecutive, but with separate flags) in the fourth bar suggests that it had words at some stage. Though suitable to be sung at the unison, the lost autograph manuscript (extant only in a published photo-facsimile) assigns the entries to voices in three different octaves. W.C.

K^3 562c ***Canon in C major, 4 voices in 1 (K^1 Anh 191)***

Origin: Vienna? 1780s?

For this canon there exists an undatable sketch in F major. Like Mozart's other F-major "pedagogical" canons it is an interval canon: each voice enters a 2nd (or 9th) below the previous voice. In view of its four-voice texture, it is arguably the most complex of all the interval canons. The C-major version is unique among Mozart's canons in assigning each voice to a specific instrument: two violins, viola, and "basso." The occasion of this arrangement is unknown. W.C.

TWO
INSTRUMENTAL MUSIC

8

Church Sonatas

A sacred concert. Anonymous engraving, Florence, 1780s.

In this stylized presentation of a concert in a chapel, a maestro beats time, an organist plays basso continuo, *and a nine-member, all-male choir sings. The orchestra consists of six violins and violas (one rescuing his music), two double basses, two oboes, two horns, two trumpets, and timpani. This engraving was used by the Florentine firm of Giovanni Chiari as a passe-partout title page for hand-copied sacred works. The title and author of the piece would be written above or below and the opening measures copied on the music scroll held in the eagle's beak.*

BACKGROUND AND OVERVIEW

Apart from three pieces for mechanical organ, and perhaps the fugues K. 154a and K. 401, the only organ music of Mozart extant is the collection of seventeen *sonate da chiesa,* church sonatas—or, as they are often known, epistle sonatas, since they were played during the celebration of the Mass between the Epistle and the Gospel (or in terms of the music, between the Gloria and Credo). The sonatas date from between 1772 and 1780, and were written for Salzburg Cathedral. All are short pieces of only one movement and all are in major keys.

Three of the sonatas are scored for an orchestra that includes oboes, horns, trumpets, and timpani; the rest are for organ and strings (without violas, as was the regular practice for music written for the cathedral). For nine of the sonatas Mozart limited the organ part to accompanying from a figured bass; the other eight sonatas also have obbligato solos for the organ. A.R.

K. 67 *Church Sonata in E-flat major, No. 1 (K⁶ 41h)*

Origin: Salzburg, 1772
Scoring: 2 violins, basso continuo

This first sonata moves, atypically, at a moderately paced tempo. In triple time, its mood is peacefully devotional. The first violins take the lead with a graceful melody. A.R.

K. 68 *Church Sonata in B-flat major, No. 2 (K⁶ 41i)*

Origin: Salzburg, 1772
Scoring: 2 violins, basso continuo

This is a typically Italianate movement, lively, optimistic, and full of inventive melodic ideas, with occasional tentative polyphonic excursions. A.R.

K. 69 *Church Sonata in D major, No. 3 (K⁶ 41k)*

Origin: Salzburg, 1772
Scoring: 2 violins, basso continuo

K. 69 is the most jubilant of this first set of sonatas. Held chords in the *continuo* contrast brightly with busily rushing violin scales. There is a short and more relaxed second subject. A.R.

K. 144 *Church Sonata in D major, No. 4 (K⁶ 124a)*

Origin: Salzburg, 1774
Scoring: 2 violins, basso continuo

The next two sonatas postdate the first group by two years. They show clearly how Mozart, at the age of sixteen, had already gained a firm grasp of symphonic form. A bright and particularly jolly motif introduces and dominates this movement, but is varied to provide contrasts of major and minor, loud and soft. A.R.

K. 145 *Church Sonata in F major, No. 5 (K⁶ 124b)*

Origin: Salzburg, 1774
Scoring: 2 violins, basso continuo

In triple time, this sonata is devotional in feeling, characterized by long melodic lines. A.R.

K. 212 *Church Sonata in B-flat major, No. 6*

Origin: Salzburg, July 1775
Scoring: 2 violins, basso continuo

A rather long and elaborate piece, this work sounds like the opening movement of an early symphony. Mozart has written in occasional polyphonic experiments, a little unsure perhaps, but charming nonetheless. A.R.

K. 241 *Church Sonata in G major*
Origin: Salzburg, January 1776
Scoring: 2 violins, basso continuo

Unlike the earlier sonatas, this piece has a completely realized organ part. It shares the dancelike character of the later church sonata, K. 225 (see below), although it is perhaps even more informal. A.R.

K. 244 *Church Sonata in F major No. 9*
Origin: Salzburg, April 1776
Scoring: 2 violins, basso continuo, organ obbligato

Here for the first time the organ functions independently. Once again the style is that of a stately minuet, with strings and organ alternating statement and answer. The development is boldly exploratory and there is a charming quiet ending. A.R.

K. 245 *Church Sonata in D major, No. 10*
Origin: Salzburg, April 1776
Scoring: 2 violins, basso continuo, organ obbligato

For Mozart the key of D major was the one ideally suited to virtuosity and the display of pomp. Although the organ plays a somewhat subsidiary role in this sonata, the general effect is that of confident jubilation. Contrasts are handled in a masterful fashion, there is a wealth of melody, and the development is boldly written. A.R.

K. 263 *Church Sonata in C major*
Origin: Salzburg, December 1776
Scoring: 2 trumpets, 2 violins, basso continuo, organ obbligato

In this work, strings are joined by trumpets, the organ part is prominent—written out for both hands—and the general mood is of majestic celebration. A.R.

K. 274 *Church Sonata in G major, No. 11 (K^6 271d)*
Origin: Salzburg, 1777
Scoring: 2 violins, basso continuo

Although the mood is a lyrical one, this sonata is full of playful touches. The organ part is realized again from the figured bass. The independence of the three main musical strands (first violins, second violins, and the bass line), together with ventures into polyphony, put the listener in mind of Handel. A.R.

K. 278 *Church Sonata in C major, No. 12 (K^6 271e)*
Origin: Salzburg, March or April 1777
Scoring: 2 oboes, 2 trumpets and timpani, 2 violins, basso continuo

This sonata, like K. 274 above, was composed during the Lenten season of 1777, but it may well have been intended for the Easter Mass, since oboes, trumpets, and drums join the string band, and the atmosphere is once more of joyful celebration. Mozart copes admirably with the resonant cathedral acoustics, allowing chord to build on chord in the loud passages. The chief harmonic interest is reserved for the soft passages for strings alone. A.R.

K. 329 *Church Sonata in C major, No. 14 (K^6 317a)*
Origin: Salzburg, March? 1779
Scoring: 2 oboes, 2 horns, 2 trumpets and timpani, 2 violins, basso continuo, organ obbligato

Two years passed between the composition of sonatas K. 278 (see above) and K. 329; it was the period of Mozart's visits to Mannheim, Paris, and Munich, of his mother's death, and of his failure in love. The final church sonatas reflect a new maturity, a firmer mastery of structure and contrast, a greater emotional depth.

It seems fairly certain that K. 329 was written for performance with the "Coronation" Mass, K. 317 (discussed on p. 13). It dates from the same time, the key is the same, and the instrumentation is identical, including the two horns that were rarely employed in Salzburg Cathedral. Two oboes, two trumpets, and timpani are also added to the string band. The organ part is elegantly written, and the mood is of grandeur and majesty, perfectly matching that of the Mass.

A.R.

K. 328 ***Church Sonata in C major, No. 13 (K⁶ 317c)***

Origin: Salzburg, early? 1779
Scoring: 2 violins, basso continuo, organ obbligato

Although there are no wind instruments in K. 328, the sonority is brilliant. The busy violin parts demand both virtuosity and lyricism, as Mozart explores corresponding moods of both jubilation and contemplation. The organ adds considerable brightness of color. A.R.

K. 224 ***Church Sonata in F major, No. 7 (K⁶ 241a)***

Origin: Salzburg, early 1780
Scoring: 2 violins, basso continuo, organ obbligato

The writing of this sonata is thoroughly assured. The development section is especially interesting, with cellos and double basses toying busily with the rhythmic figures of the opening. There are striking contrasts of mood and texture. A.R.

K. 225 ***Church Sonata in A major, No. 8 (K⁶ 241b)***

Origin: Salzburg, early 1780
Scoring: 2 violins, basso continuo, organ obbligato

A noble first subject, which reminds us of a courtly minuet, stands in striking contrast to the flowing melody of the second. Mozart treats the latter one with daring harmonic experimentation in the brief development. The organ is used discreetly to add color. A.R.

K. 336 ***Church Sonata in C major, No. 15 (K⁶ 336d)***

Origin: Salzburg, early 1780
Scoring: 2 violins, basso continuo, organ obbligato

Scored for organ with strings alone, this sonata is unique among the seventeen in being a typical Mozartean keyboard concerto movement. Mozart undoubtedly designed the organ part for himself; his official position at Salzburg in 1780 was court organist. The sonata was designed to be performed between the Gloria and Credo of Mozart's last Salzburg Mass, K. 337 (discussed on p. 13) a work that contains an elaborate solo for organ in its Agnus Dei. The organ part in this sonata would sound equally effective on the piano, although the upper overtones of the church instrument give the piece a delicious brightness. A.R.

9
Concertos and Concerto Movements

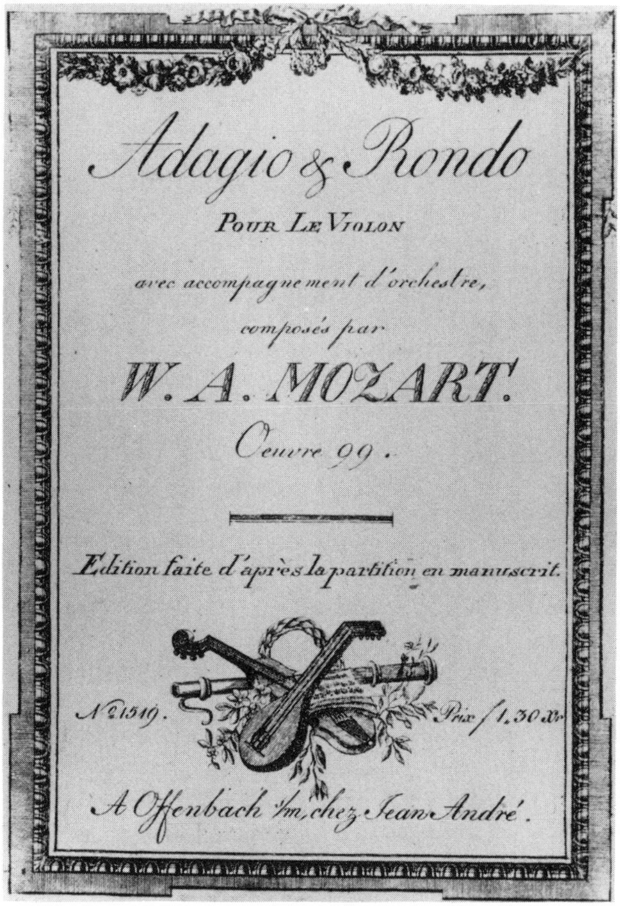

Engraved title page of the posthumous first edition (1801) of two violin concerto movements, the Adagio in E major, K. 261, and the Rondo in B-flat major, K. 269. Mozart never meant them to form a unit (their keys are incompatible), but they were linked by publisher Johann André, who bought Mozart's manuscripts from his widow.

CONCERTOS FOR PIANO

Collegium Musicum concert, Zurich, 1777. Engraving by Johann Rudolf Halzhalb.

"Concerto for obbligato harpsichord with instruments," the caption announces. The tiny "orchestra" comprises pairs of horns, violins, and flutes. This is the kind of setting for which Mozart's seven earliest keyboard concertos, K. 37, 39, 40, 41, and 107 were written.

BACKGROUND AND OVERVIEW

The Birth of the Genre

The piano concerto as a significant genre can almost be said to have been invented by Mozart. Before him, concertos for harpsichord or fortepiano and orchestra were few in number and seldom of the highest artistic quality. Exceptions are the few harpsichord concertos of the genre's putative inventor, J. S. Bach, which Mozart almost certainly did not know, and the more-than-fifty concertos of his son, Carl Philipp Emanuel, some of which Mozart may have known, but which are different enough from his own concertos that they can hardly have been his principal models. The handful of keyboard concertos by Joseph Haydn are minor works, as are the many by Johann Georg Lang and Johann Christian Bach, and the few of Johann Christoph Friedrich and Wilhelm Friedemann Bach, Franz and Georg Benda, Jean-Frédéric Edelmann, Carl Heinrich and Johann Gottlieb Graun, Johann Wilhelm Hertel, Leontzi Honauer, Johann Gottfield Müthel, Johann Schobert, Johann Samuel Schröter, Georg Christoph Wagenseil, et al. (It is noteworthy that, although they worked in many parts of Europe, these composers all were German-speaking.) Italian music also profoundly influenced the young Mozart, but the same points can be made—that styles are distant from Mozart's and artistic content is modest—concerning the twenty-three extant Italian harpsichord concertos of the mid-eighteenth century, by Domenico Auletta the elder, Francesco Durante, Giovanni Battista Martini, Giovanni Battista Pergolesi, Giovanni Benedetto Platti, and Giuseppe Sammartini. Yet in spite of the fact that Mozart lent the genre an entirely new stature, and in spite of repeated performances of his concertos by himself, his pupils, his sister, and his admirers, there was nothing written about them in the press or elsewhere, making it difficult to divine their contemporary significance. This silence has recently been explained:

> The difficulty in documenting the reception of a Mozart work results—as with Bach—from the eighteenth century's point of view, the consideration of compositions less as individual "works" than as constituent parts of a complete oeuvre or as specimens of a genre, which were dedicated not to the constituting of a repertory but to the carrying on of musical "daily business." If one disregards a few operas, which were already "repertory pieces" in his lifetime, hardly one contemporary text is devoted to a single, unique, completely determined work by Mozart (W. Kluppelholz and H. Busch [eds.], *Musik gedeutet und gewertet,* 1983, p. 36).

Thus, for Mozart's immediate contemporaries, his concertos were not "classics" but "popular music," to be enjoyed, used up, and replaced by newer works. Nonetheless, by the 1780s western Europe already had its connoisseurs and collectors of "art for art's sake," who must have recognized the extraordinary qualities of Mozart's music, as is suggested by the outpourings of editions of his music in the decade following his death. A sort of tacit approval of Mozart's piano concertos even by his contemporaries can perhaps be detected in the fact that, whereas only three of his more-than-fifty symphonies were published during his lifetime, some seven of his twenty-one original concertos for solo piano attained that distinction.

Mozart's Heyday

The period from approximately 1782 to 1785 was the most prosperous and perhaps also the happiest of Mozart's life. He was much in demand in Vienna as a composer, performer, and teacher, and he managed to make a handsome living from his freelance activities. In the early- and mid-1780s Vienna experienced a boom in public and private concert-giving, which lasted until war and recession, and the death of Emperor Joseph II in 1790, caused a decline. Mozart not only participated in this development but was himself partly responsible for it. He seems to have been the first, for instance, to give Lenten subscription concerts, which immediately became a local custom. Indeed, his activities during Lent are scarcely to be believed, for he played somewhere every evening for many weeks running. His father, visiting him during Lent 1785, wrote to his sister Nannerl about this frenetic activity:

On the same Friday [February 11] around 6 o'clock, we drove to his first subscription concert, at which a great many members of the aristocracy were present. . . . [For the rest of this passage, see K. 466, on page 131.] On Saturday evening Joseph Haydn and the two Barons Tinti came to see us and the [three] new quartets were performed. . . . On Sunday the Italian singer, Madame Laschi, who is leaving for Italy, gave a concert in the theater, at which she sang two arias. A cello concerto was performed, a tenor and a bass each sang an aria, and your brother played a glorious concerto. . . . When your brother left [the stage] the Emperor tipped his hat and called out "Bravo, Mozart!" And when he came on to play, there was a great deal of clapping. We were not at the theater yesterday, for every day there is a concert. . . . This evening there is again a concert in the theater, at which your brother is again playing a concerto. . . . Yesterday, the 15th, there was again a recital in the theater given by a girl who sings charmingly.

Your brother played his great new concerto in D [minor] most magnificently. Today we are going to a concert given at the house of the Salzburg agent von Ployer. . . .

This evening your brother is performing at a grand concert at Count Zichy's . . . but your sister-in-law and Marchand have gone to the concert at Herr von Ployer's. . . . As usual, it will probably be one o'clock before we get to bed. . . . On Friday, the 18th . . . we drove to your brother's second concert at the Mehlgrube at seven o'clock. This concert too was a splendid success. . . . The two concerts which Herr Le Brun and his wife are giving in the theater are on Wednesday, the 23rd, and Monday the 28th. By the 18th boxes for the first concert were no longer to be had. These people are going to make an enormous amount of money. . . .

In three concerts Herr Le Brun and his wife made, astonishingly, at the first 1,100 gulden, at the second 900 gulden, and at the third 500 gulden. Your brother made 559 gulden at his [benefit] concert, which we never expected, as he is giving six subscription concerts at the Mehlgrube to over 150 people, each of whom pays a souverain d'or for the six. Besides, as a favor he has been playing frequently at other concerts in the theater. . . . We never get to bed before one o'clock and I never get up before nine. We lunch at two or half past. . . . Every day there are concerts; and constant teaching, performing, composing, etc. I feel rather out of it all. If only the concerts were over! It is impossible for me to describe the rush and bustle. Since my arrival your brother's fortepiano has been taken at least a dozen times from the house to the theater or to some other house. . . . It is taken to the Mehlgrube every Friday and has also been taken to Count Zichy's and to Prince Kaunitz's. . . . Now it is dark, and I must finish and drive to the concert in the theater. . . . Tomorrow, and on Sunday, the 2nd, is the [benefit] concert for the widows [of musicians]. . . . (translations by Emily Anderson).

Leopold Mozart's letters reveal the circumstances in which, between 1782 and 1785, Wolfgang completed twelve piano concertos (along with two additional piano-concerto finales) and began two others, as well as the fact that these difficult works were usually performed without a rehearsal or, at best, with but a single run-through beforehand. From this and other evidence, we know that the orchestral musicians of Vienna must have been particularly accomplished—Leopold's and Wolfgang's standards were high.

Mozart's Decline

Between 1767 and 1791 Mozart composed twenty-eight solo keyboard concertos, two additional rondo-finales, and 2 concertos for two or three keyboard soloists. However, these thirty-two works, far from appearing at a steady rate of one or two a year, were irregularly produced: seven in the first five years (all pastiches of works by other composers), four in the next five, in the next five only two, but then seventeen in the period from the end of 1782 to 1786. By contrast, in his last five years Mozart wrote only two piano concertos. Conditions in Vienna were probably responsible both for the exceptional number of concertos in the first half of the 1780s and for his loss of interest in the genre during the latter part of that decade.

As the capital of the Austrian Empire, Vienna was the economic, political, and cultural center not just of Austria and Hungary, but for substantial portions of present-day Czechoslovakia, Germany, Italy, Yugoslavia, Poland, Russia, and Rumania. Many noble families from those regions maintained homes in Vienna, where they lived during the "season." A surprising number of the members of these families were musically literate and demanded a steady supply of good music. The intensity of this patronage helps to explain why Gluck, Haydn, Mozart, and Beethoven—none of them natives—preferred Vienna to all other cities.

The early 1780s in Vienna saw the first serious flourishings of firms devoted to music publishing (especially Artaria and Co.) and to commercial music-copying (especially Johann Traeg), who dealt widely in central Europe; public concerts (especially benefit concerts and subscription series) also flourished. At the same time, the number of private concerts reached an unprecedented level, and, during Lent, Mozart performed at one noble home or another on almost every evening not already taken up with public performances. Most of these were orchestral concerts, with symphonies, arias, and concertos; and Mozart's piano concertos became their mainstays and the principal means by which he appeared before his admiring patrons.

An advertisement in the *Wiener Zeitung* for February 25, 1784, captures something of the spirit of this vigorous activity:

> Johann Traeg, on the first floor of the Pilate House by Saint Peter's, has the honor to certify to the highly esteemed public that, encouraged by the success thus far granted him, he has drawn up a plan that will be most welcome to music lovers, by means of which they will be enabled at little cost to entertain themselves with the best pieces by the greatest masters. There are many families of this very city that amuse themselves with large or small musical gatherings. Many of them do not wish to be overloaded with sheet music, or at very least to have an introductory hearing of the things that they have a mind to buy. Inasmuch as I now possess a fine stock, which I endeavor daily to enlarge further, of the best and newest music of all types, I

therefore offer to hire out weekly either three symphonies or six quintets, six quartets, six trios, etc. for a quarterly payment in advance of three florin. If anyone wishes to give concerts twice a week and, accordingly, requires six symphonies or twelve other pieces for that purpose, he likewise can subscribe that way and pay quarterly only five florin. However, because I must strive to serve everyone fairly, no-one should have misgivings at returning the pieces received directly the following day. Because of my broad acquaintanceship with the best local musicians, I can also provide skilled musicians for large and small concerts at a very reasonable price. In order best to be able to execute these commissions, I request that people place their orders at my establishment any time before midday.

Traeg's stock included an up-to-date selection of Mozart's chamber music, arias, symphonies, and concertos.

Mozart's patrons—who usually did not have to acquire his music from Traeg or Artaria and Co. but dealt directly with him, employing him to lead their concerts—came from Viennese high society. To this class belonged both the homes in which he played and the subscribers to his concerts. The subscription list survives for a series of Lenten concerts that Mozart gave on three consecutive Wednesdays in March 1784, in the hall of the casino owned by his friend Johann von Trattner. For these subscription concerts Mozart composed three concertos (K. 449, 450, 451) and also gave their premieres. A recent study shows that, of the 174 names on the list, fifty percent came from the highest nobility, forty-two percent from the lesser nobility or from wealthy commoners with purchased titles, and a mere eight percent from the bourgeoisie (H. Schuler, *Die Subskribenten der Mozart'schen Mittwochskonzerte im Trattnersaal zu Wien anno 1784*, Neustadt a. d. Aisch, 1983). Some eighty-three percent on the list were men, in striking contrast with Parisian salon concerts of the period, which were dominated by women. Braun, Esterházy, Fries, Galitzin (Golitsïn), Harrach, Lichnowsky, Lobkowitz, Schwarzenberg, Swieten, Waldstein: what resonance these names from Mozart's list of subscribers have as patrons of the music of Haydn, Mozart, and Beethoven!

In the late 1780s this demand for new concertos diminished as Austria experienced rebellion in its Netherlands territory and a war with Turkey, the resulting economic strain causing a severe recession. Then, terrified by the political developments in France, the Emperors Joseph II and Leopold II rescinded various liberalizing reforms and instituted repressive measures. The combination of these factors led to a stifling of cultural life and a decline both of public concerts and of private patronage. Many noblemen let go their private bands, opportunities for performances were drastically curtailed, and Mozart virtually stopped composing piano concertos. N.Z.

K. 37 *Piano Concerto in F major, No. 1*
Origin: Salzburg, April 1767
Scoring: keyboard solo, 2 oboes, 2 horns, strings
Movements: Allegro (Raupach). Andante (anonymous). [Allegro] (Honauer).

K. 39 *Piano Concerto in B-flat major, No. 2*
Origin: Salzburg, June 1767
Scoring: keyboard solo, 2 oboes, 2 horns, strings
Movements: Allegro spiritoso (Raupach). Andante (Schobert). Molto allegro (Raupach).

K. 40 *Piano Concerto in D major, No. 3*
Origin: Salzburg, July 1767
Scoring: keyboard solo, 2 oboes, 2 horns, strings
Movements: Allegro maestoso (Honauer). Andante (Eckard). Presto (C. P. E. Bach).

K. 41 *Piano Concerto in G major, No. 4*
Origin: Salzburg, July 1767
Scoring: keyboard solo, 2 oboes, 2 horns, strings
Movements: Allegro (Honauer). Andante (Raupach). Molto allegro (Honauer).

K. 107/1 *Piano Concerto in D major (K³ 21b/1)*
Origin: Salzburg, c. 1771
Scoring: keyboard solo, 2 violins, basso continuo
Movements: Allegro. Andante. Tempo di Menuetto.

K. 107/2 *Piano Concerto in G major (K³ 21b/2)*
Origin: Salzburg, c. 1771
Scoring: keyboard solo, 2 violins, basso continuo
Movements: Allegro. Allegretto.

K. 107/3 *Piano Concerto in E-flat major (K³ 21b/3)*
Origin: Salzburg, c. 1771
Scoring: keyboard solo, 2 violins, basso continuo
Movements: Allegro. Allegretto.

These seven keyboard concertos are apparently the result of an ingenious series of assignments given Mozart by his father: to take the materials of some up-to-date *galant* keyboard-sonata movements by Hermann Friedrich Raupach, Leontzi Honauer, Johann Schobert, Johann Gottfried Eckard, C. P. E. Bach (K. 37–41) and, especially, J. C. Bach (K. 107) and turn them into concerto movements. Such a pastiche technique would not only have familiarized the ten-year-old composer with potential compositional models, but would also have taught him the difference between the sonata and concerto genres.

On their own terms these miniature concertos work well. Their contribution to the apparent miracle of K. 175 (Mozart's first original piano concerto), which is sometimes portrayed as Athena springing fully armed from the head of Zeus, has probably not yet been properly explained.

The scorn or indifference sometimes heaped upon the seven pastiche concertos is a vestigial residue of a Romantic attitude to art, which values originality above craft, stormy affect above *galant* airiness, complexity above simplicity. Without making exaggerated claims for the seven earliest concertos, we should perhaps throw off such unhelpful notions and accept the works for what they are.

N.Z.

K. 175 *Piano Concerto in D major, No. 5*
Origin: Salzburg, December 1773
Scoring: solo piano or harpsichord, 2 oboes, 2 horns, 2 trumpets and timpani, strings
Movements: Allegro. Andante ma un poco adagio. Allegro.

K. 382 *Rondo in D major*
Origin: Vienna, March 1782
Scoring: solo piano, flute, 2 oboes, 2 horns, 2 trumpets and timpani, strings

The Köchel Catalogue calls the Concerto in D major, K. 175, "Mozart's first piano concerto"; and this it is, aside from the seven early pastiche works just discussed. But it would be mistaken to infer from this that K. 175, completed when its composer was a month shy of his eighteenth birthday, is in any sense an apprentice work, for there is nothing halting or tentative about it. Its style is clearly Mozart's, its ideas attractive and skillfully organized, and its formal outlines similar to those of its better-known successors. Mozart himself seems to have recognized the success of his first attempt, and kept K. 175 in his repertory for a decade.

This ground-breaking work was composed in Salzburg in December 1773, probably for the use of Mozart and his sister in house and court concerts during Carnival and Lent. (During Advent no concerts took place in Salzburg.) Mozart took his "first" concerto on tour to Munich in 1774 and to Mannheim and Paris in 1777–78, writing home to his father of a concert at the house of the composer and concertmaster (leader) of the Mannheim orchestra, Christian Cannabich, "I played my old concerto in D major, because it is such a favorite here." In Mannheim the twenty-two-year-old Mozart fell in love with the singer Aloysia Weber, the older sister of his future wife Constanze; for Aloysia he composed the Metastasian *scena* "Alcandro, lo confesso . . . Non sò d'onde viene" (K. 294), which contains a (possibly unconscious) amorous allusion in the form of two passages quoted from the Andante of K. 175 at the words "I know not whence comes . . . that unfamiliar motion from within my breast."

K. 175 was published in Paris and Mainz around 1785, probably signaling the end of its usefulness to Mozart as a personal display piece. Before that, however, ~~the concerto~~ had undergone a transformation: the wind orchestration in all three movements was reworked and then, in preparation for a busy Lenten concert season in Vienna in 1782, the entirely new Finale (K. 382) found in the editions of 1785 was composed. In February 1783 Mozart sent his sister cadenzas for the first two movements of K. 175 along with an *Eingang* ("lead-in"—a brief cadenza) for its new Finale.

Despite its undeniable charm, K. 175 may reveal certain signs of Mozart's inexperience, in particular an apparent fear of emptiness manifested, for instance, in his doubling the first solo entry of the piano with the violins (something he never again did), in his occasionally accompanying the soloist's right-hand melody with tremolos in the orchestra plus a busy Alberti bass in the left hand, or in his repeating too often the Finale's opening theme. While these modern asthetic judgments are open to dispute, Mozart's own view of the work's viability can probably be inferred from the existence of the second Finale and reworked wind parts.

The two Finales show him grappling with problems of evolving taste, seeking—as Bernd Sponheuer has suggested in a recent article (*Archiv für Musikwissenschaft,* 1985)—a new synthesis of the "learned" and *"galant"* styles. Posterity's verdict seems to be that a "rigorous sonata-form movement with rich contrapuntal content" (German musicologist Hermann Abert) was replaced by a rondo with "a series of insipid variations which are a poor substitute for the beautiful original" movement (English writer Cuthbert Girdlestone). But this opinion was held neither by Mozart nor by his contemporaries. He reported with delight to his father in 1782 that the Rondo—which he called "a gem"—was "making such a great furor in Vienna" and, a year later, that the success of the new Finale was such that during one of his public Lenten concerts he had had to repeat it; then, to his sister and to the publishers he sent the version of the concerto with the Rondo, not with the sonata-form movement. N.Z.

K. 238 *Piano Concerto in B-flat major, No. 6*

Origin: Salzburg, January 1776
Scoring: piano solo, 2 flutes, 2 oboes, 2 horns, strings
Movements: Allegro aperto. [Andante un poco adagio]. Rondeau: Allegro.

This, Mozart's second piano concerto (not counting the seven early pastiche concertos) was written presumably to show off the brilliant keyboard skills of the twenty-year-old composer at court and in local salons during the traditional carnival and Lent concerts. His sister, Nannerl, who was an accomplished pianist, also performed her brother's concertos in Salzburg. In 1777 Mozart took K. 238 with him on tour, performing it at concerts in Augsburg and Mannheim. The cadenzas for the first two movements and the *Eingang* for the third surviving in a manuscript in Leopold Mozart's hand are presumed to be Wolfgang's. The concerto remained unpublished until the year after Mozart's death. N.Z.

K. 242 *Triple Piano Concerto in F major, "Lodron," No. 7*

Origin: Salzburg, February 1776
Scoring: 3 pianos soli, 2 oboes, 2 horns, strings
Movements: Allegro. Adagio. Rondeau: Tempo di Menuetto.

K. 242 also exists in a version for two pianos, probably made for use by the Mozart siblings, but in its original conception it was a concerto for three pianos or harpsichords. A presentation copy of the first version bore the inscription: "Dedicated to the incomparable merit of Her Excellency, Her Ladyship the Countess Lodron, *née* Countess d'Arco, and her daughters, their Ladyships the Countesses Aloisia and Giuseppa . . . by their most devoted servant, Wolfgango Mozart." Mozart tailor-made the solo parts to fit the abilities of the dedicatees, providing two solo parts of moderate difficulty, and a third—for the younger daughter—of modest requirements. The Lodron family figures elsewhere in Mozart's creative life: the Divertimento in F, K. 247, was written for the Countess's name day in 1776 and the Divertimento in B flat, K. 287, was probably written for the same occasion a year later. N.Z.

K. 246 *Piano Concerto in C major, "Lützow," No. 8*

Origin: Salzburg, April 1776
Scoring: piano solo, 2 oboes, 2 horns, strings
Movements: Allegro aperto. Andante. Rondeau: Tempo di Menuetto.

The Concerto in C major, K. 246, was written for the twenty-six-year-old Countess Antonie Lützow, wife of the commander of the Hohensalzburg Fortress and, it is thought, a pupil of Leopold Mozart's. The circumstances of its first performance are unknown, although it has been speculated that the Countess may have performed her concerto at the Salzburg court during Whitsuntide 1776, when members of her family visited from Prague. Some notion of the sort of occasion (besides court concerts) at which the *Kenner und Liebhaber* (connoisseurs and amateurs) of Salzburg heard Mozart's works may perhaps be gleaned from a wry letter from Leopold Mozart in 1778—even if, on this occasion, the planned piano-concerto performance came to nought:

> Count Czernin is not content with fiddling at Court, and as he would like to direct, he has collected an amateur ensemble that is to meet in Count Lodron's hall every Sunday from three o'clock. Count Sigmund Lodron came by to invite Nannerl (as an amateur) to play

the keyboard instrument and to ask me [as a professional] to keep the second violins in order. A week ago today, on the 5th [April], we had our first concert. There was Count Czernin, the *primo violino,* then Baron Babbius, Sigmund Lodron, young Wienrother, Kolb, Kolb's student from the Nonnberg [Monastery], and a couple of young students whom I did not know. The second violins were myself, Sigmund Robinig, Cusetti, Count Altham, Cajetan Andretter, a student, and [the castrato] Ceccarelli, *la coda dei secondi* [the tail of the seconds]. The two violas were the two ex-Jesuits, Bullinger and Wishofer; the two oboes were the lackey Weiser and Schulze's son, who acted in the Linz play. Two apprentice waits [town musicians] played the horns. The double basses were Cassl and Count Wolfegg, with Ranftl doing duty occasionally. The cellos were the new young canons, Count Zeill and Count Spaur, Court Councillor Mölk, Sigmund Andretter, and Ranftl. Nannerl accompanied all the symphonies and she also accompanied Ceccarelli, who sang an *aria per l'apertura della accademia di dilettanti* [for the opening of the amateur concert]. After the symphony Count Czernin played a beautifully written concerto by [Magdalena] Sirmen *alla* Brunetti, and *dopo una altra sinfonia* [after another symphony] Count Altham played a horrible trio, no-one being able to say whether it was scraped or fiddled—whether it was in 3/4 or common time, or perhaps even in some newly invented and hitherto unknown time. Nannerl was to have played a concerto, but as the Countess [Lodron] wouldn't deliver up her good concert keyboard-instrument (which is solely *Casus reservatus pro summo Pontifice* [reserved for Her Holiness]), and only the Egedacher one with gilt legs was there, she didn't perform (translation by Emily Anderson).

This description must not be taken as wholly typical, for other letters suggest that some Salzburg domestic concerts, especially those under the Mozarts' direct supervision, attained a high artistic level.

If the Countess Lützow was capable of giving a reasonable account of K. 246, then she must have been exceptionally talented for a noble dilettante. Although the work is in the "easy" key of C major, eschews the technical brilliance of such works as K. 175 and 271, and seems to project a certain ingenuousness, it nevertheless embraces a wide range of musical thought, calls for considerable digital virtuosity in the solo part, and presumes the sophistication of performers and audience alike. The Finale, in particular, is a marvelously ironic commentary on the dance that was the very symbol of the *ancien régime.* Indeed, by presenting an archetypal minuet and then subtly undermining it, Mozart's treatment brings to mind Parisian commentaries written on the eve of the Revolution, one of which reports that at balls a few minuets were played at the beginning for grandfather and grandmother, after which nothing but contredanses were heard; another of which states: "Nowadays we hardly dance minuets any longer, for the same reason that the fox [in Aesop's *Fables*] gave in refusing to eat the grapes."

K. 246 too went with Mozart to Mannheim and Paris in 1777–78, and he performed it in Vienna in the early 1780s. Three sets of cadenzas survive for the first two movements, perhaps representing an early, simple set conceived for the Countess, a more challenging but still concise set used by Mozart and his sister in the 1770s, and an extended set written in the early 1780s. N.Z.

K. 271 *Piano Concerto in E-flat major, "Jeunehomme," No. 9*

Origin: Salzburg, January 1777

Scoring: piano solo, 2 oboes, 2 horns, strings

Movements: Allegro. Andantino. Rondeau: Presto.

In January 1777 Mozart turned twenty-one. This concerto—a work of emotional depth and virtuosity written in that month—marks his musical coming-of-age. The presumed cause for this sudden artistic maturation was a visit to Salzburg in the winter of 1776–77 by a French keyboard player, one Mlle Jeunehomme. Was she a great artist? Was she young and beautiful? Nothing at all is known of her except that she provided the inspiration for this concerto, and that Mozart may have encountered her again during his half-year in Paris in 1778.

K. 271 must have remained high in Mozart's esteem, for he took it with him on his tour to Mannheim and Paris in 1777–78, and he was still performing it in Vienna in the 1780s. If, as is probable, K. 271 is the concerto listed in catalogues of 1779–81 of the Parisian music publisher Madame Gertrude Heina, then it was the first of Mozart's concertos to be published. No copy of that edition survives, but a set of parts, which includes a piano part copied by Mozart's sister Nannerl and edited by his father, is to be found in Salzburg; and the autograph score itself, after being inaccessible for four decades, can now be seen in the Jagiellońska Library in Cracow.

The first movement begins with a brief orchestral fanfare, which is answered immediately by the piano. This novelty—the introduction of the soloist into the opening tutti—alerts us at once to the special nature of the work. The marchlike ideas that open and close the orchestral ritornello are softened by appoggiaturas and a contrasting theme having the character of a contredanse. The piano reenters with a trill while the strings and winds are still playing the ritornello's concluding cadences, and it then dominates the proceedings for much of the movement, even adding its voice to the closing orchestral ritornello.

Andante in Mozart's time meant a moderate tempo slightly slower than allegretto, and andantino meant something slightly slower than that. In this extraordinary C-minor Andantino the elegiac utterances of the soloist and the dramatic punctuation of the orchestra have the character of an accompanied recitative with aria, a type of music reserved in *opera seria* for movements of heightened emotion and flights of rhetorical expression.

The Finale is immediately off and running, with the soloist setting the pace—and run it does, pausing only for a pair of brief cadenzas and for the interpolation of a Minuet as one of the episodes of the Rondo. This ironic insertion of a courtly dance into the hustle and bustle of the finales serves both to amuse us and temporarily to distance us from a movement that an instant earlier had us completely absorbed. It may also be a witty allusion to the nationality of the concerto's dedicatee.

The first two movements of K. 271 call for full cadenzas, and the Rondo for a pair of brief ones—so-called *Eingänge* or "lead-ins." Cadenzas, although in an improvisatory style, required preparation beforehand, and two different cadenzas for the first movement, two for the second movement, and three pairs of *Eingänge* for the finale have come down to us in the hands of Mozart, his sister, and his father. N.Z.

K. 365 *Double Piano Concerto in E-flat major, No. 10 (K⁶ 316a)*
Origin: Salzburg, c. 1775 to 1777
Scoring: two pianos soli, 2 oboes, 2 bassoons, 2 horns, strings (2 clarinets, 2 trumpets and timpani added in 1781)
Movements: Allegro. Andante. Rondeaux: Allegro.

On their grand tour of 1764–66 Leopold Mozart displayed his precocious children in pieces for two harpsichords, which was not a new idea, and for four-hands at a single keyboard instrument, which was a virtually unheard-of notion apparently popularized by the Mozarts. The repertory performed by the two *Wunderkinder* is mostly unknown, except for Wolfgang's little four-hand sonata, K. 19d, and a concerto for two harpsichords by the widely admired Viennese composer Georg Christoph Wagenseil (1715–77), whom the Mozarts had met in 1762. Wolfgang and Nannerl continued to play together, for a British visitor to Salzburg in 1772 (Louis de Vismes) heard them perform four-hands. So it was probably inevitable that, once Mozart turned to composing concertos, he would compose one to perform with his sister. That would seem to be the origin of K. 365, which has traditionally been dated from around the beginning of 1779, although British scholar Alan Tyson has shown that the cadenzas for the first and second movements, partly in Wolfgang's and partly in Leopold's hand, are on a kind of paper that Mozart used between approximately August 1775 and January 1777. Mozart had his father send him a copy of this concerto to Vienna in 1781. There he added clarinets, trumpets, and kettledrums to the outer movements and performed the work with his pupil and patron Josepha Barbara von Auernhammer, at a private concert at the Auernhammer's on November 23rd of that year and at a public concert in the Augarten (Vienna's central park) on May 26th of the following year. N.Z.

K. 382 *Rondo in D major.*

See the note for K. 175, Piano Concerto in D major, No. 5, on p. 119.

K. 414 *Piano Concerto in A major, No. 12 (K³ 386a, K⁶ 385p)*
Origin: Vienna, 1782
Scoring: piano solo, 2 oboes, 2 horns, strings
Movements: Allegro. Andante. Allegretto.

K. 414 was the first of Mozart's great series of Viennese piano concertos, and (with K. 413 and 415) also the first of a set of three that he performed at his Lenten concerts of 1783. It is thus the first piano concerto Mozart wrote after breaking with the archbishop of Salzburg and in 1781 settling in Vienna, where he established himself as a freelance musician. As part of his new existence he gave an extraordinary number of concerts, which explains the outpouring of piano concertos in the mid-1780s. In an often-quoted passage from a letter of December 28, 1782, to his father, Mozart described his situation:

> I must write in the greatest haste, as it is already half past five and I have asked some people to come here at six for a little concert. Although I have so much to do that often I do not know whether I am on my head or my heels, I spend the whole forenoon giving lessons until two o'clock, when we eat. After this meal I must give my poor stomach an hour for digestion. The evening is therefore the only time I have for composing and of that I can never be sure, as I am often asked to perform at Concerts. There are still two concertos wanting to make up the series of subscription concertos. These concertos are a happy medium between what is too easy and too difficult; they are very brilliant, pleasing

to the ear, and natural, without being vapid. There are also passages here and there from which *connoisseurs alone* can derive satisfaction; but these passages are written in such a way that the less discriminating cannot fail to be pleased, though without knowing why. I am distributing tickets for six ducats in cash.

Mozart was referring to the set of three piano concertos, K. 413–15, of which only K. 414 had yet been completed. He intended to sell manuscript copies of all three by subscription: from January 15, 1783, "three new, recently finished piano concertos" were announced for sale by subscription in manuscript copies, and by January 22 Mozart wrote of them as if completed. This manuscript edition of the concertos could at first be ordered directly from Mozart and later from the Viennese copying firm of Johann Traeg. But although he lowered his asking price from six to four ducats, his subscription venture apparently foundered. In April 1783 he tried without success to sell the three concertos to the Parisian publisher Jean-Georges Sieber. They were finally engraved and published in March 1785 as Opus 4 by the Viennese firm of Artaria and Co. The autograph manuscript of K. 414 in the Jagiellońska Library, Crakow, is undated. N.Z.

K. 386 *Rondo in A major*
Origin: Vienna, October 19, 1782
Scoring: solo piano, 2 oboes, 2 horns, strings with violoncello obbligato

The history of the Rondo in A major, K. 386, is a tortuous one. The autograph manuscript of this unpublished work, in Mozart's possession at his death, was included in Johann Anton André's purchase in 1799 of the composer's manuscripts from his widow. But as K. 386 was missing its last leaf, André, instead of publishing it, sold it to England, where it came into the possession of Sir William Sterndale Bennett. In 1838 Cipriani Potter published in London an arrangement of the entire work for piano alone, presumably with an ending of his own construction. Subsequently, Mozart's autograph was dismembered and distributed to many people, and bits and pieces of it have surfaced from time to time. When American musicologist Alfred Einstein came to investigate K. 386, he could locate only two leaves from the autograph containing measures 136–171; using those measures as a model, he published a freely conceived orchestration of Potter's arrangement in 1936. By 1956 British musicologist Alec Hyatt King had uncovered six further leaves in England. Adding to these six another full leaf and a partial one that they had discovered (thus accounting for measures 1–78, 118–132, and 136–171), Austrian pianist Paul Badura-Skoda and Australian conductor Sir Charles Mackerras published in 1963 an excellent reconstruction, much less speculative in nature than Einstein's, since most missing passages now had a parallel one to serve as a model. This version has been widely performed, and recorded more than once. Recently the last leaf, missing since before 1799, was discovered by British scholar Alan Tyson in a manuscript miscellany in the British Library.

It was long ago suggested that K. 386 must have been connected to the Piano Concerto in A major, K. 414. The Finale of that work shares with K. 386 date of composition, key, Allegretto in 2/4, and character: an almost pastoral serenity, with few of the high jinks Mozart often tossed into his finales. As K. 386, even though completed in all its essentials, never had the final details of its orchestration filled in by Mozart, it was most likely a rejected Finale for K. 414. N.Z.

K. 413 *Piano Concerto in F major, No. 11 (K⁶ 387a)*

Origin: Vienna, 1782 or 1783
Scoring: piano solo, 2 oboes, 2 bassoons, 2 horns, strings
Movements: Allegro. Larghetto. Tempo di Menuetto.

The *galant* charm of the opening Allegro of K. 413 clearly reveals Mozart's desire to please his listeners. Something special awaits connoisseurs in the B-flat major Larghetto: not the profundity of the middle movement of the previous concerto but a gossamer creation in which the soloist spins forth a *fioritura* (rapid, lightly played ornamental passages) of extraordinary subtlety. The Tempo di Menuetto Finale expands what was merely an episode in the Finale of K. 271 into a well-wrought Rondo.

The Finale requires no *Eingänge*. Cadenzas for the other two movements have come down to us in Leopold Mozart's hand with a now incomplete set of parts in Salzburg dating from the summer or autumn of 1783, made by a professional copyist but with corrections in the hands of both Mozart and his father. N.Z.

K. 415 *Piano Concerto in C major, No. 13 (K⁶ 387b)*

Origin: Vienna, winter 1782–83
Scoring: piano solo, 2 oboes, 2 bassoons, 2 horns, 2 trumpets and timpani, strings
Movements: Allegro. Andante. Allegro.

Completed by January 1783, this concerto belongs to a group of three that Mozart performed at his Lenten concerts of that year and published two years later as "Opus IV." It calls for the festive or military trumpets and kettledrums often associated with C major in Mozart's orchestral music.

Eighteenth-century writers on music agreed that keys had inherent characters, but often disagreed about precisely what those were. Georg Joseph Vogler (1779) thought C major "pure"; Christian Schubart (1784) found it not only pure but also "innocent, simple, naive"; to Justin Heinrich Knecht (1792) it was "cheerful, pure"; to Francesco Galeazzi (1796) "grandiose, military, serious, majestic"; and to André-Ernest-Modeste Grétry (1797) "noble and frank." For Joseph Haydn C major was the key of light, which he showed emerging from chaos in *The Creation*. A series of C-major masterpieces—among them the piano concertos K. 467 and 503, the "Jupiter" Symphony K. 551, and the string quintet K. 515—suggests that Mozart may have had similar associations.

The first movement of K. 415, with its bright orchestral palette and profusion of ideas, may be regarded in this context. The orchestra is treated with such affection that, as English writer Philip Radcliffe suggests, "we sometimes have the impression of a potential symphony [or is it an Italian overture?] into which a part for piano solo has strayed."

The following Andante relaxes into the cooler regions of the subdominant, F major (Vogler: "dead calm"; Schubart: "complaisance, calm"; Knecht: "gentle, calm"; Galeazzi: "majestic, shrill"[!]; Grétry: "mixed [noble and pathetic]"). With the martial instruments temporarily silenced, it is a sort of *cantabile* aria in an almost pastoral vein. An especially magical moment occurs at the return of the opening idea and key, where Mozart provides a lesson in embellishing a melody with grace and feeling.

The return of C major and the trumpets and drums brings with it, not the martial spirits of the first movement, but a sort of *gigue en rondeau,* whose notable wit is epitomized by some roguish grace notes. Of the strongly contrasting episodes, the first and third are poignant C-minor Adagios in 2/4, while the middle episode keeps to the jig tempo and meter with, as English musicologist Arthur Hutchings put it, "a farrago of the rondo tunes and solo bravura." The spirited tripartite refrain is varied each time it recurs. In its final appearance it serves as a coda, which finally evaporates amidst shimmering trills. N.Z.

K. 449 *Piano Concerto in E-flat major, "First Ployer," No. 14*

Origin: Vienna, February 9, 1784
Scoring: piano solo, 2 oboes, 2 horns, strings
Movements: Allegro vivace. Andantino. Allegro ma non troppo.

Mozart entered this concerto in the catalogue of his works on February 9, 1784. Apparently because it was written for the exclusive use of his pupil Barbara (Babette) von Ployer, it was not published during his lifetime, although Mozart himself performed it at his benefit concert of March 17. There, he reported to his father, "it won extraordinary applause," and he sent it to Salzburg for Nannerl to perform. Subsequently he distinguished K. 449 from his later, larger-scale piano concertos, calling it "a concerto in an entirely different style and written more for a small than a large orchestra." Hence, this is a more intimate work, eschewing the resonant, extroverted, sunlit "public" keys of C and D major for one that Mozart's contemporaries thought tended to convey "night" (Vogler, 1779), "love, devotion" (Schubart, 1784), or "splendor, solemnity" (Knecht, 1792).

The autograph manuscript, formerly in Berlin but now in Crakow, is inscribed "Di Wolfgango Amadeo Mozart per la Sig^ra^ Barbara de Ployer / Viena [*sic*] li 9 di Feb^ro^ 1784." There is also in Salzburg a set of parts prepared by Nannerl for her own use. N.Z.

K. 450 *Piano Concerto in B-flat major, No. 15*

Origin: Vienna, March 15, 1784
Scoring: piano solo, flute, 2 oboes, 2 bassoons, 2 horns, strings
Movements: Allegro. [Andante.] Allegro.

Mozart entered this concerto in his catalogue of his works on March 15, 1784. This time the winds are all obligatory, according to a letter to his father. In a subsequent letter he added that K. 450 was a work "bound to make the performer sweat." With the concertos K. 449 and 451, it forms an opus of "three grand concertos" (so-called by Mozart) which he planned first to hold back for his own and his patrons' exclusive use, and to publish only later. In fact, however, the three works remained unpublished until after his death.

The term "grand" must refer to the breadth of the works' conception and the expanded role of the the wind instruments. In the piano concertos of this period Mozart first brought to full flower the new style of orchestration that distinguished his late operas and concertos and the last three symphonies. This feature of his music forcibly struck his contemporaries, some of the more conservative of whom criticized his use of the winds either as being impracticably difficult or for overloading the accompaniments. Mozart had, in fact, arrived at a new conception of the concerto in which the orchestra did not merely accompany the fortepiano but was its equal. To the role of the winds in the late seventeenth and early eighteenth centuries (doubling the strings or answering them antiphonally) and to that of the mid-eighteenth (providing a harmonic background of sustained chords in the tuttis) Mozart now added a third possibility: sharing fully in the work's thematic development. This, the basis of nineteenth-century orchestration, is the so-called *durchbrochene Arbeit*—"openwork" or "filigree." Mozart was surely aware of the nature of his innovation, and in K. 450 he threw down the gauntlet by beginning unconventionally with the winds supported only by the bass line.

N.Z.

K. 451 *Piano Concerto in D major, No. 16*

Origin: Vienna, March 22, 1784
Scoring: piano solo, flute, 2 oboes, 2 bassoons, 2 horns, 2 trumpets and timpani, strings
Movements: Allegro assai. [Andante.] Allegro di molto.

This concerto and the next, dated respectively March 22 and April 12, 1784, by Mozart, were among those few published in his lifetime—K. 451 in Paris around 1785 and K. 453 in Speyer in 1787. The latter must have sold well, for in late 1791 its publisher Heinrich Philipp Carl Bossler also produced an edition of K. 451. This elicited a heretofore overlooked review in the Speyer magazine *Musical Correspondence of the German Philharmonic Society* (May 16, 1792), which provides a rare glimpse of how one of Mozart's contemporaries viewed these works:

> To every friend and admirer of the Mozartean muse this composition . . . can be nothing but very precious. The original style of composition, which is unmistakable here, the fullness of the harmony, the striking turns of phrase, the skilled distribution of shade and light, and many other excellent qualities, all give us cause to feel very deeply the loss of Mozart, a paragon of his era. The concerto under review is in D major, and is one of the most beautiful and most brilliant that we have from this master, in the ritornellos as well as in the solos. The opening Allegro takes up the first twelve pages, and we miss nothing in it but the figuring of the bass line in the tuttis. The Andante in G major that follows next is a kind of *romanza* in 4/4—very elegant and touching. The Finale is an Allegro di molto in 2/4, which, however, turns into 3/8 on the last page but one. In this movement the greatest difficulties certainly prevail, but there are also exceptionally beautiful modulations. It is only to be regretted that this masterly keyboard concerto is impracticable in smaller musical circles because of the number of instruments for which it is scored (and which are in part obbligato instruments), and is usable only with a strong, well-manned orchestra. The engraving is very clear and correct, and does true honor to Councillor Bossler's printing-shop.

While we are unlikely to disagree with the reviewer's critical judgments—"striking . . . skilled . . . excellent . . . most beautiful and most brilliant . . . very elegant and touching"—neither can we learn much from them except that the anonymous writer (perhaps Johann Friedrich Christmann) recognized the music's superior quality. (He must have heard a performance, as—following the usual practice—the work was published only in parts, not in score). Nevertheless, the review does touch on those aspects of Mozart's style which, contemporaneous reviews of his operas suggest, most forcibly struck his audiences as being different from other music they were encountering: the full scoring and technical difficulties for the orchestra, the chromaticism, the wide variety of texture and nuance, and the characteristic Mozartean turns of phrase. Also noteworthy here is the indication that a professional soloist, according to the performance practices of the period, would be expected to play *continuo* in the tuttis, and that, in the absence of a score, the tutti bass lines of the soloist's part might have been figured (as was, indeed, the piano part copied by Mozart's sister Nannerl).

A fact not commented upon by the reviewer was, however, noticed by Nannerl. Mozart had sent K. 451 to Nannerl and their father on May 15, 1784, and she complained that something was missing from the Andante. Mozart replied on June 12, confirming that she was quite right (he had left room for himself to improvise during performance), and he eventually sent her an ornamented version of eight measures of the Andante as well as cadenzas for the first and third movements. These survive and serve as precious examples of what Mozart expected of his piano soloists. N.Z.

K. 453 *Piano Concerto in G major, "Second Ployer," No. 17*

Origin: Vienna, April 12, 1784
Scoring: piano solo, flute, 2 oboes, 2 bassoons, 2 horns, strings
Movements: Allegro. Andante. Allegretto.

If K. 451 was written for Mozart's own use and may have received its first performance at a private concert he gave on March 31, 1784, K. 453 was written for his pupil Barbara (Babette) von Ployer who, according to Mozart, paid him handsomely for it. Her father, Gottfried Ignaz von Ployer, an agent of the Salzburg court in Vienna, hired an orchestra and the premiere took place at their summer place in the suburb of Döbling on June 13, 1784; Mozart brought along the Italian composer Giovanni Paisiello, to show off his pupil and his music. Babette von Ployer, for whom the concerto K. 449 was also written, must have been a fine performer; on the occasion of the premiere of K. 453, Mozart played his two-piano sonata K. 448 with her.

The bourrée or contredanse tune Mozart invented as the subject of the Variation-Finale of K. 453 clearly had a special place in his heart, since he taught his pet starling to sing it—although, much to his amusement, the bird sang a certain note wrong each time and held another note too long. In his cash book (May 27, 1784) Mozart commented ironically on the bird's version: "Das war schön!" (That was fine!) N.Z.

K. 456 *Piano Concerto in B-flat major, "Paradis," No. 18*

Origin: Vienna, September 30, 1784
Scoring: piano solo, flute, 2 oboes, 2 bassoons, 2 horns, strings
Movements: Allegro vivace. Andante un poco sostenuto. Allegro vivace.

The autograph manuscript of this concerto is undated; Mozart entered the work in his catalogue with the date September 30, 1784. It is thought to be the work that Mozart performed at a Lenten concert in Vienna on February 13, 1785, and that his father (who was present) referred to as

> a masterful concerto that he wrote for [the blind virtuosa Maria Theresa von] Paradis. . . . I . . . had the great pleasure of hearing all the interplay of the instruments so clearly that for sheer delight tears came to my eyes. When your brother left the stage, the Emperor tipped his hat and called out "Bravo Mozart!" and when he came on to play, there was a great deal of clapping.

The first movement begins, like those of the neighboring concertos K. 451, 453, and 459, with a favorite martial rhythm; but this proves merely an opening gambit and much of the rest of the movement is intimate, almost like chamber music, spiced with humorous (perhaps even satirical) passages and purple patches of chromaticism. This intimacy continues in a more poignant vein in the G-minor Andante, whose beautiful binary theme is given five striking (mostly double) variations and a coda functioning as a sixth. Here Mozart exploits the tone color of the wind instruments to the fullest. The refrain of the sonata-rondo Finale, with its hunting-horn fanfares, is thrown into sharp relief not only by the movement that precedes it but also by a stirring B-minor episode, in which the winds in 2/4 are pitted against the strings in 6/8, while the soloist seems torn between the two. This conflict is soon amicably resolved, and the Finale ends cheerfully. N.Z.

K. 459 *Piano Concerto in F major, "First Coronation," No. 19*

Origin: Vienna, December 11, 1784
Scoring: piano solo, flute, 2 oboes, 2 bassoons, 2 horns, strings
Movements: Allegro. Allegretto. Allegro assai.

Like the autograph of K. 456, that of K. 459 is undated. It is entered in Mozart's catalogue under December 11, 1784, and was thus perhaps intended for an Advent concert. In any case, Mozart would almost certainly have performed it at one of the Lenten subscription concerts he gave in the Mehlgrube on the six Fridays between February 11 and March 18, 1785. This concerto must have remained high in Mozart's esteem, for he took it on tour with him in 1790, performing it in Frankfurt at a concert during the coronation festivities of the Emperor Leopold II. In his catalogue Mozart listed K. 459 as having trumpets and kettledrums, even though it is in a key in which (with the exception of the Andante of the "Linz" Symphony, K. 425) he did not usually use those instruments. Those parts, if they even existed, have been lost; perhaps there is an error in Mozart's catalogue entry, or perhaps the trumpet parts were notated separately (as in the Symphony in G major, K. 318, where they are also in the "wrong" key).

The first movement (Allegro in the autograph, Allegro vivace in Mozart's catalogue) presents a brilliant profusion of ideas, held together not only by Mozart's seemingly infallible sense of continuity and contrast, but also by the way in which the opening martial rhythm pervades the texture, appearing in 165 of the 400 measures, as well as in Mozart's own cadenza. Indeed, the movement might well be considered a kind of debate between this "strict" rhythm and the more *galant* triplets that also occur with great frequency, especially in the solo part.

The middle movement, in C major, is accorded the (for a "slow" movement) brisk tempo of Allegretto, as Haydn had done in the string quartet Op. 54, No. 1, and as Beethoven would do in his Eighth Symphony. This idyll, in sonata form without development section, is not without an occasional touch of pathos. Once again, Mozart's bold wind orchestration provided glorious splashes of color.

At the time that Mozart composed K. 459 he was also completing his six string quartets dedicated to Joseph Haydn, and Haydn's music must have been on his mind: the refrain of this concerto's Finale is derived (as American musicologist, pianist, and conductor Joshua Rifkin has pointed out) from a theme in the middle of the Finale of the older master's Symphony No. 78 in C minor of 1782. The theme of the concerto, a kind of contredanse treated in the spirit of *opera buffa,* is the perfect foil for a fugato that appears three times, once worked out at some length as a development section, and that is also alluded to in Mozart's cadenza for the movement.

In addition to the autograph, there is a manuscript score with corrections in Mozart's hand owned by the Glinka Museum of Musical Culture, Moscow. N.Z.

K. 466 *Piano Concerto in D minor, No. 20*

Origin: Vienna, February 10, 1785
Scoring: solo piano, flute, 2 oboes, 2 bassoons, 2 horns, 2 trumpets and timpani, strings
Movements: Allegro. Romance. Rondo [Allegro assai].

The autograph manuscript of the Concerto in D minor, K. 466 (in the Gesellschaft der Musikfreunde, Vienna), is undated, but Mozart entered the work in his catalogue on February 10, 1785. On that very day Leopold Mozart arrived to spend a few weeks with his son and daughter-in-law. He reported to his daughter Nannerl:

> We arrived at one o'clock. . . . The copyist was still copying [K. 466] when we arrived, and your brother did not even have time to play through the Rondo, as he had to supervise the copying. . . . On the same evening we drove to his first subscription concert [of six], at which a great many members of the aristocracy were present. Each person pays a souverain d'or or three ducats for these Lenten concerts. Your brother is giving them at the Mehlgrube and only pays half a souverain d'or each time for the hall. [There were more than 150 subscribers.] The concert was magnificent and the orchestra played splendidly. In addition to the symphonies, a female singer from the Italian theater sang two arias. Then we had [the] new and very fine concerto. . . . (translation by Emily Anderson).

The orchestra musicians must have been outstanding and well acquainted with Mozart's idiom to have satisfied his sophisticated father and the Viennese audience in a sightread performance of this subtle, difficult work. Perhaps because of its wide range of affect, brooding chromaticism, and stormy outbursts, K. 466—one of only two concertos Mozart composed in minor keys—was a favorite in the nineteenth century, even though its final seventy-five measures in D major represent a clear instance of an eighteenth-century *lieto fine* (happy ending), which nineteenth-century musicians found so hard to accept. The young Beethoven had K. 466 in his repertory and wrote cadenzas for it, as did Mozart's pianist-composer son, Franz Xaver Wolfgang. However, Mozart himself did not leave any cadenzas. N.Z.

K. 467 *Piano Concerto in C major, No. 21*

Origin: Vienna, March 9, 1785
Scoring: piano solo, flute, 2 oboes, 2 bassoons, 2 horns, 2 trumpets and timpani, strings
Movements: [Allegro maestoso.] Andante. Allegro vivace assai.

The autograph manuscript of the Concerto in C major, K. 467 (in the Morgan Library, New York), is dated "nel febraio 1785" and entered in Mozart's catalogue on March 9. This pellucid work was written, therefore, between the completion of the D-minor concerto and the latter date, or a period of twenty-seven days during which Mozart also taught private pupils, entertained his father, held a quartet party to play through with Joseph Haydn and his father some of the new quartets dedicated to Haydn, and participated in perhaps another dozen public and private concerts. A handbill announcing the premiere of K. 467 reads:

> On Thursday, 10th March 1785, Kapellmeister Mozart will have the honor of giving at the I. & R. National Court Theater a Grand Musical Concert for his benefit, at which not only a new, just finished Forte piano Con-

certo will be played by him, but also an especially large Forte piano pedale will be used by him in improvising. The remaining pieces will be announced by the large poster on the day itself.

The "especially large Forte piano pedale" refers to a device that Mozart had custom built for his Viennese concerts. It was essentially another, legless fortepiano which lay on the floor underneath his regular piano. It was played by means of a pedalboard with the feet, as an organ is played (and Mozart was a skilled organist). Mozart used it to reinforce the low notes in improvising fantasias and playing piano concertos.

Leopold Mozart reported that his son took in 559 gulden. K. 467 (or at least its Andante) has made a great deal of money in recent years too, in the soundtrack of the movie *Elvira Madigan;* as the movie is forgotten, its trivialization of K. 467 fades and the work maintains its status as a masterpiece. Again, no cadenzas by Mozart survive. N.Z.

K. 482 ***Piano Concerto in E-flat major, No. 22***

Origin: Vienna, December 16, 1785
Scoring: piano solo, flute, 2 clarinets, 2 bassoons, 2 horns, 2 trumpets and timpani, strings
Movements: Allegro. Andante. Rondo: Allegro.

Mozart dated the Concerto in E flat, K. 482, "Vienna, 16 December 1785," and on that very day performed it between the acts of Carl Ditters von Dittersdorf's oratorio *Esther.* When he repeated the work at one of three Advent concerts that he presented to 120 subscribers at about the same time, the Andante received so much applause that he had to repeat it. The Concerto in A, K. 488, dated "Vienna, 2 March 1786," was intended, along with K. 482 and one other piano concerto (K. 491), for Lenten concerts of that year. None of these three concertos written for Mozart's own use was published in his lifetime, and only for K. 488 does a cadenza of his come down to us. N.Z.

K. 488 ***Piano Concerto in A major, No. 23***

Origin: Vienna, March 2, 1786
Scoring: piano solo, flute, 2 clarinets, 2 bassoons, 2 horns, strings
Movements: Allegro. Adagio. Allegro assai.

The Concerto in A, K. 488, dated "Vienna, 2 March 1786," was intended, along with K. 482 and 491, for Lenten concerts of that year. The A major concerto was one of five (with K. 451, 453, 456, and 459), copies of which Mozart offered in August of the same year to his childhood patron, the Prince von Fürstenberg. In a letter Mozart claimed that, since these concertos were "compositions which I keep for myself or for a small circle of music-lovers and connoisseurs (who promise not to let them out of their hands)," therefore they "cannot possibly be known elsewhere, as they are not even known in Vienna," asking the Prince likewise "not to let them out of his hands."

Since its publication in 1800 by Johann Anton André (who purchased Mozart's musical estate from his widow), K. 488 has been one of Mozart's most popular piano concertos. Reasons are not hard to find. The special melodic charm of the first movement, along with its striking orchestral timbre created by the key of A, which is resonant and brilliant for the strings, and by the pair of clarinets in place of the usual oboes; the seriousness of the middle movement, Adagio in place of the usual Andante and in the rare key of F-sharp minor, which transforms a siciliano into a passionate drama; the bouyancy of the sonata-rondo Finale, in which the piano and orchestra cavort jointly and severally in an exhilarating and satisfying manner—all these features combine to create one of Mozart's seemingly most perfect masterpieces. N.Z.

K. 491 *Piano Concerto in C minor, No. 24*

Origin: Vienna, March 24, 1786
Scoring: piano solo, flute, 2 oboes, 2 clarinets, 2 bassoons, 2 horns, 2 trumpets and timpani, strings
Movements: [Allegro.] Larghetto. [Allegretto.]

Mozart gave a concert for his own benefit in Vienna at the Burgtheater on April 7, 1786, his last concert in that venue. Because his C-minor Concerto, K. 491, is dated March 24, 1786, commentators have assumed (entirely reasonably) that it received its premiere on that occasion, whose program is unknown. As one of Mozart's only two concertos in a minor key, K. 491 has long been the recipient of especial attention and favor. The darkened mood, chromatic instabilities, and stormy patches all endeared it to nineteenth-century performers and audiences. Nowadays, Mozart's other, less romantic concertos have risen in popular estimation, but K. 491 has lost none of its attractiveness.

For a pianist, the C-minor Concerto offers special challenges even beyond those posed by any such towering masterpiece. One challenge concerns the first-movement cadenza. Mozart not only failed to leave a cadenza, but unlike all the other concertos (except K. 488 where a cadenza is written into the score instead of on a separate sheet of paper), there is no trill at the *fermata* which signals the cadenza. Some performers follow, therefore, the precedure in Mozart's cadenza for the third movement of K. 466, in which the trill does not end the cadenza but is followed by a solo thematic statement leading to the final ritornello. A movement as weighty as the first movement of K. 491 would seem to demand a cadenza to match. It may be not unreasonable to incorporate into the cadenza a contrapuntal section such as that found in the cadenza written for this movement by Mozart's pupil J. N. Hummel.

Another challenge is the state of the autograph manuscript, which is the property of the Royal College of Music but deposited in the British Library, and has been published in facsimile. Unlike Mozart's other piano concerto autographs, which mostly give the appearance of fair copies, K. 491 shows signs of almost Beethovenian creative struggle and indecision. In a passage like the third variation in the Finale, for instance, Mozart essayed several versions and never arrived at a final one. No definitive version is possible in such passages and each artist must, in effect, decide for himself which of Mozart's ideas works best.

N.Z.

K. 503 *Piano Concerto in C major, No. 25*

Origin: Vienna, December 4, 1786
Scoring: piano solo, flute, 2 oboes, 2 bassoons, 2 horns, 2 trumpets, strings
Movements: Allegro maestoso. Andante. [Allegretto.]

This concerto and the "Prague" symphony, K. 504, were apparently written for a series of four Advent subscription concerts that Mozart planned for December 1786 in the hall of Johann Trattner's Viennese casino. The concerto may have been repeated at a Lenten benefit concert in the Kärntnerthortheater on March 7, 1787, and probably also at Mozart's concert in the Leipzig Gewandhaus on May 12, 1789. This pellucid work was first published in 1798 by Mozart's widow Constanze as an unhappy venture in self-publication that had no sequel. N.Z.

K. 537 ***Piano Concerto in D major, "Second Coronation," No. 26***

Origin: Vienna, February 24, 1788
Scoring: solo piano, flute, 2 oboes, 2 bassoons, 2 horns, 2 trumpets and timpani, strings
Movements: Allegro. Larghetto. [Allegretto.]

The Concerto in D major, K. 537, was perhaps written by Mozart for a private Lenten concert, although no record of such an occasion exists. In one of his many letters begging money from his fellow Mason, Michael Puchberg, written in summer 1788, Mozart claimed that a concert series of his was to begin in Trattner's casino in a week which would have called for piano concertos. These concerts traditionally have been thought never to have taken place, but H. C. Robbins Landon has recently argued persuasively that they did in fact occur. Mozart took K. 537 with him to Frankfurt for a concert he gave on October 15, 1790 in connection with the installation of Leopold II as Holy Roman Emperor, thus the nickname "Coronation" Concerto (see also p. 130).

Like most of Mozart's piano concertos, K. 503 (see above) and 537 were written for his own use. Unlike many of the others, however, these two were never prepared by him for presentation to a pupil, a patron, or a publisher. As a result, no cadenzas were written down, certain melodies in the right hand of the piano parts of both works remained in outline form, and the entire left hand of K. 537 was left blank. In the first edition of the latter work (1794) the publisher Johann Anton André supplied the left hand—in part derived from the orchestral bass lines and in part invented—which has appeared in all subsequent editions. N.Z.

K. 595 ***Piano Concerto in B-flat major, No. 27***

Origin: Vienna, January 5, 1791
Scoring: piano solo, flute, 2 oboes, 2 bassoons, 2 horns, strings
Movements: Allegro. Larghetto. Allegro.

This is Mozart's last piano concerto and last concerto of any sort except K. 622, written for his clarinetist friend Anton Stadler. Two months after it was entered into his catalogue, he performed it at a benefit concert for the clarinetist (Johann) Joseph Beer, held in the great room of Ignaz Jahn's inn in the Himmelpfortgasse. Mozart's sister-in-law, first love, and former pupil Aloysia Weber Lange sang in the same program. It was Mozart's last public appearance as a concerto soloist. Mozart left cadenzas for the first two movements and two lead-ins for the Finale, which, however, also requires a third lead-in.

In Mozart's catalogue of his works the very next entry after K. 595 is a little strophic lied, "Sehnsucht nach dem Frühlinge" (Longing for Spring), K. 596, for soprano or tenor and fortepiano. The poem's first verse reads:

> Komm, lieber Mai, und mache
> Die Bäume wieder grün,
> Und lass mir an dem Bache,
> Die kleinen Veilchen blüh'n!
>
> (Come, sweet May, and turn
> the trees green again,
> and make the little violets
> bloom for me by the brook.)

The tune of the song is also the refrain of the piano concerto's Finale. It was to be Mozart's last spring. N.Z.

CONCERTOS FOR STRINGS

A private concert. Engraving by Johann Ernst Mansfeld, 1784.

The musicians include two violinists, a violist, a cellist (holding his bow in the old-fashioned, backhanded manner), a flutist, and a harpsichordist or pianist. In house concerts of the sort portrayed here, it was common to perform concertos, arias, and symphonies with one player per part.

BACKGROUND AND OVERVIEW

"Wolfgang had a little violin that he got as a present in Vienna . . .," wrote musician Johann Andreas Schachtner, a friend of the Mozart family, of an incident which took place in January 1763. "We were going to play trios, Papa [Leopold] playing the bass with his viola, Wenzl the first violin, and I was to play the second violin. Wolfgang had asked to be allowed to play the second violin, but Papa refused him this foolish request, because he had not yet had the least instruction in the violin, and Papa thought he could not possibly play anything. Wolfgang said, 'You don't need to have studied in order to play second violin,' and when Papa insisted that he should go away and not bother us any more, Wolfgang began to weep bitterly and stamped off with his little violin. I asked them to let him play with me. Papa eventually said, 'Play with Herr Schachtner, but so softly that we can't hear you, or you will have to go.' And so it was. Wolfgang played with me. I soon noticed with astonishment that I was quite superfluous. I quietly put my violin down, and looked at your Papa; tears of wonder and comfort ran down his cheeks at this scene."

A mere four months later the Augsburg newspaper published this report from a Salzburg correspondent: "I am credibly informed that the boy can now not only play from the violin clef, but also from the soprano and bass clefs, and takes part in everything on a small *violino piccolo* made specially for him, having already appeared with a solo and a concerto at the Salzburg court. Has he then learned this since the New Year?"

In the 1770s Mozart was heard in Salzburg, Vienna, Augsburg, and Munich as violin soloist, playing his own and other composers' works. On one occasion in Munich in 1777—after playing one of his own orchestral serenades with movements for solo violin—Mozart wrote to his father, Leopold, with a touch of irony, "I played as if I were the greatest fiddler in all of Europe." His father replied to him: "You yourself do not know how well you play the violin; if only you will *do yourself credit and play with energy, with your whole heart and mind, yes, just as if you were the first violinist in Europe.* Many people do not even know that you play the violin, since you have been known from childhood as a keyboard player."

One might suppose Leopold Mozart's judgment was colored by the fact that in 1756, the year of his son's birth, he had published an important textbook on the violin, a book that went through three editions, was translated into several languages, and is still in use. But his evaluation is confirmed by the violin virtuoso and first concertmaster of the Salzburg court orchestra, Antonio Brunetti, who, when he heard Leopold remark with deliberate understatement that his son could play the violin passably, blurted out, "What? Nonsense! Why, he could play anything!"

Mozart's works for violin and orchestra were written mostly in Salzburg between the years 1773 and 1776. Leaving aside two concertos of disputed authenticity (K. 268 and 271a) and two sinfonie concertante that were never completed (K. 315f and 320e), they include five orchestral serenades containing one, two, or three violin-concerto movements, five independent violin concertos, four single violin-concerto movements, and two sinfonie concertante. This is a total of some thirty-seven movements involving solo violin and orchestra—a sizable body of music. One single movement (K. 470, an Andante in A major), the last that Mozart wrote for this combination, is unfortunately lost.

To the modern music lover, violin concertos are associated with performances in formal concert halls. But in Mozart's day they were also played out-of-doors, in gardens and piazzas, as part of orchestral serenades, and were sometimes used as entr'acte music in the theater. The most common setting for violin concertos, however—at least in Northern Italy and Austria—was in church, where they embellished the Mass or Vespers service. Giuseppe Tartini and many other great violinists of the period frequently reached the general public by church performances, and this tradition was known to Mozart too.

We may guess how Mozart played the violin, for he valued in performers what we value in his music: beauty, clarity, logic, balance. When he was pleased with a performance, he reported that "It went smoothly as oil." Not for him the pyrotechnics of the violinists Pietro Antonio Locatelli or Giovanni Battista Viotti. Once, after hearing a difficult violin concerto well performed, he informed his father that he enjoyed it, but added, "You know that I am no lover of difficulties." The paradox is that Mozart's playing down of virtuosity for its own sake in his violin concertos makes them harder, not easier, to perform well. Sheer technique and bravura cannot be used in these works to compensate for a lack of thoughtful, sensitive musicianship. N.Z.

K. 207 *Violin Concerto in B-flat major, No. 1*

Origin: Salzburg, April 14, 1773 (or 1775)
Scoring: violin solo, 2 oboes, 2 horns, strings
Movements: Allegro moderato. Adagio. Presto.

It has long been thought that Mozart wrote all five of his violin concertos within a space of eight months from April 14 to December 20, 1775, in accordance with the dates written by the composer on the original manuscripts. German musicologist Wolfgang Plath has recently shown, however, that on all five manuscripts the last two digits of the date have been tampered with: it appears that all were changed to read *1780* at some point, and then changed back to *1775* later. Judging from the evidence of handwriting and watermarks, Plath argues that 1775 is probably correct for the last four concertos, but that the first concerto probably originally bore a date of 1773.

We do not know if Mozart wrote these concertos initially for his own use, although we do know that he played them in public on at least a few occasions. They cannot originally have been intended (as has often erroneously been stated) for the first concertmaster of the Salzburg orchestra, Antonio Brunetti, even though Brunetti eventually did perform some of them, because the Italian violinist assumed that post only in 1776. Mozart himself had held the title of concertmaster since July 9, 1772.

One concerto is described in a letter to Mozart from his father as "the concerto you wrote for Kolb." This refers to the Salzburg violinist Franz Xaver Kolb, who is recorded in the Mozart family's correspondence as having performed the concerto with success in Salzburg in September 1777 and July 1778. It may well have been the same concerto that Kolb played in August 1777, at a concert given by the Mozart family in their large room known as the Dancing-Master's Hall. We do not know which, if any, of the five concertos in question was the one written for Kolb, as the frequent pairing of him with this first violin concerto in the Mozart literature is nothing more than guesswork.

The great artistic distance that Mozart traveled in the period between his first and fifth violin concertos has frequently been remarked upon. And it is undeniably true that his last contributions to the genre have a kind of pristine perfection that defies explanation. Less frequently noticed, however, is the excellence of this first concerto. It is difficult to say what led up to this auspicious beginning. We know that Mozart admired the violin concertos of "the divine Bohemian," Josef Mysliveček (1737–81), and that he had in his repertory a violin concerto, also in B-flat major, by another fine Bohemian composer, Johann Baptist Vanhal (1739–1813).

The seriousness with which Mozart approached this first violin concerto is suggested by the fact that all three movements are in sonata form—the form reserved by the composers of the Classical period for many of their weightier utterances. Another hint is that the slow movement is marked Adagio, rather than the less intense Andante that Mozart often chose for his more *galant* notions.

The rollicking first movement is notable for its treatment of a varying series of themes and also at one point for an oddly un-Mozartean sort of musical stutter. It opens with a relatively brief orchestral ritornello, or passage without soloist, that features a theme reminiscent of the music of Johann Christian Bach, whom Mozart knew as a child.

The Adagio opens with a poignant section reminiscent of a Mozartean aria for a soprano heroine longing for her distant lover. The brief development section is dominated by the passionate pleadings of the soloist. Soloist and orchestra join forces for the recapitulation, formed of a striking reshuffling of the ideas of the exposition, this leading to the cadenza and a brief closing tutti.

The Finale begins in the style of a quickstep march. Both orchestra and soloist then show off their skill at rapid scales, arpeggios and *bariolage*—rapid alternation of stopped and open strings. Only the briefest interludes of lyricism are permitted to intrude upon the general hustle-bustle and high spirits, and these brief passages are usually brusquely interrupted by a rude remark from the orchestra or a blaze of virtuosity from the soloist. The development section leans heavily upon the soloist and (as in the first movement) the use of triplet figurations. The recapitulation also exploits the soloist to the fullest, but the opening quickstep is suppressed, never to reappear. Like many concerto finales, this one presents the soloist with opportunities for a couple of short cadenzas in addition to the longer one in its usual location near the end. Mozart and his contemporaries called this kind of shorter cadenza an *Eingang,* which means "lead-in," and its purpose, in fact, is to lead in to a return of one or another of the main themes of the movement.

N.Z.

K. 190 *Concertone in C major (K^3 166b, K^6 186E)*

Origin: Salzburg, May 31, 1774
Scoring: 2 violins soli, 2 oboes, 2 horns, 2 trumpets, strings
Movements: Allegro spiritoso. Andantino grazioso. Tempo di Menuetto.

Mozart's autograph manuscript of this work, now in private possession in Switzerland, is inscribed in his own hand:

"Concertone. / di Wolfgango Amadeo Mozart/à Salisburgo li 31 maggio / 1774." Mozart was eighteen years old. A few months earlier he had completed his much-admired "little" G-minor Symphony, K. 183, as well as his first piano concerto, K. 175, and he was soon to begin work on an opera for Munich for the Carnival of 1774–75, *La finta giardiniera*. For what performers the Concertone was created is, unfortunately, not documented, but the addition of trumpets to the usual oboes and horns suggests that the occasion may have been a festive one.

The unusual title "Concertone" was one in limited use in Southern Germany, Austria, and Northern Italy during the mid-eighteenth century. It means literally "grand concerto" which is similar to the Italian concerto grosso. In Mannheim, Paris, or London, such a work would probably have been entitled "sinfonia concertante." These were all different ways of labeling a concerto with more than one soloist. In the case of the present work, the two solo violins are active throughout, the solo oboe has important contributions to make in all three movements, and the solo cello is heard only briefly in each movement. Mozart's concertone resembles (at least in its quirky selection of solo instruments) three of Joseph Haydn's early programmatic symphonies, *Le Matin, Le Midi,* and *Le Soir* (Nos. 6, 7, and 8).

Mozart must have thought highly of the Concertone, for he took it with him on his journey to Mannheim, Munich, and Paris (1777–78) in search of a job. His father urged him to have it performed at Mannheim, but Mozart succeeded only in playing it at the piano for a fellow composer, who advised him that it was the sort of work in fashion in Paris. He also played it more than once for a famous connoisseur, the Baron von Bagge, then at Mannheim but known in Paris for his musical salon. According to Mozart, von Bagge liked the piece so much that he was "quite beside himself." But as far as we know, the Concertone was never performed in Paris.

The first movement is in the easy, *galant* style of Bach's youngest son, Johann Christian. The beautifully written out cadenza accomplishes in a few bars what many a longer cadenza has failed to do: it gives a dramatic summation of the movement.

The slow unfolding of the thirty-two-bar tutti that begins the Andantino suggests immediately the large scale on which this movement is constructed. The long, graceful melodies both here and in the solos that follow remind us of a society in which time passed more slowly and the fastest ways people could get where they were going were on horseback or aboard a sailing vessel.

The Finale is, rather exceptionally, cast in the form of a Minuet and Trio. Although not of extraordinary length for the finale of a concerto whose previous movements are on such a grand scale, the movement is large for a minuet. Mozart's ballroom minuets with trio from this period average about thirty-four measures, his symphonic minuets about sixty, but the Finale of the Concertone reaches 151 measures. The movement is the most conventional of the three; what individuality it has comes from the cavorting of the soloists in the Trio, punctuated by some fine writing for the orchestra's oboes and horns, forming an impromptu wind band.

N.Z.

K. 211 *Violin Concerto in D major, No. 2*
Origin: Salzburg, June 14, 1775
Scoring: violin solo, 2 oboes, 2 horns, strings
Movements: Allegro moderato. Andante. Rondeau: Allegro.

K. 211 is the first of four violin concertos—K. 211, 216, 218, and 219—that Mozart composed within a six-month period from June 14 to December 20, 1775. More than two years had passed since he had written his first violin concerto. In the meantime he had written the Concertone (1774), as well as two Serenades, K. 185 (1773) and 203 (1774), each of which contained a miniature three-movement violin concerto within its eight-movement format—a pattern that Mozart was soon to repeat in Serenades K. 204 (1775) and 250 (1776). The second violin concerto stands at the chronological threshold of Mozart's greatest accomplishments in the string concerto medium.

If one may venture a guess about what Mozart learned from his first concerto, it was to be more economical with his materials. Although the difference between the two concertos in playing time is slight, the second is tighter in structure and more organic in relationships between themes and sections. The sound of the second concerto is brighter, too, because a sharp key calls into play the resonance of the open strings of the violins. Although Mozart eschewed virtuosity for its own sake, the demands made on the soloist in this concerto are not inconsiderable. Yet, when the work was first published in 1802, it was under the title *Concerto facile* (Easy Concerto). This reveals the attitude of the early nineteenth century, which was increasingly fascinated by the possibilities of transcendental virtuosity. Beethoven's violin concerto of 1806, for instance, owes more to the example of the famous composer-virtuoso Giovanni Battista Viotti than to that of Mozart.

The first movement finds Mozart exploring several avenues not visited in the earlier work, including some interesting touches of chromaticism and a few moments of delicious irony (as in those passages in which an "oom-pah" bass line suggests that Mozart's tongue is firmly planted in his cheek).

The Andante, in G major, is filled from beginning to end with a serene lyricism. There is no touch of pathos, except perhaps for a few unexpected silences, during which the listener may well wonder whether the world can really be as lacking in tension as it is portrayed here.

The fact that Mozart labeled the Finale in French ("rondeau") rather than in Italian ("rondo") has given rise to speculation about possible French models or influences at work in the movement. It should not be overlooked, however, that Mozart was at no pains to hide his dislike of most of the French music of his time. In the 1770s the Italian-speaking composers and their imitators were preeminent in opera, the German-speaking composers in instrumental music, and the French in dance music. Mozart's Rondeau refrain is, in fact, in the style of a French minuet, while the working out of the movement as a whole is strictly in the German-Italian style. The Minuet recurs three times. N.Z.

K. 216 *Violin Concerto in G major, "Strassburg," No. 3*
Origin: Salzburg, September 12, 1775
Scoring: solo violin, 2 oboes, 2 horns, strings
Movements: Allegro. Adagio. Rondeau: Allegro.

Mozart's activities during the summer of 1775 are not known to have been extraordinary. He is credited with composing a church sonata (K. 212), a divertimento (K. 213), a serenade (K. 204), and a march (K. 214). There is recorded no personal or musical experience that would explain a striking elevation of his style. Yet every commentator has noted that the first two violin concertos, fine as they are, are on a lower plane of inspiration than the last three. It is perhaps in the nature of Mozart's precocious genius that no explanation for this can be or need be given, for as long as he practiced his art he continued to grow.

The first movement opens with a ritornello that, in quite another form and key, Mozart had used elsewhere. He had invented this cheerful opening as the ritornello of an aria in his serenata *Il rè pastore*. K. 208, which had had its first performance (probably only an unstaged, concert version, however) in Salzburg on April 23, 1775. The aria, "Aer tranquillo," is sung by the nobly born foundling Aminta, the "shepherd king" of the opera's title. The text is in two sections, the first expressing Aminta's satisfaction with his lot as a shepherd, the second begging the gods to help him if he must give up this simple life.

A comparison between the aria and the concerto movement reinforces the often-stated notion that a concerto is a species of musical drama in which the violinist and the orchestra are protagonists. And the sense of an ongoing drama is heightened in the first movement of the present concerto by the increasingly articulate role assigned the orchestra during the solo passages, as well as by a recitative-like section.

In tone, the Adagio, in the dominant key of D major, differs not only from the previous movement but from the middle movements of the two previous concertos. Certain aspects of this new sound are straightforwardly attributable to the substitution of two flutes for the two oboes (in Mozart's orchestra they would have been played by the same performers), to the horns moving to a lower key, to the muting of the orchestral violins, and to the pizzicati of the cellos and basses. In addition, however, there is a further change, much more subtle and harder to define. Perhaps some of the mystery may lie in the flawless way in which, when the opening of the movement returns near the end, the melodies are provided with a delicate overlay of *fioritura*. And some of it may be the seemingly careless manner in which the melody occasionally ignores the triplets of the accompaniment and goes its own way with groups of two or four notes. But to touch on these important aspects is still to fall short of a full explanation of this movement's surpassing beauty.

In a letter written to his son at the beginning of October 1777, Leopold Mozart reported that at a performance of a play in Salzburg, "Brunetti had to play a concerto during an intermission while costumes were being changed, and it was the one of yours that contains the 'Strassburger.' He played extremely well, but in both Allegros was occasionally out of tune, and once nearly overextended himself in a cadenza." A few weeks later Mozart wrote to his father that he had gone with his uncle (Leopold's brother) to spend the day at the Holy Cross Monastery in Augsburg. Mozart performed various pieces of his at lunch and in the evening, including his "Strassburg concerto", "which went like oil. Everyone praised my beautiful, pure tone." In most writings on Mozart, the "Strassburg" Concerto is identified as the Concerto No. 4 in D Major, K. 218. But as we shall see, research by Hungarian musicologist Dénes Bartha has demonstrated conclusively that K. 216 is Mozart's "Strassburg" Concerto.

The Rondo Finale develops in the more or less expected pattern, and we progress as far as **A-B-A-C-A-D** when, long before the **D** section can reach any sort of conclusion, it breaks off abruptly with three tutti chords. After a brief pause, the Allegro in 3/8 time is replaced by an Andante *alla breve,* and the solo violin performs an elegant gavotte in G minor, accompanied by the string section playing pizzicato. But before it reaches its conclusion, the music breaks off once again in mid-phrase and Mozart launches into yet another tune, a lusty one, also in *alla breve* time but now Allegretto and returning to G major. It is this gay tune that Bartha's researches have shown is a song known in Mozart's day under the title "The Strassburger." (Unfortunately, only the tune without any words has been recovered; perhaps it was dance and not a song.)

After another brief pause comes the return of the jig, and, soon, of the Rondo refrain itself. Then, one more episode and the movement ends as it began, with the winds having the last word. N.Z.

K. 218 ***Violin Concerto in D major, No. 4***
Origin: Salzburg, October 1775
Scoring: violin solo, 2 oboes, 2 horns, strings
Movements: Allegro. Andante cantabile. Rondeau: Andante grazioso.

Like the opening of the previous concerto, the fourth concerto begins in martial fashion, but this time Mozart introduces a beautifully contrasting section into the orchestral ritornello and returns to the noisy energy of the opening for only the last few measures before the soloist enters. That entrance is effected with the ritornello's opening fanfare, but transposed up two octaves. In fact, throughout the movement Mozart seems to have taken special pleasure in lifting the solo violin out of the orchestral texture and highlighting its activities. It is undoubtedly the heightening of simultaneous expressivity and virtuosity in this movement that has made it such a perennial favorite with violinists and audiences alike.

The Andante cantabile, in the dominant key of A major, is just what its heading suggests: a "singing" movement. The quiet contentment of this piece is established from the very first note of the broad opening theme, which recurs in the middle of the movement, and (disguised somewhat) in the coda. The virtuosity of the outer movements is absent here, replaced by an unabashed melodic outpouring. An especially lovely touch is furnished by the little canonic echoes that the oboe offers the soloist just prior to the return of the opening material in the middle of the movement. The opening idea of the Andante cantabile is one that Mozart used briefly earlier in a subsidiary role in the Finale of his concertone. It also serves in this concerto, speeded up and turned into 6/8 in the Allegro ma non troppo section of the Finale.

The brief, dance-inspired Andante grazioso in 2/4 that opens the finale recurs three times during the course of the movement. It is always followed by a larger, jig-like Allegro ma non troppo section in 6/8, but whereas the Andante is always the same, the Allegro only begins the same way in its four appearances and then branches off into something new.

Between the second and third occurrence of this andante-allegro unit, there is an interruption rather similar in effect to the interruption in the Finale of the previous concerto. The new tune introduced at this point is in G major, in cut time, and is marked Andante grazioso.

Like the "Strassburger" tune, it is a contredanse and includes a rustic drone. This melody may have folk, or popular, origins as well, as some commentators have suggested, but no source for it has yet been uncovered. We do know, however, that Mozart revised it and turned it into the first of a set of four contredanses, K. 269b (see the note on p. 219). N.Z.

K. 219 *Violin Concerto in A major, "Turkish," No. 5*

Origin: Salzburg, December 20, 1775
Scoring: violin solo, 2 oboes, 2 horns, strings
Movements: Allegro aperto. Adagio. Rondeau: Tempo di Menuetto.

With this concerto we reach the last of the group of five works that constitute Mozart's central contribution to the violin concerto repertory. Once again we are in the dark about the precise occasion for which the piece was written. All five of Mozart's violin concertos are filled with witty and humorous moments. Sometimes we smile, hardly knowing why; at other times the joke is plain. English music scholar, composer, and pianist Sir Donald Tovey writes of this aspect of young Mozart's style as a "special vein of epigrammatic comedy," and this is nowhere more evident than in the present concerto. But the pervasive good humor of the splendid first movement does not hide its underlying poetry.

The opening ritornello begins with great energy and conviction, introducing a number of attractive ideas. The innocuous upward arpeggio with which the orchestral introduction ends—a most improbable idea—is developed later on in the movement and serves to end it. The violinist enters not in the usual way, with either a return to the beginning of the movement or a transitional flourish leading to that return, but rather with a totally unexpected six-bar Adagio.

The slow movement, an Adagio in E major, has been thought by some critics to bear a resemblance to the aria "O wie ängstlich, o wie feurig" from *The Abduction from the Seraglio,* an aria in which Belmonte expresses his eager anticipation at being reunited with his love, Constanze. The movement is on a larger scale than the slow movements of any of the previous violin concertos.

The Finale gives this concerto its nickname. Like the finales of the two previous violin concertos, it is a Rondo organized around an interruption. The refrain of the Rondo is a Minuet, as are the first episodes. The courtly elegance of the Minuet places us firmly in the West, ready for a confrontation with the infidel East, which appears in the form of a "Turkish" section: the interruption.

Turkish subjects were popular in Western Europe at this time. Mozart, Gluck, Haydn, Grétry, and others wrote operas with Turkish settings. But of course Mozart's "Turkish" music is not really Turkish, for even had he known such music firsthand (which is improbable), the notation he used could not have conveyed, nor could the musicians for whom he wrote have performed, its microtonal intervals and "irrational" rhythms. What then is the origin of his "Turkish" music? (It is found not only in this concerto, but in *The Abduction,* in the Finale of the A major piano sonata, K. 331, and in a couple of other pieces.) The answer, worked out with great clarity by the late Hungarian musicologist Bence Szabolcsi, is this: Hungarian and gypsy music from areas abutting the Ottoman Empire.

In those areas, in which there had long been both peaceful and warlike interactions with the Muslims, the Christian peasants and the gypsies were influenced in their music-making by the Eastern music they heard and sometimes imitated or parodied. Some of the features that Mozart picked up in his desire to convey a sense of the exotic to his listeners include: a leaping melody, a drone bass with percussive repeated notes, odd chromatic touches to the melody, swirling ornamentation, mostly in the form of grace notes, trills, and turns, and a lively march-like tempo. In one area of Hungary the peasants call this style of music *Törökös,* which means precisely the same as Mozart's own "alla turca," namely, "in the Turkish manner."

The invigorating result of this borrowing is not a transcription of eighteenth-century Turkish music, but, rather, a parody of a parody. Although this music is in a completely Western manner, it evokes something foreign that is simultaneously the subject of admiration, fear, and ridicule. As to where Mozart could have heard such music, it may have been in Pressburg, Hungary (now the Czechoslovakian city of Bratislava), which he visited briefly in 1762, not long before his seventh birthday. Or it may have been on his extensive travels in Western Europe, during which he encountered itinerant musicians from many nations. But most likely it came from his senior colleague at Salzburg, Michael Haydn, who, before assuming his post there, had worked in Hungary and who spiced several of his own pieces with pseudo-Turkish elements.

The form of this Rondo could be schematized as **A-B-A-C-A-D-A-B-A,** but this would be somewhat misleading since the **D** section, which is the "Turkish" interruption, is much longer than any of the others and is itself a rondo structure. Hence, we have a pair of rondos, or a rondo within a rondo. In the "Turkish" section there occurs three times a characteristic leaping theme that was not new to Mozart when he included it in this Finale. He had already used it in a ballet entitled *Le gelosie del Serraglio* (Jealousy in the Harem), K. 135a, written in December 1772 in Milan for performance with his just-completed opera, *Lucio Silla,* K. 135. The completed version of this ballet is lost, but sketches survive that show Mozart intended to employ the leaping theme in A major as a brief contredanse, and then in A minor as a more extended finale. The title of the lost ballet confirms the symbolism assigned to the exotic portion of the violin concerto. N.Z.

K. 261 *Adagio in E major*
Origin: Salzburg, 1776
Scoring: violin solo, 2 flutes, 2 horns, strings

K. 269 *Rondo in B-flat major (K⁶ 261a)*
Origin: Salzburg, 1776
Scoring: violin solo, 2 oboes, 2 horns, strings

K. 373 *Rondo in C major*
Origin: Vienna, April 2, 1781
Scoring: violin solo, 2 oboes, 2 horns, strings

These three independent movements were written for the Salzburg concertmaster Antonio Brunetti, as we learn from the Mozart family's correspondence.

The Adagio, K. 261, and the Rondo, K. 269, have often been linked, because Leopold Mozart mentioned them in a letter of September to his son as "the Adagio and Rondo that you composed for Brunetti," and because they were first published together as "Adagio et Rondo pour le Violin, oeuvre 99." But there can be no question of the two works having been intended as a unit, for the key relation between them does not permit that. In fact, they may have been written as substitute movements for the fifth and first violin concertos respectively.

The autograph of the Adagio, K. 261, bears the brief note, "Di Amadeo Wolfgango Mozart, 1776." It was undoubtedly this work that Leopold referred to in his letter of October 9, 1777, as "the Adagio you wrote specially for Brunetti, because he found the other one too artificial." "The other one" must refer to the slow movement of the A major Concerto (No. 5), K. 219, which is the only one that could accommodate a slow movement in E major.

Mozart returns here to his idea in the slow movement of the third concerto of muting the orchestral violins and replacing the oboes with flutes. With the horns tuned a fourth lower (E instead of A), the orchestra takes on a new sheen, which would provide a fine foil for the bright sounds of the outer movements of K. 219. Whether or not the movement can truly be said to be less "artificial" than the original slow movement is a question difficult to answer. If Brunetti was looking for a somewhat simpler piece containing less artifice than the original slow movement, he was probably disappointed. The movement begins in a serene *cantabile* vein, but soon enough musical complexities and a certain amount of melodic (but not harmonic) chromaticism are introduced. To modern ears the result is attractive but not superior to the original slow movement of K. 219. The new movement is, in any case, noticeably shorter than the old one, and this may perhaps have been something that Brunetti requested.

Toward the end of his life Mozart was commissioned to write some pieces (K. 594, 608, and 616) for what were then called musical clocks but what we would now call music boxes. The existence in a Leipzig collection of one such instrument of the period that plays an arrangement of the Adagio, K. 261, suggests that Mozart himself may have returned to his beautiful piece a decade after he wrote it and reworked it for another purpose.

The Rondo in B-flat major, K. 269, bears only the inscription "Rondeaux" on the autograph manuscript, but since it was, as we have seen, mentioned in Leopold's letter in the same breath with the Adagio, K. 261, which is dated 1776, that date has been assigned to it too. It is not clear why this work is usually known under the title "Rondo Concertante." Speculation about the work's origin suggests that Mozart eventually came to consider that the original sonata-form Finale of his first concerto was unsuccessful, and wrote (for one of Brunetti's Salzburg performances) this brief Rondo Finale more in line with his later thinking on the matter.

The attractive tune with which the Rondo begins must have appealed to Mozart, because he planned to use it in a ballet in Paris in 1778—a project that never came to fruition. The slender plot of the unfinished, untitled ballet (K. 299c), as well as it can be made out from Mozart's sketches, involves a man who dares to dance with another woman while his wife is temporarily absent. The little tune that forms the refrain of the concerto was to have been the *pas de deux* in which the man dances with the other woman.

Unlike most of the other works for violin and orchestra, the creation of the Rondo in C major, K. 373, is documented. In 1781 Mozart, along with Brunetti and the castrato Francesco Ceccarelli, was ordered to accompany the archbishop of Salzburg on a visit to Vienna. On April 8 the archbishop commanded that a concert be given, and that evening Mozart wrote to his father: "Today (for I am writing at 11 o'clock at night) we had a concert, where three of my compositions were performed—new ones, of course; a concerto-rondo for Brunetti [K. 373]; a sonata for myself with violin accompaniment [K. 379], which I composed last night between 11 and 12 (but in order to be able to finish it, I wrote out only the accompaniment for Brunetti and retained my own part in my head); and then a rondo [K. 374] for Ceccarelli, which he had to repeat." The autograph of K. 373 has gone astray, but it reportedly bore the legend, "Wien am 2. April 1781," confirming that the work was indeed new—just six days old—when it received its first performance.

It would be inaccurate to state that K. 373 shows signs of haste in its composition, because it is perfectly wrought, and charming of its sort. But in comparing it to Mozart's several other violin concerto rondos, we cannot but notice that this one is briefer and less seriously worked out. Or to put it another way, had Mozart written this rondo after writing two other concerto movements, he most likely would have made it a bit weightier than this admittedly delightful occasional piece. N.Z.

K. 364 ***Sinfonia Concertante in E-flat major (K⁶ 320d)***

Origin: Salzburg, 1779

Scoring: violin and viola soli, 2 oboes, 2 horns, strings

Movements: Allegro maestoso. Andante. Presto.

We know even less about the genesis of the Sinfonia Concertante, K. 364, than about that of the Concertone, K. 190. The original score is lost, and the brief autograph fragments that do survive bear no indications of date or provenance. The work is thought to date from the summer of 1779, when Mozart was twenty-three years old. It has generally been supposed that after his return from Paris, where works in sinfonia-concertante form were all the rage, Mozart may have wished to introduce the genre to Salzburg, and that this work was the result.

About the same time that he wrote K. 364, Mozart also attempted a sinfonia concertante for violin, viola, cello, and orchestra (K. 320e), but he abandoned it and it remained only a noble torso. The two works have a technical peculiarity in common: the solo viola part is transposed to a lower key, forcing the violist to tune the instrument higher in order to sound in the same key as the other instruments. In the present work, the viola part is notated in D major, and the violist must tune each string a half step higher to sound in E-flat major.

Mozart's reasons for taking this unusual step may be surmised: the higher tuning makes the tone of the viola more brilliant and increases the ease with which rapid passages can be articulated. Furthermore, the viola playing in D on open strings has added resonance that will be lacking to the violin playing in E flat. Thus the usually milder viola is put on a more equal footing with the customarily more brilliant violin. Mozart was an excellent violist as well as violinist, and he treats the two instruments with absolute equality throughout this double concerto, often giving to the viola in the recapitulations what he had given to the violin in the expositions.

This work has many fervent admirers. Alec Hyatt King, an English musicologist, calls it a giant in comparison with Mozart's other music of the period: "It towers up as would the Matterhorn if transplanted to stand among the gentle foothills and lesser peaks that rise from the Salzburg plain." Although the orchestra calls for only oboes and horns with the usual strings, Mozart deepens and enriches it partly through passages where the various string choirs are divided, partly through the frequently *concertante* treatment of the oboes and horns in the outer movements.

The long first movement is so full of thematic substance—some six motifs in the opening tutti, followed by about six new ones when the soloists enter—that the listener cannot take everything in at a first hearing but must come back to the movement again and again to do it full justice.

With the Andante, the music ceases to be *galant* and amusing, the key shifts to C minor, and the whole takes on a demeanor of the utmost seriousness. In fact, the grave atmosphere of this movement transcends anything found in the other works for violin and orchestra. Some of the writing sounds deliberately archaic. The model seems to be not the carefree extroversion of the London Bach, Johann Christian, who served Mozart as a model so often, but rather the sensitive introspection of the Berlin and Hamburg Bach, Carl Philipp Emanuel.

In listening to this movement, it is hard to avoid the notion that we are witnessing the expression of some inner emotions, and at least one commentator has speculated that Mozart may have been paying tribute to his mother, who had died in 1778 at the age of fifty-seven, while accompanying him on his trip to Paris.

The Finale returns to the happier realms of the first movement, and in typical finale fashion presents us with a Rondo based upon lively, dancelike tunes. Mozart is not so lavish with his melodies here as in the opening movement, but still quite lavish enough.

N.Z.

CONCERTOS FOR WINDS

Frederick the Great playing a flute concerto with his court musicians at San Souci, Potsdam. Engraving by P. Haas.

Frederick did this daily almost without interruption throughout his reign. Only close associates and family were admitted to these royal musicales where the repertory centered on concertos written by the king himself or by his flute teacher, Johann Joachim Quantz.

BACKGROUND AND OVERVIEW

Mozart possessed a consuming interest in the solo qualities of wind instruments. In his compositions for orchestra, and especially in his piano concertos, concert arias, and operas, he gave winds an importance and an independence that was unprecedented in the music of his time. Not only did he give them passages in which they speak as a band totally unsupported by strings, but he often gave them solo and ensemble passages of obbligato proportions. From the horn obbligato in the early opera *Mitridate,* K. 87, to the one for trombone in the Requiem, K. 626, at one time or another the composer gave a prominent role to every standard wind instrument that was available to him (he even wrote a trumpet concerto, a work that has, unfortunately, been lost).

The strongly individual flavors of the

different wind instruments impressed Mozart deeply. But, as with singers, his readiness to write for them was dependent ultimately upon his knowledge of the abilities of the performers themselves. He came to know intimately many wind players who possessed talents of the highest order. But curiously it was the personalities of these performers as much as their artistry that seem to have attracted the composer. He was stimulated by their company and, paradoxically perhaps, even by their human shortcomings. Thus Mozart was inspired by the brilliance of the wind players in Mannheim and elsewhere, and he seemed curiously accepting of their sometimes loose morals. The clarinet virtuoso Anton Stadler—a man whom one can sense Mozart loved deeply—apparently cheated Mozart mercilessly and actually was in debt to him for 500 gulden at the time of the composer's death, a sum greater than one half the annual income of either man. Yet it was for Stadler that Mozart wrote many of his most heartfelt compositions for the clarinet.

With the wind concertos the paradox goes even deeper, because writing them proved to be economically disastrous for Mozart. He received half his fee for the flute concertos (but then he delivered only half the number he had promised) and no payment at all for the flute and harp concerto. The horn concertos were probably presents to a friend of his, the horn player Joseph Leutgeb, and the clarinet concerto certainly can be included as part of Stadler's unpaid debt to Mozart. Fortunately none of these hazards seems to have deterred him. The concertos come from the pen of a man whose understanding of wind instruments had never before been approached and whose wide experience with them was unparalleled. R.H.

K. 191 *Bassoon Concerto in B-flat major (K⁶ 186e)*

Origin: Salzburg, June 4, 1774
Scoring: bassoon solo, 2 oboes, 2 horns, strings
Movements: Allegro. Andante ma adagio. Rondo: Tempo di Menuetto.

It is possible that Mozart wrote as many as five bassoon concertos; only one survives. In all likelihood, this concerto was written for one of the two bassoonists employed by the archbishop in Salzburg—Johann Heinrich Schulz or Melchoir Sandmayr. It is the first of Mozart's extant concertos for a wind instrument, and, by common consent, a little masterpiece.

To accompany the bassoon, Mozart employed his standard orchestra of strings, oboes, and horns, though use of the wind instruments is reserved mainly for the orchestral passages and, in the solos, to those sections in which the soloist is confined to long notes.

The concerto bears witness to Mozart's skilled use of the orchestra to accompany an instrument that has limitations both of range and power. In compensating for these shortcomings the composer is able positively to embrace the bassoon's virtues—its lyrical gift, its agility, its rich sonorities, its wit, and its wide-stepping ability. Mozart has thus achieved a concerto intrinsically for the bassoon (as any cellist who has attempted to arrange the work for his own instrument will readily testify).

The opening orchestral passage falls naturally into three parts, beginning with a truncated version of the first subject and ending with an arpeggiated codetta that, throughout the movement, the orchestra always reserves for itself, and with which it marks off the various sections.

The British critic Alec Hyatt King refers

to the second movement as a "dreamy arioso." Certainly there is an operatic quality about the serene melody entrusted to the bassoon that extends beyond its possibly accidental similarity to the Countess's aria "Porgi amor" from *The Marriage of Figaro,* K. 492; the feeling of somberness is also intensified by the strings, muted throughout the movement.

The last movement is one of Mozart's minuet finales; that is, a movement based on the rhythm, rather than the actual form, of a minuet. He called it a Rondo, but it is in fact a mixture of rondo and variation. R.H.

K³ 271k *Oboe Concerto in C major*

Origin: Salzburg, 1777
Scoring: oboe solo, 2 oboes, 2 horns, strings
Movements: Allegro aperto. Andante ma non troppo. Allegro.

During his years in Salzburg in the mid-1770s Mozart's interest in wind instruments grew. For instance, he wrote five divertimenti for oboes, bassoons, and horns for the archbishop's dinner table, and he employed a solo oboe prominently in the Concertone for Two Violins and Orchestra, K. 190. He also wrote, sometime before October 1777, a concerto in C major for the principal oboist in Salzburg, Giuseppe Ferlendis. For many years the work was assumed to be yet another in the tragically long list of lost works by Mozart, but research has established that the Flute Concerto in D major, K. 314, written in Mannheim in 1778, is in fact nothing other than a reworking of this earlier oboe concerto.

The oboe concerto remained a favorite with Mozart. He made a present of it to Friedrich Ramm, the oboist of the Mannheim orchestra, and recorded that Ramm was "quite crazy with delight," and that in February 1778 "Herr Ramm (by way of a change) played for the fifth time my oboe concerto written for Ferlendis, which is making a great sensation here. It is now Ramm's *cheval de bataille* [war horse]." The oboist's delight in the gift was no doubt due to the flood of beautiful melodies that Mozart offered his soloist.

The concerto opens with the normal orchestral ritornello, ending with a downward-curving orchestral tailpiece that Mozart uses constantly in this movement at decisive moments. Hard upon this the soloist enters with a seemingly unending melody that is replete with pure joyousness. Mozart here found much to his liking a new method of accompanying the soloist by means of the violins only. He frequently returned to the device in this concerto, and in others requiring light accompaniment for a relatively light-voiced solo instrument.

After a sonorous orchestral introduction, the soloist dominates the slow movement with an expansive and highly decorated melody, much of which is again accompanied only by the violins.

The Finale is a beautifully integrated rondo in which ideas from the opening portion find their way into the two subsequent episodes. The Rondo theme itself inspired Mozart when he came to compose his opera *The Abduction from the Seraglio,* K. 384; it has strong similarities with Blonde's aria, "Welche Wonne, welche Lust." R.H.

K. 313 *Flute Concerto in G major (K⁶ 285c)*

Origin: Mannheim, early 1778
Scoring: flute solo, 2 oboes, 2 horns, strings

Movements: Allegro maestoso. Adagio non troppo. Rondeau: Tempo di Menuetto.

On September 23, 1777, Mozart set out from Salzburg on a tour that took him principally to Mannheim and Paris. It is well known that he was overwhelmed by the brilliance of the Mannheim orchestra in the employ of Karl Theodor, Elector Palatine. This orchestra had achieved a Continental reputation for the precision of its ensemble, its bowing, its dynamic effects, and the accuracy of its phrasing. Mozart was particularly impressed by Mannheim's wind players, as much (it would appear) for their readiness to befriend him as for the brilliance of their playing. His letters frequently reflect his enthusiasm for Johann Baptist Wendling, Friedrich Ramm, and Georg Wenzel Ritter, respectively principals on flute, oboe, and bassoon.

The twenty-one-year-old composer came to know Wendling's family intimately—he orchestrated one of Wendling's flute concertos, composed several works for members of his family, frequently took his meals with them, and eventually lodged with them. Wendling, for his part, interceded with the Elector to obtain commissions or employment for Mozart. When this did not work, and there was a very real risk that Mozart would have to leave Mannheim, Wendling found other freelance work for him, including a commission to write some concertos and quartets for a wealthy amateur flutist named Ferdinand de Jean. Mozart was to receive 200 gulden for these pieces—a sizable sum that many musicians would have taken more than six months to earn.

To his father Mozart stressed his determination to complete the commission within two months. But even at this stage Leopold Mozart evidently had reservations about these assurances and by the end of January 1778 it was apparent that he was indeed right: his son was procrastinating and the commission was probably more extensive than he had at first admitted. Mozart's dilatory attitude served only to make his father extremely angry. His fear was that if Wolfgang did not soon complete the works he would not receive his money.

He was more than half right. On February 14 Mozart told his father that Wendling and Ramm were leaving Mannheim for Paris, adding, "M. de Jean is also leaving for Paris tomorrow and, because I have only finished two concertos and three quartets for him, has sent me 96 gulden [that is, 4 gulden short of the total]; but he must pay me in full, for that was my agreement with the Wendlings, and I can send him the other pieces later."

Leopold, who was not deficient in simple arithmetic, immediately perceived that the commission must have been for four concertos and six quartets, since his son was given only half the agreed sum. In a blistering letter he upbraided Wolfgang for lying to him. Wolfgang produced some lame excuses, concluding with an astonishing sentence that has troubled commentators on his flute music ever since it was published: "Moreover, you know that I become quite powerless whenever I am obliged to write for an instrument that I cannot bear." The sentence, if it has been properly interpreted, presents us with the extraordinary paradox of a composer creating some of the most charming and idiomatic flute music ever conceived—and detesting the flute!

It seems that Mozart was lucky to receive as much money from de Jean as he did, assuming that the flute pieces we know of now are the sum of his finished work. Three quartets at the most can be attributed to the commission, and no more than two concertos and a single extra movement—and of the concertos, the one in D (K. 314) was no more than an arrangement of his earlier Concerto in C for oboe (271k) (see the notes for the Flute Quartets K. 285, 285a, and 285b, p. 261.) Ramm's many performances of this work must have been known by de Jean, so he would hardly have been grateful for a second-hand composition. Mozart really had no grounds to complain.

The Flute Concerto in G major, K. 313, seems therefore to have been the only original one to come from de Jean's commission. Yet it gives no sign of Mozart's possible distaste for the instrument. It is full of humor, warmth, and refined good taste. As with every instrument he wrote for, he learned and assimilated the flute's technical potential and never embarrassed the performer by exceeding it. He uses his customary orchestra of strings, oboes, and horns for the outer movements.

The opening orchestral ritornello presents the somewhat pompous first subject, merely hints at the second, and adds a rhythmically arpeggiated codetta of its own that recurs throughout the movement at moments of structural significance, very much as in the first movement of the oboe concerto.

In the slow movement Mozart replaces his oboes with two flutes, which, against an accompaniment of muted strings, spell out in harmony the sensuous melody later to be played alone by the soloist. Their soft sound rather than the penetrating timbre of the oboes seems exactly what Mozart required in this warm and gentle movement.

The Finale, in sonata rondo form, is one of Mozart's elegant finales in minuet tempo. Its quality has inspired many tributes: American musicologist Alfred Einstein speaks of it as "a veritable fountain of good spirits and fresh invention," while British musicologist Alec Hyatt King refers to its "easy graceful style which conceals a wealth of imaginative detail and clever formal planning." R.H.

K. 314 *Flute Concerto in D major (K^6 285d)*

This work is Mozart's arrangement of the Oboe Concerto in C major, K. 271k. See the notes for the Oboe Concerto, K. 271k, and for the Flute Concerto in G major, K. 313, above.

K. 299 *Flute and Harp Concerto in C major (K^6 297c)*

Origin: Paris, April 1778
Scoring: flute and harp soli, 2 oboes, 2 horns, strings
Movements: Allegro. Andantino. Rondeau: Allegro.

Among the other compositions Mozart was working on during his stay in Paris was the Concerto for Flute and Harp. His mother made the first, somewhat confused, reference to it as "two concertos, one for the flute and one for the harp." Mozart can seldom have found a commission more distasteful than this one, disliking as he apparently did both the flute and the harp. Once again an ironical twist of fate was to confront him with a disagreeable task, and once again the expected recompense was not forthcoming. Even though he completed a concerto full of lyrical beauty and of technical complexity almost ideally suited to its exponents, he was to be deprived of his fee.

Baron Grimm, a lifelong friend of

Mozart's family, introduced him to the Count of Guines, who commissioned this concerto. Adrien-Louis Bonnière de Souastre, Comte de Guines (his complete title), was at the time governor of the province of Artois. He had been a French diplomatic representative in Berlin from 1769 and then in London until February 1776, when his service there was cut short by a lawsuit accusing him of bribery and speculation. This resulted in his recall to France. With such a background it is hardly surprising that this French aristocrat did not feel bound by debts owed to an impecunious and powerless young musician from Austria.

The Concerto for Flute and Harp is a salon piece, as befits the delicate nature of the solo instruments, but while externally it savors of Mozart's most polite *galant* style, there are stronger, more personal forces at work in the beautiful slow movement, where the impersonal *arioso* style of his earlier years gives place to the more individual romance that would become characteristic of his mature years in Vienna. Each movement is compactly formed, but with an unusual abundance of melodic material—perhaps Mozart's antidote to the sound of the solo instruments, which he may have found tedious. If so he need not have worried; his instinct for combinations of instrumental sounds and the best use of them is as accurate and vivid here as ever.

In fact, a constantly changing tonal palette is a feature of the entire composition, and the two soloists, when they enter, add to the possibilities—even though Mozart very rarely allows his orchestral wind players to accompany them lest they overbalance them.

Oboes and horns are omitted from the exquisite slow movement, and if the sonorities of the string writing seem even more luxurious than usual it is because Mozart allowed himself two viola parts.

The last movement is a Rondo in the style of a gavotte. If Mozart wrote such music for instruments he is reputed to have disliked, how would he have dealt with them had they been instruments he loved? R.H.

K. *320 *Sinfonia Concertante in G major*

Origin: Salzburg, August 3, 1779
Scoring: 2 flutes soli, 2 oboes soli, 2 bassoons soli, strings
Movements: Andante grazioso. Rondeau: Allegro ma non troppo.

This work consists of movements three and four of the "Post Horn" Serenade in D major, K. 320, used by Mozart as a sinfonia concertante. Mozart also used movements one, five, and seven as a symphony (K. *320). See the notes on pp. 201, and on pp. 236.

K. 315 *Andante in C major (K^6 285e)*

Origin: Salzburg? 1779 or 1780
Scoring: flute solo, 2 oboes, 2 horns, strings

The autograph manuscript of this pellucidly beautiful movement for flute and orchestra is undated, but the paper on which Mozart wrote was of a kind he used in Salzburg only in the years 1777–79. It has long been considered part of the commission of flute works Mozart undertook in Mannheim for the amateur de Jean and perhaps a substitute slow movement for the G major flute concerto, K. 313. These hypotheses are plausible, but remain unproven. This work's continued popularity with flutists and audiences arises from the elegantly simple manner in which the flute pours forth its joy and sadness, above the sympathetic murmurings of the orchestra, like the heroine of a pastoral opera of the period. N.Z.

K. 371 *Rondo in E-flat major*
Origin: Vienna, March 21, 1781
Scoring: horn solo, 2 oboes, 2 horns, strings

In March of 1781 Mozart had just left the service of the Archbishop of Salzburg for Vienna and the life of a freelance composer, performer, and teacher. It is probable that at the earliest opportunity he sought out the company of the horn player Joseph Leutgeb, who as principal horn in the Salzburg orchestra since 1763 had been one of Mozart's closest friends during his formative years. Leutgeb had performed as a soloist in Paris in 1770, and when Mozart and his father were in Italy in 1772 and 1773, he joined them as a traveling horn virtuoso. "He will certainly make his mark here," Mozart predicted to his sister, and indeed Leutgeb does appear to have caused a sensation when he arrived in Milan in February of 1773. "He will make quite a fortune here, for he is extraordinarily popular," reported Leopold Mozart. "If the concert takes place that the courtiers want to arrange for him, I wager that he will get 100 *cigliati* on the spot. The archduke too wants to hear him."

In spite of these early auguries of a distinguished career, Leutgeb for some reason never achieved the financial security or fame that by rights his prowess on the horn should have brought him. He moved to Vienna in 1777, having borrowed the money from Leopold Mozart in order to do so—money that was still owing five years afterward when a sympathetic Wolfgang, who was continually in money trouble himself, asked his father: "Please have a little patience with poor Leutgeb. If you knew his circumstances and saw how he has to muddle along, you would certainly feel sorry for him. I shall have a word with him and I feel sure that he will pay you, at any rate by installments."

Leutgeb's name turns up in some of Mozart's last letters to his wife, who was taking the cure at Baden: "I am sleeping tonight at Leutgeb's," he notes, and again, "I am going to give Leutgeb a surprise by going out to breakfast with him." In his penultimate surviving letter, he tells Constanze that he twice took Leutgeb to see *The Magic Flute,* K. 260. Obviously Mozart loved the man.

Many writers have made assessments of Leutgeb's ability as a horn player, but it is the music that Mozart wrote for him that bears the most vivid testimony: four concertos, a quintet for horn and strings, and probably also the Rondo, K. 371, as well as other fragmentary compositions.

All of these works were of course written for the hand horn (or natural horn), an instrument that lacked the valves of the modern instrument, which is fully chromatic throughout its compass. In contrast, the only notes naturally available on the hand horn were those of the harmonic series (the instrument's overtones but not its fundamental tone). There were large gaps between the notes that could be sounded in the lower register. But many of the missing intermediate notes could be achieved by inserting the hand into the bell of the instrument at different depths; this method markedly altered the timbre of many of these "stopped" notes, a fact that sensitive composers like Mozart exploited to full advantage. This technique was not ordinarily expected of orchestral performers, but chamber music soloists and concerto players could achieve little without the ability to coordinate lip and hand.

In spite of his renowned buffoonery in the horn concertos, Mozart was sensitive to the characteristics of both instrument and soloist. His understanding of the technique of the hand horn player was masterly; the frequency of breathing points and the general conciseness of the concertos were only practical and not musical concessions to his soloist's lungs and lips; the four horn concertos remain difficult to play well, on natural horns or modern valved horns. The slow movements bear witness to Leutgeb's evident talent for intensely lyrical playing. All four concerto finales are children of their instrument, resplendent with lively rhythms drawn from the horn calls of the hunting field. During Mozart's lifetime, hunting rhythms were common fodder in the concert hall when an exuberant finale was required, but the composer here transforms a cliché into consummate art.

Leutgeb asked Mozart for a concerto as early as 1777, when he transferred to Vienna, but the earliest work for solo horn and orchestra is K. 371, which dates from March 21, 1781. It was the first work Mozart wrote in Vienna as a freelance composer. He left it incomplete after dashing off the entire solo line and orchestrating the first page; thereafter he made only sporadic indications of the orchestral accompaniment. After Mozart's death, one of his pupils completed the scoring. Mozart's sixteen-page manuscript had always been considered to contain the entire Rondo, but in 1990 an additional four pages came to light, completing the work for the first time.

One of the most obvious features of the jaunty Rondo theme is the repeated off-beat stresses of its final measures, a figure that Mozart uses extensively throughout the Rondo and to which he was to return five years later in the first-act Finale of *The Marriage of Figaro*.

R.H.

K. 417 *Horn Concerto in E-flat major, No. 2*

Origin: Vienna, May 27, 1783
Scoring: horn solo, 2 oboes, 2 horns, strings
Movements: Allegro maestoso. Andante. Rondo.

This was the first of Mozart's horn concertos to be completed. The superscription on the autograph manuscript ("Wolfgang Amadè Mozart takes pity on Leutgeb, ass, ox, and simpleton, at Vienna 27 May 1783") is not inconsistent with several anecdotes that reflect Mozart's somewhat brutal, if affectionate, ridiculing of Leutgeb; the composer, it is said, would sit down and write a horn concerto only if Leutgeb was on hands and knees picking up and re-sorting pages of symphonies and concertos that Mozart had flung onto the floor. Another time, Leutgeb had to kneel down behind the stove while Mozart wrote. "I can never resist making a fool of Leutgeb," he is reputed to have said. The image is at once funny and sad. In so many ways, Mozart was the kindest of men: witness the fact that he was composing these wonderful horn concertos for Leutgeb probably without expecting compensation. But, like other mortals, he had some puzzling and strangely insensitive sides to his character.

The spacious first movement is planned more broadly than the opening movements of later horn concertos and holds a wealth of melodic ideas. The slow movement, in the dominant key of B flat, has a simple songlike structure, preceded by an orchestral introduction of the first half of the melody. There are two complete "verses," virtually identical except that the pitch of the second is suddenly altered during its second phase in order to fortify the sense of the home key. A third "verse" begins, only to break off, leading to a short coda and the conclusion of the movement.

The Rondo is full of gaiety and fun. The opening hunting theme is ideally suited to the solo horn, and its orchestral repeat is predominantly colored by wind instruments. The range of the horn is at its widest in this movement, especially in the first episode, where it stretches more than two octaves. R.H.

K. 495 ***Horn Concerto in E-flat major, No. 4***

Origin: Vienna, June 26, 1786
Scoring: horn solo, 2 oboes, 2 horns, strings
Movements: Allegro moderato. Romanza: Andante. Rondo: Allegro vivace.

"Ein Waldhorn Konzert für den Leutgeb" (A hunting-horn concerto for Leutgeb) was entered by Mozart into his personal catalogue of compositions on June 26, 1786. This was the horn concerto, K. 495. Mozart was again back in humorous vein, copying out his autograph manuscript in a gay variety of different-colored inks: black, red, blue, and green. He returned also to his conventional orchestra of strings, oboes, and horns.

Mozart tricks us at the outset; we are led to believe that the strongly rhythmic violin melody (reminiscent of the opening of his masonic cantata *Die Maurerfreude*, K. 471, written the previous year) is the principal theme, but in fact it is the melody in long notes pursued by the oboes that that soloist adopts as his choice. The orchestral exposition follows its normal course, introducing the second subject and another curiously similar theme as a codetta, a theme the soloist cannot wait to play, coming in well before his traditional point of entrance.

In the recapitulation Mozart significantly reorders the material of the first subject group, and elements of both orchestral and solo expositions come together in new and hitherto untried relationships. Traditionally, the soloist bows from the scene after playing his cadenza, but here he puts in one last belated appearance at the end, sharing the codetta theme with the oboes over a whispery violin accompaniment.

The music of the slow movement is on a higher plane, and tests the soloist severely, both spiritually and physically. The impassioned principal theme is virtually identical to that in the slow movement of the four-hand Piano Sonata in F major, K. 497, composed just over a month later, except for its softer rhythms, which offer a greater expressive potential to the horn soloist. And curiously, Mozart's self-quoting continues with the melody of the first episode, which recalls the beginning of the Piano Quartet in G minor, K. 478.

The highly vivacious hunting Finale immediately dispels all traces of sadness. This could very well be the liveliest of all Mozart's hunting finales. Many years later Richard Strauss paid this type of finale the compliment of brilliantly caricaturing it in his own two horn concertos. R.H.

K. 447 ***Horn Concerto in E-flat major, No. 3***

Origin: Vienna, 1787 or 1788
Scoring: horn solo, 2 clarinets, 2 bassoons, strings
Movements: Allegro. Romance: Larghetto. Allegro.

The third horn concerto, K. 447, has the most enigmatic history of them all. Its date is uncertain, but the composer's handwriting, the paper of the autograph, and stylistic considerations all suggest that it was probably written considerably later than the commonly accepted 1783 date, perhaps even later than the fourth horn concerto. It is the least humorous of the horn concertos—at least in its opening two movements—and had the composer not added Joseph Leutgeb's name to his manuscript at two cadence points in the Finale, we would be tempted to speculate that he did not write it for his friend.

Curious also are the two title pages and two sets of page numbers, one for the first movement and one for the remainder, suggesting the distinct possibility that Mozart originally composed the Romance and Finale, and only later added a first movement to turn the work into a three-movement concerto. Its most unusual feature is its orchestration: Mozart abandoned his customary oboes and orchestral horns and chose instead clarinets and bassoons to join the strings. The additional warmth of these instruments, coupled with a more lyrical musical style, and a slow movement entitled "Romance" in the subdominant key of A-flat major, resulted in a work less extroverted than its companions, but of greater beauty and intimacy.

These qualities are apparent from the start as the violins play a lush and warm melody in their low register. Even before the first idea is ended we are made aware that chromatic alterations to both melody and harmony are to play an important part in this concerto. The second subject is curiously identical to the one in the Piano Concerto in C major, K. 467, except that its accentuation is exactly reversed.

In the development section we enter the dark and romantic tonal regions of D-flat major. Despite the difficult key, Mozart still finds enough notes possible on the natural horn to offer his soloist a new theme, and then the development continues with a series of remote modulations, with the sixteenth-note motive from the exposition on the violins over a pedal bass, the whole linked together by pivotal long notes from the horn. The English scholar Cuthbert Girdlestone considered this "one of the most remarkable symphonic passages in all Mozart." Following it, most of the material of the recapitulation is familiar. As in the previous horn concerto Mozart felt the need for a cadenza, though he left it to Leutgeb to invent one.

We hear the exquisitely lyrical opening melody of the slow movement no fewer than five times. The first two, one for the soloist and one for the orchestra, following each other immediately. The Rondo Finale, in contrast, is positively teeming with thematic ideas; there are probably six or more in the opening refrain alone of which Mozart makes constant use, either integrally or as seeds for later development. The end of the second episode is the scene of one of his most inspired jokes. The orchestra, in octaves at the end of the second refrain, suddenly swerves off course into the key of the slow movement, and the solo horn repeats—now in tallyho hunting rhythms—the beautiful theme that was its constant companion there. When the refrain returns for the last time, Mozart's purposes are made plain as all the member fragments of this vast Rondo theme come together. R.H.

K. 412 *Horn Concerto in D major, No. 1 (K¹ 514, K⁶ 386b)*

Origin: Vienna, first movement begun c. 1786 to 1788, completed in 1791; Rondò begun in 1791, incomplete.
Scoring: horn solo, 2 oboes, 2 bassoons, strings
Movements: Allegro. Rondò: Allegro.

Like the Rondo, K. 371, this work was left incomplete. Mozart's original manuscript is undated. It includes the completed first movement, scored for strings, oboes, and bassoons; this leads into a full-length sketch of the Finale with a score layout for solo horn and strings only. There is a second, completed manuscript of this second movement (Ludwig Köchel listed it separately as K. 514). It is in the hand of Franz Xaver Süssmayr, who completed his teacher's fragmentary Rondo.

The first movement begins quietly with an enchantingly lyrical melody that seems on first hearing more suited to strings than to the horn. In fact, it proves as beautiful on the horn as on strings, but when the soloist turns to the second subject, he rejects out of hand the orchestra's suggestion and invents a delightfully happy idea of his own.

The Rondo has three episodes, and at every turn there is ample evidence of Mozart's gaiety and humor. He is laughing when he uses a canon, the most learned of devices, to link the end of the first episode to the Rondo theme. He is laughing still louder as he continues by trying out the Rondo theme itself in canon—and of course it works perfectly. In the lengthy second episode it is another of Mozart's jokes to write for the horn, tonally a most conservative instrument, a melody in a foreign key. And not just any melody, either, for, as Alec Hyatt King has pointed out, Mozart (or, rather, Süssmayr) here adapts almost literally a wildly inappropriate Gregorian chant that would have been familiar to the Viennese as part of the Easter service, from the Lamentations of Jeremiah. When the Rondo theme returns for the fourth time the newly decorated violin accompaniment is pure joy, and Mozart, ever inventive, elaborates the idea further in the closing stages of the movement. In his sketch of this Rondo Finale, Mozart jotted down a stream of jocular directions or abuse in Italian for Joseph Leutgeb, who frequently was the butt of the composer's somewhat caustic sense of humor, such as "Ah, infamous pig," "Take a breather," "A sheep could trill like that" and (after the fourth repetition of the Rondo theme) "You're going to bore me a fourth time, and thank God it's the last." Even the tempo marking is a joke: Adagio in the horn part and Allegro for the strings, perhaps an allusion to Leutgeb's tendency to drag the tempo.

R.H.

K. 622 ***Clarinet Concerto in A major***

Origin: Vienna, October 1791

Scoring: clarinet solo, 2 flutes, 2 bassoons, 2 horns, strings

Movements: Allegro. Adagio. Rondo: Allegro.

Mozart wrote only two more concertos after finishing his last horn concerto: one for the piano (K. 595, in B-flat major) and one for the clarinet. The clarinet concerto turned out to be his valediction to instrumental composition: it was completed a mere two months before his death.

He first became enraptured by the clarinet during the months he spent in Mannheim in 1777 and 1778. "Ah, if only we had clarinets too! You cannot imagine the glorious effect of a symphony with flutes, oboes, and clarinets," he later wrote his father. Then he met Anton Stadler and his brother Johann in Vienna, where they had been freelance clarinetists for some eight years, and Mozart's love of the instrument became absolute. Mozart was especially inspired by Anton's playing; for him he composed the piano and wind quintet, K. 452, the clarinet trio, K. 498, the clarinet quintet, K. 581, and the two arias in the opera *La clemenza di Tito* that employ obbligato clarinet and basset horn (an alto clarinet). And finally and most wonderful of all, the clarinet concerto.

Anton was always fascinated by the deep notes of his instrument, so he sat second to his brother in orchestra and *Harmonie* (wind band). As his interest grew he designed, in collaboration with a local clarinetist and instrument maker, Theodor Lotz, a clarinet that would play two tones lower than normal, down to a written C, two octaves below middle C. It was for this clarinet that Mozart wrote the quintet, K. 581, the concerto, and the aria "Parto, parto" from *La clemenza di Tito*.

The work began as a concerto in G major for basset horn; 199 measures of the first movement survive in this form. They are virtually identical to the clarinet concerto, but whether it was Mozart's or Anton Stadler's decision to begin again a tone higher, utilizing the extended clarinet instead, we do not know.

The autograph manuscript of the concerto is lost. This is particularly unfortunate in the case of a work written specifically for Stadler's clarinet. What we know today is an anonymous arrangement for the conventional clarinet; the notes Mozart would have allotted to the very bottom of Stadler's instrument have been rewritten. But even in its slightly inauthentic state, this is Mozart's greatest wind concerto. The *galant* era of the flute, oboe, and bassoon concertos is past, the almost concertino-like succinctness of the horn concertos is now unnecessary. The clarinet concerto is of the same depth and breadth of conception as the late piano concertos, and possesses the same serenity and sublimity as the very last, K. 595.

Mozart chooses a quiet orchestral background. He rejects the piercing oboes for the soft sound of flutes, uses horns as usual, and decides upon a pair of bassoons; these were an addition to the original instrumental line-up of the aborted basset horn version. Furthermore Mozart often writes the bass line for the cellos, unsupported by double basses. But this is just one of the many subtle instrumental refinements that are part of his orchestral palette at the end of his life. His harmonic palette has been enriched too with a wealth of chromatic detail that he always uses tastefully and relevantly. And his understanding of the technical abilities of the clarinet is nothing short of masterly. Its full compass and range of tone color are exploited, its capacity to sustain a *cantabile* melody has never been bettered, and the ease with which it can play scales and arpeggios makes it a natural instrument of accompaniment, as the interplay between soloist and orchestra in this concerto demonstrates. Yet Mozart shunned technical virtuosity for its own sake, and found even cadenzas irrelevant.

The concerto opens with a theme in the same limpid, easy-paced, and lyrical mold that characterizes Mozart's late works in A major: the clarinet quintet and the Piano Concerto in A major (K. 488). Both seem immediately to strike the same mood. The amazing wealth of moods, colors, and images of the development are purely the result of Mozart's mastery in transforming and reshaping the music of the exposition: he no longer has any need to invent new themes. The recapitulation, markedly shorter than the exposition, nonetheless follows the same course in a more concentrated and often subtly altered form.

As Alec Hyatt King says, "The Adagio, in D, is music of utter simplicity, which seems to reflect the timeless and beatific vision of a mind at peace with itself." Mozart chooses that simplest of musical shapes for it, song form **(A-B-**

A), concluding with a coda. The melody is one of Mozart's most naïve and yet most mature utterances. Except for the few bars that make up the middle section, the music clings to its home key of D major throughout. Commenting on this tonality, American musicologist H. C. Robbins Landon notes, "There are times when an unbearable sadness seems to linger in the music, the more profound and tragic because it smilingly emerges from the serenity of a bright major key."

The Finale is a generously conceived Rondo, yet it is remarkable how concentrated and close-knit its various musical elements actually are. The soloist introduces the Rondo theme, and its working out involves a long discussion between soloist and orchestra, including some typically warm Mozartean instrumental touches.

Every such detail contributes to our awe at Mozart's technical mastery in his last concerto. The ear marvels, but only the heart can understand the deeper message of this miraculous work. Its quiet resignation has often been noted, perhaps suggesting that when writing it Mozart understood the extent of his own illness. The poignancy of the slow movement is proof enough of this, but a hidden sorrow pervades the movements that flank it, as well. H. C. Robbins Landon found in Shakespeare the perfect words to describe the paradox of these great Allegro movements: "The heart dances, but not for joy."

R.H.

10

Symphonies and Symphonic Movements

A secular concert. *Open-air Orchestra,* ca. 1790. Engraving by Giuseppe Servolini.

Like the engraving of a sacred concert on p. 109 above, this served the firm of Giovanni Chiari as a passe-partout title page for hand-copied music, in this case secular music. Space is provided on the masonry walls in the right and left foreground for the particular work's title and author, and in the center bottom for its opening measures. In the center at the back sits the maestro at his spinettone (a large, rectangular harpsichord especially designed for playing in opera orchestras) surrounded by a male and female singer, a cellist, and a double bass player. The rest of the orchestra comprises eight violinists and pairs of violists, oboists, horn players, and trumpet players. The setting is a topiary garden.

BACKGROUND AND OVERVIEW

Mozart's first symphony was written in 1764, his last in 1788; in the former year Jean-Philippe Rameau died, in the latter Ludwig van Beethoven turned eighteen. During this quarter-century significant changes in musical style occurred, which can be observed in Mozart's more-than-fifty symphonies as well as in the symphonies of his contemporaries.

Many writers about Mozart's symphonies have made the mistake of confusing the general change in symphonic style during his lifetime with his personal development as a composer. These style changes were closely related to a gradual shift in the function and valuation of symphonies, from works intended to provide entertaining but conventional introductions to plays, operas, ballets, concerts, serenades, and a variety of other social, religious, or civic events, to works viewed as art for art's sake and the principal attractions of formal concerts.

Examination of Mozart's symphonies of the late 1770s and early 1780s reveals the emergence of essential elements of the new style. A key technical and stylistic change was the dissolution of the composite bass line of the early symphonies into independent parts for cello, double bass, and bassoon. The last symphony in which bassoons merely play along on the bass line is K. 208 + 102 of 1775, and the first in which the cellos and double basses are systematically written for separately is K. 319 of 1779.

Another noteworthy development was the definitive separation of the overture-sinfonia and the concert-sinfonia. These two genres were intertwined for most of the eighteenth century, not only in their forms and functions but in the interchangeability of the labels "overture" and "sinfonia". The last opera overture refurbished by Mozart as a symphony was *Il rè pastore,* K. 208 + 102, of 1775. The last concert symphony used as an overture with his consent was K. 318 of 1779. The first overture that Mozart did not recycle as a concert symphony was the overture from *Idomeneo* of 1781.

Then there was the new style of orchestration. To the winds' Baroque function as instruments doubling the strings, opposing the strings in concerto grosso fashion, or appearing as soloists, and to their mid-century function of sustaining slow-moving background harmonies in the tuttis, was now added a new function: ongoing participation in the presentation, fragmentation, and development of important thematic materials. This new treatment of the wind instruments, by no means entirely absent from the symphonies of the 1770s, is clearly adumbrated in the "Linz" Symphony of 1783, K. 425, but it first appears fully developed in the "Prague" Symphony, K. 504, having been brilliantly evolved in the piano concertos and operas of the early 1780s. The increased virtuosity demanded of the wind players meant a decline in the practice of doubling: the last of Mozart's symphonies requiring the oboists to play the flute is K. 250 of 1776.

The increased difficulty was not limited to the wind parts, however. It generally went along with increases in length, in contrapuntal textures, and in chromaticism, which, taken together, amounted to a new seriousness and complexity in the symphony as a genre. The symphonies that Mozart wrote between his symphonic debut as an eight-and-a-half-year-old prodigy and the "Haffner" Symphony of 1782 (K. 385) display the growth of the genre, the evolution of the musical style of the period, the maturing of Mozart's own style, and his increasing command of the métier. They do not show much development in technical or conceptual difficulty, which seems to have awaited Mozart's break with the conservative influences of Salzburg, his father, and the archbishop, and his freely breathing the more bracing atmosphere of Emperor Joseph II's Vienna.

Looking back on these striking changes in the form and function of symphonies from the viewpoint of the early nineteenth century, German writer and composer E. T. A. Hoffmann summarized the matter succinctly:

> In earlier days one regarded symphonies only as introductory pieces to any larger production whatsoever; the opera overtures themselves mostly consisted of several movements and were entitled "sinfonia." Since then our great masters of instrumental music—Haydn, Mozart, Beethoven—bestowed upon the symphony a tendency such that nowadays it has become an autonomous whole and, at the same time, the highest type of instrumental music.

The enumeration of Mozart's symphonies requires a brief explanation. Of the traditional forty-one numbered symphonies, four are now considered spurious, Nos. 2, 3, 11, and 37. (However, No. 37 does contain a short introductory passage by Mozart that is discussed below in the note for Symphony No. 36, K. 425.) Two more symphonies have recently come to be regarded as authentic, K. 19a and 45a. This yields a total of thirty-nine symphonies conceived originally as such by Mozart.

One must add to them, however, thirteen more symphonies that Mozart derived from his own previous compositions. Six of these symphonies were extracted from extended Salzburg serenades, K. 100, 185, 203, 204, 250, and 320, by the exclusion of various "extra" movements. Three more symphonies originated as three-movement overtures to *Mitridate, La Betulia liberata,* and *Lucio Silla.* The remaining four symphonies borrow their first two movements from the overtures to *Ascanio in Alba, Il sogno di Scipione, La finta giardiniera,* and *Il re pastore,* and in each case Mozart composed a new concluding (third) movement. The inclusion of these thirteen works brings the total number of Mozart's symphonies to fifty-two. N.Z.

K. 16 *Symphony in E-flat major, No. 1*
Origin: London, end of 1764
Scoring: 2 oboes, 2 horns, strings
Movements: Molto Allegro. Andante. Presto.

Late in April 1764 the Mozarts, on a grand tour of western Europe, left Paris and settled in London. How Wolfgang came to write his first symphony there was recalled after his death by his sister Nannerl:

> On the fifth of August [we] had to rent a country house in Chelsea, outside the city of London, so that father could recover from a dangerous throat ailment, which brought him almost to death's door. [. . .] Our father lay dangerously ill; we were forbidden to touch the keyboard. And so, in order to occupy himself, Mozart composed his first symphony with all the instruments of the orchestra, especially trumpets and kettledrums. I had to transcribe it as I sat at his side. While he composed and I copied he said to me, "Remind me to give the horn something worthwhile to do!" [. . .] At last after two months, as father had completely recovered, [we] returned to London.

The earliest symphony listed by Köchel, and No. 1 in collected editions of Mozart's symphonies, is the Symphony in E flat, K. 16. The autograph manuscript bears the superscription

"Sinfonia / di / Sig. Wolfgang / Mozart / a london / 1764." But is this the symphony described in Nannerl's account? She mentioned that she copied Wolfgang's first symphony, whereas the score of K. 16 is in Wolfgang's hand with corrections by his father, Leopold. Perhaps Nannerl may simply have meant she had to copy parts for her brother; other symphonies from this period (K. 19, 19a, 45a) survive as sets of parts copied by Leopold and Nannerl. She also mentioned that Wolfgang wrote for trumpets and kettledrums, instruments not used in K. 16. As for giving the horn "something worthwhile to do," that is perhaps satisfied by a passage in the Andante, where the horn plays the motive "do-re-fa-mi," best known from the Finale of the "Jupiter" Symphony, K. 551, but found in other works by Mozart and his contemporaries. Yet all this sounds too much like special pleading: the discrepancies between the symphony in Nannerl's anecdote and K. 16 suggest that the latter may not be the symphony described as his first by his sister.

If the heading "Sinfonia / di Sig. Wolfgang / Mozart / a london / 1764" is correct, the work must date from after Leopold's illness but before the New Year—from October, November, or December. The manuscript begins tidily, but soon numerous corrections are entered by Wolfgang and Leopold in larger, cruder hands, attesting to artistic and mechanical struggles in the creation of what is probably Wolfgang's earliest surviving symphony.

The first movement opens with a three-measure fanfare in octaves, immediately contrasted by a quieter eight-measure series of suspensions, all of which is repeated. This leads to a brief *agitato* section, and the first group of ideas is brought to a close on the dominant. At this point the winds fall silent, and the initial idea of the second group is heard, extended by a passage of rising scales in the lower strings accompanied by tremolo in the violins. A brief coda concludes the exposition, which is repeated. The second half of the movement, also repeated, covers the same ground as the first, working its way through the dominant and the relative minor to reach the tonic at the beginning of the second group. The movement faithfully captures the early symphonic vocabulary, with its alternations of loud and soft, syncopations, unisons, tremolos, rapid scales, and repeated notes. Only the singsong melody at measures 37–43 and 99–106 seems to fall flat. Here Wolfgang originally wrote independent parts for first and second violins, but Leopold changed them to play in unison; even so, the melody projects weakly in these passages.

The brevity and lack of development of the Andante—a binary movement in C minor—give it an aphoristic character. Sustained winds, triplets in the upper strings, and duplets in the bass instruments combine effectively to paint a *scena* that would have been at home in an opera of the period, perhaps accompanying a nocturnal rendezvous. Brief as this movement is, however, it wanders a bit. That is, the immature composer had a good idea but perhaps not yet the craft to develop it cogently.

At the beginning of the Presto a new fanfare launches a jig-like Finale in the form of a truncated rondo with a diatonic refrain and intervening episodes containing touches of chromaticism in the *galant* manner.

Writers who, wishing to chronicle Mozart's progress, have taken pains to point out the great differences in length, complexity, and originality between this earliest surviving symphony and his last few, may have missed a crucial point: there is little difference in length, complexity, or originality between K. 16 and the symphonies of Johann Christian Bach's Op. 3 and Carl Friedrich Abel's Op. 7, which were apparently among Mozart's chief models. The change in Mozart's symphonies over his lifetime must be explained not only by his own artistic and technical development, but by the stylistic evolution of the period. N.Z.

K. 19 ***Symphony in D major, No. 4***
Origin: London, 1765
Scoring: 2 oboes, 2 horns, strings
Movements: Allegro. Andante. Allegro.

The wrapper that held the original set of parts for K. 19 survives; it is inscribed "Sinfonia / à 2 Violinj / 2 Hautbois / 2 Corni / Viola / e / Basso / in F [overwritten with] C [crossed out in pencil and added alongside] D." These notations in Leopold's hand apparently indicate that the wrapper had served first for a Symphony in F (presumably K^6 19a), and then for one in C (the missing K^6 19b?), before being pressed into service for K. 19. The three symphonies were probably not intended to form an "opus," since each replaced the one before it.

The first movement begins with a fanfare of the kind used for signaling by post horns or military trumpets, which sounds twice and is never heard again. The movement has the bright timbre that sharp keys impart to the strings. Like the first movements of K. 16 and K^6 19a, this one is binary form, here without repeats. An especially nice touch is the unprepared A-sharp with which the second half begins—the kind of quirky chromatic twist much in evidence in Mozart's published sonatas of the period.

The G-major Andante, *sempre piano,* possesses a conventional, pastoral serenity, its "yodeling" melodies and droning accompaniments evoking thoughts of hurdy-gurdies and bagpipes. This movement had its models in certain types of melodies originating in Naples and popular in those parts of Europe to which Italian opera had penetrated. An occasional "yodeling" in the melody of the Finale, a binary movement in jig style with both sections repeated, ties it to the previous movement. N.Z.

K^3 19a ***Symphony in F major (K^1 Anh 223)***
Origin: London? first half of 1765?
Scoring: 2 oboes, 2 horns, strings
Movements: Allegro assai. Andante. Presto.

The existence of this long-lost work was known from the beginning of its first violin part, written on the wrapper of the previous symphony. That it was a completed work and not a fragment had also been known, from its incipit in the early-nineteenth-century Breitkopf & Härtel Manuscript Catalogue, with an indication of instrumentation. K. 19a reappeared at the beginning of February 1981, when press dispatches from Munich reported the discovery of a set of parts in Leopold's hand, found among some private papers.

Leopold entitled the work, "Sinfonia / in F / à / 2 Violinj / 2 Hautb: / 2 Cornj / Viola / e / Basso / di Wolfgango Mozart / compositore de 9 Añj." The paper on which Leopold copied K. 19a is French, but as Wolfgang was in England and Holland during his ninth year, it must have been exported from France. Since Mozart turned nine years old on January 27, 1765, the symphony, if it was in fact created in London as suggested by the number K. 19a given it by Alfred Einstein in K^3, would then have to be placed in February, March, or April of that year, in time for either the concert of February 21 or perhaps one of the famous London concert series run by J. C. Bach and Carl Friedrich Abel, which was in its first season. But Alfred Einstein's dating of K. 19a was based upon its link to K. 19, whose dating is also uncertain, so K. 19a may possibly belong to the time between the Mozarts' arrival in Holland in September 1765 and Wolfgang's tenth birthday in January 1766.

The first movement opens with a broad melody in the first violins, accompanied by sustained harmonies in the winds, broken chords in the inner voices, and repeated notes in the bass instruments. A brief bit of imitative writing leads to a cadence on the dominant and the introduction of a contrasting second subject. Tremolos in the upper strings accompanying a triadic, striding bass line lead to a closing subject. The second half of the movement presents the same succession of ideas as the first, and both sections are repeated. As the harmonic movement is from tonic to dominant in the first half and from dominant to tonic in the second, with little that could be described as developmental in the use of themes or harmonies, and as the double return of a recapitulation is absent, the movement is nearer to binary than to sonata form. In this regard the first movements of K. 16 and 19a are alike; in another regard the first movement of K. 19a seems superior: the kind of lapse in the handling of thematic material mentioned above in the discussion of K. 16 is no longer in evidence.

The oboes are silent in the B-flat Andante, which, like the first movement, consists of two approximately equal sections, both repeated. The bass line instruments and horns are assigned supporting roles, and a dialogue between first violins and violas is mediated by the second violins, which join now one, now the other.

Finales in 3/8, 6/8, 9/8, or 12/8 were common at the time K. 19a was written, and usually took on the character of an Italianate *giga*. Here, however, the rondo refrain has a different sort of rustic character. Many a play and opera on the London stage had a hornpipe, reel, or highland fling danced in it; these "exotic" touches perhaps tickled the fancy of a nine-year-old composer, who may have tried to capture their spirit in this Finale. N.Z.

K. 22 ***Symphony in B-flat major, No. 5***
Origin: The Hague, December 1765
Scoring: 2 oboes, 2 horns, strings
Movements: [Allegro.] Andante. Allegro molto.

At the top of Leopold's score of K. 22, which is written on Dutch paper, is the inscription "Synfonia / di Wolfg. Mozart à la Haye nel mese December 1765." The work was almost certainly composed for the Mozart's public concert at The Hague on January 22, 1766.

The opening movement, binary and without repeats, has no tempo indication, which by eighteenth-century convention is therefore understood to be a generic "Allegro." It begins with a tonic pedal in the bass for fourteen measures, in a manner usually associated with the Mannheim symphonists but which originated in Italy and which by 1765 could be heard in many parts of western Europe. A contrasting second subject, a dialogue between the first and second violins, is followed by the apparently mandatory theme in the bass instruments accompanied by tremolo in the upper strings. A brief transition section puts the opening idea through the keys of F minor and C minor, returning to the home key shortly after the recapitulation of the second subject, with the rest following essentially as in the exposition.

The G-minor Andante, a simple **A-B-A–coda,** exhibits chromaticism, imitative textures, and occasional stern unisons. German musicologist Hermann Abert even thought that he heard foreshadowings here of the Andante of Mozart's penultimate symphony, K. 550, but such a comparison does injustice to both works, which were composed two decades apart in disparate styles, for varying purposes and different audiences. As if the Andante's intensity of feeling were dangerous in a work intended for polite society, the Finale—a sort of brisk minuet in the form of a rondo, originally marked Allegro moderato—makes amends by leaning in the other direction. N.Z.

K. 43 ***Symphony in F major, No. 6***
Origin: Vienna, 1767
Scoring: 2 oboes (doubling flutes), 2 horns, strings
Movements: [Allegro.] Andante. Menuetto. Allegro.

The autograph manuscript, a beautifully written fair copy, bears the heading "Sinfonia di Wolfgango Mozart à Vienne 1767." Above "1767" was written (apparently in Leopold's hand) "a olmutz 1767," but this was subsequently crossed out. The Mozarts visited the North Moravian town of Olomouc (Olmütz) on only one, unhappy occasion, between approximately October 26 and December 23, 1767. They had fled there from Vienna hoping to avoid an outbreak of smallpox, which, however, both Wolfgang and Nannerl did eventually contract. From the inscriptions on the autograph, Alfred Einstein in K^3 concluded that K. 43 must have been either begun in Vienna in the autumn and completed in Olomouc, or begun in Olomouc and completed in Vienna at the end of December, and the editors of K^6 concur. But K. 43 cannot have been completed in Vienna at the end of December 1767, for although the Mozarts did leave Olomouc around December 23, they reached Vienna only on January 10 of the new year. The reason for the slowness of their journey was this: in the course of fleeing from Vienna they had stopped at Brno (Brünn), where the Count von Schrattenbach, brother of the archbishop of Salzburg, had arranged a concert. But Leopold wanted his children even further from Vienna's smallpox epidemic, so he postponed the concert until their return trip. Hence the Mozarts returned to Brno on Christmas Eve and on December 30 gave their concert, which was duly noted in the diary of a local clergyman:

> In the evening . . . I attended a musical concert in a house in the city known as the "Taverna," at which a Salzburg boy of eleven years and his sister of fifteen years, accompanied on various instruments by inhabitants of Brno, excited everyone's admiration; but he could not endure the trumpets, because they were incapable of playing completely in tune with one another.

This report of Wolfgang's reaction has the ring of truth to it, for extreme sensitivity to trumpets in his childhood is documented elsewhere. Trumpets aside, however, if Leopold Mozart was anything other than pleased with the local orchestra, he was politic enough to hide the fact, for the leader of the Brno town musicians reported that "Mr. Mozart, Kapellmeister of Salzburg, was completely satisfied with the orchestra here and would not have believed that my colleagues could accompany so well at the first rehearsal."

There is one more fact to consider about the genesis of K. 43: the paper on which it was written is of Salzburg origin. Perhaps the symphony was begun prior to departure for Vienna and completed later, but this is not a necessary assumption, as the Mozarts would have carried some music paper with them when traveling. We may therefore propose the following hypothetical scenario for K. 43: it was drafted in Vienna between September 15 and October 23, 1767 (and perhaps also in Salzburg before September 13), completed, revised, or recopied in Olomouc after Wolfgang's recovery from smallpox, and may have received its premiere on December 30 in Brno. As all of Mozart's unquestionably genuine symphonies datable to before the end of 1767 are in three movements, K. 43 may provisionally be regarded as his earliest four-movement symphony.

The first movement opens with a fanfare virtually identical to one used by J. C. Bach, Johann Stamitz, Carl Joseph Toeschi, Carl Ditters von Dittersdorf, and undoubtedly others to open symphony movements. Then follows a passage built over a pedal and probably implying a *crescendo,* the turn to the dominant, the opening fanfare in the bass with tremolo above, a lilting theme (strings alone, piano), and the energetic closing section of the exposition. A concise development section, based on the fanfare in the bass and some new material, leads to the lilting theme, now in the tonic, and then the rest of the exposition by way of recapitulation. The movement thus lacks the "double return" of opening theme and key of Wolfgang's later symphonies.

The Andante of K. 43 is based upon the eighth number of his "Latin comedy" (we should perhaps call it a "cantata" or "serenata") *Apollo et Hyacinthus,* K. 38 (see the note on p. 42). In the libretto for K. 38 Hyacinth and Zephyr are friends, and Zephyr loves Hyacinth's sister Melia. But Apollo also loves Melia and seeks the friendship of Hyacinth. Zephyr, in a jealous rage, mortally wounds Hyacinth by flinging a discus at him, and then blames Apollo, causing Melia to renounce Apollo. Discovered by his father, Hyacinth reveals in his dying breath that Zephyr, not Apollo, was his murderer. In the duet which became the Andante of K. 43, the King, having vented his grief and rage at the death of his son, reveals the true story to his daughter, and they beg Apollo's forgiveness. This supplication has the desired effect: Apollo reappears, turns Zephyr into a wind, transforms Hyacinth's body into a bed of flowers, and agrees to marry Melia.

Responding not to the sense of anxiety in the text but rather to the mood of supplication, the youthful composer composed a movement of almost sublime serenity. In both versions the movement displays the characteristic orchestral color of Mozart's symphony andantes of this period, here created by a change of key (C major), flutes replacing oboes, first violins muted, second violins and bass instruments pizzicato, and violas, *divisi,* murmuring in sixteenth notes.

The Minuet, rather legato compared to the others of the period, exploits descending triplet upbeats in the first section, ascending ones in the second. The Trio, in the subdominant, also makes use of triplets, with the wind silent and the articulation more detached. In the second section of the Trio the theme appears in the bass and then, returning to the violins, is interrupted and terminated by an unforeseen touch of chromaticism. The Finale, a binary movement with both halves repeated, is as notable for its careful writing for the strings, including playful dialogues between first and second violins, as for the conservative role assigned the winds, which support the strings and seldom venture out on their own. N.Z.

K. 45 *Symphony in D major, No. 7*

Origin: Vienna, January 16, 1768

Scoring: 2 oboes, 2 horns, 2 trumpets and timpani, strings

Movements: Allegro. Andante. Menuetto. [Allegro.]

The autograph of K. 45 bears the inscription "Sinfonia di Sig[no]re Wolfgang Mozart / 1768, 16 Jener"—thus it was completed just a few days after the return to Vienna from the journey to Olomouc and Brno discussed above. It is written on paper of a particularly large, coarse type, which bespeaks purchase in a provincial place (undoubtedly, in this instance, Brno or Olomouc), where large paper of good quality could not be had.

There is no record of the Mozarts' giving a public concert at this time, so we must assume that this symphony was written for a private concert. The Mozarts did have a two-and-a-half-hour audience with Empress Maria Theresa and her son, the recently crowned Emperor Joseph II, only three days after the completion of K. 45. During the audience Wolfgang and Nannerl performed and music was discussed, but as none of the court musicians were present, no orchestral music can have been played. The earliest documented occasion on which K. 45 could have been heard was near the end of March at a grand Lenten concert which, Leopold reported to his friends in Salzburg, "was given for us at the house of His Highness Prince von Galitzin, the Russian Ambassador."

By the time of the Russian ambassador's concert, Leopold had overstayed the leave of absence granted him from his duties at the Salzburg court, and the archbishop had issued an order stopping his pay until he returned. The reason Leopold had not returned to Salzburg was that (following the Emperor's suggestion) Wolfgang had composed a comic opera, *La finta semplice,* K. 51, whose production was repeatedly delayed by intrigues on the part of envious Viennese musicians. Malicious rumors circulated that Wolfgang was a fraud, and that his father did his composing for him. Leopold, a man with an acute sense of honor, felt that he could not leave Vienna before he and his son were vindicated. Yet although he battled valiantly against his opponents, the opera remained unperformed in Vienna.

The overture for the ill-fated *La finta semplice* was a reworking of K. 45. And this new version was, in its turn, used as an independent symphony. To turn a concert- or chamber-symphony into an overture-symphony Mozart omitted the Minuet and Trio. He altered the orchestration of the remaining movements, adding pairs of flutes and obbligato bassoons to the original pairs of oboes and horns, while dropping the trumpets and kettledrums. Mozart added a considerable number of phrasing and dynamic indications to the reworked symphony, as well as a few changes of rhythm and pitch. In the Andante he also altered the meter from common time to *alla breve,* and the eighth notes of the melody to dotted eighths and sixteenths. Finally, he added two additional bars of music to the first movement and four to the Finale. In the Finale the repeats of both halves were eliminated and changes were made to the ending.

The Finale is based on the kind of idea that, if found in a set of dances, would have been called a contredanse, that is, a popular rather than courtly dance. A closely related tune circulated in London around 1800 under the name "Del Caro's Hornpipe," while another appears in the Intrada (introductory movement) of Leopold Mozart's divertimento, *Die musikalische Schlittenfahrt* (The Musical Sleighride). The origins of this vernacular tune-type may be lost in the mists of oral tradition. N.Z.

K[3] 45a *Symphony in G major, "Lambach" (K[1] Anh 221)*

Origin: The Hague, late 1765 or early 1766; revised Salzburg, 1767
Scoring: 2 oboes, 2 horns, strings
Movements: Allegro maestoso. Andante. Presto.

The Benedictine monastery at Lambach, in Upper Austria near Wels, was a convenient way station for the Mozart family on their journeys between Salzburg and Vienna. Like many other Bavarian and Austrian monasteries of the time, Lambach provided rooms and meals for travelers, and maintained a musical establishment to ornament its liturgy and to provide entertainment. Amandus Schickmayr, a friend of Leopold Mozart's, was at Lambach from 1738 and had become abbot of the monastery in 1746. At the beginning of January 1769 the Mozart family, returning to Salzburg from their stay of more than a year in Vienna, stopped at Lambach. The visit, not mentioned in the family's surviving letters and diaries, is known solely from inscriptions on two musical manuscripts.

The manuscripts in question are sets of parts for two symphonies in G, one inscribed "Sinfonia / à / 2 Violini / 2 Oboe / 2 Corni / Viola / e / Basso. / Del Sig[re] Wolfgango / Mozart. / Dono Authoris / 4ta Jan: 769," and the other bearing a similar inscription but with "Leopoldo Mozart / Maestro di Capella di S: A: R: / à / Salis[go]" in place of "Wolfgango Mozart." For convenience of reference, the symphony at Lambach ascribed to Wolfgang will be referred to as K. 45a, that ascribed to Leopold as G16. The two manuscripts, neither of which is an autograph, were discovered in the monastery's archives by the Austrian musicologist Wilhelm Fischer, who in 1923 published K. 45a. Prior to that, however, an entry for K. 45a could be found in the first and second editions of the Köchel Catalogue as Anh. 221, one of ten symphonies known to Köchel solely by the opening measures of their first movements in the Breitkopf & Härtel Manuscript Catalogue.

In K[3] Alfred Einstein placed the rediscovered Symphony in G, K. Anh. 221, in the chronology of authentic works according to the date on the Lambach manuscript. Speculating that the symphony had been written during the Mozarts' just ended sojourn of more than a year in Vienna, he assigned it the number 45a representing early 1768. The editors of K[6] accepted Einstein's and Fischer's opinion of the authenticity of Anh. 221 = 45a, as did the French writer Georges Saint-Foix and others who wrote about Wolfgang's early symphonies. And Einstein's placing of K. 45a in Vienna in early 1768 was generally accepted too.

In 1964 the German musicologist Anna Amalie Abert published a startling hypothesis about the two G major "Lambach" symphonies. She had come to believe that—like the accidental interchange of infants that underlies the plots of a number of plays and operas—the two symphonies had been mixed up, perhaps by a monkish librarian at Lambach. Abert based her opinion on a stylistic examination of the two, and on comparisons between them and other symphonies thought to have been written by Leopold and Wolfgang at about the same time.

In February 1982, however, new evidence was published confirming the correctness of arguments in favor of Wolfgang's authorship of, and an earlier date for, K. 45a. The Bavarian State Library in Munich had acquired the recently discovered, original set of parts for K. 45a. They comprise first and second violin parts apparently in the hand of a professional copyist, a *basso* part in Nannerl's hand, and the other parts in Leopold's hand. The title page of the rediscovered manuscript, also in Leopold's hand, reads: "Sinfonia / à 2 Violini / 2 Hautbois / 2 Corni / Viola / et / Basso / di Wolfgango / Mozart di Salisburgo / à la Haye 1766." K. 45a therefore forms a pendant to the Symphony in B flat, K. 22, also composed at The Hague, where the reception granted the Mozarts appears to have been enthusiastic. K. 45a may have been written (along with the *Gallimathias musicum,* K. 32) for the investiture of Prince William V of Orange, in which case it would have been part of what Leopold referred to in a letter to Salzburg when he said that Wolfgang "had to compose something for the Prince's concert."

The first movement of K. 45a is one of only two of Mozart's more-than-fifty symphonies (the other being the Symphony in D major K. 185) that begin with the melody in the bass, a texture he otherwise reserved for near the ends of expositions and of recapitulations. In a number of his early symphonies the beginnings of the first and final movements are related in melodic contour. In K. 45a something else occurs: the second or lyrical subjects of the first and third movements are the ones that are connected. (A related procedure is found in the Piano Concerto in F major, K. 414, in which the first theme of the opening Allegro reappears transformed as the second theme of the Andante.) The Finale of K. 45a is so much of a piece with the Finales of K. 16, 19, 19a, and 22 that all may be said to belong to the same general conception and, keys aside, to be virtually interchangeable. As for the Andante, the revised version is the first of Wolfgang's symphonic andantes to use an orchestral texture that would be his favorite for a number of years: in these movements (the Andantes of K. 43, 100, 113, 183, 201, 203, and 200) the winds are either silent or reduced, the violins are muted, and the cellos and basses play pizzicato.

It remains to be said on the subject of K. 45a that between the copying of the original set of parts in The Hague in 1766 and the copying of the Lambach parts in Salzburg in 1767, the work underwent a careful revision. The two versions are very much the same work: no bars of music have been added or deleted and no new ideas introduced. Rather, numerous details large and small have been altered, mostly in the inner parts. As Wolfgang would scarcely have revised his symphony merely as an academic exercise, he probably had occasion to perform the second version of K. 45a in Salzburg between the return from the grand tour in December 1766 and the departure for Vienna in October 1767, and the success of the Salzburg performance (or performances) must have encouraged Leopold to take the work on tour to Vienna.

N.Z.

K. 48 *Symphony in D major, No. 8*
Origin: Vienna, December 13, 1768
Scoring: 2 oboes, 2 horns, 2 trumpets and timpani, strings
Movements: [Allegro.] Andante. Menuetto. [Allegro.]

Why, on the eve of his departure from Vienna after a stay of more than a year, did Wolfgang write another symphony? The autograph manuscript of K. 48 is inscribed "Sinfonia / di W: Mozart / 1768 / à Vienna / den 13ten dec:." The very next day Leopold wrote a final letter to Salzburg, yet mentioned no forthcoming event that might explain the need for a new symphony. Indeed, he would seem to have been deliberately mysterious about the obligations keeping them in Vienna:

> As very much as I wished and hoped to be in Salzburg on His Highness the Archbishop's consecration day [December 21], nonetheless it was impossible, for we could not bring our affairs to a conclusion earlier, even though I endeavored strenuously to do so. However, we will still set out from here before the Christmas holiday.

As the Mozarts were long overdue at Salzburg and Leopold's pay was being withheld, one might expect that they would have left Vienna immediately after their vindication on December 7, when, at the consecration of a new church, Wolfgang led performances of his own newly composed Mass, Offertory, and trumpet concerto in the presence of the Imperial court and a large audience. Yet something held the Mozarts in Vienna for more than two weeks longer. That "something" may have been the unknown occasion for which K. 48 was written, most likely a farewell concert in the palace of one of the nobility.

Like K. 45, K. 48 is in the festive key of D and calls for trumpets and kettledrums in addition to the usual strings and pairs of oboes and horns. Like both K. 43 and 45, K. 48 is in four movements. Its opening Allegro begins with a striking idea featuring dotted half notes alternating *forte* and *piano*. In the space of a mere six bars this melody covers a range of two and a half octaves. This wide-ranging melody is accompanied by nervous eighth notes in the bass line soon followed by running sixteenth notes in the violins which, with an occasional comment from the oboes and one dramatic silence, bring the bustling exposition to its conclusion. The movement, like all four in this symphony, has both sections repeated. Exceptionally for first movements of symphonies from this period in Mozart's life, the development section of K. 48 is nearly as long as its exposition; in the course of its modulations it reviews the ideas already heard. The recapitulation gives them again in full (for the first time in his symphonies), and the movement thus provides a lucid demonstration of American musicologist James Webster's apparently paradoxical description of sonata form as "a two-part tonal structure, articulated in three main sections."

The Andante, in G major for strings alone, is a little song in binary form. The peculiar character of the opening idea results from its harmonization in parallel $^6_3$ chords and the singsong quality of its melody, rather like a nursery-rhyme tune. This leads, however, to a second, more Italianate, idea, which, with its larger range and insistent appoggiaturas, conveys a more worldly, perhaps even operatic, ethos.

The Minuet reinstates the winds, although the trumpets and drums drop out for the contrasting G-major Trio. Here Mozart perfectly captured the stately pomp that Viennese symphonic minuets of the time provided as a kind of aesthetic stepping-stone between the Apollonian slow movements and the Dionysian finales, which in this case is a jig in a large binary design. N.Z.

K[3] 61g/I *Symphonic Minuet in A major*
Origin: Italy? 1770?
Scoring: 2 flutes, strings

Several German Mozart scholars have suggested that this A-major Minuet, K. 61g, No. I, was originally intended for the Symphony in A major, K. 114, of December 1771, but according to Mozart's writing in the work's autograph it probably dates from as early as 1770, and the paper on which he wrote it is a type he used in Italy that very year. Furthermore, the work is scored for flutes and strings, and lacks the horns called for by K. 114. That K. 61g, No. I may have had some sort of symphonic connection, though, is suggested by the fact that, unlike Mozart's ballroom minuets, it does call for violas. N.Z.

K. *100 *Symphony in D major, "Serenade" (K[6] *62a)*
Origin: Salzburg, autumn? 1769
Scoring: 2 oboes (doubling flutes), 2 horns, 2 trumpets, strings
Movements: Allegro. Menuetto. Andante. Menuetto. Allegro.

This work consists of movements one, five, six, seven, and eight of the Serenade in D major, K. 100, used by Mozart as a symphony. See the note on p. 230.

N.Z.

K. 73 *Symphony in C major, No. 9 (K[3] 75a, K[6] 73)*
Origin: Salzburg or Italy? late 1769 or early 1770?
Scoring: 2 oboes (doubling flutes), 2 horns, 2 trumpets and timpani, strings
Movements: Allegro. Andante. Menuetto. Allegro molto.

The autograph manuscript of K. 73 bears only the inscription "Sinfonie" in Wolfgang's hand. The date "1769" was added in another hand, perhaps Leopold's, perhaps Johann Anton André's. Köchel accepted that date, and the editors of K[6] have reverted to it, thus calling into question Alfred Einstein's attempt in K[3] to redate the work to the summer of 1771. Because a sketch for the Minuet of this symphony is found in the autograph of a series of minuets (K. 103) that K[3] and K[6] claim Wolfgang wrote for carnival 1769, it might seem logical to propose that the symphony was completed around the same time, in which case even the Köchel No. 73 would be too high. But the dating of the minuets themselves rests on vague stylistic grounds and should only with great caution be used as a basis for dating the symphony. From Wolfgang's writing, German musicologist Wolfgang Plath assigns the manuscript of the minuets, K. 103, to early summer 1772, while Oxford scholar Alan Tyson reports that its paper is a type used by Wolfgang in the spring of 1772. Again on the basis of writing, the manuscript of the symphony was originally dated "probably not before early summer 1772" by Plath, but more recently—after examining the autograph in Cracow—he has reverted to Köchel's estimate of late 1769 or early 1770. Tyson reports that the paper of K. 73 is a Salzburg type that cannot be closely dated.

The evidence connecting K. 73 with Italy is also ambiguous: there is a single leaf that began its existence as an attempt by Leopold to copy out a *basso* part for this symphony. For unknown reasons, he abandoned his effort after only twelve measures, and Wolfgang later used the mostly empty sheet of music paper to work out a puzzle canon from the second volume of Padre Martini's *Storia della musica,* a book that came into the Mozarts' possession in Bologna in early October 1770. But this provides only a starting date, as Wolfgang continued to work sporadically on Martini's puzzle canons for a few years. In sum, even with its autograph, the *basso* fragment, and the other version of the Minuet available for examination, K. 73 has so far resisted efforts firmly to date or place it.

German musician Detlef Schultz wrote of the first movement that its "principal theme departs from the overture-type. It is a hybrid form in which a first phrase, built of chordal figurations in the Italian style, gives way to a *cantabile* phrase in a manner unknown to the theater symphony. In other respects the movement still bears a pronounced overture character." Likewise indicative of the movement's hybrid nature is that fact that, even though the symphony as a whole is a four-movement concert symphony along Germanic lines rather than a three-movement Italianate overture-symphony, the first movement lacks the repeats usually found in the former genre.

The Andante, a subdominant binary movement with both halves repeated, is treated similarly to the andantes of a number of Wolfgang's symphonies of the period: the horns, trumpets, and kettledrums drop out and the oboists, taking up their flutes, soar above the treble staff coloring the movement from beginning to end. Danish musicologist Jens Peter Larsen singles out this movement from Wolfgang's symphonies of the period "for its fine *cantabile.*"

In their monumental biography of Mozart, Théodore de Wyzewa and Georges Saint-Foix find the stately Minuet Haydnesque, and especially the Trio, which is for strings alone, even though both are more foursquare than the older master's best minuets. The violas, by their simple doubling of the bass line in the Minuet, reveal the movement's ballroom origin. (Other symphony minuets that exist also in versions for the ballroom and likewise lack independent viola parts are found in K. 112 and 320.)

The Finale is a gavotte (or contredanse) *en rondeau.* Although the movement is marked Allegro molto 2/4, its rondo theme is based on an underlying moderate tempo 2/2 gavotte, which can be sensed by beating time once in a measure, starting with an upbeat. The Finale is 176 measures long, but Wolfgang only wrote out eight passages totaling seventy-two measures. These he numbered one to twenty in such a way that an alert copyist could piece together the whole movement. Over the first eight measures, for instance, he wrote "1 2 5 6 8 9 16 17," signifying the four pairs of appearances of the movement's refrain. This method, which saved time, paper, and ink, suggests how clearly Wolfgang must have had the movement's straightforward structure **(A-B-A-C-A-D-A)** in mind as he came to write it down. The whole projects an impression of deliberate naïveté, from the nursery-rhyme character of the refrain to the comically singsong quality of the **D** section in C minor. N.Z.

K. 74 *Symphony in G major, No. 10*

Origin: Rome, April 1770
Scoring: 2 oboes, 2 horns, strings
Movements: Allegro. [Andante.] [Allegro.]

The autograph of K. 74 bears neither date nor title, although at the end of the last movement Mozart expressed his gratitude (or perhaps relief?) at its completion by writing "Finis Laus Deo." At the beginning someone else wrote "Ouverture (zur Oper Mitridate)," but this incorrect inscription was subsequently crossed out. Unable in the early 1970s to examine the autograph of K. 74, Wolfgang Plath had to content himself with echoing the Köchel Catalogue's "probably 1770 in Milan." Alan Tyson, more fortunate a few years later, discovered that K. 74 is written on the same rare type of paper that Wolfgang used for the aria "Se ardire, e speranza," K. 82, composed in Rome in April 1770. This places the work reasonably securely.

K. 74 is written in Italian overture style, that is, the first movement is in sonata form without repeats in which, after a complete recapitulation, an altered codetta flows into the second movement not only without a halt but even without a new tempo indication or double barline. At this juncture the eighth notes in the oboes continue on unperturbed, as the meter shifts from common time to 3/8 and the key from G major to C major. The Finale is marked simply "Rondeau," whose spelling gives a hint of the character of its refrain, which is that of a French contredanse. Noteworthy in this movement is an "exotic" episode in G minor, perhaps the earliest manifestation of Wolfgang's interest in "Turkish" music, discussed in connection with the Violin Concerto in A major, K. 219 (see p. 143).

A remarkable aspect of the Mozart family's voluminous correspondence is its almost exclusive concentration on people and their creations. Did they never look out the windows of the carriages in which they traveled or of the buildings in which they stayed? Did they fail to look about themselves when they went out walking? It is as if in their view of the world nature hardly existed or was little worthy of comment. But in Rome in the spring of 1770 the fourteen-year-old Mozart perhaps did notice something, for in the first movement of K. 74 at measures 17–22 and the parallel passage in the recapitulation (measures 77–82) there occurs what appears to be the call of the *cinciallegra* or titmouse. N.Z.

K. *87 *Symphony in D major, "Mitridate" (K⁶ *74a)*

Origin: 1770

Scoring: 2 flutes, 2 oboes, 2 horns, 2 trumpets, strings

Movements: Allegro. Andante grazioso. Presto.

This work consists of the Overture to the opera *Mitridate, rè di Ponto* used by Mozart as a symphony. See the note on p. 45.

N.Z.

K. *118 *Symphony in D minor, "La Betulia liberata" (K⁶ *74c)*

Origin: Italy and Salzburg, between March and July 1771

Scoring: 2 flutes, 2 oboes, 2 bassoons, 4 horns, 2 trumpets, strings

Movements: [Allegro.] Andante. Presto.

This work consists of the Overture to the oratorio *La Betulia liberata* used by Mozart as a symphony. See the note on p. 32.

N.Z.

K. 110 *Symphony in G major, No. 12 (K⁶ 75b)*

Origin: Salzburg, July 1771

Scoring: 2 oboes (doubling flutes), 2 bassoons, 2 horns, strings

Movements: Allegro. [Andante]. Menuetto. Allegro molto.

Wolfgang headed the autograph manuscript of this work, "Sinfonia / del Sgr. Cavaliere Amadeo / Wolfg. Mozart in Salisburgo / nel Luglio 1771." The title "Cavaliere" refers to the Cross of the Golden Spur, or Knighthood of the

Golden Order, which the Pope conferred upon the fourteen-year-old prodigy in Rome in July 1770. A year later plans were already well advanced for a second trip to Italy, and this symphony was doubtless intended for (undocumented) concerts in Salzburg that summer and (documented) concerts during his second Italian journey, in Milan (November 22 or 23) and Brixen (December 11 and 12).

It is difficult to regard this symphony as having been born of the same creative impulses that spawned K. 73. It is worked out on a grander scale and apparently with more care. The care is manifested in all movements in the more contrapuntal conception of the inner parts and, especially, of the bass line. The opening Allegro tends toward the monothematic, a tendency that has been noted in the symphonies K. 114 and 134. That is, the opening idea reappears, somewhat transformed, in the dominant as a "second subject" and again in its original guise in the closing section of the exposition. The development section is based on an imitatively treated descending scale, followed by striding eighth notes in the bass, an idea previously heard in the closing section of the exposition. The recapitulation is not literal, with the retransition extended in a developmental way.

The second movement of K. 110 bears no tempo indication, although it is without question an Andante or Andantino. The oboes are replaced by flutes, the horns fall silent, and a pair of bassoons, previously and subsequently tacitly subsumed along with the cellos, double basses, and harpsichord (under the rubric *basso*), suddenly blossoms forth with obbligato parts. If the movement had been given a title, it might have been "romanza." It is in the "simple" key of C major and is in sonata form with two repeated sections. Many of the movement's two-measure phrases are immediately repeated, creating a kind of musical construction that the French called "couplets." The carefully wrought inner parts in Mozart's movement reveal the German craftsman hidden beneath the French finery, while a touch of harmonic color is provided by the major chord on the flatted sixth degree, which sounds twice near the end of each section.

The Minuet is canonic, a device found in a number of Joseph Haydn's symphony minuets of this period, and one to which Mozart would occasionally return, for instance, in the F-major Symphony, K. 130, the C-minor Wind Serenade, K. 388, and the G-minor Symphony, K. 550. This application of learned canonic devices to the insouciant ballroom minuet may be considered an attempt to render the dance more "symphonic." The aggressively striding Minuet is set off by the more sedate E-minor Trio for strings alone.

Like the Finale of K. 73, the present Finale is a 2/4 Allegro in which one can sense the moderate tempo 2/2 gavotte or contredanse underlying the theme by beating time half as often. This Rondo has a G minor middle section, itself binary in structure, which is exotic in character; the origins and associations of such exoticism are explored in connection with the violin concerto K. 219 on p. 143.

N.Z.

K. *111 + 120 *Symphony in D major, "Ascanio in Alba" (K⁶ *111 + 111a)*

Origin: Salzburg, between December 1771 and October 1772

Scoring: 2 flutes, 2 oboes, 2 horns, 2 trumpets and timpani, strings

Movements: Allegro assai. [Andante grazioso?] Presto.

This symphony also began its life as an overture, in this case to the serenata *Ascanio in Alba,* K. 111, written for the celebrations surrounding the wedding of the Austrian Archduke Ferdinand and Princess Maria Beatrice Ricciarda d'Este of Modena. Mozart began work on the opera in late August 1771, completing it by September 23. Its first performance in Milan on October 17 was a success, apparently eclipsing a new opera by the veteran Johann Adolf Hasse, which was also part of the festivities. That the great choreographer Jean-Georges Noverre created the ballets in *Ascanio* doubtless added to its brilliance.

In this instance Mozart went against his usual custom and composed the overture first, because he had decided to integrate the end of his overture into the beginning of the serenata. Thus, following the opening Allegro, the Andante served as a ballet, to be danced by "the Graces." The libretto explains the setting that the Andante was to accompany:

> A spacious area, intended for a solemn pastoral setting, bordered by a circle of very tall and leafy oaks which, gracefully distributed all around, cast a very cool and holy shade. Between the trees are grassy mounds, formed by Nature but adapted by human skill to provide seats where the shepherds can sit with graceful informality. In the middle is a rustic altar on which may be seen a relief depicting the fabulous beast from whom, according to legend, the City of Alba derived its name. A delicious, smiling countryside—dotted with cottages and encircled by pleasant, not-too-distant hills from which issue abundant and limpid streams—is visible through the spaces between the trees. The horizon is bounded by very blue mountains, which merge into a most pure and serene sky.

For a Finale, the overture had an Allegro in 3/4 with choruses of spirits and graces singing and dancing, thus anticipating (in a most diminutive way) Beethoven's innovation in his Ninth Symphony. When Mozart decided to turn the overture into a concert symphony, he kept the first two movements unchanged, replacing the choral Finale with a brief *giga* in the form **A-B-A-coda**. On the basis of Mozart's writing, the autograph of the new Finale has been dated "probably the end of October or beginning of November 1771 in Milan." But as the paper employed in the Finale is of Salzburg manufacture, this symphony Finale was more likely written sometime between the second half of December 1771 and the beginning of October 1772. N.Z.

K. 112 *Symphony in F major, No. 13*
Origin: Milan, November 2, 1771
Scoring: 2 oboes, 2 horns, strings
Movements: Allegro. Andante. Menuetto. Molto Allegro.

The autograph manuscript is a clearly written fair copy inscribed "Sinfonia / del Sig^{re} Cavaliere Amadeo / Wolfgango Mozart / à Milano 2 di Novemb. / 1771" (the first word in Wolfgang's hand, the remainder in Leopold's). Its first performance was probably at an orchestral concert *(eine starke Musik)* that Leopold and Wolfgang gave in Milan on November 22 or 23 at the residence of Albert Michael von Mayr, keeper of the privy purse to Archduke Ferdinand, governor of Lombardy and son of Empress Maria Theresa.

That K. 112 was conceived as a concert piece and not an overture can be seen in the first, second, and fourth movements, in which all sections but the coda of the Finale are repeated. Whereas three previous symphonies require five to seven minutes each to perform, K. 112 takes about fifteen minutes. From the beautifully proportioned sonata form of the first movement, through the careful part-writing of the B-flat Andante (for strings alone) to the characteristic jig-like Rondo-Finale, a spirit of confidence and solid workmanship seems to emanate from this symphony, fruits perhaps garnered from the success of *Ascanio in Alba* the previous month.

In the Minuet the violas, instead of having an independent part to play, as is customary in Mozart's symphonic minuets, double the bass line. Given that his ballroom dances are without viola parts, this feature of the Minuet of K. 112 may mean either that it had fulfilled another function before being pressed into service in this symphony, or that, with this sonority, Mozart wished to evoke memories of the ballroom in his listeners. In the Trio (for strings alone), however, the violas do carry an independent part. That the Minuet probably existed before the rest of the symphony is suggested by the fact that it (but not the Trio or the rest of the symphony) is copied into Wolfgang's manuscript in Leopold's hand. N.Z.

K. 114 ***Symphony in A major, No. 14***
Origin: Salzburg, December 30, 1771
Scoring: 2 flutes (doubling oboes), 2 horns, strings
Movements: Allegro moderato. Andante. Menuetto. Molto allegro.

K. 114 ***Symphonic Minuet in A major***
Origin: Salzburg, December 30, 1771
Scoring: 2 oboes, 2 horns, strings

This is the first of a series of eight symphonies written for Salzburg in the period of less than a year between the Mozarts' second and third Italian trips. Presumably practical motives lay behind this outpouring. The Italian trips had not proven lucrative, and a portion of Leopold's salary had been withheld during his absence. The time had come for him and his son to dig in their heels at home, in order to reestablish their usefulness there and to pay off their debts. Wolfgang and Leopold returned from Italy on December 15, 1771, and next day the Archbishop Sigismund von Schrattenbach died. The autograph manuscript of K. 114 is dated two weeks later. Symphonies may have been needed for the period of mourning, for muted carnival festivities, for Lent, and for the installation of the new archbishop in March. In addition, Wolfgang sought a promotion, for his title of concertmaster had been honorary. Having proven his mettle, the sixteen-year-old was decreed a regularly paid member of the court orchestra on August 9, 1772 by the archbishop, at the modest annual salary of 150 florins.

It has been suggested that in this symphony Wolfgang declared himself for the "Viennese" or "Austrian" symphonic style, while still keeping key Italian elements. In this context, "Austrian" refers to the greater length, more extensive use of winds, more contrapuntal texture, four-movement format, and greater use of non-*cantabile* thematic materials. But the first theme, with its mid-measure syncopation, is closer to the style of J. C. Bach than to that of Vienna. Danish musicologist Jens Peter Larsen considers K. 114 "one of the most inspired [symphonies] of the period. One could point out many beauties in this work, such as [in the first movement] the developmental transition, the second subject with its hint of quartet style, and the short, but delicately wrought development with elegant wind and string dialogue." Even the gentle opening bars, which forgo loud chords or fanfares and begin *piano,* suggest something new. The relatively high-pitched horns in A were probably responsible for suggesting to Mozart that flutes be used in place of oboes; once the decision was made on technical grounds, however, the whole symphony seems to have been colored by it. The sole conservative trait of this strikingly modern movement is the handling of the winds in the development section, more in a concerto-grosso style than in a symphonic style.

In a number of symphonies Mozart required that the oboists take up flutes in the andantes; here the reverse is the case, oboes replacing flutes and the horns dropping out. The movement is in sonata form with both sections repeated. The violas, which had already had a *divisi* passage in the development section of the first movement, here form an important series of duets, often doubling the oboes at the octave below or engaging in dialogue with them. The development section, written in continuous eighth notes, gives the somewhat old-fashioned impression of Baroque style intercalated between the more characteristic Classical style of the exposition and recapitulation.

The autograph manuscript of K. 114 contains an extra, fully scored Minuet, without Trio, that Mozart crossed out. The opening theme of the rejected movement is a reworking of the theme of the Andante. The Minuet Mozart finally provided is a particularly stately one, spiced with some well-placed secondary-dominant chords near the end of each section. Its Trio, in A minor, is in a mock-pathetic vein. The pathos is provided by the repeated-note melody on the fifth degree of the scale rising the semitone to the flatted sixth; this melodic shape would have been familiar to Mozart from such plainchant settings as that for the somber Holy Week text "Miserere mei Deus." The mocking comes from the second violins, which, with their triplets and trills, wander about as if making variations on a comic-opera tune. The intention behind the juxtaposition of high and low styles was probably ironic or parodistic.

The Finale begins with a three-note fanfare and a response, once repeated. Then something strange happens. Instead of developing the fanfare or introducing a proper first theme, Mozart has the orchestra play, twice in a conspicuous manner, the harmony-primer chord progression I–IV–V–I. This is apparently an allusion to the *bergamasca,* a kind of dance or song in which a melody is composed or improvised over many repetitions of these four chords. In German-speaking countries a text commonly sung to the tune most often associated with the *bergamasca* reads:

> Kraut und Rüben haben mich vertrieben,
> Hätte meine Mutter Fleisch gekocht,
> So wär ich länger blieben.
>
> (Cabbages and turnips drove me away.
> Had my mother cooked some meat,
> Then I'd have stayed longer.)

J. S. Bach quoted the "Kraut und Rüben" tune at the end of his Goldberg Variations. Mozart did not quote the tune, but the presence of his little joke in the Finale supports the suggestion that this symphony may have been composed with carnival in mind. The rest of the movement, in sonata form with both sections repeated, is also in high, if more conventionally symphonic, spirits.

The mockery of the Trio and the *bergamasca* of the Finale's exposition and recapitulation bring to mind the remarks of a German visitor to Salzburg in the mid-1770s, surely describing carnival: "Here everyone breathes the spirit of fun and mirth. People smoke, dance, make music, make love, and indulge in riotous revelry, and I have yet to see another place where one can with so little money enjoy so much sensuousness." N.Z.

K. 124 *Symphony in G major, No. 15*
Origin: Salzburg, February 21, 1772
Scoring: 2 oboes, 2 horns, strings
Movements: Allegro. Andante. Menuetto. Presto.

Carnival ends on Mardi gras (Shrove Tuesday) and with the next day, Ash Wednesday, the forty days of Lent begin; in 1772 these days fell on February 3 and 4 respectively. Mozart wrote at the top of the autograph manuscript of K. 124, "Sinfonia / del Sig^{re} Cavaliere Wolfgango Amadeo Mozart Salisburgo 21 Febrario 1772." Hence the work may have been intended either for a Lenten concert or for the new archbishop, who took office on April 29. The archbishop was an amateur violinist who liked to join his orchestra in performing symphonies, standing next to the concertmaster, perhaps for maximum professional guidance or perhaps to be seen symbolically at the orchestra's center of power.

The first movement of K. 124 has a character quite different from that of the previous symphony. Its angular opening theme is of a more abrupt sort than the genial theme of K. 114, although, curiously, the two themes outline the same scale degrees: do-sol-mi-re-sol-fa-mi. For the rest, the first movement of K. 124 is more compact, less inclined to a "fullness of ideas" than that of K. 114. An attractive touch is the ambiguous rhythm of the second subject, which for an instant leaves the listener unsure of whether he is hearing 3/4 or 6/8. A pause on a diminished chord allows listeners and performers alike to catch one last breath before plunging with great momentum toward the final cadence of the exposition. The development section begins calmly, but a false reprise in E minor soon introduces some of the agitated effects often associated with symphonic development. The recapitulation is literal, with a four-bar codetta added. Both main sections are repeated.

The C-major Andante, a binary movement with both halves repeated, is notable for its *concertante* writing for horns and oboes. The Minuet and Trio (for strings only) illustrate German theorist Johann Philipp Kirnberger's description of the minuet as "ruled by *galant* agreeableness united with calm dignity. There is hardly another dance where so much elegance, noble decorum, and such a highly pleasing manner is to be met."

The Rondo-Finale begins with the same fanfare as does the Finale of K. 114, but here it is not instantly repeated, and the movement continues in an apparently straightforward manner. The joke (and it surely is one) comes in the coda, where the melody suddenly evaporates, leaving only some chords, syncopations, tremolos, an oom-pah bass, and a fanfare or two. N.Z.

K. 128 *Symphony in C major, No. 16*
Origin: Salzburg, May 1772
Scoring: 2 oboes, 2 horns, strings
Movements: Allegro maestoso. Andantino grazioso. Allegro.

The autograph manuscripts of the symphonies K. 129 and 130 are in the West Berlin library, while K. 128 is in East Berlin. Each of these three manuscripts and that of the Regina coeli, K. 127, also in West Berlin, is inscribed "nel mese di maggio 1772 Salisburgo," an exceptional output for a single month even for the prolific sixteen-year-old Mozart. Was this fire lit under him by a desire to attract the favorable notice of the newly installed archbishop? Perhaps, too, Mozart was girding his loins for the third (and final) trip to Italy from October 1772 to March 1773, which would require new symphonies.

That the opening movement of the first of these works is marked not simply "allegro" but also "maestoso" suggests something broader in tempo than the typical first movement of this period of Mozart's symphonic production. It is notated in 3/4, but, as the rhythm of the first half of the exposition comprises entirely eighth note triplets, the listener at first takes it for 9/8. The second theme, a memorable leaping melody, first reveals the true underlying meter. After a touch of the second theme in the minor, an energetic bass line figure ushers in the closing section. The exposition is repeated but the rest is not. The development section is announced by the sudden appearance of an E-flat chord, which proves to be a herald of D minor. Then follow in rapid succession hints of E minor, A minor, G major, F major, and again G major, the dominant needed to establish the recapitulation. The development takes only thirty-one measures during which the thematic material is almost entirely scales, yet it is so tightly and logically constructed that one has the impression of having traversed great tonal distances. The recapitulation is not literal, containing a number of telling developmental touches.

Just as the previous Allegro was maestoso, so the Andante is grazioso, which has equally the result of slowing the movement's tempo and deepening its affect. The movement, for strings only, is in sonata form with both sections repeated. A chamber-music texture involves the players in dialogue, most often between the first and second violins or between the upper and lower strings.

The Finale is a jig in the form of an oddly proportioned rondo: **A-A-B-A-B-A-C-A-coda**, in which the **B** section is roughly five times the length of the **A** section. When the end of the Finale is nearly reached and the listener thinks that Mozart has already showed his hand, he kicks up his heels with a series of hunting-horn calls. This is all the more unexpected as the wind writing in the rest of the symphony is conservative. N.Z.

K. 129 *Symphony in G major, No. 17*

Origin: Salzburg, May 1772
Scoring: 2 oboes, 2 horns, strings
Movements: Allegro. Andante. Allegro.

The autograph manuscript of K. 129 has the usual sort of heading that Wolfgang, with or without the help of his father, put on his works during this period: "Sinfonia / del Sg^{re} Cavaliere Amadeo Wolfgango / Mozart nel mese di Maggio 1772 / Salisburgo." Such inscriptions have been, and generally must be, taken at face value, for they are often the only information about the provenance of Wolfgang's instrumental works, which usually do not leave behind additional clues, the way operas and other occasional works do. The studies (often referred to here) of the evolution of Wolfgang's writing and of the paper types used in his music manuscripts have confirmed the reliability of most of the dates on the manuscripts. The same studies show that K. 129 was begun, put aside, and then resumed at a later time. This in turn could suggest either that the symphony was begun in May 1772 and completed at a later date, or that it was begun earlier and completed on that date. (The latter suggestion is most likely the correct one.)

The first movement of K. 129 begins with a great chord reinforced by quadruple stops in the violins. There follows an odd little tune, based on the so-called Scottish snap (also known as the Lombard rhythm). To identify this rhythm, sing the following Scottish folksong, noting the rhythm to which the italicized syllables are set: "When a *Laddie* meets a *Lassie, Comin'* through the rye." This rhythm is heard again as part of the second subject and as the most important motive of the development section. A repetitive passage over a pedal, probably calling for a *crescendo,* leads into the closing section of the exposition, in which the first and second violins engage in witty repartee. Both sections of this sonata-form movement are repeated. A temperamental development section alternates brief moments of lyricism with *forte* outbursts of the Scottish snap; the recapitulation is literal.

The C-major Andante begins like a serene song with the strings playing alone. The oboes and horns join and the song is repeated. For the rest of the exposition no other striking ideas are introduced, but Mozart spins a magical web of commonplace melodic fragments. The "development" section is a concise eight-measure *fugato,* leading to a literal recapitulation. Again both halves are repeated.

The Finale begins with a hunting-horn flourish virtually identical to one Mozart was to use in 1773 played by horns as the trio of a minuet of the Divertimento, K. 205, and again years later to begin his piano sonata K. 576. This, then, may have been the kind of symphony which English historian Charles Burney denigrated for having its Finale based on "a minuet degenerated into a jigg." Although the movement consists of two repeated sections with the sonata-form modulatory scheme, at the moment the tonic returns, the opening theme is merely hinted at and no true recapitulation occurs. The movement is thus perhaps best considered in rounded binary rather than sonata form. The function of jig-finales like the present one is analogous to that which Mozart later ascribed to the Finale of an act of *Die Entführung aus dem Serail,* which "must go very fast—and the ending must make a truly great racket . . . the more noise the better—the shorter the better—so that the audience doesn't grow cold before the time comes to applaud."

N.Z.

K. 130 *Symphony in F major, No. 18*
Origin: Salzburg, May 1772
Scoring: 2 flutes, 4 horns, strings
Movements: Allegro. Andantino grazioso. Menuetto. Molto allegro.

Mozart inscribed the autograph of this work simply "Sinfonia," to which his father added "del Sg^{re} Cavaliere Amadeo Wolfg: Mozart / à Salisburgo nel Maggio 1772." Several commentators, following French scholar Georges Saint-Foix, have regarded K. 130 as the first of Mozart's "great" symphonies, and, it must be admitted, the piece does contain inspired ideas, beautifully worked out. In addition to its fine ideas, this symphony also has a distinctive timbre, arising from the key, which is unusual for Mozart's symphonies; from flutes in place of, and occupying a higher tessitura than, oboes; and from the two pairs of horns in C-alto and F (or F and B-flat *basso* in the Andantino grazioso).

Mozart had begun the first movement with the customary single pair of horns in mind, and continued that way through the Andantino. By the time he reached the Minuet, however, he decided to add another pair of horns, found in this movement and the Finale, and he subsequently went back and wrote parts for the additional horns on blank staves between systems in the first and second movements. Mozart's change of mind may have been motivated by the return to Salzburg from a European tour of the horn virtuoso Joseph Leutgeb, for whom he was later to write his horn quintet and horn concertos.

The first movement, in sonata form with the first section repeated, begins quietly without fanfare. The opening motive, also heard at the end of the exposition, in the development section, and at the beginning and end of the recapitulation, prominently features the short-long rhythm mentioned in connection with the first movement of the previous symphony—a rhythm associated not only with Lombardy and Scotland but also with Hungarian folk music, some of which Mozart may have encountered in his travels or heard from Michael Haydn, who had worked in Hungary before moving to Salzburg.

The Andantino grazioso is a placid movement in binary form, whose opening idea features three-measure phrases rather than the usual even-numbered ones. Once again the violins are muted, the cellos and basses pizzicato; as in other andantes that feature this orchestration, the violas are without mutes, perhaps confirming a puzzling feature of so many of the orchestras of the period: the tiny number of violas. The meter is 3/8 rather than the customary 2/4. Joseph Haydn first wrote symphonic andantes in 3/8 in four symphonies from the years 1770–72. Could Mozart have known and imitated any of them in K. 130, or was the timing mere coincidence?

The Minuet is wittily constructed around a canon between the bass line and the violins in octaves, with the violas adding a rustic drone wobbling back and forth between C and B natural, in good-natured contradiction of the F-major harmonies. The Trio offers a bit of musical slapstick: quasi-modal harmonies and stratospheric high horn writing. The French writers Théodore de Wyzewa and Georges Saint-Foix called this Trio (along with that of K. 132) "daring and bizarre," which it is. Here was something special for the recently returned Leutgeb. Lest the gay exterior of this movement deceive, however, note that Mozart crossed out and rewrote a ten-bar passage in the Trio on the way to achieving the unassuming perfection of his final results.

The Finale, marked Molto Allegro in pencil, probably in Leopold's hand, balances the first movement in length and substance, and, like it, is in sonata form; it thus departs from the short, dancelike finales of the Italian symphonists and of many of Wolfgang's own earlier symphonies, imparting new substance to a formerly lightweight design. The movement is filled with rushing scales, sudden changes of dynamic, tremolos, and other joyous sounds much in favor in symphonies of the period. Although Leopold once referred to such writing in the symphonies of Johann Stamitz as "nothing but noise," Wolfgang understood how to make brilliant use of the style. N.Z.

K. 132 *Symphony in E-flat major, No. 19*
Origin: Salzburg, July 1772
Scoring: 2 oboes, 4 horns, strings
Movements: Allegro. Andante. Menuetto. Allegro.

K. 132 *Symphonic Andantino grazioso in B-flat major*
Origin: Salzburg, July 1772
Scoring: 2 oboes, 2 horns, strings

Leopold's hand is in evidence in the autograph manuscript of this symphony too.

Besides adding to Wolfgang's heading "Sinfonia" the information "del Sg[re] Cavaliere Amadeo Wolfgango Mozart / nel Luglio 1772 Salisburgo," he also provided the tempo indications for the first, second, and fourth movements.

The triadic figure with trill, which opens the first movement of K. 132, also serves as the beginning of the piano concerto K. 482. Although the movement's orchestration is conservative (that is, the winds are used as a choir rather than as soloists), few symphony movements of the 1770s show better Mozart's extraordinary ear for orchestral sonorities. Indeed, the movement seems to be as much about orchestral sonorities as about themes or modulations.

Two complete slow movements survive for this symphony: an Andante in 3/8 found in the expected position between the first movement and the Minuet, and a substitute movement, an Andantino grazioso in 2/4, added in the manuscript after the Finale. (In both movements one pair of horns is silent.) The 3/8 movement is based in part upon borrowed materials. Its opening melody reproduces the first seven notes of a Gregorian Credo. Later in the movement there appears a variant of a popular German Christmas carol, "Joseph, lieber Joseph mein," also known with the Latin text "Resonet in laudibus." The residents of Salzburg were familiar with this version of "Joseph, lieber Joseph mein," as it was played by the mechanical carillon in a tower of the Hohensalzburg Castle each Christmas season. That instrument has survived and may occasionally still be faintly heard above the noises of the modern city, although it no longer plays the tune in question. Mozart tucked the quotation into the second violin part in measures 37–56 and the parallel passage at measures 128–47.

Although unaware of the presence of musical quotations, musicologist Alfred Einstein found Mozart's first Andante "full of personal spiritual unrest and rebellion" and even "expressionistic," and Italian critic Luigi Della Croce, so "personal" as to require replacement. Besides its other eccentricities, the movement was too long, as may be seen by comparing it with the andantes of the seven other symphonies written around the same time, which in performance average roughly five-and-three-quarter minutes, whereas K. 132's first Andante lasts about nine-and-a-half minutes. This exceptional movement must have had some local significance, an allusion to Salzburg affairs or a private joke, but whatever that may have been is lost to us. Perhaps its very specificity led to its being replaced by an all-purpose, "abstract" movement, containing (as far as anyone knows) no quotations. This new, more conventional movement features a simple but elegant melody shared between violins and oboes and maintaining a dialogue with the rest of the orchestra.

The Minuet begins with a canonic exchange between the first and second violins. This tune is soon imitated by the bass instruments and then heard in one voice or another throughout the piece, including after a humorously timed pause just before the return of the opening theme in the middle of the second section. As mentioned above, the Trio, for strings only, was called "daring and bizarre" by the French writers Théodore de Wyzewa and Georges Saint-Foix, while the Austrian scholar Hermann Abert too noted a "tendency toward eccentricity." It appears to be based upon a melody in the style of a psalm tone (the most monotonous type of Gregorian chant), set as a parody of a post-Renaissance motet. A brief outburst of ballroom gaiety at the beginning of the second section is the only intrusion of the secular world into the mock-sanctity of the psalmody. Was this Mozart's commentary on the curious mix of secular and sacred at the court of the prince-archbishops of Salzburg?

The Finale, a substantial movement in the form of a gavotte or contredanse *en rondeau,* is as French as Mozart's symphonic music ever becomes. The Rondo resounds with a kind of mock naïveté of which, one imagines, members of the French nobility who enjoyed playing at shepherds and shepherdesses would have approved. Mozart had harsh things to say about most French music of his time, exasperatedly calling it "trash" and "wretched," and he was loath to admit any indebtedness to it. Yet in 1778 he wrote of a group of his symphonies that "most of them are not in the Parisian taste," implying, of course, that some of them were in that taste. N.Z.

K. 133 *Symphony in D major, No. 20*
Origin: Salzburg, July 1772
Scoring: 2 oboes (1 doubling flute), 2 horns, strings
Movements: [Allegro.] Andante. Menuetto. [Allegro molto.]

The autograph bears the characteristic inscription "Sinfonia / del Sgre Cavaliere Amadeo Wolfgango / Mozart. nel Luglio 1772 à Salisburgo." The first movement opens with three tutti chords, after which a rising sequential theme with trills follows in the strings. (The theme of this rising sequence is related to the opening idea from a sonata of J. C. Bach's, which Mozart used as the basis of the first movement of his pastiche piano concerto, K. 107/3.) Flourishes from the trumpets, as well as from the other winds, define this as a festive work, and there is much dialogue between the winds and strings throughout the movement. A contrasting lyrical section of the exposition features the Scottish or Lombardic rhythm noted in several other of Mozart's symphonies of this period (see p. 182). Both halves are repeated. A well-worked-out development section returns to the tonic key without presenting the opening theme. That theme Mozart saves for the end, where it is heard in the strings and then, in a grand apotheosis, heard again doubled by the trumpets. This handling of sonata form thus creates a kind of mirror form, which works especially well here because the closing theme of the exposition is derived from (and both precedes and follows) the primary theme, imparting to the movement striking unity despite an apparent variety of themes.

Exceptionally, the binary Andante is in the dominant instead of the subdominant. It is scored for strings (once again violins muted and the bass instruments pizzicato), with the addition of a solitary "flauto traverso obbligato." The translucent timbre of the orchestra, with the flute doubling the first violins at the octave above and occasionally venturing forth as a soloist, is handled with felicity. Did Mozart know the similar writing for solo flute found in the Andante of Joseph Haydn's Symphony in C major, Hob. I:30, of 1765?

The Minuet is short, simple, and fast, something Mozart favored at this time judging by his complaint about Italian minuets that "generally have plenty of notes, are played slowly, and are many bars long." The Trio, for strings accompanied by the oboes, once again provided an opportunity for him to shake a few tricks from his sleeve, in this case syncopations, suspensions, and other contrapuntal devices, or an ironic negation of the homophonic texture normally found in dance music.

The Finale is an enormous jig in sonata form that, once begun, continues virtually without rest to its breathless conclusion. This movement bears no tempo indication, and none would have been needed, as jig-finales were common and everyone knew how they went. In addition, the finales of symphonies were usually faster than their first movements. Thus the first and last movements of this symphony should bear the generic, editorial tempo indications "[Allegro]" and "[Allegro molto]" respectively. N.Z.

K. 134 *Symphony in A major, No. 21*
Origin: Salzburg, August 1772
Scoring: 2 flutes, 2 horns, strings
Movements: Allegro. Andante. Menuetto. Allegro.

With their customary division of labor, Wolfgang headed the autograph manuscript of K. 134 "Sinfonia" and his father added "del Sgre Caval: Amadeo Wolfg: Mozart. / in Salisburgo nel Agosto 1772." Since the symphonies K. 128, 129, 130, 132, 133, and 134 are dated May (three works), July (two works), and August 1772 respectively, there must have been a pressing need for new symphonies. It may have been the Mozarts' intention to form an "opus" of six, although as the works' manuscripts come down to us, they consist of two separate works (K. 128, 129) and then the four others bound together in the nineteenth century.

The first movement eschews a more usual march-like, common-time opening in favor of one in 3/4. For Mozart, this is an exceptionally monothematic movement. The opening idea is heard repeatedly in the tuttis of the exposition and recapitulation and in the development section as well. Perhaps the approach to monothematicism is the reason that Mozart felt the need, rather unusual for him during this period, to add an eighteen-measure coda in which, after a brief allusion to the principal theme, a few triadic flourishes assure even an inattentive listener that the close has been reached.

The Andante, like several others of the period, is in 2/4 and in the subdominant. It opens with a melody that Mozart may have been inspired to write by Gluck's aria "Che farò senza Euridice?" from *Orfeo ed Euridice*. The movement's *cantabile* beginning is spun out into a sonata-form movement of considerable subtlety, its texture carefully worked out, with an elaborate second violin part and divided violas.

The Minuet has a brusque quality audible in a number of Mozart's and Joseph Haydn's symphonic minuets. The courtly Minuet gives way to an anti-courtly Trio, with its virtually non-melodic first section and, in the second section, chords tossed antiphonally between winds and violins, pizzicato, over a drone in the violas, arriving at a peculiarly chromatic passage to prepare the return of the opening "non-melody."

The Finale begins with a *bourrée*, which is subjected to full development in sonata form with coda. One might expect a dance turned into a symphonic finale to be in the "lighter" form of a rondo rather than sonata form; but apparently this was not seen by Mozart as an aesthetic problem of disparity between form and content, and the Finale of his penultimate symphony, K. 550, observes the same procedure. The spirit of the dance continually peers through the symphonic facade. N.Z.

K. *135 *Symphony in D major, "Lucio Silla"*
Origin: Salzburg? 1772
Scoring: 2 flutes, 2 oboes, 2 bassoons, 2 horns,

2 trumpets and timpani, strings
Movements: Molto allegro. Andante. Molto allegro.

This works consists of the Overture to the opera *Lucio Silla* used by Mozart as a symphony. *See the note on p. 47.

N.Z.

K. 161 + 163 *Symphony in D major, "Il sogno di Scipione" (K[6] 141a)*

Origin: Salzburg, between May and October 1772
Scoring: 2 flutes, 2 oboes, 2 horns, 2 trumpets and timpani, strings
Movements: Allegro. Andante. [Presto.]

Until recently it was believed that Mozart's setting of Metastasio's *serenata drammatica Il sogno di Scipione,* K. 126, was composed for ceremonies connected with the installation of the new archbishop of Salzburg, and performed in early May 1772. This was logical enough, as on the autograph could be seen the date 1772, apparently in Leopold's hand, and the Italian name "Girolamo" (that is, Hieronymus Colloredo) appears in the text. It now emerges, however, that "Girolamo" was written over an erasure, which can be deciphered as "Sigismondo," the Italian form of the name of the previous archbishop, Sigismund Christoph von Schrattenbach, who died on December 16, 1771. Hence, this occasional cantata must date from between April and August of 1771, when the Mozarts were in Salzburg between Italian sojourns, and it was probably revived in 1772 with the necessary change of name. The overture of K. 126 (to which Köchel originally gave the separate number K. 161) consisted of an Allegro moderato and an Andante; Mozart later added a Finale (originally numbered K. 163), to make an autonomous symphony.

On the basis of the writing in the autograph manuscript of the Finale, the German musicologist Wolfgang Plath believes it to date from the summer of either 1773 or 1774, when Mozart was in Salzburg, but the English scholar Alan Tyson reports that the paper on which it is written is a type used by Mozart mostly between May and October 1772, although a few bits of it were used somewhat later. The symphony version thus most likely belongs with the six other symphonies produced in the busy summer of 1772.

Metastasio's *azione teatrale* of 1735, *Il sogno di Scipione,* based on Cicero's *Somnium Scipioris* with personae and incidents from Roman history, offers much philosophy and little *"azione"* (action), featuring among its cast of characters the allegorical figures of Constancy and Fortune. Instead of trying to create some kind of music of the spheres, Mozart responded to the libretto's abstractions with an all-purpose sinfonia that would have been at home in any church, chamber, or theater of the period, regardless of the occasion.

The first movement opens in unison, a device that Mozart would later mock as a mannerism of Mannheim symphonies. The exposition continues in the most brilliant Italian-overture style, with the requisite lyrical interlude. The development section jumps into B minor, leaving behind it the tremolo of the exposition, and—in a reversal of the common pattern—deals with newly introduced, calmer material. After twenty measures of the recapitulation, it is interrupted by new developments, which abbreviate the section and lead it to the Andante, a movement of pastoral serenity. The three movements of K[6] 141a, linked by incomplete cadences, are played without a break, the Finale even beginning on a dominant seventh rather than a tonic chord, an unusual gesture that may also be heard at the beginning of the Finale of Schubert's second symphony. (In Schubert's case, however, the dominant seventh is just a transition heard once, whereas in K^6 141a it is essential to the movement's opening idea and, as such, is repeated.) The Finale, whose Presto indication is written in pencil by an unknown hand (perhaps Leopold's), is a kind of minuet in the form of a rondo under a strong sonata-form influence. N.Z.

K. 184 *Symphony in E-flat major, No. 26 (K^3 166a, K^6 161a)*

Origin: Salzburg, March 30, 1773

Scoring: 2 flutes, 2 oboes, 2 bassoons, 2 horns, 2 trumpets, strings

Movements: Molto presto. Andante. Allegro.

The first two pages of the autograph manuscript of K. 184 were written by Leopold, the remainder of the first movement by a professional copyist, and the other movements by Wolfgang. Recent examination of the heavily defaced date confirms that it probably reads "30 March 1773" following the usual inscription "Del Sig^re: Cavaliere Amadeo Mozart." This was about a month after the seventeen-year-old composer and his father returned from their third and last Italian journey.

Every commentator has remarked on the dramatic character of this work; for instance, Georges Saint-Foix in his typically extravagant diction: "The violence of the first movement followed by the infinite despair of the Andante (in the minor), and the ardent and joyous rhythms of the Finale mark this symphony as something quite apart; romantic exaltation here reaches its climax." In addition, the work seems filled with familiar ideas. The intense opening gesture of the Molto presto later served Mozart as a model for the more relaxed openings of two other E-flat pieces: the Sinfonia Concertante, K. 364, and the Serenade for Winds, K. 375. The C-minor Andante, replete with sighing appoggiaturas and other effects borrowed from tragic Italian arias, is the first in a series of powerful C-minor andantes. The theme of the jig-like Finale of K. 184 resembles that of the rondo-finale of the horn concerto, K. 495, again in E flat. Thus, Mozart had in mind a group of ideas associated with E-flat major and C minor, which reappeared in various guises over a period of years. Throughout all three movements of K. 184, *concertante* writing for the winds is prominent for this period.

The jig-finale makes no attempt to maintain the high drama of the two previous movements. That Mozart thought of its function as relaxing the tension generated earlier appears in the reversal of the tempo indications of the first and third movements from his usual practice.

There are two clues about the possible origins of this exceptionally serious symphony: its three movements are played without a break, in the manner associated with many Italian overture-sinfonias, and the orchestration calls for pairs of flutes and oboes to play simultaneously. Mozart's practice in his orchestral serenades and earlier symphonies was to use either oboes or flutes, not both, and in his last symphonies to use a pair of oboes plus a single flute. With the exception of K. 297, written for Paris, the relatively few symphonies requiring pairs of flutes and oboes played simultaneously originated as overtures to theatrical works: *Die Schuldigkeit des ersten Gebots,* K. 35; *La finta semplice,* K. 51; *Mitridate, rè di Ponto,* K. 87; *Ascanio in Alba,* K. 111; and *Il sogno di Scipione,* K. 126. Especially telling in this regard is the overture to *La finta semplice,* which began life as the concert symphony, K. 45, with oboes, and then had a pair of flutes added to it for the theater. Hence, K. 184 was likely intended from the start to serve in the theater as an overture, a function that would not then have precluded (nor should it now preclude) its use in concerts.

Appropriately, therefore, K. 184 was pressed into service during the 1780s, apparently with Mozart's consent, by the traveling theatrical troupe of Johann Heinrich Böhm as the overture to *Lanassa* by the Berlin playwright Karl Martin Plümicke, which concerns the plight of a Hindu widow who, unable to reconcile herself to her husband's death, eventually flings herself onto a funeral pyre. Böhm's production of *Lanassa* not only employed K. 184 as an overture, but was decked out with the not-inconsiderable incidental music Mozart had composed for *Thamos, King of Egypt* (K. 345), to which new texts had been set. This is undoubtedly why one sometimes reads the probably erroneous statement that K. 184 was originally intended as an overture for *Thamos* itself. N.Z.

K. 199 *Symphony in G major, No. 27 (K³ 162a, K⁶ 161b)*

Origin: Salzburg, April 10 [16?], 1773
Scoring: 2 flutes, 2 horns, strings
Movements: Allegro. Andantino grazioso. Presto.

The date on the autograph is, once again, defaced and difficult to decipher with confidence; the paper is a type used by Mozart between about March 1773 and May 1775. The first movement of K. 199 is a small-scale, finely proportioned sonata-form movement exuding high spirits. As in the first movement of K. 124, an attractive metric ambiguity is hinted at.

In the D-major Andantino grazioso the upper strings are muted, the lower ones play mostly pizzicato, and the flutes, previously limited to reinforcing the tuttis, come into their own, offering up the kind of air sung beneath the balconies of young women in many an eighteenth-century Italian opera. With its mild parallel sixths and thirds and flowing triplets, the movement offers only a touch of chromaticism occasioned by augmented sixth chords toward the end of each of its two repeated sections to hint that the world might contain any darkness.

The Finale begins with some contrapuntal gestures, which coexist uneasily with the *galant* ideas in the rest of the movement. Georges Saint-Foix describes the effect as "a sort of fugato that soon takes on a waltz rhythm." The subject of the fugato, G–C–F♯–G, is derived from the opening theme of the first movement. Mozart would later comment wryly on this sort of quasi-contrapuntal writing in the Finale of his *Musikalischer Spass* (Musical Joke), K. 522. The short-windedness of the opening is somewhat redeemed by a more extended version of the same material that occurs at the recapitulation, where it serves both as main theme and as retransition. (As discussed below in connection with the Symphony in B flat, K. 319, such suggested rather than actual counterpoint was an essential element of symphonic style of the period.) Counterpoint aside, the jig-like Finale brings the symphony to a lively conclusion. N.Z.

K. 162 *Symphony in C major, No. 22*
Origin: Salzburg, April 19 [29?], 1773
Scoring: 2 oboes, 2 horns, 2 trumpets, strings
Movements: Allegro assai. Andantino grazioso. Presto assai.

This symphony calls for a pair of "long trumpets" *(trombe lunghe)* in addition to the usual strings and pairs of oboes and horns. If kettledrum parts once existed, they have been lost. The date on the autograph has been tampered with, but perhaps reads April 19 or 29, 1773; this date is contradicted neither by the form of Mozart's writing nor by the paper employed, a type used by Mozart in Salzburg between about March 1773 and May 1775.

The opening gestures of the first movement establish the festive character of the entire work, by an alternation of tutti outbursts with a quiet staccato motive. These first twelve measures are absent at the beginning of the recapitulation, reserved for the end where they serve as closing section. This is thus a mirror-form movement of the sort discussed in connection with the first movement of K. 133. The Andantino grazioso in F major temporarily retires the trumpets and adheres to the customary pastoral spirit of such movements. The prominently featured *concertante* writing for the oboes and horns brings this movement close in style to several of the andantes in Mozart's orchestral serenades of the period. The jig-like Finale—which brings back the trumpets with a vengeance, opening with a transformation of the fanfare that, in the bass instruments, began the first movement—is worked out in a concise sonata form. N.Z.

K. 181 *Symphony in D major, No. 23 (K⁶ 162b)*
Origin: Salzburg, May 19, 1773
Scoring: 2 oboes, 2 horns, 2 trumpets, strings
Movements: Allegro spiritoso. Andantino grazioso. Presto assai.

This symphony and K. 162 open with similar flourishes. The present first movement, with the unusual tempo indication Allegro spiritoso, is an essay in the use of orchestral "noises" to form a coherent and satisfying whole. That is, there are few memorable melodies, but rather a succession of timbral devices, including repeated notes, fanfares, arpeggios, sudden *fortes* and *pianos,* scales, syncopations, dotted rhythms, and so on. Eighteenth-century debates about the aesthetics of such a musical style show striking similarities to twentieth-century discussions of abstract art.

The G-major Andantino grazioso follows the first movement without pause. The trumpets again fall silent, and the movement in some sense compensates for the previous lack of beautiful melody, offering an oboe solo in the style of a siciliano, a kind of lilting, slow-motion jig vastly popular in eighteenth-century operas and instrumental music and originating in the folksong of Sicily. This leads, again without break, straight into a rondo in the style of a contredanse or march, to which Georges Saint-Foix correctly applied the eighteenth-century appellation "quick step." N.Z.

K. *185 *Symphony in D major, "Serenade" (K⁶ *167a)*

Origin: Salzburg, autumn 1773?
Scoring: 2 oboes (doubling flutes), 2 horns, 2 trumpets, strings
Movements: Allegro assai. Andante grazioso. Menuetto. Adagio—Allegro assai.

This work consists of movements one, five, six, and seven of the Serenade in D Major, K. 185, used by Mozart as a symphony. *See the note on p. 232. N.Z.

K. 182 *Symphony in B-flat major, No. 24 (K³ 166c, K⁶ 173dA)*

Origin: Salzburg, October 3, 1773
Scoring: 2 oboes (doubling flutes), 2 horns, strings
Movements: Allegro spiritoso. Andantino grazioso. Allegro.

The autograph manuscript bears the inscription "Sinfonia / del Sig^re^ Cavaliere / Wolfgango Amadeo Mozart il 3 d'ottobre / a Salisburgo 1773," with the date strongly crossed out. This symphony has been undervalued by modern commentators and conductors, yet Mozart must have thought well of it, for a decade after he composed it, he wrote from Vienna to his father in Salzburg requesting that it be sent (along with other works) for use in his concerts in the Austrian capital.

Although the opening movement is nearly as dependent on orchestral "noises" for its content as the first movement of K. 181, a few melodies of note emerge including one in which the Scottish or Lombardic rhythm again features prominently. The Andantino grazioso, with its muted violins, change of key to E flat putting the horns a fifth lower, and substitution of a pair of flutes for oboes, providing a characteristic contrast of timbre and mood, is a simple *cantilena* in **A-A-B-A** form. This is a reversal of Mozart's previous practice of associating flutes with higher pitched horns and oboes with lower pitched horns. The jig-Finale that concludes this Dionysian work is pure *opera buffa* from start to finish.

N.Z.

K. 183 *Symphony in G minor, No. 25 (K⁶ 173dB)*

Origin: Salzburg, October 5, 1773
Scoring: 2 oboes, 2 bassoons, 4 horns, strings
Movements: Allegro con brio. Andante. Menuetto. Allegro.

Debussy once wrote of Beethoven's Ninth Symphony that it "has long been surrounded by a haze of adjectives. Together with the Mona Lisa's smile—which for some strange reason has always been labeled 'mysterious'—it is the masterpiece about which the most stupid comments have been made. It's a wonder it hasn't been submerged entirely beneath the mass of words it has excited." On a more modest scale, the same might be said of the verbiage surrounding Mozart's two G-minor symphonies—the famous one, K. 550, and the so-called "Little" G minor, K. 183. The vast majority of eighteenth-century symphonies are in major keys and appear to convey the optimistic "grand, festive, and noble" character mentioned by the contemporary writer Johann Abraham Peter Schulz, rather than the darker, more pessimistic or more passionate feelings of the few minor works. The "haze of adjectives" can be at least partially dissipated by attempting to view K. 183 (and other minor-key works of the period) looking forward from the first two-thirds of the eighteenth century, rather than backwards from the nineteenth century.

The sounds of the minor-key symphonies of the early 1770s were not entirely new ones. These tempestuous effects had been invented in the opera houses to portray nature's storms as well as storms of human emotion. A thorough investigation of *opere serie* of the 1760s might reveal the musical sources of the so-called *Sturm und Drang* symphonies of the 1770s.

Both the opening Allegro con brio and the closing Allegro of K. 183 display, in addition to their often-mentioned stormy character, large-scale sonata form with both halves repeated plus a coda. The special sound of the symphony's outer movements is partly a result of four horns in place of the usual two, which not only impart a certain solidity to the work's texture, but, as the two pairs of horns are in different keys (G and B-flat), gave Mozart a wider palette of pitches to exploit in writing his horn parts, enabling him to allow those primarily diatonic instruments to participate in some of the work's chromaticism. The first movement, which has recently acquired notoriety in the sound-track of the film *Amadeus,* exhibits, in British musicologist Stanley Sadie's words, the "urgent tone of the repeated syncopated notes . . . the dramatic falling diminished seventh and the repeated thrusting phrases that follow. The increased force of the musical thinking is seen in the strong sense of harmonic direction, the taking up of melodic figuration by the bass instruments, and the echo sections, which are no longer merely decorative but add intensity."

The Andante in E-flat major is also in sonata form with both halves repeated, but without coda. Here storminess gives way to other passions, portrayed by the appoggiaturas of longing and sadness. These are tossed back and forth between the muted violins and the obbligato bassoons, and also heard in the violas, cellos, and basses. An especially fine moment occurs eight measures into the recapitulation where, in a passage not present in the exposition, a rising sequence of sighs touches in rapid succession upon F, G, and C minor, and then A-flat, E-flat, and B-flat major.

The Minuet's stern unisons and chromaticism contradict received ideas about the polite social graces of that dance, illustrating J. A. P. Schulz's remark that "because minuets of this type are really not for dancing, composers have departed from the original conception." The four-measures phrases and rounded binary form are traditional, but the movement's darkened demeanor is no longer that of the ballroom. This disparity between what is expected of a minuet and what Mozart wrote in K. 183 is pointed up by the genial G-major Trio, written for *Harmonie*—that is, for the favorite Austrian wind band consisting of pairs of oboes, horns, and bassoons. Such groups were much employed in and around Vienna to provide music for banquets, out-of-doors social occasions, evening serenades, and the like. Wind players provided English historian Charles Burney with dinner music during his stay at the Viennese inn "At the Sign of the Golden Ox," and a decade later Mozart wrote a wind serenade, K. 375, and then was pleasantly surprised by a sextet of itinerant musicians playing it under his window on his name day. The Trio of K. 183 offers a breath of fresh air and relaxation, as it were, placing in sharp relief the sterner Minuet that flanks it.

That the first movement of K. 183 is marked Allegro con brio and the last only Allegro may appear to contradict the principle that the tempos of last movements are generally faster than those of first movements. Here, however, the first movement includes sixteenth notes and important rhythmic, harmonic, or melodic events on all four quarter notes of the measure, whereas the most rapid notes in the Finale are eighth notes and important events tend to occur only twice per measure. American musicologist H. C. Robbins Landon has suggested that this extraordinary work may have been modeled on, or inspired by, Joseph Haydn's equally extraordinary Symphony No. 39 of the late 1760s, which is also in G minor with four horns. N.Z.

K. 201 *Symphony in A major, No. 29 (K[6] 186a)*

Origin: Salzburg, April 6, 1774
Scoring: 2 oboes, 2 horns, strings
Movements: Allegro moderato. Andante. Menuetto. Allegro con spirito.

Much of what was stated about K. 183 could be repeated about this work, including (despite its major key) the agitated and serious character of the first and last movements, the use of sonata form in three of the four movements, the strongly contrasted character of the Andante (in this case perhaps noble serenity rather than longing), the symphonic rather than dance quality of the minuet, and the basing of the opening of the Finale on a transformation of the opening of the first movement. The thoroughgoing excellence of this symphony has long been recognized; it and K. 183 are the earliest of Mozart's symphonies in the repertories of major orchestras.

The first movement begins *piano,* without the more usual loud chords or fanfare. The opening theme consists of an octave drop (which reappears at the begining of the Finale) and a group of forward-moving eighth notes leading to a second octave drop, and so on in a rising sequence, the whole then repeated an octave higher, *tutti,* and in canon between the violins and the lower strings. Several subjects of contrasted character appear in the dominant, leading to a closing section with repeated notes and arpeggios. The compact development section, bustling with scalewise passages, repeated notes, modulations, and syncopations, leads to a literal recapitulation. Both sections are repeated, and the movement is brought to its jubilant close by a coda based upon the opening idea heard in canon.

The Andante and Minuet have in common the prominent use of dotted and double-dotted rhythms, characteristic of marches and of the slow sections of French *ouvertures* and considered to convey stateliness, nobility, and even godliness. The Andante, another with muted strings, is perhaps the most eloquent of the several that Mozart wrote in this vein. The energy of the outer movements spills over into the Minuet, which seems presided over more by the spirit of Mars than by that of Terpsichore.

Despite its fully worked-out sonata form, including a development section that Alfred Einstein described as "the richest and most dramatic Mozart had written up to this time," the Finale has the character of a *chasse* (a piece based on hunting-horn calls), with its mandatory repeated notes and other fanfares. At the ends of the exposition, development, recapitulation, and coda, Mozart gave the violins a rapid ascending scale: clear aural signposts to articulate the movement's formal structure. In this symphony Mozart seems to have achieved a successful equilibrium between the lyrical elements and the abstract, instrumental ones. N.Z.

K. 202 ***Symphony in D major, No. 30 (K[6] 186b)***

Origin: Salzburg, May 5, 1774
Scoring: 2 oboes, 2 horns, 2 trumpets, strings
Movements: Molto allegro. Andantino con moto. Menuetto. Presto.

The first and last movements begin with a melody constructed around the descending tonic triad D–A–F♯–D. The first movement is in a tightly knit sonata form, featuring manipulations of a cliché trill figure that occurs unobtrusively on D in the fourth measure, with more emphasis on E some nineteen measures later, then eleven measures after that with considerable force on A as an interruption of a lyrical theme, and finally invades the texture toward the end of the exposition, like a hive of musical bumblebees trying to sing polyphony.

The Andantino con moto, in A major, is in a diminutive sonata form and scored for strings alone. The apparent simplicity of its *cantabile* melodies belies the care that Mozart must have taken to make all four voices active and interesting. The Minuet and Trio exude a ballroom spirit, but comparison with sixteen minuets, K. 176, which Mozart wrote for carnival of 1774, reveals some differences: the ballroom minuets are shorter, more homophonic, and always omit violas. The simpler textures and more symmetrical phrase structures of K. 176 were apparently designed to be easily perceptible in a noisy social setting, whereas the more elaborate symphony minuet was meant to have closer attention paid to it by both performers and listeners.

The Finale, like the first movement in sonata form with both sections repeated and a coda, displays a bold mixture of serious and not-so-serious ideas. The opening fanfare in dotted rhythms is in the spirit of a quickstep. This march-like opening is contrasted however with patches of lyricism; and if the development section, with its diminished chords and abrupt pauses, causes us momentarily to be quite serious, then the way in which the coda simply evaporates rather than offering a "proper" ending reminds us that the composer was, after all, an eighteen-year-old with a well-developed sense of humor.

Georges Saint-Foix, Alfred Einstein, and other commentators have detected a retrenchment in this symphony, a return to the sheer entertainment and *galanterie* of earlier works after the greater seriousness of K. 183 and 201. Whether this is a cause for regret or pleasure depends upon one's aesthetic; for Saint-Foix and Einstein it was the former. But why should a festive work in D with trumpets be "serious," and what anachronistic (i.e., romantic) overvaluation of "seriousness" is implied? Who knows what gala occasion in Salzburg may have required just such spirited music as this? N.Z.

K. *203 ***Symphony in D major, "Serenade" (K[6] *189b)***

Origin: Salzburg, autumn? 1774
Scoring: 2 oboes, 2 horns, 2 trumpets, strings
Movements: Andante maestoso—Allegro assai. [Andante.] Menuetto. Prestissimo.

This work consists of movements one, six, seven, and eight of the Serenade in D Major, K. 203, used by Mozart as a symphony. See the note on p. 233.

N.Z.

K. 200 ***Symphony in C major, No. 28 (K[3] 173e, K[6] 189k)***

Origin: Salzburg, November 17 [12?], 1774 [1773?]

Scoring: 2 oboes, 2 horns, 2 trumpets and timpani, strings
Movements: Allegro spiritoso. Andante. Menuetto. Presto.

The autograph of K. 200 is apparently dated November 17, 1774, although because the date has again been tampered with, the day can also be read as November 12 or the year as 1773. The paper used by Mozart was a type that appears in works of his dated between about March 1773 and May 1775. If the date November 17 (or 12), 1774 is correct, then K. 200 brings to an end the outpouring of symphonies composed for Salzburg in the early 1770s. After this he was not to write another symphony proper until he arrived in Paris in 1778.

Several commentators have heard echoes of other music in this piece. German musicologist Hermann Abert pointed to the similarity between the first movement and that of the symphony in B flat, K. 182. Théodore de Wyzewa and Georges Saint-Foix heard Joseph Haydn's influence in the first movement. They judged the opening idea of the Andante to be in the style of a German popular song, and they considered the Minuet "like a first draft of the minuet from the Jupiter Symphony." (The present writer, however, finds the opening of the Minuet closer to that of the minuet of Haydn's Farewell Symphony, No. 45.) French author J.-V. Hocquard is reminded of *Die Zauberflöte,* finding in the symphony's Finale musical motives that recur in this opera. This game of "find the tune" and "name the influence" is difficult to resist and, as several studies have been devoted largely to it, one should try to understand what may lie behind it. Composers of the period were not as interested in originality per se as were those of a later period. As more attention was paid to craft and less to inspiration, great works could be based upon common materials. This may be compared to the attitude of a skilled cabinetmaker commissioned to build a fine table: his choice of materials and shape need not be novel for the table to be beautiful to look at and well functioning, provided he knows how to choose wood and work with it. N.Z.

K. *196+121 *Symphony in D major, "La finta giardiniera" (K⁶* 196+207a)*

Origin: Salzburg, spring? 1775?
Scoring: 2 oboes, 2 horns, strings
Movements: Allegro molto. Andantino grazioso. Allegro.

Mozart visited Munich from December 6, 1774 to March 7, 1775, to attend the rehearsals and performances of *La finta giardiniera* (K. 196). This new Italian comic opera was performed on January 13, 1775 and had a favorable reception. Later on the work was given, in a translation supervised by Mozart, in a number of German-speaking cities as a Singspiel, *Die Gärtnerin aus Liebe* (or sometimes as *Das verstellte Gärtner-Mädchen*), with the recitatives as spoken dialogue. As befitted its function, the first movement of the overture is shorter and less serious than first movements of other symphonies Mozart had recently written. The brief Andantino grazioso in A major is for strings alone. At some other time, in a separate manuscript, Mozart wrote a lightweight but brilliant Finale, K. 121 = 207a. On the basis of the writing in the autograph of this Finale the date of spring 1775 has been suggested, but the paper is a Milanese type from the third Italian journey, used mainly between November 1772 and early 1773. Was the paper left over from Italy, or did Mozart have an older movement around that he decided to press into service when a finale for the *Finta giardiniera* overture was needed?

Mozart's overture-symphony is neither programmatic nor even pyschological in nature. But as it was his practice to write the overture of an opera after he had familiarized himself with the story and composed most of the music, a brief summary of the opera's intrigues may serve to suggest why the symphony's first movement is so gay and its second so *galant*. The Marchesa Violante, slighted by Count Belfiore whom she loves, disguises herself and her valet as gardeners and the two seek employment at the Podesta's palace. The Podesta is charmed by Violante, and the Podesta's maid by the valet. Meanwhile, Count Belfiore is about to marry the Podesta's niece who is, in turn, being pursued by Ramiro. All appears lost, but the plot receives the necessary twists and Violante and the Count, the valet and the maid, and Ramiro and the niece are joined together in pairs by mutual love, leaving only the Podesta alone. N.Z.

K. *204 *Symphony in D major, "Serenade" (K⁶ *213a)*

Origin: Salzburg, autumn? 1775
Scoring: 2 oboes (doubling flutes), bassoon, 2 horns, 2 trumpets, strings
Movements: Allegro assai. [Andante.] Menuetto. Andantino grazioso—Allegro.

This work consists of movements one, five, six, and seven of the Serenade in D major, K. 204, used by Mozart as a symphony. See the note on p. 234. N.Z.

K. *208+102 *Symphony in C major, "Il rè pastore" (K⁶* 208+213c)*

Origin: Salzburg, 1776 or 1777
Scoring: 2 oboes (doubling flutes), 2 horns, 2 trumpets, strings
Movements: Molto allegro. Andantino. Presto assai.

This Symphony in C major is derived from the overture to Mozart's serenata *Il rè pastore* (The shepherd king), K. 208, a famous libretto by Metastasio set by an extraordinary number of composers including Christoph Willibald Gluck, Francesco Uttini, Giuseppe Sarti, Johann Friedrich Agricola, Johann Adolf Hasse, Niccolò Piccinni, Baldassare Galuppi, Niccolò Jommelli, Felice Giardini, and many others. The work, which Mozart composed in the space of about six weeks before its premiere in Salzburg on April 23, 1775, had been commissioned to celebrate the visit to Salzburg by Archduke Maximilian Franz, youngest son of Empress Maria Theresa. As Salzburg lacked a proper opera house, this work was cast as a serenata and given in concert form; the archduke's travel diary, therefore, speaks only of attending a "cantata."

The story concerns the conflicts between love and duty in a foundling prince who, having been raised a shepherd, is reluctant to give up rustic pleasures for the burdens of the throne. Mozart's one-movement "overtura" to the opera has the same opening gesture as the previous symphony, but there follows in this case a movement more concise and Italianate. In the concert symphony version this leads directly into an Andantino that Mozart manufactured from the first aria of the opera. This he accomplished by substituting a solo oboe for the shepherd king Aminta (sung by a castrato) and by writing eight new measures that lead, again without halt, into an entirely new Finale. The aria, of which the middle movement of the symphony is a barely altered arrangement, finds

Aminta on the banks of a stream with shepherd's pipes in hand (the orchestration features a pair of flutes), wondering what fate holds for him and his shepherdess.

The newly created Finale, a rondo in the style of a country dance, is written on a type of paper that Mozart used in the Litany, K. 243 (March 1776), in the symphony version of the Serenade, K. 250 (probably the second half of 1776 or first half of 1777), and in the entr'actes to *Thamos, King of Egypt,* K. 345 (undatable), so the symphony must have been created in 1776 or 1777. N.Z.

K. *250 *Symphony in D major, "Serenade" (K⁶ *248b)*

Origin: Salzburg, autumn? 1776

Scoring: 2 oboes (doubling flutes), 2 bassoons, 2 horns, 2 trumpets, strings

Movements: Allegro maestoso. Menuetto galante. Andante. Menuetto. Adagio—Allegro assai.

This work consists of movements one, five, six, seven, and eight of the "Haffner" Serenade in D Major, K. 250, used by Mozart as a symphony. See the note on p. 235. N.Z.

K. 297 *Symphony in D major, "Paris," No. 31 (K⁶ 300a)*

Origin: Paris, June 1778

Scoring: 2 flutes, 2 oboes, 2 clarinets, 2 bassoons, 2 horns, 2 trumpets and timpani, strings

Movements: Allegro assai. Andantino. Allegro.

K. 297 *Symphonic Andante in G major (K⁶ 300a)*

Origin: Paris, ?July 1778

Scoring: flute, oboe, 2 bassoons, 2 horns, strings

Mozart must have completed this symphony by June 12, 1778, on which date he wrote to his father reporting that earlier in the day he had played it through at the keyboard for the singer Anton Raaff and Count Carl Heinrich Joseph Sickingen, minister of the Palatinate, after lunch at the latter's house. The symphony had its premiere at the Concert spirituel on Corpus Christi (June 18) after only one rehearsal—the usual practice—on the previous day. Mozart reported:

I was very nervous at the rehearsal, for never in my life have I heard a worse performance; you cannot imagine how they twice bumbled and scraped through it. It was really in a terrible state and would gladly have rehearsed it again, but as there is always so much to rehearse there was no time left. So I had to go to bed with an anxious heart and in a discontented and angry frame of mind. Next day I had decided not to go to the concert at all; but in the evening, the weather being fine, I at last made up my mind to go, determined that if [my symphony] went as badly as it had at the rehearsal I would certainly go up to the orchestra, take the violin from the hands of Lahoussaye, the first violinist, and lead myself! I prayed to God that it might go well, for it is all to His greater honor and glory; and *Ecce,* the symphony began. . . . Right in the middle of the first Allegro was a passage that I knew they would like; the whole audience was thrilled by it and there was a tremendous burst of applause; but as I knew when I wrote it what kind of an effect it would produce, I repeated it again at the end—when there were shouts of "Da capo." The Andante also found favor, but particularly the last Allegro because, having observed that here all final as well as first allegros begin with all the instruments playing together and generally *unisono,* I began mine with the two violin[-section]s only, piano for the first eight bars—followed instantly by a *forte;* the audience, as I expected, said "Shh!" at the soft beginning, and then, as soon as they heard the *forte* that followed, immediately began to clap their hands. I was so happy that as soon as the symphony was over I went off to the Palais royal where I had a large ice, said the rosary as I had vowed to do—and went home.

In a perceptive commentary on this letter, Austrian conductor and cellist Nikolaus Harnoncourt remarks on differences between Mozart's audiences and ours: the 1778 audience required new music and expressed its appreciation and understanding not only after each movement but—exceptionally—during a movement. Harnoncourt also suggests that the passage in the first movement of K. 297 which so pleased the members of the Parisian audience that they burst into applause may be measures 65–73, recurring at 220–27, where a spiccato (bouncing bow) melody in the violins supported above by sustaining wind and below by cellos and basses pizzicato creates a brilliant effect.

On the other hand, Stanley Sadie (following Théodore de Wyzewa and Georges Saint-Foix) has proposed a different identification for the passage that Mozart "knew they would like." The passage in question occurs in the exposition at measures 84–92, then in the recapitulation at measures 238–50, and finally in the coda at measures 257–69.

The success of the new symphony is to some extent confirmed by a brief review, which remarked that "This artist, who from the tenderest age had made a name for himself among harpsichordists, can today be placed among the ablest composers," and by the director of the Concert spirtuel, Joseph Legros's decision to publish it as, presumably, one of the best symphonies in his repertory.

After the performance of his symphony, Mozart had a falling-out with Legros, because of the latter's failure to perform his (now lost) Sinfonia concertante, K. Anh 9=297B). Then one day the two men had a chance encounter:

I told you already that my symphony at the Concert spirituel was a tremendous success. . . . Monsieur Legros, the director, is amazingly taken with me. You must know that, although I used to be with him every day, I have not been near him since Easter; I felt so indignant at his not having performed my sinfonia concertante. I often went to the same house to visit Monsieur Raaff and each time I had to pass his rooms. His servant and maids often saw me and I always sent him my compliments. It is really a pity that he did not perform it, as it would have made a great hit—but now he no longer has an opportunity of doing so, for [the Mannheim wind players having returned home] where could four such players be found to perform it? One day, when I went to call on Raaff, I was told that he was out but would certainly be home very soon and I therefore waited. M. Legros came into the room and said: "It is really quite wonderful to have the pleasure of seeing you again." "Yes, I have a great deal to do." "I hope you will stay to lunch with us today?" "I am very sorry, but I am already engaged." "M. Mozart, we really must spend a day together again soon." "That will give me much pleasure." A long pause; at length, "Apropos. Will you not write a grand symphony for me for Corpus Christi?" "Why not?" "Can I then rely on this?" "Oh yes, if I may rely with certainty on its being performed, and that it will not have the same fate as my sinfonia concertante." Then the dance began. He excused himself as well as he could but did not find much to say. In short, the symphony was highly approved of—and Legros is so pleased with it that he says it is his very best symphony. But the Andante has not had the good fortune to satisfy him; he says that it has too many modulations and that it is too long. He derives this opinion, however, from the fact that the audience forgot to clap their hands as loudly and as long as they did at the end of the first and last movements. For indeed the Andante has won the greatest approval from me, from all connoisseurs, music-lovers, and the majority of those who have heard it. It is just the reverse of what Legros says—for it is quite simple and short. But in order to satisfy him (and, as he maintains, several others) I have composed another Andante. Each is good in its own way—for each has a different character. But the new one pleases me even more. . . . On 15 August, the Feast of the Assumption, my symphony is to be performed for the second time—with the new Andante.

The order of events narrated in this letter is not easily grasped. Mozart is distracted (understandably, under the circumstances; the letter was written just after his mother died) and seems to be relating events by free association rather than by any systematic method. This tendency to chronological incoherence in his letters, which Leopold had noticed and complained about while Mozart was still in Mannheim, can only have been exacerbated by his mother's death, his failure to find suitable employment, and his defensive need to persuade his father that things were going better than in reality they were. In any case, the portion of Mozart's letter suggesting the creation of a second Andante for K. 297 is confirmed by the sources: the Berlin and Salzburg autographs contain one Andante (in 6/8) while the Parisian first edition has an entirely different one (in 3/4). There remains some confusion about which is the earlier movement and which the later, and the experts continue to debate the matter. N.Z.

K. 318 *Symphony in G major, No. 32*
Origin: Salzburg, April 26, 1779
Scoring: 2 flutes, 2 oboes, 2 bassoons, 4 horns, 2 trumpets and timpani, strings
Movements: Allegro spiritoso. Andante. Tempo Primo.

This was the first symphony Mozart composed after his unfortunate trip to Paris. Because its format bears a resemblance to some Parisian *opéra comique* overtures by André Grétry, biographers have exerted themselves trying to guess for which stage work this "overture" may have been intended. German writer Hermann Deiters suggested that K. 318 was intended for *Thamos, König in Ägypten,* K. 345, while Alfred Einstein thought that it was for the untitled and never completed Singspiel now known as *Zaide,* K. 344. But this symphony, dated April 26, 1779, was composed too late for the first version of *Thamos* (1773) and almost certainly too early for *Zaide* (1779–80) or the second version of *Thamos* (winter? 1779–80). Furthermore, when in the 1780s the music to *Thamos* was reused with new words as incidental music to a Viennese play, not K. 318 but the E-flat symphony, K. 184, was the overture. Finally, the one-movement da capo form for sinfonias was not the invention of Grétry and other composers of *opéras comiques,* but had been taken over by them from Italian models; Mozart had previously composed such a work in the D minor overture for his oratorio *La Betulia liberata,* K. 118.

Most editions of K. 318 give it the subtitle "Ouverture," and the widely-circulated Breitkopf & Härtel edition dubs the work "Ouvertüre in italien Stile." However justified these labels may seem, there is no authority for them. They were apparently intended to make a distinction between concert symphonies and theater overtures—a distinction that in Mozart's time was largely observed in the breach thereof, as his own practices reveal. He gave the score no title at all, simply writing "di Wolfgango Amadeo Mozart mpr. d. 26 April 79." Certainly he approved the work's use in the theater (as he probably would have done with most of his symphonies): in 1785 he provided it (along with two new vocal numbers, the quartet "Dite almeno, in che mancai," K. 479, and the trio "Mandina amabile," K. 480) as the overture for a Viennese production of Francesco Bianchi's *opera buffa, La villanella rapita* (The Abducted Country Girl), which was how the symphony was published and known in the nineteenth century.

The work's opening Allegro spiritoso is a sonata form movement in which, for almost the first time in Mozart's symphonies, the *basso* of Baroque tradition is in several passages resolved into independent parts for bassoon, cello, and double bass, creating novel timbral effects. (Could this have been part of what struck a correspondent of the music newspaper, the *Allgemeine musikalische Zeitung,* in 1822 as too modern to have been written by Mozart?) At the point in the movement where the recapitulation might be expected, the Allegro breaks off at a grand pause and a G major Andante, organized in the form of a rondo **A-B-A′-C-A″-B′**, is heard. After ninety-eight measures this too breaks off, leading without pause to a *Tempo primo* which, after a few bars of transition, presents a literal recapitulation not from the beginning but from six bars before the return of the so-called "second subject," telescoping the exposition's 109 measures to sixty-seven. The "missing" opening of the recapitulation finally sounds at the end, functioning as a brilliant coda. The resulting shape is an asymmetrical arch- or mirror-form, which, if the opening group of ideas is **A**, the second group of ideas **B**, and the Andante **C**, has the design **A-B-C-B′-A′**. N.Z.

K. 319 *Symphony in B-flat major, No. 33*
Origin: Salzburg, July 9, 1779
Scoring: 2 oboes, 2 bassoons, 2 horns, strings
Movements: Allegro assai. Andante moderato. Menuetto. Allegro assai.

The autograph is headed "di Wolfgango Amadeo Mozart mpr. Salisburgo li 9 di giuglio 1779." The pages from Nannerl's diary covering the period between June 16 and September 14 of that year are missing, and no other document gives us a clue to Mozart's reason for having written this symphony. If intended for something other than the usual round of church, court, or private concerts, K. 319 was probably for Johann Heinrich Böhm's theatrical troupe. Böhm's troupe, which had in its repertory at least two of Mozart's works (*Thamos* and the Italian *opera buffa La finta gardiniera* transformed into a Singspiel as *Die verstellte Gärtnerin*), was first in Salzburg from late April to early June 1779, at which time the Mozarts became acquainted with him and a number of his leading players. The company of nearly fifty actors, dancers, and singers returned to Salzburg in early September and stayed until the beginning of Lent 1780. K. 319 thus may have been written in anticipation of their return.

This symphony originally had only three movements, but some time after he moved to Vienna Mozart added a Minuet and Trio. The added movement was inserted into the autograph on paper of a type that he used mainly from June to the end of 1785 but also in one or two scores of the previous year. This work enjoyed considerable circulation, with early sets of parts found in Salzburg, Schwerin, the Reichersberg Monastery in Upper Austria, Bozen, Prague, Modena, Frankfurt, Donaueschingen, and Graz.

All three of the original movements of K. 319 are in sonata form, share thematic resemblances, and begin their development sections with new ideas rather than with manipulations of previously presented ones. In the development section of the first movement the four-note motto "do-re-fa-mi" sounds at measures 143–46 and 151–54, and again, altered, in the Andante at measures 44–47, and the Minuet (9–12) and Trio (1–4). The Andante is in the form **A-B-A′-B′-A-coda**, with the **A′** section written in imitative texture, first in the strings in the dominant, then in the winds in the tonic.

The Finale begins as if it were simply one more brisk jig; but the jig's triplets alternate with a march's duplets (and in four passages the two overlap), the wind writing is more prominent than earlier, and the development section offers an example of that kind of pseudo-counterpoint which, while never exceeding two real voices, creates the illusion of many-layered polyphony. This way of handling counterpoint has important implications for the technique of symphony composition in the eighteenth century. It may also be connected to Mozart's methods of sketching and of writing out his music; indeed, to his conception of that music. Among the sketches that survive, some are on a single line, but many occupy two lines on which are found the principal melodic line and the lowest-sounding part. From those scores that Mozart began as fair copies and then abandoned, and from scores in which he changed ink or quill while writing, one sees that those two structural voices were written first, and the others filled in later. A report suggesting that Joseph Haydn employed and taught a similar way of composing symphonies comes from his pupil, the composer and pianist Frédéric Kalkbrenner, who wrote concerning imitation: "The best are the imitations in two parts, which were the only ones that Haydn used, even in his symphonies for full orchestra. He said that imitations of more than two parts 'befuddle the ear.' "

N.Z.

K. *320 ***Symphony in D major, "Serenade"***

Origin: Salzburg, autumn? 1779
Scoring: 2 oboes, 2 bassoons, 2 horns, 2 trumpets, timpani, strings
Movements: Adagio maestoso—Allegro con spirito. Andantino. Presto.

This work consists of movements one, five and seven of the "Post Horn" Serenade in D major, K. 320, used by Mozart as a symphony. Mozart also used movements 3 and 4 as a sinfonia concertante (K. *320). See the notes on p. 236, and on p. 153. N.Z.

K. 338 ***Symphony in C major, No. 34***

Origin: Salzburg, August 29, 1780
Scoring: 2 oboes, 2 bassoons, 2 horns, 2 trumpets and timpani, strings
Movements: Allegro vivace. Andante di molto. Allegro vivace.

This, the last symphony Mozart wrote in (although not the last he wrote for) Salzburg, is inscribed "Sinfonia di Wolfgango Amadeo Mozart mpr. li 29 Agosto, Salsbourg 1780." Nannerl's diary reports that her brother played at court on September 2, 3, and 4; one of those dates probably was the premiere of K. 338. By then Mozart knew that he was to leave for Munich in a few weeks to oversee the preparation of *Idomeneo,* so this symphony could have served both as farewell to Salzburg and as introduction to Munich. No Munich performance is in fact recorded, however; K. 338 was indeed performed by Mozart in Vienna in the early 1780s, and in 1786 he sold a set of parts with corrections in his own hand to

Prince Joseph Wenzel von Fürstenberg, still found in the archives at Donaueschingen. Other early sets of parts survive at Salzburg, Berlin, Vienna, and Prague, but the work was not published before 1797.

The first movement of K. 338—originally headed "Allegro," to which Mozart added "vivace"—is in sonata form without repeats. The opening fanfare is the prototype for the nearly identical gestures that begin the overtures of *Così fan tutte* and *La clemenza di Tito;* but here, by inserting echoes and extensions of the material that follows, Mozart has created an entirely different shape and character.

The first movement was originally followed by a minuet, or at least Mozart began one, but it has been torn from the autograph, leaving only the first fourteen measures, which are on the back of the last page of the first movement. A number of four-movement symphonies by other composers of the period place the minuet second instead of third, but as Mozart's practice was the latter pattern, this fragmentary minuet is an enigma. (See also the discussion of the symphonic minuet, K. 409, below.)

In the autograph Mozart labeled the middle movement of K. 338 "Andante di molto," but he must have found that it was performed more slowly than he wished, for in the concertmaster's part that he sent to Donaueschingen he added "più tosto allegretto." The Finale, another large jig in sonata form with both sections repeated, gives a special *concertante* role to the oboes, yet this is still not the kind of elaborate writing for winds that would be a hallmark of Mozart's Viennese orchestration of the 1780s. After K. 338, Mozart abandoned the commonplace jig-finale forever in his symphonies.

Mozart was to write one more symphony for the musicians of Salzburg with whom he had such ambivalent relations: the "Haffner" Symphony, K. 385. By the time he composed it, however, he was permanently installed in Vienna, far from his father, the archbishop, the "coarse, slovenly, dissolute court musicians," and the other citizens of Salzburg with whom he found it "impossible to mix freely." N.Z.

K. 409 *Symphonic Minuet in C major (K^6 383f)*

Origin: Vienna, May 1782
Scoring: 2 flutes, 2 oboes, 2 bassoons, 2 horns, 2 trumpets and timpani, strings

The notion promulgated by Alfred Einstein in K^3 that this C-major Symphonic Minuet was written to be added to K. 338 is improbable. K. 409 is too long to fit the proportions of K. 338, and calls for a pair of flutes not found in it. The editors of K^6 suggest that Mozart could have added flutes to the first and last movements of K. 338, as he did to the Viennese version of K. 385; but there is not a shred of evidence to suggest that he actually did so. From its large scoring, length, relative complexity of texture, and the presence of violas, K. 409 must have been intended as a concert piece and not as dance music. N.Z.

K. 385 *Symphony in D major, "Haffner," No. 35*

Origin: Vienna, July or August 1782
Scoring: 2 oboes, (2 flutes and 2 clarinets added later), 2 bassoons, 2 horns, 2 trumpets and timpani, strings
Movements: Allegro con spirito. [Andante.] Menuetto. Presto.

The circumstances surrounding the creation of K. 385 are more fully documented than those of any other of Mozart's symphonies. In mid-July 1782 Leopold wrote requesting a new symphony for celebrations for the ennoblement of Wolfgang's childhood friend Sigmund Haffner (the younger). On July 20, Wolfgang replied:

> Well, I am up to my eyes in work. By Sunday week I have to arrange my opera *[Die Entführung aus dem Serail]* for wind instruments, otherwise someone will beat me to it and secure the profits instead of me. And now you ask me to write a new symphony too! How on earth am I to do so? You have no idea how difficult it is to arrange a work of this kind for wind instruments, so that it suits these instruments and yet loses none of its effects. Well, I must just spend the night over it, for that is the only way; and to you, dearest father, I sacrifice it. You may rely on having something from me by every post. I shall work as fast as possible and, as far as haste permits, I shall write something good.

Although Wolfgang was prone to procrastination and making excuses in letters to his father, in this instance his complaints were possibly justified; he had just completed the arduous task of launching his new opera (the premiere was July 16) and was preparing to move house on July 23 in anticipation of his marriage. Under the circumstances, it is hardly surprising that a week later Mozart reported to his father:

> You will be surprised and disappointed to find that this contains only the first Allegro; but it has been quite impossible to do more for you, for I have had to compose in a great hurry a serenade [probably K. 375], but for wind instruments only (otherwise I could have used it for you too). On Wednesday the 31st I shall send the two minuets, the Andante and the last movement. If I can manage to do so, I shall send a march too. If not, you will just have to use the one [K. 249] from the Haffner music [K. 250], which hardly anyone knows. I have composed my symphony in D major, because you prefer that key.

On July 29 Sigmund Haffner was ennobled, adding to his name "von Imbachhausen." On the 31st, however, Mozart could write only that:

> You see that my intentions are good—only what one cannot do, one cannot! I am really unable to scribble off inferior stuff. So I cannot send you the whole symphony until next post-day. I could have let you have the last movement, but I prefer to dispatch it all together, for then it will cost only one fee. What I have sent you has already cost me three gulden.

On August 4 Wolfgang and Constanze Weber were married in Vienna without yet having received Leopold's grudging approval, which arrived the following day. Meanwhile, the other movements must have been completed and sent off, for on August 7 Wolfgang wrote to his father: "I send you herewith a short march [probably K. 408, No. 2]. I only hope that all will reach you in good time, and be to your taste. The first Allegro must be played with great fire, the last—as fast as possible." Given the speed at which the "Linz" Symphony could be produced a year later, one may be justified in suspecting that the slow progress of the "Haffner" Symphony had more than a little to do with Mozart's disaffection toward Salzburg and anger at his father.

Precisely when the party celebrating Haffner's ennoblement took place is not known, for Leopold's letter reporting the event is lost. However, the fact that in a later letter Wolfgang was unsure whether orchestral parts had been copied (see below) suggests that the symphony had not arrived in time. Be that as it may, either the work was performed in Salzburg prior to August 24 or Leopold had studied it in score and had indicated his approval, for on that day Wolfgang responded, "I am delighted that the symphony is to your taste."

Three months after the premiere of K. 385 in Salzburg the symphony again entered the Mozarts' correspondence, when Mozart wrote to his father on December 4, in a letter that went astray, asking for its return. He wrote again on the 21st, summarizing the lost letter, including the remark: "I also asked you to send me at the first opportunity which presents itself the new symphony that I composed for Haffner at your request. I should like to have it for certain before Lent, for I should very much like to have it performed at my concert." On January 4, 1783 he returned to the subject: "It is all the same to me whether you send me the symphony of the last Haffner music which I composed in Vienna, in the original score or copied out [into parts] for, as it is, I shall have to have several additional copies made for my concert." Mozart then asked in addition to be sent four other symphonies: K. 204, 201, 182, and 183. On the 22nd he again reminded his father, "Please send me the symphonies I asked for as soon as possible, for I really need them now," and on the 5th of February yet again, this time with renewed urgency:

> Please send the symphonies, especially the *last one,* as soon as possible, for my concert is to take place on the third Sunday in Lent, that is, on March 23rd, and I must have several duplicate string parts made. I think, therefore, that if it is not copied [into orchestral parts] already, it would be better to send me back the original score just as I sent it to you; and remember to put in the minuets.

Finally, on February 15 Wolfgang could write, "Most heartfelt thanks for the music you have sent me . . . ," adding (ironically?), "My new Haffner symphony has positively amazed me, for I had forgotten every single note of it. It must surely produce a good effect."

Mozart then proceeded to rework the score of K. 385 sent from Salzburg by putting aside the March, deleting the repeats in the first movement, and adding pairs of flutes and clarinets in the first and last movements, primarily to reinforce the tuttis and requiring no further changes in the already existing orchestration of those movements. The added instruments are written in a lighter ink than the rest of the score and can be easily distinguished in the autograph manuscript and in the facsimile edition.

Mozart's academy (concert) duly took place on Sunday, March 23, in the Hofburgtheater. He reported to his father:

> The theater could not have been more crowded and . . . every box was full. But what pleased me most of all was that His Majesty the Emperor was present and, goodness!—how delighted he was and how he applauded me! It is his custom to send money to the box office before going to the theater; otherwise I should have been fully justified in counting on a larger sum, for really his delight was beyond all bounds. He sent 25 ducats.

In its broad outlines Mozart's account is confirmed by a report published in the *Magazin der Musik,* Hamburg:

> Vienna, 23 March, 1783. . . . Tonight the famous Chevalier Mozart held a concert in the National Theater, at which pieces of his already highly admired composition were performed. The concert was honored with an exceptionally large crowd, and the two new concertos and other fantasies that Mr. Mozart played on the fortepiano were received with the loudest applause. Our Monarch, who, against his habit, attended the whole of the concert, as well as the entire audience, accorded him such animous applause as has never been heard of here. The receipts of the concert are

estimated to amount to 1,600 gulden in all. N.Z.

K. 425 *Symphony in C major, "Linz," No. 36*

Origin: Linz, October or November 1783
Scoring: 2 oboes, 2 bassoons, 2 horns, 2 trumpets and timpani, strings
Movements: Adagio—Allegro spiritoso. Poco Adagio. Menuetto. Presto.

Mozart's letters from Vienna in the months following his marriage are filled with promises of a journey to Salzburg to enable his father, his sister, and their friends to meet his bride. Excuse after excuse was found to postpone this trip, not only because Mozart was painfully aware of his father's and sister's disapproval of his choice of wife, but also because he feared forcible detention in Salzburg for having left the archbishop's service. On being reassured by his father concerning the latter point, Wolfgang and Constanze finally set out, arriving in Salzburg toward the end of July 1783 and remaining there until the end of October. From what little is known of the visit, it must have been difficult for all concerned.

On the return trip to Vienna the couple had to pass through the town of Linz. What took place there is recounted in Mozart's letter of October 31 to his father:

> We arrived here safely yesterday morning at 9 o'clock. We spent the first night in Vöcklabruck and reached Lambach Monastery next morning, where I arrived just in time to accompany the Agnus Dei on the organ. The abbot [Amandus Schickmayr] was absolutely delighted to see me again. . . . We spent the whole day there, and I played both on the organ and on a clavichord. I heard that an opera was to be given next day at Ebelsberg at the house of the Prefect Steurer . . . and that almost all of Linz was to be assembled. I resolved therefore to be present and we drove there. Young Count Thun (brother of the Thun at Vienna) called on me immediately and said that his father had been expecting me for a fortnight and would I please drive to his house at once for I was to stay with him. I told him that I could easily put up at an inn. But when we reached the gates of Linz on the following day, we found a servant waiting there to drive us to Count Thun's, at whose house we are now staying. I really cannot tell you what kindnesses the family are showering on us. On Tuesday, November 4th, I am giving a concert in the theater here and, as I have not a single symphony with me, I am writing a new one at breakneck speed, which must be finished by that time. Well, I must close, because I really must set to work.

If Mozart is to be believed, then between October 30 and November 4 he wrote a new symphony, copied the parts (or had them copied), and perhaps even had time to rehearse the work once before its premiere. The concert took place in the main room of the Ballhaus in Linz. Nothing is known of the orchestra, which was probably that of the Counts Thun, junior and senior, and which Mozart would reencounter in Prague in 1787, and which Franz Xaver Niemetschek, in a passage cited below, called "first rate." It may have had a fair complement of players, to judge by the full instrumentation of K. 425.

The new symphony was taken to Vienna where Mozart performed it again at his "academy" of April 1, 1784.

From the moment the noble, double-dotted rhythms of the opening Adagio sound, the listener is plunged into the musical world of Mozart's late masterpieces. The fruits of the artistic freedom of Vienna, of working with that city's outstanding orchestral musicians, of experience in orchestration gained in piano concertos and *Die Entführung,* and of a more serious approach to the symphony in general, are apparent in the "Linz" Symphony. The large scale of the first movement, its perfectly proportioned form, the skill of the orchestration—none of these gives the slightest clue to the hurried circumstances under which the work was created.

The presence in the Andante of trumpets and drums—instruments otherwise silent in slow movements and in all movements in F major—changes what might have been simply an exquisite *cantilena* into a movement of occasionally almost apocalyptic intensity. Beethoven apparently took note of the effectiveness of this movement when he decided to use the trumpets and drums in similar ways in the same key in the Andante of his First Symphony of 1799–1800. Joseph Haydn had earlier tried trumpets and drums in slow movements of symphonies probably unknown to Beethoven, but in general it remained a special effect rarely used in the classical symphony.

The Minuet and Trio of the "Linz" Symphony form the most conventional of its four movements, the pomp of the former set off by the mock innocence of the oboe and bassoon duet in the latter—but none of the high jinks here that Mozart sometimes put into his trios for Salzburg consumption.

The Finale of the "Linz" Symphony is akin to that of the "Haffner" Symphony of the previous year and, like it, was undoubtedly meant to be performed observing Mozart's injunction to play "as fast as possible." As a foil to the brilliant homophonic texture dominating this spirited movement, and by way of development, Mozart inserted passages of the characteristic kind of pseudo-polyphony already noted in the Finale of K. 319.

Among Mozart's possessions found after his death was the score of a symphony, containing a slow introduction, the following Allegro and half of the Andante in his hand, but the rest of the Andante, the Minuet and Trio, and the Finale in another hand. The work, K. 444, has frequently been performed as Mozart's Symphony No. 37, despite the fact that as early as 1907 it was known—without its slow introduction—as a symphony by Michael Haydn (Perger No. 16 = K^6 Anh A 53), written for the installation of a new abbot at the Michaelbeuern Monastery in May 1783.

Otto Jahn and Ludwig Köchel had stated that Mozart created K. 444 in 1783 on the same occasion he created K. 425, when, as discussed above, he was asked without warning to give a concert during a stopover in Linz. Investigation suggests that the notion that Mozart's version of Haydn's symphony was written in Linz originated with Johann André, upon whose researches Jahn and Köchel relied considerably. André thought that K. 444 was the symphony which Mozart had composed so rapidly in Linz. By the time the true "Linz" Symphony, K. 425, was identified, the original (false) reason for K. 444's connection with that city had been forgotten, and a myth was born. Thus, every Mozart biography, as well as all editions of the Köchel Catalogue, place Mozart's version of Haydn's symphony in Linz in 1783. As it is based upon André's incorrect hypothesis, this explanation of the origin of K. 444 is groundless; and Alan Tyson's researches have now shown that Mozart's manuscript is written on a type of paper that he used only after his return from Salzburg via Linz to Vienna in 1783, and mainly in the months February–April 1784. N.Z.

K. 504 *Symphony in D major, "Prague," No. 38*

Origin: Vienna, December 6, 1786
Scoring: 2 flutes, 2 oboes, 2 bassoons, 2 horns, 2 trumpets and timpani, strings
Movements: Adagio—Allegro. Andante. Presto.

Mozart's relations with the citizens of Prague form a happy chapter in the sad story of his last years. At a time when Vienna seemed to grow indifferent to him and his music, Prague apparently could not get enough of either. The success of his visit to supervise a production of *Le nozze di Figaro* was such that he was commissioned to write an opera especially for Prague, which turned out to be *Don Giovanni;* and his final opera too, *La clemenza di Tito,* was written for the Bohemian capital. The Prague schoolmaster Franz Niemetschek, who after Mozart's death was entrusted with the education of his son Karl, has left an eyewitness account of the premiere of the "Prague" Symphony and of Mozart's relationship with the Prague orchestra. Written a decade after the events it describes, and certainly idealized, Niemetschek's account is accurate in broad outline if not always in detail:

> . . . [Mozart] came to Prague in 1787 (to supervise the premiere of *Don Giovanni*); on the day of his arrival *Figaro* was performed and Mozart appeared in it. At once the news of his presence spread in the stalls, and as soon as the overture had ended every one broke into welcoming applause.
>
> In answer to a universal request, he gave a piano recital at a grand concert in the opera house [on 19 January]. The theater had never been so full as on this occasion; never had there been such unanimous enthusiasm as that awakened by his heavenly playing. We did not, in fact, know what to admire most, whether the extraordinary compositions or his extraordinary playing; together they made such an overwhelming impression on us that we felt we had been bewitched. When Mozart had finished the concert he continued improvising alone on the piano for half-an-hour. We were beside ourselves with joy and gave vent to our overwrought feelings in enthusiastic applause. In reality his improvisations exceeded anything that can be imagined in the way of piano-playing, as the highest degree of the composer's art was combined with perfection of playing. This concert was quite a unique occasion for the people of Prague. Mozart likewise counted this day as one of the happiest of his life.
>
> The symphonies *[sic]* which he composed for this occasion are real masterpieces of instrumental composition, which are played with great élan and fire, so that the very soul is carried to sublime heights. This applied particularly to the grand Symphony in D major, which is still always a favorite in Prague, although it has no doubt been heard a hundred times.
>
> . . . [Mozart] had experienced how much the Bohemians appreciated his music and how well they executed it. This he often mentioned to his acquaintances in Prague, where a hero-worshipping, responsive public and real friends carried him, so to speak, on their shoulders. He warmly thanked the opera orchestra in a letter to Mr Strobach, who was director at the time, and attributed the greater part of the ovation which his music had received in Prague to their excellent rendering.

The "Prague" symphony distinguishes itself from the fifty-odd symphonies that Mozart had previously written by being noticeably more difficult: it is harder to perform and more challenging conceptually. As early as December 1780, when Wolfgang was composing and rehearsing *Idomeneo* with the famous Mannheim orchestra, then transplanted to Munich, Leopold twice warned him of the dangers of the demands he placed upon the orchestral musicians: ". . . when your music is performed by a mediocre orchestra, it will always be the loser, because it is composed with so much discernment for the various instruments and is far from being conventional, as, on the whole, Italian music is," and, three weeks later,

> . . . do your best to keep the whole orchestra in good humor; flatter them, and, by praising them, keep them all well-disposed toward you. For I know your style of composition—it requires unusually close attention from the players of every type of instrument; and to keep the whole orchestra at such a pitch of industry and alertness for at least three hours is no joke.

In the years following *Idomeneo* and the "Haffner" and "Linz" Symphonies Mozart had been exposed to the extraordinary wind playing of Vienna and, in his operas and piano concertos of those years, he had gone beyond the already advanced techniques found in the works of 1780–83, forging entirely new methods of orchestration. The change in orchestration did not occur in isolation, for Mozart's style had deepened in all major genres in the mid-1780s, becoming more contrapuntal, more chromatic, and more extreme in expression. The "Prague" Symphony benefited not only from this newly elaborated orchestration and deepening of style, but also from the more serious role that, increasingly, was assigned to symphonies, which were now expected to exhibit artistic depth rather than serving merely as elaborate fanfares to open and close concerts.

In German-speaking countries K. 504 is often dubbed "the symphony without minuet." This designation arises from a retrospective point of view, for although thousands of eighteenth-century symphonies (including many of Mozart's) are in three movements, the Classical symphonies most performed in the nineteenth and early twentieth centuries—Mozart's last six, Haydn's twelve "London" symphonies, and all the symphonies of Beethoven and Schubert—are, except for K. 504, in four movements. If K. 504 is the only famous Classical symphony to lack a minuet or scherzo, then there must be something special about it, at least according to this anachronistic notion—hence the *soubriquet*. N.Z.

K. 543 *Symphony in E-flat major, No. 39*
Origin: Vienna, June 26, 1788
Scoring: 1 flute, 2 clarinets, 2 bassoons, 2 horns, 2 trumpets and timpani, strings
Movements: Adagio—Allegro. Andante con moto. Menuetto. Allegro.

The Symphony in E flat, K. 543, dated June 26, 1788 in Mozart's catalogue, is the least studied of the final trilogy. Compared to the extensive critical and analytical literature devoted K. 550 and 551, that for K. 543 is modest. As this symphony exhibits no lack of workmanlike construction or sublime inspiration, its relative neglect is a puzzle. Could this be because it has neither the proto-Romanticism of the G-minor Symphony nor the nickname and extraordinary Finale of the "Jupiter"? Could it be that the kinds of ideas Mozart chose to explore in this work survive the translation from the lean, transparent sounds of eighteenth-century instruments to the powerful, opaque sounds of modern instruments less well than the more muscular ideas of the G-minor and "Jupiter" symphonies? That the flat key, which creates a somewhat muted string sound compared to the brilliance of C major (K. 425, 551) or D major (K. 297, 385, 504), makes less of an impression in large modern halls on twentieth-century instruments than it did in small halls with the instruments of the period? It is also Mozart's only symphony, and one of his very few orchestral works in any genre, without oboes, which imparts to it a particular timbre.

Mozart's introduction is an amalgam of noble dotted rhythms, descended from the openings of French *ouvertures,* with the insinuating chromaticism that pervades all movements of the symphony. The introduction rises majestically from the tonic stepwise to the dominant in eight measures and then ornaments the latter for seventeen measures, creating a sense of expectancy. The opening of the Allegro is an interesting case of strong ideas presented in a deceptively understated way. Beginning with a thin, imitative texture, *piano,* the exposition works itself into an agitated state, with such momentum that much of it sounds developmental in character, and when the dominant is reached, the calmer "second group" of ideas sounds more like a transition to the closing section than a stable presentation of contrasting material. The development section gives an idea from the "second group" another chance to assert itself, but this is soon driven out by some of the agitated motives which, after an abrupt general pause, seem to evaporate mysteriously, making way for the quiet beginning of the recapitulation.

The Andante con moto presents its main subject in binary form with both sections repeated, leading to a stormy section, which, together with the opening subject, recurs frequently, the development of the two accounting for virtually the entire movement. This economy of means was commented upon by an early reviewer, who singled out the tune of the first measure-and-a-half as "an in itself insignificant theme admirably developed in an artful and agreeable manner."

The courtly Minuet is set off by a Trio that is not merely in the style of a *Ländler* (an Alpine folkdance which is the forerunner of waltz), like several of Mozart's earlier trios, but is actually based on a real one, given out by a pair of clarinets, which were favorite Alpine village instruments. Thus the rusticism of Mozart's earlier trios remains in this late Trio, if in a more suave guise.

The perpetual motion of Mozart's monothematic Finale exhibits the kind of good humor for which Joseph Haydn's finales are known and loved, in this case resembling in its hurtling high spirits the Finale of Haydn's eighty-eighth symphony, composed about 1787. There is something profoundly comical about the juxtaposition of the trivial contredanse tunes on which these movements are based with the intense thematic and harmonic manipulations to which those tunes are subjected in the working out of the form. The aura of elevated irony thus created is sometimes lost in too-pious performances, which may attempt to minimize the movements' pervasive humor by smoothing over the rough edges and unexpected turns of direction. N.Z.

K. 550 *Symphony in G minor, No. 40*

Origin: Vienna, July 25, 1788

Scoring: 1 flute, 2 oboes, (2 clarinets added later), 2 bassoons, 2 horns, strings

Movements: Molto allegro. Andante. Menuetto. Allegro assai.

The G-minor Symphony, K. 550, dated July 25, 1788, in Mozart's own catalogue of his work (and also on the autograph, although probably not in his hand), was as early as 1793 advertised by the Viennese music dealer Johann Traeg as "one of the last and most beautiful of this master." The work's intensity, unconventionality, chromaticism, thematic working-out, abundance of ideas, and ambiguity—all of these brought it close to the hearts of early nineteenth-century musicians and critics, who praised its richness of detail and called it "romantic" (meaning, apparently, "modern" and "good"). Not that there was agreement about its "meaning," for some found it filled with "the agitation of passion, the desires and regrets of an unhappy love" while others attributed to it "Grecian lightness and grace."

Whatever it may have been thought to mean, the work was widely known, performed, and imitated. By beginning the first allegro of a symphony with a quiet, *cantabile* utterance, as in K. 543 and 550, Mozart had ignored contemporary symphonic norms. The opening of K. 550 in particular, *piano,* with no brilliant opening chords but merely an accompaniment waiting for a tune to accompany, reverberated through the nineteenth century, and can be heard at the beginnings of Beethoven's Ninth Symphony, Schubert's A-minor string quartet, Mendelssohn's violin concerto, and more than one Bruckner symphony.

Even earlier, Joseph Haydn quoted from K. 550's E-flat slow movement in his oratorio *Die Jahreszeiten* (The Seasons) in the E-flat aria, No. 38, "Erblicke hier, bethörter Mensch" (See here, deceived mankind), where winter is compared to old age. The quotation occurs following the words "exhausted is the summer's strength," by which Haydn perhaps offered simultaneously a gloss on Mozart's music, a commemoration of the loss of his admired younger colleague, and a commentary upon the approaching end of his own career. Schubert took note also of the Minuet of K. 550, using it—in a general way—as a model for the G-minor Minuet of his Fifth Symphony; Schubert's copy of the beginning of Mozart's Minuet survives.

No symphony of Mozart's, not even the "Jupiter," has aroused so much comment as this one. A vast body of criticism and analysis has been published in several languages, to say nothing of hundreds of pages of program notes. This is perhaps to be expected of a work in the regular repertory of most conductors and orchestras and widely disseminated in recordings, but the intensity of the interest in K. 550 is even greater than that in many other works which likewise belong to the regular repertory. In addition to being a pillar of the repertory and one of the most flawless exemplars of the Classical style, the G-minor Symphony is a key work in understanding the link between musical Classicism and musical Romanticism, and perhaps even a mournful hint of what Mozart might have composed had he lived a normal lifespan.

Numerous articles and whole books have been written trying to describe or analyze the miraculous construction and effects of K. 550. What more can one write about the stormy yet lyrical first movement with its distant modulations and insistent anapest rhythms? About the E-flat major Andante with its throbbing eighth notes, sighing appoggiaturas, and twitching pairs of thirty-second notes? About the darkly canonic Minuet and its surprisingly sunny, *alfresco* Trio? About the brilliant Finale, which takes a bourrée rhythm, attaches it to a Mannheim "rocket" (a rapid upward arpeggio), and turns the unlikely mixture into a propulsive sonata form movement of enormous proportions? With all of its repeats observed, Mozart's great penultimate symphony lasts more than half an hour, taking on Beethovenian proportions.

N.Z.

K. 551 *Symphony in C major, "Jupiter," No. 41*

Origin: Vienna, August 10, 1788
Scoring: 1 flute, 2 oboes, 2 bassoons, 2 horns, 2 trumpets and timpani, strings
Movements: Allegro vivace. Andante cantabile. Menuetto. Molto allegro.

In German-speaking countries during the first half of the nineteenth century, K. 551 was known as "the symphony with the fugal finale" or "the symphony with the fugue at the end." The nickname "Jupiter" originated in Britain. Mozart's son Franz Xaver told publishers Vincent and Mary Novello that the *sobriquet* was coined by Haydn's sponsor in London, the violinist and orchestra leader Johann Peter Salomon. Certainly, the earliest manifestations of the title were British: the first appearance of the "Jupiter" subtitle on concert programs, which occurred in Edinburgh on October 20, 1819, followed by its use in a London Philharmonic Society concert of March 26, 1821; and the earliest edition to bear the subtitle, a piano arrangement of the work made by Muzio Clementi and published in London in 1823.

There is no reason to deny how revolutionary a work the "Jupiter" Symphony is in its ideas and their working out. To what other symphonies prior to 1788 can it be compared? What political and social motivations could have been responsible for Mozart's abandonment of the familiar style of so many earlier symphonies for something so elaborate and large-scale? His discontent or idealism must have been great to have released him from normal constraints, allowing this symphony to transcend the musical, technical, and philosophical bounds that polite society generally placed on symphonies. What, for instance, could Mozart have had in mind when he permitted himself the harmonic daring, when he constructed his contrapuntal finale, and when he decided to juxtapose prominently these features with the dotted rhythms and abrupt scalewide passages of the French *ouverture* of the *ancien régime*—rhythms used in hundreds of eighteenth-century operas, cantatas, oratorios, and liturgical works to symbolize nobility or godliness? (Was it these rhythms, found to some extent in every movement except the Minuet and Trio, that inspired the symphony's British admirers to style it the "Jupiter"?)

What Mozart had in mind will never be known, for he "forgot" to write the words to his melodies. Or nearly so, for in the first movement he quoted a recent aria, "Un bacio di mano," K. 541 (see the note on p. 87). Composed for insertion into Anfossi's opera *Le gelosie fortunate* for performances in Vienna from June 2, 1788, the aria has a witty Frenchman, Monsieur Girò, warning an inexperienced, would-be lover, Don Pompeo, about the dangers of wooing women (the quoted portion italicized):

Un bacio di mano vi fa maraviglia,
E poi bella figlia volete sposar,
Voi siete un po' tondo, mio car Pompeo,
L'usanze del mondo andate a studiar.
Un uom, che si sposa con giovin vezzosa,
A certi capricci, dee pria rinunciar,
Dee libere voglie lasciar alla moglie,
Dee sempre le porte aperte lasciar,
Dee chiudere gli occhi, gli orecchi, la bocca,
Se il re degli sciocchi non vuole sembrar.

(A kiss on her hand astonishes you,
And then you wish to marry the beautiful girl.
You are a bit innocent, my dear Pompeo.
Go study the ways of the world.
A man who marries a pretty young thing,

Must first be prepared to renounce certain of
his own whims,
To let his wife have her way,
To always leave the doors open,
His eyes, ears, and mouth shut,
If he does not wish to seem the king of fools)

The verse is thought to be the work of da Ponte and, indeed, both text and music are very much of a piece with similar scenes of sexual comedy in *Le nozze de Figaro* and *Così fan tutte*. But what has this to do with Jupiter, ruler of the gods (or at least, with those musical features which tempted musicians to coin the *sobriquet*)? A partial answer is suggested by Stanley Sadie, who remarks that the first movement of K. 551 is embued with the spirit of Mozart's comic operas of the period. And those operas are of the genre known as *semiseria* (or *dramma giocoso,* as the libretto of *Don Giovanni* has it), a new hybrid mixing the formerly separate genres of *opera buffa* with its lower-class characters, *opera seria* with its kings, queens, gods, and goddesses, and the sentimental *opéra comique* with its middle-class characters. Thus in the first movement of K. 551 characters of all classes—Jupiter (if it is he), Monsieur Girò, Don Pompeo, and doubtless others to whom we have not been properly introduced—could strut upon the same stage on a more-or-less equal footing, something the *ancien régime* had invariably striven to suppress. And into the mix, along with the *seria, buffo,* and middlebrow characters, went the Revolutionary (Mozart himself?) with his abrupt outbursts, shocking modulations, heroic wind orchestration, and pleasure in puncturing the too-comfortable received truths of society.

The Andante cantabile of the "Jupiter" Symphony not only moves, it profoundly disturbs. Its opening theme seems to express some inchoate yearnings to which the rude *fortes* reply with a brusque *"Nein,"* rather like what Beethoven would write many years later in the instrumental recitative in the Finale of his Ninth Symphony. After this theme with its negation reappears, now in the bass, a section of agitated chromaticism, syncopations, accents, and off-beat sixteenth notes (measures 19ff.) introduces elements of tension and instability that cannot be completely dispelled by the calming sextuplets of the closing section (measures 28ff). The repeat of this exposition only increases the sense of unresolution, which reaches such a pitch in the development section (based upon the ideas of the agitated section from measures 19ff.) that when the opening idea returns in the tonic at measure 60 it cannot prevail, and is swept away by more development. This further development extends until the reintroduction of the calming closing subject in the tonic at measure 76, which the third time is even less able to contain the underlying instability than it was the first two times. Finally, the opening, thwarted at the false recapitulation, returns as a coda, but a sense of true resolution proves elusive and, although the tonic cadence is affirmed three times, this proves insufficient to clear the air, which is left ringing with mysterious reverberations of unease.

Even in the Minuet and Trio—the archetypal musical symbol of the *ancien régime*—one hears a host of contrapuntal and motivic complexities murmuring uneasily beneath a *galant* exterior, and threatening at any moment to break through the facade. The Trio (so often reserved by Mozart for some kind of joke) also has a special character, as it puts the cart before the horse, or, rather, the cadence before the melody it would normally terminate. The rounded binary form of Mozart's minuets in general is here enlarged to such a point that it functions like a monothematic sonata form movement, with the apposite rhythmic drive and developmental textures. Thus, the earlier symphony scheme of four movements in contrasting forms (sonata-binary-dance-rondo) has now been replaced by four essays in sonata form, by four parallel structures. Besides the Minuet's pervasive chromaticism, so alien to eighteenth-century dance music, another technical clue to the further removal of the dance from its ballroom origins is found in the bass line, where, for the first (and only) time in a symphony minuet, Mozart writes separate parts for the cellos and for the double basses (measures 9–13, 52–55).

And what, finally, could Mozart have intended in using a contrapuntal tag of liturgical music (the notorious do-re-fa-mi motive) for the opening of the Finale? (A surely coincidental closure to Mozart's career as a symphonist is effected by the presence of the same motive in his "first" symphony, K. 16, written nearly a quarter-century earlier.) This motive, derived from Gregorian chant and probably best known in the eighteenth century as the beginning of the hymn *Lucis creator,* was a commonplace of the Fuxian species of counterpoint in which Mozart was trained and upon which he in turn trained his own pupils. It appears in the works of dozens of composers from Palestrina to Brahms. Something of what it may have meant to Mozart in the Finale of the "Jupiter" Symphony is suggested by the Credo of his Missa brevis in F major, K. 192, based on the same motive, where the continuation on the words "in unum Deum, Patrem omnipotentem" is closely related to what follows in the "Jupiter" Finale at that point. Does this work, then, contain Mozart's Creed?

American musicologist Leonard Ratner has plausibly demonstrated that the fugato in the coda of the Finale of the "Jupiter" Symphony (and by implication the entire sonata form movement leading up to it, as if by fortunate accident) is an instance of *musica combinatoria*—"that part [of music theory] which teaches the manner of combining sounds; that is, of changing their place and figure in as many manners as possible." Musicians of the second half of the century were so fascinated by this possibility, and the periodic style was so conducive to its methods, that between 1757 and 1813 more than a dozen musical games were published which enabled one to compose simple dance movements by a throw of the dice or some other system of random choice. These parlor games were commercial manifestations of a method of compositional manipulation that helped composers and would-be composers generate new ideas that could, by means of craft, be turned into binary, ternary, rondo, sonata, or other forms.

In the "Jupiter" Finale six themes heard during the exposition, development, and recapitulation function as they might in any brilliantly worked out sonata-form movement of a symphony (given Mozart's propensity for "fullness of ideas"), and only in the coda is his secret plan revealed: five of these themes can be combined to create a fugato in five-part invertible counterpoint (see the table below). A sixth theme, the continuation of the opening motive, does not enter into the fugato. In the "open" form that the sixth theme takes in measures 5–8 of the exposition and recapitulation, it appears not at all in the coda, but in the "closed" form given it in measures 13–19 it brings the fugato to a scintillating conclusion by resolving the complex polyphony into a powerful homophonic gesture that prepares the closing fanfares in the brass over which are superimposed the rest of the orchestra repeating one of the other themes in unison and octaves, in a triadically rising sequence. (See table below.)

In the last decade of his life, Mozart must have read or heard some of the complaints that his music had too great a profusion of ideas or was too densely textured: the elaborate orchestration, chromaticism, contrapuntally conceived part-writing, and extraordinary number of ideas that he used to construct an instrumental movement or aria posed problems for some of his contemporaries, as being inimical to "that sense of unity, that clarity and directness of presentation" that one critic found wanting in his symphonies, although not in Haydn's. This perceived "problem" in the symphonies was neatly expressed by a Swedish admirer of Mozart's as his "distractions."

What a response the coda of the Finale of K. 551 makes to accusations of incoherence caused by too many ideas of varied character! as if to say, "Yes, these ideas do belong together, if only you can see it my way," or—to rephrase this with reference to the earlier metaphor—"Yes, these people do belong together on the same stage."

Just before the coda of the last movement of his last symphony, Wolfgang may have thought of his father and Salzburg, and added a seventh theme to the already generous complement of six on which the rest of the movement is based. This theme can easily be missed, appearing as it does in the midst of a complex texture and just before a powerful cadence that draws attention from it. No matter whether this theme is a quotation of something remembered from long ago or merely an evocation of all such conventional themes on which Wolfgang's early symphonies were based but which find so little place in his last five. What does matter is that this conventional theme is presented in a work that puts behind it the style in which Leopold wrote and on which he trained Wolfgang. Yet the new style was not exclusive but inclusive, for it could combine into an artistic whole ideas of the most diverse sorts. Hence, Leopold's *galant* style was not rejected but had become merely one option among many.

When Mozart wrote the Finale of the "Jupiter" Symphony, he cannot have known that it would be his valedictory essay in the genre, for he had every reason to expect to live into the nineteenth century. Yet had he known, he could hardly have found a more telling summation of the journey he had traveled in his symphonies from lighthearted entertainment and formal articulation of other,

PERMUTATIONS OF THEMES IN THE CODA OF THE FINALE OF K. 551
(WIND-INSTRUMENT DOUBLINGS OMITTED)

INSTRUMENT	THEME							
vn. I			2	1	3	4+3	5	1
vn. II		2	1	3	4+3	5	2	3
va.	2	1	3	4+3	5	2	1	2
vc.	1	3	4+3	5	2	1	3	4
db.				2	1	3	4+3	5
(from measure:)	(369)	(373)	(377)	(381)	(385)	(389)	(393)	(397)

After L. Ratner, 'Ars Combinatoria: Chance and Choice in Eighteenth-Century Music,' in H. C. Robbins Landon and R. E. Chapman (eds.), *Studies in Eighteenth-Century Music: A Tribute to Karl Geiringer on His Seventieth Birthday* (New York, 1970), pp. 343–63, here p. 361.

more important works to serious works of art at the center of the musical universe. The fugato in the coda of the "Jupiter" Finale presents an apotheosis in which a contrapuntal motive representing faith, and four of the movement's other themes are presented simultaneously in strict style in many combinations and permutations, introduced and (so to speak) presided over by a conventional theme not previously heard, which, however, is not permitted to enter into the final synthesis. This perhaps gives us a glimpse of Mozart's dream of escaping his oppressive past and giving utterance to his fondest hopes and highest aspirations for the future. That fugal writing might go beyond its *stile antico* association with established religion to carry such Enlightenment symbolism was clearly stated by the Abbé Georg Joseph Vogler, seven years Mozart's senior but writing in the 1790s: "The fugue is a conversation among a multitude of singers. . . . The fugue is thus a musical artwork where no one accompanies, no one submits, where nobody plays a secondary role, but each a principal part."

N.Z.

11

Dances

A ball in the Redoutensaal in the Hofburg, Vienna, ca. 1800. Engraving by Joseph Schütz.

Each year at carnival time, fashionable Viennese society, joined by Mozart, his wife, and their friends, flocked to public balls in the Redoutensaal and elsewhere. The sets of contredanses, minuets, German dances, and Ländler that Mozart composed in the last four years of his life for the officially sponsored balls in this hall in the imperial palace discharged his obligations to the court. The dance band is visible in the balcony at the extreme left.

BACKGROUND AND OVERVIEW

Mozart was involved with dance music and dancing at every stage of his life. The first pieces he learned at the harpsichord as an infant were minuets, as were many of his earliest attempts at composition. He, his family, and his friends all loved dancing, which they did at home as well as at parties and balls, especially during carnival, the festive season between Christmas and Lent. The house in which the Mozart family lived in Salzburg from 1773 had a large room, the dancing-master's room, in which they held rehearsals, concerts, and dances.

Mozart's dances range from the informality of *Ländlers,* Alpine folkdances that were the forerunner of the waltz, to the popularity of German dances and contredanses, descended from English country dances, to the old-fashioned formality of minuets, to the brilliance of formal ballets choreographed for professional dancers in the theater. N.Z.

The dances fall into three main chronological groups: works of his childhood and youth until 1778, written for various Salzburg festivities and simply scored; the ballet *Les petits riens,* 1778, and the ballets for *Lucio Silla,* 1772, and for *Idomeneo,* 1780–81; and finally, the most important group, the dances written for the Redoutensaal, the famous ballroom that still stands in Vienna, once the scene of carnival balls that were patronized by the Emperor and attended by people of all classes. These last dances owe their existence to Mozart's appointment on December 7, 1787, as *k. k. Kammerkompositeur* (Royal Imperial Chamber Composer); they were mostly composed for the carnivals of 1789 and 1791—that is, after the last three symphonies (K. 543, 550, and 551). Here Mozart evolves within the set eight-measure periods a rich and subtle scoring of a kind not found anywhere else in his music. Whoever would know Mozart, must hear this music.

E.S.

K[6] 33B *Untitled Piece [Contredanse] in F major*

Origin: Zurich, October 1766
Scoring: piano? orchestra?

On the return home from London, via The Hague and Paris, the Mozart family paused in Zurich to give a concert. Wolfgang scrawled this short binary piece on the back of a handbill advertising the concert, perhaps as an impromptu demonstration of his talent. It consists of a melody and bass line notated in piano score. In modern times it has been orchestrated and performed. W.C.

K[2] 65a *7 Minuets (K[6] 61b)*

Origin: Salzburg, January 26, 1769
Scoring: 2 violins, basso
Keys of Dances: G, D, A, F, C, G, D

These are the first minuets Mozart wrote for dancing, only for strings but full of interest. Oddly enough, they depart frequently from the inevitable eight-measure periods of the later dances, and they vary greatly in mood. They are, moreover, the only of Mozart's Salzburg dances to have been precisely dated by the composer. E.S.

K[3] 61g/II *Minuet in C major*

Origin: Salzburg, early 1769
Scoring: piano? orchestra?

Mozart wrote this minuet on the back of a single sheet on which he wrote the Symphonic Minuet in A major, K. 61g/I (see the note on p. 173). The Trio is almost identical with that of the orchestral minuet K. 104, No. 1, probably written about two years later (see below). Thus it seems possible that the dance was originally conceived for orchestra. E.S.

K. 94 ***Minuet in D major (K⁶ 73h)***
Origin: Salzburg, 1769
Scoring: piano? orchestra?

This minuet, without trio, exists only in piano score, but it could not have been intended for keyboard for it contains some unplayable tenths. The manuscript is in the hand of Leopold Mozart, but the music might well be genuine Mozart.

E.S.

K. 123 ***Contredanse in B-flat major (K⁶ 73g)***
Origin: Rome, April 13 or 14, 1770
Scoring: 2 oboes, 2 horns, 2 violins, basso

In April 1770 Leopold Mozart arrived in Rome with his son. "After luncheon we went to St. Peter's," he proudly wrote home, ". . . and actually stood near the Pope." Leopold continued in his leisurely way about the weather, acquaintances, and digestive powders, concluding with greetings from Wolfgang, who is feeling fine and "encloses a Contredanse." K. 123 is this very dance. This tiny piece is a jewel of unusual perfection, a sort of child's view of Handel, utterly disarming in its innocence. E.S.

K. 122 ***Minuet in E-flat major (K⁶ 73t)***
Origin: Bologna, August 1770
Scoring: 2 oboes, 2 horns, 2 violins, basso

During the Mozarts' first tour to Italy, both Wolfgang's and Leopold's letters contain occasional references to dance music being sent home. One of these is the contredanse K. 123 (see above). Another, a minuet "danced by Monsieur Pick" (Carlo de Picq) on stage in Milan, is mentioned in a letter of April 1770, but the music is not preserved. In the same vein, the short minuet K. 122 appears to have been included in a letter of August 1770, to judge from a postscript remark in Leopold's hand on the autograph manuscript, but its origin and purpose are unknown. Since, like K. 123, it lacks a viola part, it was presumably intended for the ballroom rather than the stage or concert hall. W.C.

K. 104 ***6 Minuets (K⁶ 61e)***
Origin: Salzburg, late 1770 or early 1771
Scoring: 2 oboes (1 doubling piccolo), 2 horns, 2 trumpets, 2 violins, basso
Keys of Dances: C, F, C, A★, G, G
[★without trio]

The first two minuets of K. 104 are practically identical to two by Michael Haydn which were almost certainly written earlier. The manuscript of K. 104 is in Mozart's own hand, so it is clear that he did not hesitate to "borrow" these compositions. We know from Mozart's letters to his sister in these years that he was always interested in Haydn's latest dances. E.S.

K. 103 ***19 Minuets (K⁶ 61d)***
Origin: Salzburg, early summer 1772
Scoring: 2 oboes (doubling flutes), 2 horns, 2 trumpets, 2 violins, basso
Keys of Dances: C, G, D, F, C, A★, D, F, C, G, F, C, G, B♭, E♭, E★, A★, D,★ G★
[★without trio]

These pieces were written hurriedly; this is certain from the writing, from four consecutive fifths (grammatical errors which were rare in Mozart), and from his general habit in composing music of this kind. Originally Mozart composed twenty minuets, but he seems to have grouped and regrouped them on three occasions. The first twelve finally emerged in the present order, but his intentions for the rest remain unknown. E.S.

K. 164 ***6 Minuets (K⁶ 130a)***
Origin: Salzburg, June 1772
Scoring: 2 oboes (1 doubling flute), 2 horns (doubling trumpets), 2 violins, basso
Keys of Dances: D, D, D, G, G, G

In this set there are three minuets in D with oboes and trumpets, then three in G with oboes and horns, while each trio is for strings, the flute being almost constantly in octaves with the first violins. Some of the dances may well have been borrowed from Michael Haydn (see note on K. 104 on p. 218), but in their simple way they are beautifully written. E.S.

K. 176 ***16 Minuets***
Origin: Salzburg, December 1773
Scoring: 2 oboes (doubling flutes), bassoon, 2 horns (doubling trumpets), 2 violins, basso
Keys of Dances: C, G, E♭, B♭*, F, D, A, C, G, B♭*, F, D, G, F, C, D [*without trio]*

In the minuets K. 176 we find again the tuneful charm and rich colors of the earlier sets but little change toward the elaborate wind writing of later years, except that the oboes and horns occasionally have an obbligato part and the bassoon sometimes moves independently of the bass. Eleven of these minuets also exist in an original piano arrangement. E.S.

K. 101 ***4 Contredanses, "Serenade" (K⁶ 250a)***
Origin: Salzburg, early 1776?
Scoring: 2 oboes (1 doubling flute), bassoon, 2 horns, 2 violins, basso
Keys of Dances: F, G, D, F

Formerly thought to have been composed in 1769, this set is now placed in the first half of 1776 in Salzburg. Except for the first sixteen measures, the first violin part is in the hand of Leopold Mozart, who also wrote "Ständchen" at the head of the manuscript, with the result that for years this set of dances was classified among the serenades. Suspicions are aroused that Leopold was in fact the composer of this music. However, the middle two dances are included with two others in a piano score in Mozart's hand probably written at about the same time (see K⁶ 269b below); though this is only fragmentary, it may be taken as an indication for accepting Nos. 2 and 3 as being Wolfgang's. E.S.

K⁶ 269b ***4 Contredanses***
Origin: Salzburg, early 1776?
Scoring: piano? orchestra?
Keys of Dances: G, G, C, D

These dances in piano score were discovered in Czechoslovakia in 1956. Unfortunately only the first page of the set, containing No. 1, No. 2, and No. 3 (incomplete), and the last page with No. 12 were found. Nos. 2 and 12 are Nos. 2 and 3 of K. 101, but Nos. 1 and 3 are certainly also reduced from orchestral score. No. 1 is based on the same folksong as the G-major section of the Finale of the violin concerto, K. 218, the first eight measures being practically identical. E.S.

K. 267 ***4 Contredanses (K⁶ 271c)***
Origin: Salzburg, early 1777
Scoring: 2 oboes (1 doubling flute), bassoon, 2 horns, 2 violins, basso
Keys of Dances: G, E♭, A, D

These were probably written for the Salzburg carnival in February 1777, Mozart's last untroubled year at home before the journey to Mannheim and Paris.

These four pieces have a slightly archaic character that is not characteristically Mozartean. The first is a gigue with jolly horn calls, the next two are gavottes—one more tender, the other more brisk—the last a running 2/4 Allegro, full of melodic invention. E.S.

K[2] 315a *8 Minuets (K[6] 315g)*
Origin: Salzburg, late 1778
Scoring: piano? orchestra?
Keys of Dances: C, G, D, C, F, D, A, G

These eight minuets for keyboard are doubtless a reduction from an orchestral score. The melody of the Trio of No. 4 is also that of the slow movement of the piano concerto K. 414. In fact, it had started life as the slow movement of J. C. Bach's Sinfonia for the 1763 London revival of Baldassare Galuppi's *La calamità de'cuori*. The trio to No. 8 is on a separate manuscript and may not belong to the set at all. E.S.

K. 363 *3 Minuets*
Origin: Vienna or Salzburg, c. 1782 to 1783?
Scoring: 2 oboes, 2 bassoons, 2 horns, 2 trumpets and timpani, 2 violins, basso
Keys of Dances: D, B♭, D [all without trios]

The purpose of these three minuets without trios and the date of their composition are unknown. To judge from the handwriting and watermarks of his undated manuscript, Mozart may have written them—along with part of K. 463 (see below)—during his 1783 visit to Salzburg, perhaps with the upcoming Viennese carnival season in mind. E.S.

K. 463 *2 Minuets with Contredanses, "Quadrilles" (K[6] 448c)*
Origin: Salzburg or Vienna, late 1783 or early 1784
Scoring: 2 oboes, bassoon, 2 horns, 2 violins, basso
Keys of Dances: F, B♭ [both minuets without trio]

In each piece a slow stately minuet (Mozart himself wrote "Menuetto cantabile Adagio" over the second) of only eight measures introduces a lively contredanse and is repeated at the end. Mozart's biographer and his widow's second husband, Georg Nikolaus Nissen, wrote on the autograph manuscript "Two quadrilles," referring to the two contredanses. This must have been an anachronistic assumption on his part, however, as the quadrille as a way of dancing the contredanse did not come into being before the beginning of the nineteenth century.

From manuscript evidence, it appears likely that Mozart prepared these dances—like those of K. 363 (see above) and K. 610, 461 and 462 (see below)—for the 1784 carnival season in Vienna, perhaps while visiting Salzburg in the second half of 1783. E.S.

K. 610 *Contredanse in G major, "Les filles malicieuses"*
Origin: Vienna? 1782–84?
Scoring: 2 oboes, 2 horns, 2 violins, basso

The cryptic title of this graceful little contredanse eludes explanation: who are the "spiteful young ladies?" Likewise, Mozart's manuscript eludes precise dating, but it appears to come from about the same time as the three minuets, K. 363—perhaps during his visit to Salzburg in the fall of 1783. The piece turns up (without its title) on two later occasions as well: (1) reorchestrated as the last of the five Contredanses, K. 609, of about 1787–88, and (2) paired with the German Dance in G major, K. 611, as entered in Mozart's catalogue under March 6, 1791 (see the note for K. 611 below). Thus the seemingly ephemeral little work enjoyed surprising longevity, due either to public favor or to Mozart's own fondness for it. W.C.

K. 461 *6 Minuets (K⁶ 448a)*
Origin: Vienna, early 1784
Scoring: 2 oboes (doubling flutes), 2 bassoons, 2 horns, 2 violins, basso
Keys of Dances: C, E♭, G, B♭, F, D*
*[*without trio]*

Presumably composed just before Mozart began to keep the catalog of his works, these were to have been the usual set of six minuets, but the last one remained a fragment of eight measures. Though we are not yet among the great dances of the last years, there are many subtle touches of orchestration not found in earlier dances. E.S.

K. 462 *6 Contredanses (K⁶ 448b)*
Origin: Vienna, January 1784
Scoring: 2 violins, (2 oboes, 2 horns added later), basso
Keys of Dances: C, E♭, B♭, D, B♭, F

The scoring was originally only for strings, the wind parts being written on a separate sheet. These pieces consist of two, three, or four eight-measure sections with repeats, each entire dance being played twice. E.S.

K. 509 *6 German Dances*
Origin: Prague, February 6, 1787
Scoring: piccolo, 2 flutes, 2 oboes, 2 clarinets, 2 bassoons, 2 horns, 2 trumpets and timpani, 2 violins, basso
Keys of Dances: D, G, E♭, F, A, C

Perhaps the happiest times in Mozart's late troubled years were his first two visits to Prague. The first lasted from mid-January to mid-February, 1787. Georg Nikolaus Nissen tells the story that we owe the only composition of this month to the cunning of Count Johann von Pachta. Knowing Mozart's delight in parties, he invited him to his palace an hour before the other guests. On arrival the astonished composer was led into a study where he was served—instead of dinner—pen, ink, and paper. At the end of the hour he presented his host with a set of dances. This story must be about the "6 Tedeschi," K. 509, dated February 6, 1787. Alone among his German dances, these are in 3/8 notation, one-to-a-measure rhythm, and probably danced as a waltz. The six dances are joined together by modulating interludes; they conclude with a brilliant coda. E.S.

K. 609 *5 Contredanses*
Origin: Vienna, 1787 to 1788
Scoring: flute, side drum (in Nos. 3, 4), 2 violins, basso
Keys of Dances: C, E♭, D, C, G

The first dance is a delightful version of Figaro's "Non più andrai," still a famous tune in Vienna after four and a half years. No. 3 is a *Ländler* with three trios, although probably done as a group dance in the manner of the contredanse. E.S.

K. 534 *Contredanse in D major, "Das Donnerwetter"*
Origin: Vienna, January 14, 1788
Scoring: piccolo, 2 oboes, 2 horns, side drum, 2 violins, basso

On December 7, 1787, Mozart was appointed Royal Imperial Chamber Composer and he at once began composing dances for the coming carnival festivities in the Redoutensaal. Mozart entered this dance in his catalogue on January 14, 1788. "The Thunderstorm" is a vivid little sketch to join the other programmatic contredanses K. 535, 587, 607, and 610. E.S.

K. 535 *Contredanse in C major, "La Bataille"*
Origin: Vienna, January 23, 1788
Scoring: piccolo, 2 clarinets, bassoon, trumpet, side drum, 2 violins, basso

Composed in Vienna on January 23, 1788, this contredanse was announced in the *Wiener Zeitung* as "The Siege of Belgrade." Thus, Mozart forecast Emperor Joseph II's campaign against the Turks, which began unexpectedly as late as February. Belgrade did not fall to the Imperial armies under General Laudon until October of the following year. In the coda of "The Battle," to provide warlike sound effects, the basses are to be struck with the bow. E.S.

K. 536 *6 German Dances*
Origin: Vienna, January 27, 1788
Scoring: piccolo (doubling flute), 2 oboes (doubling flutes and clarinets), 2 bassoons, 2 trumpets (doubling horns) and timpani, 2 violins, basso
Keys of Dances: C, G, B♭, D, F, F

The wind instruments, while not being, strictly speaking, obligatory, are the salt and pepper of this music. The opening of No. 1 is simply a translation into 3/4 of the beginning of the contredanse "La Bataille" (K. 535), written four days before and itself probably based on a traditional song or march. In fact the timpani-roll in the dance is a reminder of that very innocent battle. E.S.

K. 567 *6 German Dances*
Origin: Vienna, December 6, 1788
Scoring: piccolo (doubling flute), 2 oboes (doubling flutes and clarinets), 2 bassoons, 2 horns, 2 trumpets and timpani (doubling side drum), 2 violins, basso
Keys of Dances: B♭, E♭, G, D, A, C

Though not quite as lively as the Prague dances, K. 509, these have a popular, rustic quality and quite a strong Bohemian character—as in the syncopations of the opening melody. Among the varied effects there is the *Ländler* No. 5 with its Turkish trio (A minor with percussion). Mozart composed these dances to go with the previous set in the following order: K. 536, 1–5, K. 567, 1–5, K. 536, 6, and K. 567, 6. E.S.

K. 568 *12 Minuets*
Origin: Vienna, December 24, 1788
Scoring: 2 flutes (doubling piccolos), 2 oboes (doubling clarinets), 2 bassoons, 2 horns, 2 trumpets and timpani, 2 violins, basso
Keys of Dances: C, F, B♭, E♭, G, D, A, F, B♭, D, G, C

The twelve minuets lack the codas of the foregoing German Dances with their Mannheim *crescendos,* but they are well worth attending to for many orchestral efforts not found elsewhere in Mozart's music. The double concerto for flute and bassoon which forms the trio of No. 5 is one of the most remarkable passages. Note too the "Spanish" trio of No. 6, and the solos for clarinet, oboe, and piccolo. E.S.

K. 571 *6 German Dances*
Origin: Vienna, February 21, 1789
Scoring: 2 flutes (1 doubling piccolo), 2 oboes (doubling clarinets), 2 bassoons, 2 horns, 2 trumpets and timpani, 2 violins, basso
Keys of Dances: D, A, C, G, B♭, D

Mozart is beginning to develop the remarkable scoring of his late dances.

Note especially the military campaign of the trio of No. 3, the bubbling wind runs in imitation in No. 4, and the light conversation piece which makes up its trio with a comic chromaticism so characteristic of this set. E.S.

K. 585 ***12 Minuets***
Origin: Vienna, December 1789
Scoring: 2 flutes (1 doubling piccolo), 2 oboes (doubling clarinets), 2 bassoons, 2 horns, 2 trumpets and timpani, 2 violins, basso
Keys of Dances: D, F, B♭, E♭, G, C, A, F, B♭, E♭, G, D

Each dance has its own special interest—the frankly rather displeasing discords in No. 4, the rich, romantic scoring of No. 7, the way in which horns and woodwind take charge in No. 8, No. 11 with its Mendelssohnian wind accompaniment, No. 12 exuberant in the Minuet and full of yearning in the Trio—each dance having a figuration, color, or mood not found anywhere else. E.S.

K. 586 ***12 German Dances***
Origin: Vienna, December 1789
Scoring: 2 flutes (1 doubling piccolo), 2 oboes (doubling clarinets), 2 bassoons, 2 horns, 2 trumpets and timpani, tambourine, cymbals, 2 violins, basso
Keys of Dances: C, G, B♭, F, A, D, G, E♭, B, F, A, C

There is no lack of variety in these highly imaginative compositions—though every dance consists identically of two eight-measure periods. Certain features of orchestration unusual in Mozart's music may be noted: the high horn parts, the bassoons doubling the violin melodies, the timpani rolls, the country fiddler's effect, and the "Spanish" trio of No. 5. E.S.

K. 587 ***Contredanse in C major, "Der Sieg vom Helden Koburg"***
Origin: Vienna, December 1789
Scoring: flute, oboe, bassoon, trumpet, 2 violins, basso

None of Mozart's "military" music is more delightful than "Our Hero Coburg's Victory." It is a musical tribute to the decisive victory gained by Fieldmarshal Prince Koburg-Saalfeld (or Coburg-Saalfeld) with his Austrian army and Russian allies over the Turks at Martinesti in Rumania on September 22, 1789. There is a folk-tune opening a section in the minor to indicate "here be Turks," (though oddly enough no "Turkish music" as they called percussion), constant alarums by the trumpet, and excursions by unusually resourceful wind instruments. E.S.

K. 106 ***Overture and 3 Contredanses (K⁶ 588a)***
Origin: Vienna, January 1790
Scoring: 2 oboes, 2 bassoons, 2 horns, 2 violins, basso
Keys of Dances: D, A, B♭

Mozart omitted this work from the catalogue he kept from 1784. The Overture is little more than an extended fanfare of thirty-four measures, all in D major. Each dance has four eight-measure groups, the first two or three being repeated da capo. E.S.

K. 599 ***6 Minuets***
Origin: Vienna, January 23, 1791
Scoring: 2 flutes (1 doubling piccolos), 2 oboes (doubling clarinets), 2 bassoons, 2 horns, 2 trumpets and timpani, 2 violins, basso
Keys of Dances: C, G, E♭, B♭, F, D

Mozart composed three sets of Minuets, K. 599, 601, and 604, as a group, comprising a total of twelve dances to be played in the same order as he wrote them. Here we meet the full wonder of the scoring of Mozart's late dances. Each Minuet and Trio consists of two eight-measure groups, but there is extraordinary wealth of color and rhythm. The Trio of No. 6 is unique in its scoring: the strings fill in the background, but the essence consists of two measures of timpani, then bassoons, oboes, flute, and piccolo, entering canonically to build up a marvelous tapestry of sound. E.S.

K. 600 ***6 German Dances***
Origin: Vienna, January 29, 1791
Scoring: 2 flutes (1 doubling piccolo), 2 oboes (doubling clarinets), 2 bassoons, 2 horns, 2 trumpets and timpani, 2 violins, basso
Keys of Dances: C, F, B♭, E♭, G, D

Mozart composed three sets of German Dances, K. 600, 602, and 605, as a group, comprising a total of thirteen dances to be played in the same order as he wrote them. This set is one of the best known today: it has a simple country style and almost childlike simplicity. In the trio of No. 5 the flute and piccolo in turn try to imitate a canary. E.S.

K. 601 ***4 Minuets***
Origin: Vienna, February 5, 1791
Scoring: 2 flutes (1 doubling piccolo), 2 oboes (doubling clarinets), 2 bassoons, 2 horns, 2 trumpets and timpani, hurdy-gurdy, 2 violins, basso
Keys of Dances: A, C, G, D

K. 602 ***4 German Dances***
Origin: Vienna, February 5, 1791
Scoring: 2 flutes (1 doubling piccolo), 2 oboes (doubling clarinets), 2 bassoons, 2 horns, 2 trumpets and timpani, hurdy-gurdy, 2 violins, basso
Keys of Dances: B♭, F, C, A

K. 603 ***2 Contredanses***
Origin: Vienna, February 5, 1791
Scoring: piccolo, 2 oboes, 2 bassoons, 2 horns, 2 trumpets and timpani, 2 violins, basso
Keys of Dances: D, B♭

All ten dances bear the date February 5, 1791, in Mozart's catalogue, and it is not impossible that he wrote them all in one day. Unaccountably he entered the third German Dance again in his catalogue for March 6, and it therefore received the Köchel no. 611.

Among the special "joke" effects he composed in the dances of these weeks there is the hurdy-gurdy of K. 601 and 602. The hurdy-gurdy or beggar's lyre (German *Leier*), having rather surprisingly survived from the Middle Ages, enjoyed a spell of popularity in the 1780's, especially in the shepherdess games of Marie Antoinette's court. It is a box containing two strings which are stopped (in unison) by wooden keys pushed in by the fingers of the left hand. The right hand turns a handle to rub a resined wheel against the strings. A bass string of unvarying pitch may also be brought into contact with the wheel, producing a bass drone, as in K. 602. Mozart doubtless sought, and achieved, a comic effect. E.S.

K. 604 ***2 Minuets***
Origin: Vienna, Febuary 12, 1791
Scoring: 2 flutes, 2 clarinets, 2 bassoons, 2 trumpets and timpani, 2 violins, basso
Keys of Dances: B♭, E♭

K. 605 ***3 German Dances***
Origin: Vienna, February 12, 1791
Scoring: 2 flutes (1 doubling piccolo), 2 oboes, 2 bassoons, 2 horns (doubling post horns),

2 trumpets and timpani, 5 sleigh bells,
2 violins, basso
Keys of Dances: D, G, C

In K. 605 Mozart depicts a sleigh ride with five sleigh bells and two post horns: the trio of No. 3 is entitled "Die Schlittenfahrt" (The Sleigh Ride). Sleigh rides, with bells jingling and post horns sounding, were a popular winter pastime of the court. The sleigh bell trio is based on an Austrian folk-tune; the delightful coda combines all the tunes and instruments of the third German Dance. While the two minuets have the mellow coloring of clarinets, rich harmonies, and flat keys, the simpler, rustic German Dances are suitably brighter, with occasional harsh chromaticism as in the Trio of No. 2.

E.S.

K. 607 *Contredanse in E-flat major, "Il trionfo delle donne" (K^6 605a)*

Origin: Vienna, February 28, 1791
Scoring: flute, oboe, bassoon, 2 horns,
2 violins, basso

The opera *Il trionfo delle donne* (The Triumph of Women) by Pasquale Anfossi (1727–97) was first sung in Vienna on May 15, 1786, two weeks after the premiere of *Figaro*. Mozart presumably uses tunes from it in this contredanse. Unfortunately the autograph is incomplete, breaking off at the end of four pages (fifty-three measures).

E.S.

K. 606 *6 German Dances in B-flat major, "Ländlerische"*

Origin: Vienna, February 28, 1791
Scoring: 2 violins, basso (wind parts lost)

K. 606 is presumed to have been written for full orchestra like the other sets and reduced for two violins and bass. It is only the latter version that survives. From its considerable divergence from the *incipit* in Mozart's own catalogue (which bears the title "6 Ländlerische," or "ländler-like" dances) and the clumsiness of the part-writing, one may conclude that this reduction, published in 1795, is not by Mozart.

E.S.

K. 611 *German Dance in C major, "Die Leierer"*

Origin: Vienna, March 6, 1791
Scoring: [orchestra]

On March 6, 1791, Mozart entered in his catalogue the incipits for a pair of dances in G major: the Contredanse, K. 610, and the German Dance, K. 611. No trace survives of the dances as Mozart paired them here, but both dances exist in separate earlier versions—a fact that demonstrates the occasional unreliability of Mozart's catalogue as a tool for dating. K. 610 was composed some eight or so years earlier; K. 611 was composed just a month earlier as the third of four German Dances, K. 602, the one with obbligato hurdy-gurdy (see the notes for K. 610 and 602 above).

Mozart's catalogue entry reads "1 Contredanse Die Leyerer.—1 Teutscher [German Dance] mit Leyerer Trio." Did Mozart mean to apply the title *Die Leierer* (The Organ-Grinders) to the Contredanse, the German Dance, or both? Might the "organ-grinders" have had something to do with the "spiteful young ladies" of K. 610?

W.C.

12

Serenades, Divertimentos, and Marches

Open-air wind music at a banquet of the Prague Civic Guard on Strelecky Island, Prague, 1794. Anonymous engraving.

The performers constitute the standard Harmoniemusik *or wind octet of two oboes, two clarinets, two horns, and bassoons.*

BACKGROUND AND OVERVIEW

This is a particularly delightful, puzzling category of Mozart's music. A divertimento, as its name would suggest, is music of a diverting sort—entertainment music. It is usually said (questionably, in my opinion) to be of a lighter character than "serious" genres such as sonata, string quartet, etc. But as so much of Mozart's other music is diverting, and as his divertimentos contain so much serious artistic content, the distinction would seem to be a dubious one. In Austria in the mid-eighteenth century, "divertimento" could be the title of almost any kind of instrumental music, including piano sonatas, string trios or quartets, and even orchestral works. Mozart's divertimentos include chamber music (one on a part) and orchestral works. The one-on-a-part divertimentos usually give themselves away by demanding soloist technique of the first violinist, especially concerto-like high passages, and sometimes also the more difficult to play "stopped" notes for the horns.

The original meaning of "serenade" is a love song sung by a young man under the window of his beloved. In this sense, serenades are found in Mozart's operas, the best-known of them being Don Giovanni's "Deh, vieni alla finestra." But here we are dealing with the orchestral serenade, which was an almost exclusively Salzburgian genre, composed there by Michael Haydn, Wolfgang and Leopold Mozart, and other local musicians, but virtually unknown elsewhere. A Salzburg orchestral serenade was an *omnium-gatherum,* often consisting of the following heterogeneous elements: an introductory march (and sometimes an ending march), the movements of a symphony, at least two minuets with trios (sometimes more than one trio per minuet), and one, two, or three concerto movements for one or several members of the ensemble to perform.

Salzburg serenades were usually written either for such private celebrations as weddings, birthdays or namedays, investitures, and promotions, or for the public celebrations of the end of the summer term at the university. (That is why the Mozarts referred to them as "Finalmusik".) Such a work constituted the main musical event of the celebration in question, providing a melange of marches, dances, symphony, and concerto, all rolled into one. These works were often performed out-of-doors, in the garden of a stately home or in the squares in front of the university and in front of the archbishop's palace.

One further title is associated with divertimento and serenade: cassation. The etymology of this word is obscure, but it most probably can be traced to the German idiom *gassatim gehen,* meaning "to walk about and perform in the streets." In mid-eighteenth-century Austria, in any case, it refered to the same kind of instrumental music called divertimento or serenade. In Mozart's music the title is associated with only four works (K. 32, 62+100, 63, and 99), although there is some evidence in Mozart's letters that the three terms, serenade, divertimento, and cassation, may have been used casually somewhat interchangeably. His widow Constanze, in any case, in a letter of 1801, claimed that cassation (which she spelled "gassation") was "a loathsome, misunderstood provincial expression."

N.Z.

ORCHESTRAL SERENADES, DIVERTIMENTOS, AND MARCHES

Music in the Graben (the main thoroughfare of Central Vienna) on the eve of the Feast of Saint Anne, 1805. Engraving by G. E. Opitz.

A description from a Viennese almanac for the year 1794 captures the scene: "During the summer months, if the weather is fine, one comes across serenades performed in the streets almost daily and at all hours (but usually late at night). . . . These serenades, however, do not consist of one singer with the simple accompaniment of a guitar, mandora, or another instrument, as in Italy or Spain. . . ; rather, these night-musics consist of trios and quartets (mostly from operas) of several vocal parts, of wind instruments, frequently even of an entire orchestra. . . ."

K. 32 *Gallimathias Musicum in D major (K² Anh 100a)*

Origin: The Hague, March 1766
Scoring: 2 oboes, 2 horns, [bassoon], strings, obbligato harpsichord

Writing from London early in 1765, Leopold Mozart informed his Salzburg correspondents, the Hagenauers, "We shall not go to Holland, that I can assure everyone," and "The Dutch Envoy in London several times begged me to visit the Prince of Orange at The Hague, but I let this go in by one ear and out by the other." Leopold had plans to bring his family home by way of Paris, Milan, and Venice, but then in late July 1765, at the beginning of the return journey something happened to change his mind:

On the very day of our departure the Dutch Envoy drove to our lodgings and was told that we had gone to Canterbury for the races and would then leave England immediately. He turned up at once in Canterbury and implored me at all costs to go to The Hague, as the Princess of Weilburg, sister of the Prince of Orange, was extremely anxious to see this child, about whom she had heard and read so much. In short, he and everybody talked at me so insistently and the proposal was so attractive that I had to decide to come.

This "proposal"—for the Mozarts to be official guests of the court—led to their remaining in Holland from September 1765 to April 1766. The length of their stay was in part a result of illnesses suffered by Wolfgang and Nannerl, and, in part, of the favorable reception and financial success of their concerts; but it was also owing to a desire to remain long enough to take advantage of the liberal patronage likely to accompany the installation of the eighteen-year-old Prince William V of Orange on March 11, 1766, at The Hague.

Prince William had a strong musical lineage. His mother, Princess Anne of Britain, had been Handel's loyal pupil and patron, and a patron of the violinist and composer Jean-Marie Leclair l'aîné. As she gave her son a musical upbringing, it is hardly surprising that there were considerable musical entertainments associated with his installation (as well as fireworks that Leopold characterized as "astounding"). The orchestra for these entertainments comprised twelve violins, three violas, three cellos, two double basses, pairs of winds, trumpets, and timpani, for a total of about thirty-six musicians not counting the harpischord player, who was the ten-year-old composer himself.

Written for this occasion, the *Gallimathias* is a quodlibet (a medley of tunes), some movements based on tunes known to Wolfgang and his Salzburg compatriots, some on tunes familiar to his Dutch audience. The work survives in two versions: a preliminary draft in which Wolfgang's and Leopold's hands are found intermingled, and a fair copy made by a professional copyist apparently for a performance in Donaueschingen some months later. The order and number of movements of the draft version and the Donaueschingen fair copy differ. Between them the two versions contain some twenty-one movements. Which movements, and in which order, one hears performed depends on the version chosen. Most of the movements are on a tiny scale.

With its quotations of popular songs and other special effects, the *Gallimathias* displays strongly satirical and parodistic elements. A movement entitled "Pastorella" presents the melody of the Christmas carol, "Joseph, lieber Joseph mein" *(Resonet in laudibus)* over a drone. The melody is in a particular version known to every denizen of Salzburg because it was played in the appropriate season by a mechanical carillon ("Hornwerk") in the tower of the Hohensalzburg Castle that dominates the city. (Mozart would return to this tune in 1772, quoting it in the original slow movement of his symphony, K. 132.) Two movements are marches, one a minuet, and several based on materials idiomatic to hunting horns, post horns and Alphorns. Another movement in 3/4 is based on the song "Eitelkeit! Eitelkeit! Ewigs Verderben" (Vanity! Vanity! Endless corruption). Yet another movement incorporates a Bavarian song, "Gedult beschutzet mich, wann Neid und Hass wird rasen" (Forebearance shields me when envy and hate rage). And the Finale is a fugue based appropriately, for the occasion, on the Dutch patriotic hymn "Willem van Nassau." (The previous month Mozart had published a set of keyboard variations, K. 25, on the same tune.) N.Z.

K. 63 ***Cassation in G major***
Origin: Salzburg, 1769
Scoring: 2 oboes, 2 horns, strings
Movements: Marche. Allegro. Andante. Menuet. Adagio. Menuet. Finale: Allegro assai.

In 1769 Mozart wrote his first serenade-like works for Salzburg events: the Cassations K. 63 in G major and K. 99 in B-flat major, both scored for oboes, horns, and strings, and the Serenade in D major, K. 100, scored for larger orchestra. The first of this pair of cassations was probably written very early in 1769, just after Mozart had returned from Vienna. It may have been performed as a musical contribution to the carnival season (Shrovetide), those traditional days of license and merriment immediately preceding Lent until Shrove Tuesday.

The opening March of K. 63 begins quietly. It is almost as if the marching procession is heard at first in the distance, rounds a corner, and then is suddenly upon us. For the first Minuet there is a curious twist: virtually the entire minuet is a canon, the violas, cellos, and basses following exactly one measure behind the violins. D.S.

K. 99 ***Cassation in B-flat major (K^6 63a)***
Origin: Salzburg, 1769
Scoring: 2 oboes, 2 horns, strings
Movements: Marcia. Allegro molto. Andante. Menuetto. Andante. Menuetto. Allegro.

In 1769 Mozart was content to write lighthearted outdoor music without any thought of its later use or publication; yet for all the music's ephemeral nature, he withheld none of his genius or invention. That is what makes the Cassation in B flat such a gem among his early works: it has elegance, character and a rare conviction, so that the listener feels not that he is in the midst of an experiment but that he is at the fountainhead of genuine inspiration, lavished upon music that he hopes was appreciated in its own time.

In the opening movement, the characteristic march rhythm is present in a more subtle way than usual; there is a general impression of grace as well as dignity. As in the G-major Cassation, Mozart adopts a distinctly intellectual pose for the first of his two minuets: once again a canon opens each half, strict enough to make clear that this is not simply a passage in loose imitation. The busy allegro that begins the Finale seems to be getting into its stride when an Andante in 6/8 time breaks in and changes the mood. This pattern recurs, and then a sudden pause leads back—not to the beginning of the movement but to the beginning of the cassation. We are back to the march that started things off. D.S.

K. 62 ***March in D major, "Cassation"***
Origin: Salzburg, 1769
Scoring: 2 oboes, 2 horns, 2 trumpets and timpani, strings

K. 100 ***Serenade in D Major (K^6 62a)***
Origin: Salzburg, 1769
Scoring: 2 oboes (doubling flutes), 2 horns, 2 trumpets, strings
Movements: Allegro. Andante. Menuetto. Allegro. Menuetto. Andante. Menuetto. Allegro.

This is the last of the three serenades (or cassations) written in the summer of 1769. Almost certainly intended for performance out-of-doors, the serenade combines elements of ceremony and entertainment, and it may well be the work referred to in the minutes of the Salzburg Gymnasium, or Latin grammar school: "August 6, 1769: At night, in honor of the Professor of Logic, music composed by the most excellent boy Wolfgang Mozart." The addition of wind instruments to the string ensemble helped the sound to carry and also provided the ambitious young composer with a spendid opportunity to show how skillfully he could deal with orchestral textures.

Originally this eight-movement serenade began with a march, K. 62, the opening measures of which were noted down by Mozart in a letter from Bologna dated August 4, 1770. But the march disappeared for nearly 200 years. When the Mozarts reached Milan in December of 1770, they found themselves in the midst of the myriad problems of operatic production. Wolfgang had been invited to compose an opera, *Mitridate, rè di Ponto,* and when it came time to rehearse the entry of King Mithridates the director called for a suitable march—which had not been included in the original plan. Suddenly the youthful genius, remembering that he had the score of the serenade with him, hurriedly pulled it out of a trunk, removed the pages containing the march and solved the problem without more ado. The march was lost when the run of performances came to an end. A few years ago, however, a copy of *Mitridate* was discovered that contained the march, which can now be restored in performances of both the opera and the serenade.

After the opening Allegro, there are three consecutive movements in which solo oboe and horn are highlighted, creating a kind of inset sinfonia concertante. In the second Andante, the two oboists switch to flutes, as oboe players were often expected to be able to do in Mozart's day. D.S.

K. 113 *Divertimento in E-flat major*
Origin: Milan, November 1771
Scoring: 2 clarinets, (2 oboes, 2 English horns, 2 bassoons added later), 2 horns, strings
Movements: Allegro. Andante. Menuetto. Allegro.

Despite the title "divertimento," which usually implies a "chamber" scoring with one to a part (i.e. in the strings), K. 113 appears to be a work for orchestral forces. The principal evidence is the following: (1) the use of heavy wind forces, especially in the later version, which would seem to require an orchestral string complement for adequate balance, and (2) the presence of the double title "Concerto ò sia Divertimento" written by Leopold Mozart on Wolfgang's original manuscript, which would seem to indicate an intended *concertante* effect of various solo lines emerging from an orchestral background. Whatever Mozart's intent, K. 113 is nowadays performed satisfactorily both as an orchestral work and as chamber music.

Mozart composed the divertimento on his second tour to Italy, during the month following the successful premiere of his *Ascanio in Alba* in Milan on October 17. The occasion for the work may have been an "academy," or private concert, in the home of Albert Michael von Mayr on November 22 or 23, for which Mozart may also have composed his Symphony in F major, K. 112. K. 113 is an arresting work, composed both in the four-movement form and energetic style of the modish Italian sinfonia.

The second version of K. 113, with expanded wind forces, can be dated on the basis of handwriting to early 1773. This coincides with Mozart's third and last visit to Italy, for the production of *Lucio Silla* for Milan. In connection with his stay in Milan, Mozart composed two wind divertimentos, (K. 186 and 166) that require the same forces as the revised wind complement of K. 113: pairs of oboes, clarinets, English horns, horns, and bassoons. It seems likely that Mozart had the same group of wind players in mind when he added the new parts to K. 113 as when he composed the new divertimentos.

K. 113 is Mozart's first work to use the clarinet. It is also his only four-movement orchestral serenade, although this was to become a standard format of his later wind divertimentos, and it reappears in both *Ein musikalischer Spass* and *Eine kleine Nachtmusik.* Moreover, K. 113 seems to share with many of these works a certain robust charm and alfresco atmosphere. W.C.

K. 131 *Divertimento in D major*
Origin: Salzburg, June 1772
Scoring: flute, oboe, bassoon, 4 horns, strings
Movements: [Allegro.] Adagio. Menuetto. Allegretto. Menuetto. Adagio. Allegro molto.

Like K. 113 (see above), the title "divertimento" would seem to belie the fact that this music has certain inherent orchestral qualities, particularly in its heavy scoring for wind instruments. The occasion for the composition is unknown. Its autograph date places it in the summer of 1772, a time of year for which, in 1774 and 1775, Mozart provided the serenades K. 203 and 204 respectively—be it either for the name day of Archbishop Hieronymus Colloredo or for the end of the academic year in the University (as "Finalmusik"). It is conceivable that K. 131 might have fulfilled a similar function in 1772.

Like K. 113, K. 131 makes colorful and clever use of instrumental combinations, particularly among the winds. Its format reverts, however, from the Italianate four-movement sequence of K. 113 to a more spaciously designed seven-movement sequence reminiscent of the early Salzburg cassations. Mozart specialist Alfred Einstein has remarked that K. 131 "is exactly like the Milan Divertimento (Concerto) K. 113 in character, but is transformed in style into something Salzburgian." W.C.

K. 189 *March in D major (K^6 167b)*
Origin: Vienna, July or early August 1773
Scoring: 2 flutes, 2 horns, 2 trumpets, 2 violins, basso

This was probably the march to open and close the Serenade K. 185 (see below) ordered as "Finalmusik" (music for the end of the University term in early August) by the "young Herr Andretter" in Salzburg and composed by Mozart in Vienna in the summer of 1773. E.S.

K. 185 *Serenade in D major, "Andretter" (K^6 167a)*
Origin: Vienna, July or early August 1773
Scoring: 2 oboes (doubling flutes), 2 horns, 2 trumpets, strings with violin solo in movements two, three, and six
Movements: Allegro assai. Andante. Allegro. Menuetto. Andante grazioso. Menuetto. Adagio. Allegro assai.

The "Andretter" Serenade was composed in the summer of 1773 while Mozart and his father were spending the better part of three months in Vienna on the lookout for positions at the imperial court. Nothing came of it, but there was a commission to write a festive work ("Finalmusik") in connection with the wedding of the elder son of Johann Ernst von Andretter, military counselor to the archbishop of Salzburg's court. Since writing the serenade K. 100 of 1769, Mozart had lost none of his touch as a composer of first-rate light music. The intervening years had seen the production of numerous minuets for public dancing and the divertimentos K. 113, 131, 186, and 166. It is possible that Mozart also wrote the Divertimento K. 205 for the Andretter family at about the same time (see below).

The second and third movements of the "Andretter" Serenade (as well as the first Trio of its second Minuet) call for a solo violin, a reflection of the fact that since July 9, 1772, Mozart held the resoundingly titled but poorly paid job of concertmaster of the Salzburg court orchestra, and could create opportunities to show off his facile fiddle. D.S.

K. 237 *March in D major (K^6 189c)*
Origin: Salzburg, August 1774
Scoring: 2 oboes, 2 bassoons, 2 horns, 2 trumpets, 2 violins, basso

In this march, composed to go with the serenade K. 203 (see below), Mozart uses horns in A and trumpets in D; the former are prominent in the first half (which has moved to A major) and are joined by the bassoons, the latter, along with the oboes, in the tonic key parts of the second half. As usual, Mozart makes a positive virtue of a technical limitation, and achieves sounds unusual even for him. E.S.

K. 203 *Serenade in D major (K^6 189b)*
Origin: Salzburg, August 1774
Scoring: 2 oboes (doubling flutes), bassoon, 2 horns, 2 trumpets, strings with violin solo in movements two, three and four
Movements: Andante maestoso—Allegro assai. [Andante.] Menuetto. [Allegro.] Menuetto. [Andante.] Menuetto. Prestissimo.

Composed in the summer of 1774, either for the ceremonies marking the end of an academic year or for the name day of the archbishop of Salzburg, Hieronymus Colloredo (it has sometimes been called the "Colloredo" Serenade), this work again is planned on ample lines, with no less than eight movements, including three minuets. No less, but possibly more; for like the serenade K. 100, which originally started with a March of suitable length and dignity for the entrance of the venerable ecclesiastics, professors, and city officials, this work also has a clearly related (though now separate) march, K. 237 (see above).

A subtle feature is the sudden appearance of a solo bassoon part in the Trio of the second Minuet. As in so many other orchestras, the archbishop's musicians were frequently "double-handed," and a few could even lay reasonable claim to competence on three or four instruments. It would have been perfectly possible for one of the musicians to put down his instrument and take up a bassoon for as long as it might be needed. But this was not the case here; rather, in any movement without obbligato bassoon parts, the bassoons are present anyway, playing along on the bass line with the cellos and double basses, according to standard eighteenth-century practice. In any event, the oboists were doubling on flutes, as in the serenades K. 185, 204, and 250.

The first of the serenade's two Andante movements, together with the following Minuet and Allegro, forms a miniature violin concerto, set apart from the serenade proper because of its special scoring and its choice of keys—B flat, F, then back to B flat. D.S.

K. 215 *March in D major (K^6 213b)*
Origin: Salzburg, August 1775
Scoring: 2 oboes, 2 horns, 2 trumpets, strings

This march was composed as a introduction or exit to the Serenade K. 204 (see below), which was probably composed for the feast celebrating the end of the academic year at Salzburg University.

E.S.

K. 204 *Serenade in D major (K⁶ 213a)*
Origin: Salzburg, August 5, 1775
Scoring: 2 oboes (doubling flutes), bassoon, 2 horns, 2 trumpets, strings with violin solo in movements two, three, and four
Movements: Allegro assai. Andante moderato. Allegro. Menuetto. [Andante.] Menuetto. Andantino grazioso—Allegro.

This work, probably completed on August 5, 1775, for the academic festivities, is virtually a twin of the previous serenade (K. 203). Again it offers evidence of the oboists who doubled on flutes and the bassoonist whose participation is highlighted only in the fifth movement. Once again, too, the solo violin comes to the fore and was probably played by Mozart himself. As in K. 203, the first Andante, together with the following Allegro and Minuet, form a miniature violin concerto.

The second Andante offers a further glimpse of Mozart's skill as an orchestrator. Instead of using either the two oboes or the two flutes, he asks for only one of each and adds a solo bassoon and two horns, thus creating a five-part wind harmony team.

D.S.

K. 214 *March in C major*
Origin: Salzburg, August 20, 1775
Scoring: 2 oboes, 2 horns, 2 trumpets, strings

All the other marches written in Salzburg belonged to one of the serenades or "Finalmusiken." This march cannot be attributed to any of the serenades, which are all in D. Whether it was written for a serenade now lost or as an occasional piece remains a puzzle.

E.S.

K. 239 *Serenade in D major, "Serenata Notturna"*
Origin: Salzburg, January 1776
Scoring: timpani, strings with 2 violins, viola, and double bass soli
Movements: Marcia: Maestoso. Menuetto. Rondeau: Allegretto.

This must have been a work for carnival of 1776. Despite Mozart's preference for five or more movements in serenades, there was no standard number, as this work demonstrates by proceeding directly from its opening march to a Minuet and Trio and thence to a Rondo-Finale. The orchestra consists of kettledrums and strings without double basses. However, as in nearly all the tuttis the solo double bass doubles the orchestral cellos, and the expected sixteen-foot sound is heard. The work's special color derives at least in part from the kettledrums, which, liberated from their usual role of providing the bass for a pair of trumpets, are elevated to an unwonted prominence.

The stately opening movement, Maestoso 2/4, is filled with subtleties of rhythm and orchestration, which place it outside the realm of the normal march. Fragments of fanfares and march rhythms sprinkled throughout the movement cannot disguise the fact that it was written to serve in place of a symphonic movement and for an attentive audience of amateurs and connoiseurs rather than for the parade grounds. The Minuet, as stately as the March, makes good use of the short-long rhythm known variously as the Lombardic rhythm or Scotch snap. It is neatly contrasted by a more sedate Trio, played by the soloists alone.

The 2/4 Finale, marked "Rondeau: Allegretto," reminds us of descriptions of the Salzbourgeois of Mozart's time. One traveler remarked that "The Salzburger's spirit is exceedingly inclined to low humor. Their folksongs are so comical and burlesque that one cannot listen to them without side-splitting laughter. The Punch-and-Judy spirit shines through everywhere, and the melodies are mostly excellent and inimitably beautiful." The Rondo theme is a high-spirited country dance, cheekily decked out with grace notes. The intervening episodes include a mock-pathetic Adagio in 3/4, a kind of quick-step march, an outburst of pizzicato, and a closing blaze of martial gaiety based on the quick step. N.Z.

K. 249 *March in D major*
Origin: Salzburg, July 20, 1776
Scoring: 2 oboes, 2 bassoons, 2 horns, 2 trumpets, strings

Mozart's "Haffner" Serenade, K. 250 (see below), was first played on the eve of the wedding of Marie Elisabeth Haffner, a member of the notable Salzburg family. Mozart wrote the present splendid march to open or close the evening, but it is all too rarely played with the serenade today. E.S.

K. 250 *Serenade in D major, "Haffner"*
Origin: Salzburg, July 1776
Scoring: 2 oboes (doubling flutes), 2 bassoons, 2 horns, 2 trumpets, strings with violin solo in movements two, three, and four
Movements: Allegro maestoso. Andante. Menuetto. Rondeau: Allegro. Menuetto. Andante. Menuetto. Adagio—Allegro.

In the summer of 1776, Mozart received a commission to write a full-scale serenade for the wedding of Marie Elisabeth Haffner, daughter of a wealthy merchant and burgomaster of Salzburg, Sigmund Haffner, who was a friend of Leopold Mozart and an admirer of his lively young son.

The serenade was probably a great success, for in 1782, when a member of the Haffner family attained a modest place among the nobility, Leopold immediately contacted Wolfgang—then in Vienna—about another musical contribution for the Haffners, the work now known as the "Haffner" Symphony, K. 385.

The distinguished French Mozart scholar, Georges Saint-Foix, writes illuminatingly about the serenade and its place in Mozart's development:

> This Serenade (K. 250), composed by Mozart in the middle of his twentieth year—that is to say, in the full flower of his musical inspiration, for this year, 1776, sees the full blossoming of his rarest gifts of music and poetry—this Serenade marks for us the climax, not to say the apotheosis, of the period we have designated as *galante*. It is the successor of the serenades of 1773, 1774, and 1775 [K. 185, 203, and 204], but with what a difference! Its exceptional length is perhaps due to the solemnity of Elisabeth Haffner's wedding, but it is certain that on this particular day the young master was bent on making a great impression and spreading out before his fellow-citizens all the richness his genius was able to produce.

Like K. 185, 203, and 204, the present Serenade includes a miniature violin concerto—movements 2, 3, and 4—as a showcase for Mozart's own violinistic abilities. D.S.

K. 335 *Two Marches in D major (K⁶ 320a)*
Origin: Salzburg, August 1779
Scoring: 2 flutes, 2 oboes, 2 horns, 2 trumpets, strings

Probably these two marches were intended for the "Post Horn" Serenade, K. 320 (see below). A conventional flourish opens the first march but is forgotten in the recapitulation in favor of a better idea—a melody for oboes and horns with a flowing violin counterpoint. Again, the more or less formal continuation of that first subject becomes—*piano* and *scherzoso*—a witty second subject in which the oboe is accompanied by the strings *battendo col legno,* striking the strings with the wood of the bow.

The second march contains the usual series of good tunes. In the second part, just as in the first march, Mozart disconcertingly forgets all the music of the first part, except for the first four and the last four measures, and produces a string of new tunes—a delightfully cavalier, and probably unique treatment of sonata form on an informal occasion. Among other things, trilling flutes provide bird song.

E.S.

K. 320 *Serenade in D major, "Post Horn"*
Origin: Salzburg, August 3, 1779
Scoring: 2 flutes (1 doubling piccolo), 2 oboes, 2 bassoons, 2 horns (1 doubling post horn), 2 trumpets, strings
Movements: Adagio maestoso—Allegro con spirito. Menuetto. Concertante: Andante grazioso. Rondeau: Allegro ma non troppo. Andantino. Menuetto. Finale: Presto.

Mozart's biographer and Prague acquaintance Franz Xaver Niemetschek claimed that Mozart wrote the "Post Horn" Serenade to celebrate Archbishop Colloredo's name day on September 30, 1779. But Mozart dated the work August 3 of that year, suggesting that it was intended for the end of the academic year celebrations held annually in the Kollegienplatz, the square in front of Salzburg University, in the first week in August. In seems, rather, that for the archbishop's name day Mozart revived his "Haffner" Serenade, K. 250.

The "Post Horn" Serenade is crammed full of musical jokes, and we may suspect that in some of them Mozart was slyly thumbing his nose at the archbishop and other citizens of provincial Salzburg. It is also quite possible that he was influenced by Haydn's odd Symphony No. 60, "Il Distratto" (The Absent-Minded Man), written originally as incidental music for a comedy given at Esterházy in 1774, and performed as a six-movement symphony in Pressburg the following year. Mozart heard it when it was performed in Salzburg in 1776, by a traveling theatrical troupe. The basic principle underlying the composition of both works is the use, abuse, and overuse of every sort of eighteenth-century musical cliché.

Mozart's serenade introduces itself with a majestic, slow introduction, which leads, two measures earlier than one might expect, into an Allegro con spirito. The first violins, the bassoons, and trumpets each have short rhythmic figures of their own, which interplay for eight measures; the principle of repetition with virtually no melody continues throughout the first episode, each section of the band demanding its sometimes superfluous say. The second subject is announced by a brusque preparatory measure having nothing to do with the attractive tune that follows in the violins, except that it interrupts at every fourth measure; one's ear consequently must concentrate on the oboes to catch the continuation of the melody. There is much chattery question-and-answer between instruments in the development. Then comes a variation of the slow introduction, a regular recapitulation, and a coda that emphasizes rather excessively that the key is D major and the occasion one of celebration.

The allegretto Minuet starts boldly enough, but shortly before it reaches the halfway point it comes to a modest, almost apologetic close; the process is then repeated. (Haydn's Minuet in Symphony No. 60 has a similar anticlimax.) The Trio, a dialogue between flute and bassoon, each in unison with the first violins, has the character of a charming peasant dance.

Next follow two *concertante* (soloistic) movements, with pairs of flutes and oboes acting as solo quartet in concert with their colleagues, the main burden being carried by the first flute and first oboe. (Trumpets and drums are silent but horns occasionally also play a soloistic role.) Mozart thought highly of these two movements, for he programmed them in a concert he gave in Vienna some four years later, referring to them as "the short concertante symphony from my last *Finalmusik.*"

The second Minuet is grandiose. Two instruments not hitherto heard show up in the two Trio sections of this Minuet. The piccolo, two octaves above the violins, takes the lead in the folklike first trio. In the second trio a charming melody in the violins is quite overshadowed by the call of the post horn, an instrument that gives the Serenade its subtitle. A valveless brass instrument, the post horn was designed for mail-coach guards, who would use it to announce their impending approach to the next stop along the route. Was it Mozart's way of saying how much he longed to get the deuce out of Salzburg?

The presto Finale, like the first movement, is a succession of typical musical figures of the period, ascending and descending scale and arpeggio passages, accompaniments in triplets, military brass calls, a development that begins too ambitiously and fizzles out (there is a similar moment in Haydn's Symphony No. 60), and so on. The occasional suspicion of a gloomy shadow is speedily dismissed, and this choice spoof ends, as did the opening movement, with too many emphatic repetitions of the D-major tonic chord.

It is astonishing that Mozart, in parodying indifferent music, as he does in several movements of this serenade, should nevertheless manage to produce so fresh and delightful a work. A.R.

K. 408/1 ***March in C major (K^6 383e)***
Origin: Vienna, 1782
Scoring: 2 oboes, 2 horns, 2 trumpets and timpani, strings

This was presumably composed for one of Mozart's concerts in Vienna in 1782. Constanze later claimed that he had composed it for her (1782 was the year of their marriage), and Mozart himself reduced it to piano score. There is some resemblance to the *Idomeneo* march of the previous year, but above all this tiny piece of four-and-one-half minutes (including repeats) shows how generous Mozart was with his melodies. E.S.

K. 408/3 ***March in C major (K^6 383F)***
Origin: Vienna, 1782
Scoring: 2 flutes, 2 bassoons, 2 horns, 2 trumpets and timpani, strings

This march was probably written along with K. 408, No. 1 for Mozart's Vienna concerts in 1782. Like the other marches, this one is in a richly melodic sonata form. E.S.

K. 408/2 ***March in D major (K^6 385a)***
Origin: Vienna, 1782
Scoring: 2 oboes, 2 bassoons, 2 horns, 2 trumpets and timpani, strings

The summer of 1782, his first in Vienna, was a complicated one for the twenty-six-year-old Mozart. He was eager to marry and only awaited parental approval. Leopold Mozart in Salzburg, though tardy in sending his blessing, was assiduous in his demands for compositions: first for a symphony for a Haffner family feast (and Mozart, though struggling to complete a large-scale wind piece, wrote the "Haffner" Symphony, K. 385) and then for a march to go with the symphony. Mozart writes on August 7 thanking his father for his blessing, and enclosing "a short march. I hope it arrives in time." This is the present work, intended to be performed with the first version of the "Haffner" Symphony. E.S.

NON-ORCHESTRAL SERENADES, DIVERTIMENTOS, AND MARCHES

Title-page vignette from the first edition of Mozart's *Musikalischer Spass* (Musical Joke), K. 522 (Offenbach-am-Main: Johann André, 1802).

This satirical rendering of provincial musicians represents precisely the instrumentation required not only for Mozart's K. 522, but also for his divertimentos and marches K. 247, 248, 287, 334, and 445.

K. 290 ***March in D major (K³ 173b, K⁶ 167AB)***

Origin: Salzburg, summer 1772?
Scoring: 2 horns, violin, viola, basso

This march has often been paired with the Divertimento in D major, K. 205 (see below), on the grounds of scoring: both the march and divertimento are unique among Mozart's works of these genres in their use of a single violin part, rather than first and second violins. (The fact that the divertimento contains a bassoon part, while the march does not, presents no problem, for the bassoon could have doubled the bass line, as it does throughout the divertimento.) Recently, however, handwriting analysis has suggested a date of a year earlier, in the summer of 1772. No occasion has yet come to light to correspond to this earlier date of origin. W.C.

K. 186 ***Divertimento in B-flat major (K³ 159b)***

Origin: Milan, March 1773
Scoring: 2 oboes, 2 English horns, 2 clarinets, 2 horns, 2 bassoons
Movements: Allegro assai. Menuetto. Adagio. Allegro.

The divertimentos K. 186 and 166, Mozart's first works for wind band, were almost certainly commissioned during his stay in Milan in March 1773. They were certainly not performed in Salzburg, where Mozart returned at the end of the month, for clarinets and English horns were not available there. Both works are in nine, not ten, parts, for the second bassoon always plays in unison with the first or remains silent.

The first movement of K. 186 is at the same time an opening Intrada and a simple rustic Ländler. The sturdy Minuet is contrasted by a legato Trio in which clarinets and horns are silent. The Andante, with its solemn, slow 6/8 swing and its innocent beauty, is one of those early works of Mozart which make one catch one's breath. The final Allegro is similar in mood and construction to the contredanse Finale which rounds off the companion divertimento, if a bit less boisterous. E.S.

K. 166 ***Divertimento in E-flat major (K³ 159d)***

Origin: Salzburg, March 24, 1773
Scoring: 2 oboes, 2 English horns, 2 clarinets, 2 horns, 2 bassoons
Movements: Allegro. Menuetto. Andante grazioso. Adagio. Allegro.

This is the companion divertimento to K. 186 (see above). The first movement is in binary form, for the exposition is immediately followed by a recapitulation in varied harmony. The Minuet is a sturdy martial piece. The Trio for once is really a trio—for two English horns and bassoon. The Andante grazioso is a Rondo with varied instrumentation of the theme but dominated by the curious octaves of oboe and English horn. The Adagio with its held notes, legato line, and high horn parts gives a radiant sonority. The Allegro is a high-spirited contredanse in rondo form. E.S.

K. 205 ***Divertimento in D major (K³ 173a, K⁶ 167A)***

Origin: Salzburg, July 1773
Scoring: 2 horns, bassoon, violin, viola, basso
Movements: Largo—Allegro. Menuetto. [Adagio.] Menuetto. Finale: Presto.

The origin of K. 205 is unclear, for Mozart failed to include a date on his manuscript.

Since the paper type of the manuscript is unusual for Mozart's Salzburg compositions, many historians have dated the work during Mozart's visit to Vienna in the fall of 1773. Specifically, it has often been connected with a garden concert given at the home of the Viennese physician Dr. Anton Mesmer on August 18, mentioned in a letter of Leopold Mozart three days later.

More recently, handwriting analysis has placed the work slightly earlier, in July. During this time Mozart was composing a serenade, K. 185, for the Andretter family in Salzburg—either for the elder Johann Ernst von Andretter or for his son Thaddäus. In later years, Leopold Mozart referred to his son's "Andretterin Musik," that is, a composition for a *female* member of the Andretter family. Perhaps the work was K. 205. If so, it may have been designed for the name day festivities of Maria Anna Elisabeth von Andretter, first wife of Johann Ernst, on July 26, 1773. W.C.

K. 188 *Divertimento in C major (K^6 240b)*
Origin: Salzburg, mid-1773
Scoring: 2 flutes, 5 trumpets, timpani
Movements: Andante. Allegro. Menuetto. Andante. Menuetto. [Gavotte.]

The idea of rococo chamber music for trumpets, flutes, and timpani seems odd to modern sensibilities, but it must not have to Mozart and his father. They arranged a suite of dances from Viennese ballets by Joseph Starzer and Christoph Willibald Gluck for that combination (K. 626b/28 and 159c=Anh C 17.12), and Mozart composed this original divertimento, K. 188.

Trumpet playing was an old and honorable calling; for centuries the players had belonged to guilds in which they served long apprenticeships. Along with the timpanists they made their livings as town musicians or attached to the cavalry. Their duties included such activities as sounding the hour, playing fanfares for civic, courtly, and religious ceremonial occasions including the arrival and departure of dignitaries, and (mounted on horseback) signaling maneuvers in battle and on the parade grounds. And the most skilled among them were also on call to supplement bands and orchestras for operas and concerts.

The archbishop of Salzburg supported a dozen trumpet players and a pair of timpanists for his court and cathedral. Leopold Mozart praised the first of the trumpet players, Johann Baptist Gesenberger, "who has made himself very famous for the extraordinary purity of his intonation (especially in the high register), for the rapidity of his leaps, and for his good trill." The second trumpet player, Caspar Köstler, was known for his *cantabile* tone and his performances of concertos and solos. The third trumpet player, Johann Andreas Schachtner, was a close friend of the Mozart family. "There is not one of the trumpeters or kettledrummers in the princely service who does not play the violin well," Leopold adds. These were refined, elegant musicians.

Mozart's autograph manuscript of the divertimento, K. 188, is on a kind of paper that he used in Salzburg following the return from his third and last trip to Italy in March 1773 until around 1775, and the relative immaturity of his musical hand suggests the beginning of that period; but the work cannot be more closely dated than that.

The sounds of the trumpets and flutes mingle in surprising and sometimes scintillating ways, the former giving brilliance to the latter and the latter sweetening the former. The effect resembles a manic set of stops on a Baroque organ, indeed, rather like the mechanical organ *(Hornwerk)* that sounded from a tower in the castle on the cliff overlooking Salzburg.

The divertimento's opening Andante is a stately intrada, the following Allegro a kind of diminutive sonata movement. The third and fifth movements, old-fashioned minuets without trios, frame an Andante in which Alberti-bass figurations from the flutes give the effect of a enlarged hurdy-gurdy, with a giant organ-grinder turning the crank. A brilliantly orchestrated gavotte serves as the brief Finale. N.Z.

K. 213 *Divertimento in F major*
Origin: Salzburg, July 1775
Scoring: 2 oboes, 2 horns, 2 bassoons
Movements: Allegro spiritoso. Andante. Menuetto. Contredanse en Rondeau: Molto allegro.

With this divertimento Mozart begins the series of five *Tafelmusik* (dinner music) works for wind sextet. These include K. 213, 240, 252, 253, and 270, composed between July 1775 and January 1777, presumably for the Salzburg court. The slightly gauche unison effects of the Milan divertimenti are passed, and Mozart has become complete master of the material.

The first movement of K. 213 is in miniature sonata form with a most subtly varied recapitulation. The Andante in varied ternary form (A-B-A) has the innocence and grace of some antique ballet. The Minuet is of a very Haydnesque cast; the Trio is a swinging *Ländler*. The Finale is the only one among the contredanse finales in these works actually titled thus. With its irrepressible horns it is one of Mozart's most exuberant movements. E.S.

K. 240 *Divertimento in B-flat major*
Origin: Salzburg, January 1776
Scoring: 2 oboes, 2 horns, 2 bassoons
Movements: Allegro. Andante grazioso. Menuetto. Allegro.

This is the second of the "Dinner Music" series. The first movement is more extended than in K. 213, and the second subject is fuller; the recapitulation begins with the middle of the first subject, reserving the formal opening statement for the very end of the movement. The Andante grazioso, like all these slow movements, has the dancing lilt of a gavotte. The Minuet is noteworthy for the high range of the high B-flat horns, and for its delightful concluding bars in which the instruments seem to tease each other with their dotted rhythms. The finale, unexpectedly in sonata form, is an odd movement—it makes up for a lack of melodic wealth with a wistful little phrase as a second subject, which appears like a sensitive poet at a rowdy party.
E.S.

K. 252 *Divertimento in E-flat major (K⁶ 240a)*
Origin: Salzburg, early 1776
Scoring: 2 oboes, 2 horns, 2 bassoons
Movements: Andante. Menuetto. Polonaise. Presto assai.

This is the third in the series of "Dinner Music." Mozart provides variety by opening with an Andante, a graceful siciliano but with an unusual number of dynamic marks. The Minuet with its merrily prattling first horn is one of the gayest; the Trio has the more solemn character of its key of A flat. The Polonaise appears rarely in Mozart's music (the piano sonata K. 284, the divertimento K. 287, and the divertimento K^6 439b, No. 5); this one has a delightful swagger. The Finale, based on the Austrian tune "Die Katze lässt das Mausen nicht" ("The cat won't give up chasing mice"), chases along to a brilliant conclusion. E.S.

K. 248 *March in F major*
Origin: Salzburg, June 1776
Scoring: 2 horns, 2 violins, viola, basso

This march originated with the divertimento, K. 247 (see below), which was written for the name day of Countess Antonia Lodron in Salzburg. E.S.

K. 247 *Divertimento in F major, "Lodron" No. 1*
Origin: Salzburg, June 1776
Scoring: 2 horns, 2 violins, viola, basso
Movements: Allegro. Andante grazioso. Menuetto. Adagio. Menuetto. Andante—Allegro assai.

Count Ernst Lodron was High Master of Ceremonies in Salzburg, a man in an influential position with whom Mozart always got on well, unlike his employer, the archbishop. This divertimento is the first work which the twenty-year-old composed for the name day of Lodron's wife, Countess Antonia, on June 13, 1776. The success of the piece encouraged the Lodrons to commission and Mozart to write another in the following year with the same instrumentation, the divertimento K. 287.

The first movement is in sonata form, with a wealth of melodic invention; Mozart doesn't repeat his opening four measures until the very end of the whole movement, when he uses it by way of a coda. The second movement is a kind of slow rondeau. Following the first Minuet comes an Adagio for strings only; it is largely a show piece for the first violin, as is the Trio of the second Minuet. A short Andante ushers in the lively contredanse Rondo with which the work ends. C.C.

K. 251 *Divertimento in D major*
Origin: Salzburg, July 1776
Scoring: oboe, 2 horns, 2 violins, viola, basso
Movements: Allegro molto. Menuetto. Andantino. Menuetto. Rondeau: Allegro assai. Marcia alla francese.

This work, one of the gayest and most light-hearted that Mozart ever penned, was written, some say, for the twenty-fifth birthday of Mozart's beloved and gifted sister Nannerl on July 30, 1776. The opening Allegro molto is one of Mozart's most brilliant early experiments in sonata form. In it he employs one of Haydn's favorite devices, building the whole movement out of the energetic first subject; it even appears in the dominant minor, instead of a true second subject, and rounds off both the exposition and the whole movement as a forceful coda.

The second movement is a straightforward Minuet; strings alone play the Trio. Then comes another highlight, a serenely beautiful Andantino in the form of a rondeau. Mozart's own special blend of exquisite melody and heart-searching sadness is nowhere more apparent than at the point where the solo oboe takes up the tune. A Minuet follows, most unusually serving as the theme for a set of three variations, the first featuring the solo oboe, the next the first violin, the third bringing forward the second violin. Then comes the Rondo, one of the brightest and most entertaining which Mozart ever wrote. The final March "in the French style" may have been meant to begin the divertimento as well as conclude it. C.C.

K. 253 *Divertimento in F major*
Origin: Salzburg, August 1776
Scoring: 2 oboes, 2 horns, 2 bassoons
Movements: Andante. Menuetto. Allegro assai.

This is the fourth in the series of "Dinner Music." The work opens with a Theme and Variations, as do only two other multimovement works of Mozart's (the flute quartet K. 298, and the piano sonata K. 331). But its position in the divertimento is the only unconventional feature of this movement; as a final variation the theme is repeated allegretto. As so often occurs in Mozart's dances, the Minuet is noble and expressive, the Trio more playful and dancing. The Finale combines bravura with delicacy; it is in ternary form with a coda. E.S.

K. 286 *Notturno in D major (K^6 269a)*
Origin: Salzburg, between December 1776 and January 1777
Scoring: four groups, each with 2 horns, 2 violins, viola, basso
Movements: Andante. Allegretto grazioso. Menuetto.

K. 286 may have been written for carnival of 1777. The work is exceptional both in its instrumentation and in the layout of its movements. The first of the four identical groups of players has no special designation, but the others were labeled by Mozart "First echo," "Second echo," and "Third echo," making clear their functions. The three movements are an Andante in 3/4, an Allegretto grazioso in 2/4, and a Minuet and Trio. It has been widely stated that this work must be a fragment because of its apparently unorthodox structure. This is a fallacy, for numerous Austrian works from this time have three movements with a minuet as the third.

The opening of the Andante (a leisurely sonata form with both halves repeated) has a gentle *cantabile* melody to which, however, pulsating eighth notes in the accompaniment impart a certain passion. The movement's "development" section is not one, but this is in some sense atoned for by a developmental retransition in which occur syncopations, sixteenth notes, and a touch of the minor—a "storm" that proves only a brief summer shower, passing as quickly as it came.

The perky Allegretto grazioso in 2/4 begins as if it were going to be a rondo, but (peculiarly for a work with all its movements in the same key) it seems unable to get far from D major, and instead of a rondo we get a sonata form without development section. The Minuet is closer in character to Mozart's ballroom dances than to his symphonic minuets; by its considerable length it dwarfs the brief Trio (performed by the string players of the first ensemble) that Mozart added apparently as an afterthought. In all three movements the twenty-one-year old composer amuses himself and his listeners by toying with the amount of delay between and overlap among the echoes; this is especially delightful in the Minuet when the four pairs of horns break into fanfares. N.Z.

K. 270 *Divertimento in B-flat major*
Origin: Salzburg, January 1777
Scoring: 2 oboes, 2 horns, 2 bassoons
Movements: Allegro molto. Andantino. Menuetto. Presto.

This is the fifth of the set of "Dinner Music," and perhaps the finest of all. The Allegro molto is the longest first movement of the series, being in full sonata form with a dramatic development and a deliciously varied repeat in the recapitulation. The Andantino is a graceful gavotte in miniature sonata form with a delightful Alberti-bass accompaniment for horn in the coda. The Minuet *(moderato)* has a witty tune with a sort of hiccup in the second bar, and a *Ländler* Trio. The Presto is a breathless gigue, or rather 3/8 contredanse, with a moment of glory for the bassoon in the coda. E.S.

K. 287 *Divertimento in B-flat major, "Lodron" No. 2 (K[3] 271b, K[6] 271H)*

Origin: Salzburg, June 1777
Scoring: 2 horns, 2 violins, viola, basso
Movements: Allegro. Tema con variazioni: Andante grazioso. Menuetto. Adagio. Menuetto. Andante—Allegro molto.

The B-flat Divertimento is the second of a pair written for Countess Antonia Lodron, the leading light of the music-loving aristocracy in Salzburg. The previous year Mozart had composed the Divertimento in F (K. 247) for the name day of the Countess, on June 13. She herself was an amateur pianist and Mozart had taught her two daughters piano. (In 1776 he had written his Concerto for Three Pianos, K. 242, especially for the Lodron ladies.)

The composer himself must have been proud of the B-flat Divertimento; he took it with him to Munich three months after the premiere and performed the solo violin part from memory at the home of Count Joseph von Salern, the chief manager of the Court Opera. Mozart wrote to his father afterward: "You cannot imagine how delighted Count Salern was. But he really understands music, for all the time he kept on shouting 'Bravo,' where other noblemen would take a pinch of snuff, blow their noses, clear their throats—or start a conversation." A day or two later Mozart gave a concert at Franz Albert's, the musical landlord of the Black Eagle, the inn where he was lodging. And once more, in the course of four and a half hours of music, he played the B-flat Divertimento. "They all opened their eyes!" he wrote home proudly. "I played as though I were the finest fiddler in all Europe."

The divertimento is in six substantial movements. They are worked out with such care and brilliance that one can well believe Mozart spent a good deal of effort in their making. The melody of the Theme and Variations is that of a German folksong, "Heissa, hurtig, ich bin Hans und bin ohne Sorge" (Whoopee! My name is Hans, and I haven't a care in the world).

The last movement opens with a tragic recitative for the solo violin, in the style of *opera seria;* we expect an equally tragic dramatic aria to follow. Instead, there is a sudden change of scene: in a breezy Allegro molto, in 3/8 time, the first violin plays the tune of a Tyrolean folksong, "D'Bauerin hat d'Katz verlorn" (The farmer's wife has lost the cat). A.R.

K. 445 *March in D major (K[6] 320c)*

Origin: Salzburg, summer 1780
Scoring: 2 horns, 2 violins, 2 violas, basso

This march was almost certainly written for the "Robinig von Rottenfeld" Divertimento, K. 334 (see below). It shares with the Divertimento its melodic style and somewhat virtuoso character. E.S.

K. 334 *Divertimento in D major "Robinig von Rottenfeld" (K[6] 320b)*

Origin: Salzburg, 1779 or 1780
Scoring: 2 horns, 2 violins, viola, basso
Movements: Allegro. Thema (con sei variazioni): Andante. Menuetto. Adagio. Menuetto. Rondo: Allegro.

After a fateful tour that took him to Munich, Mannheim, and Paris—during which his mother died, his hopes of gaining fame and independence were dashed, and the young soprano with whom he had fallen in love jilted him—Mozart returned to Salzburg in January 1779, staying there until 1780.

The months of travel were of immense importance to Mozart's psychic as well as his artistic development. Not only had he been exposed to some of the finest music-making in Europe, he had also discovered how it feels to be talented but no longer a *Wunderkind*. Temporary successes there had certainly been; but in the end he had been rejected for permanent posts, and, equally distressing, had been rejected in love. His new music, though still in the *galant* style, begins to show traces of deeper emotion, even of violence and anguish.

The new depths are at once evident if one compares the divertimento for Countess Lodron (K. 287), written before his journey, and the one in D (K. 334), composed a few months after his return. K. 334 was intended for his family's patrician friends, the Robinig von Rottenfelds. Though the scoring is the same—strings and two horns—its scale and sweep are grand. It demands considerable virtuosity of the first violinist.

The opening Allegro begins cheerily enough with an extended melody, promising at once a composition of substance. The first Minuet, often played as a separate piece, is one of Mozart's best-known movements, rivaled perhaps only by Boccherini's famous Minuet. It is very much in the style of a *Ländler*. The final Allegro is a Rondo in 6/8 dance rhythm. At times Mozart takes his first violin so high above the staff that the music could almost be mistaken for the high jinks of Italian violinist Niccolò Paganini, who was not yet born when this piece was written. A.R.

K. 375 ***Serenade in E-flat major***
Origin: Vienna, October 1781
Scoring: 2 clarinets, 2 horns, 2 bassoons (2 oboes added in July 1782)
Movements: Allegro maestoso. Menuetto. Adagio. Menuetto. Allegro.

In a letter to his father of November 3, 1781, Mozart explains how he came to write the original version of the Serenade, K. 375:

> I wrote it for St. Theresa's Day for Frau von Hickel's sister, or rather the sister-in-law of Herr von Hickel, court painter, at whose house it was performed for the first time. The six gentlemen who executed it are poor beggars who, however, play quite well together, particularly the first clarinet and the two horns. But the chief reason why I composed it was in order to let Herr von Strack, who goes there every day, hear something of my composition, so I wrote it rather carefully. It has won great applause too and on St. Theresa's Night it was performed in three different places: for as soon as they finished playing it in one place, they were taken off somewhere else and paid to play it.

St. Theresa's Day was October 15. Two weeks later, on Mozart's own name day, October 31, the six wind players showed up in his courtyard at eleven o'clock at night to serenade him with the same composition. "These musicians asked that the street door might be opened and, placing themselves in the center of the courtyard, surprised me, just as I was about to undress, in the most pleasant fashion imaginable with the first chord in E-flat."

The Herr von Strack for whom he composed the piece "rather carefully" was Joseph von Strack, a gentleman of the emperor's bedchamber, who Mozart hoped might report on it favorably at court. Certainly the composition is more elaborately worked out than the previous serenades, more serious in mood. A.R.

K deest *Harmoniemusik in C major, from* Die Entführung aus dem Serail

Origin: Vienna, July 1782
Scoring: 2 oboes, 2 clarinets, 2 horns, 2 bassoons
Movements: Overture and 16 numbers

This transcription of music from *The Abduction from the Seraglio* is one of many such operatic transcriptions for wind ensemble that enjoyed a vogue in Vienna in the early 1780s. In a letter to his father on July 20, 1782, four days after the premier of *The Abduction,* Mozart wrote:

> Well, I have a big piece of work in front of me because I have to arrange my opera for *Harmonie* [wind ensemble] by a week from Sunday. If I don't someone else will beat me to it and take my profit. . . . You don't realize how hard it is to arrange a work of this kind for *Harmonie* so that it suits wind instruments and yet loses none of its effect. I'll have to spend the night over it because that's what it takes to bring it off. . . .

Indeed, besides the present transcription, another wind arrangement of music from *The Abduction* is known—in two extant versions—by the leading Viennese wind-band arranger of the day, Johann Nepomuk Went.

In a recent monograph, the Dutch conductor and musicologist Bastiaan Blomhert has for the first time stated the case for Mozart's authorship of this arrangement, which was formerly attributed, on slender evidence, to Franz Joseph Rosinack. Blomhert's argument focuses primarily on the technique of transcription, which in the case of this work is far more innovative and ambitious than that of standard, routine wind-band transcriptions of the time. Moreover the techniques of the present arrangement manifest similarities to certain Mozartean peculiarities of wind scoring, such as one finds in the wind-band arrangements of popular opera tunes in *Don Giovanni,* Act II, and in Mozart's original compositions for wind ensembles.

The transcription contains the Overture (with a newly composed ending) and sixteen of the opera's twenty-one numbers, thus encompassing most of the original score. W.C.

K. 388 *Serenade in C minor, (K^6 384a)*

Origin: Vienna, July 1782 or late 1783
Scoring: 2 oboes, 2 clarinets, 2 horns, 2 bassoons
Movements: Allegro. Andante. Menuetto in canone. Allegro.

July 1782 was an exceptionally busy month for Mozart. The first two weeks were taken up by the premiere of *The Abduction from the Seraglio,* on the 23rd Mozart changed his residence, and he was involved in considerable dilemmas and intrigues with the Weber family preceding his marriage. To crown it all, his father wrote, asking Wolfgang to compose a symphony (K. 385) to celebrate young Sigmund Haffner's ennoblement. "You will be astonished to see only the first Allegro," Wolfgang answered in a letter of July 27, "but I could do no more because I had hurriedly to write a serenade, but only for wind instruments (or I could have used it for you too)!" The other serenade, or "Night Music" as Mozart calls it in this letter, may have been the present work. It was perhaps written for one of the Princes Liechtenstein, but there is no record of its performance.

If Mozart said that the E-flat Serenade (K. 375) was "rather carefully" written, he might have said of this one that it was composed "with the utmost care." It shows no sign of hurried creation; it is tightly structured, and superbly wrought.

The Minuet and Trio might be said to be an act of contrapuntal homage to J.S. Bach and George Frideric Handel. Although the Minuet is not fugal, it is a canon: the oboes play the melody one measure ahead of the answering bassoons and two octaves above, with the clarinets and horns filling in the harmony. The Trio, in the major key, is a canon *al rovescio,* that is, with the answer played upside down.

Mozart later made a masterly arrangement of this Serenade for string quintet, K. 406 (see the note on p. 255). A.R.

K. 410 ***Adagio in F major (K[3] 440d, K[6] 484d)***

Origin: Vienna, 1782 or 1783?
Scoring: 2 basset horns, bassoon

K. 411 ***Adagio in B-flat major (K[3] 440a, K[6] 484a)***

Origin: Vienna, 1782 or 1783?
Scoring: 2 clarinets, 3 basset horns

The two Adagio movements K. 410 and 411 are of a somewhat serious character. Mozart fell in love with the basset horn during his Vienna period, encouraged by his friend and virtuoso of this instrument, Anton Stadler. Anton and his brother Johann are surely to be regarded as the first performers of these works. We know that the art of the Stadler brothers and the depth of the pleasant, secretive sound of these instruments induced the Vienna Freemasons to make use of them during solemn occasions in the Lodges. Both pieces were apparently created around 1783 and were intended for performance on such a festive occasion, with which the seriousness and the style of their construction is in harmony. K. 410 presents a quietly flowing canon in the two clarinets over a freely moving bass in the bassoon, a small contrapuntal masterpiece. It is countered by the rich harmonic structure of K. 411, a tonal gem and, at the same time, one of the most solemn and transfigured of Mozart's creations. E.F.S.

K[3] 439b ***Five Divertimentos in B-flat major (K[1] Anh 229 + 229a)***

Origin: Vienna, 1783 or later
Scoring: 3 basset horns
Movements
No. 1: Allegro. Menuetto: Allegretto. Adagio. Menuetto. Rondo: Allegro.
No. 2: Allegro. Menuetto. Larghetto. Menuetto. Rondo: Allegro.
No. 3: Allegro. Menuetto. Adagio. Menuetto. Rondo.
No. 4: Allegro. Larghetto. Menuetto. Adagio. Allegro: Rondo.
No. 5: Adagio. Menuetto. Adagio. Andante: Romance. Polonaise.

The history of the three-part pieces K. 439b is complicated. The salient points are (a) that on May 31, 1800, Mozart's widow wrote to the publisher Johann Anton André that the clarinetist Anton Stadler still had in his possession copies of trios by Mozart for basset horns, and (b) that in 1803, some pieces for two basset horns and bassoon (!) were published under Mozart's name by Breitkopf & Härtel. In a later issue (by Simrock of Bonn), twenty-five pieces were published, divided into five "Serenades" of five pieces each. The scoring was given as two clarinets and bassoon. All later editions and arrangements were based on this Simrock issue. There are, however, indications that Constanze was quite right in believing in the existence of some trios for basset horns by her husband, and that they were these very pieces. For one thing, the lowest part sounds better on a basset horn than on a bassoon. Another indication is in the relation of the parts to each other: in the version for two clarinets and bassoon, there is often too great a distance between upper parts and bass. (In the reconstructed version for basset horns, the music is written in the key of F major, but it still sounds a fifth lower in B-flat major.) It is perhaps worth mentioning that Mozart repeatedly experimented with pieces for homogeneous wind instrumentation, analogous to string quartet or quintet. M.F.

K. 361 ***Serenade in B-flat major (K⁶ 370a)***
Origin: Vienna, late 1783 or early 1784?
Scoring: 2 oboes, 2 clarinets, 2 basset horns, 4 horns, 2 bassoons, double bass
Movements: Largo—Molto allegro. Menuetto. Adagio. Menuetto: Allegretto. Romance: Adagio—Allegretto—Adagio. [Tema con variazioni: Andante.] Finale: Molto allegro.

This great work is often called "Gran Partitta," but not by Mozart (this title on his manuscript is in a foreign hand). Its origin is uncertain. Alan Tyson's research assigns the paper of the manuscript a 1782 dating. On the other hand, stylistic evidence suggests that the work was commissioned somewhat later by Anton Stadler, the clarinet virtuoso for whom Mozart later composed his clarinet quintet (K. 581) and concerto (K. 622). On March 23, 1784, four movements of the B-flat Serenade were premiered by Stadler and twelve other musicians at the National-Hoftheater in Vienna. The performance was announced in the newspaper *Wienerblättchen* and was chronicled with great admiration by Johann Friedrich Schink, who attended the concert and described in his *Memoirs* his delight and admiration for Stadler's performance and Mozart's work.

Mozart was quite possibly referring to this Serenade when he remarked to his father, in a letter dated February 10, 1784, "There are pieces I must write that will bring me money *right now—but not later.*" When would he ever again be likely to capitalize on a piece with such a singular instrumentation?

The work has a great number of stylistic similarities with pieces in the K. 450's. A striking example is the largo introduction, with dotted fanfares and *dolce* responses. This device appears again immediately in the piano and wind quintet K. 452 and the piano and violin sonata K. 454. The syncopated accompaniment figure that immediately follows this opening in K. 454 is precisely the ostinato accompaniment figure in the sublime Adagio of the wind serenade.

Although the work is sometimes performed with contrabassoon, Mozart's autograph is unequivocally scored for string bass, with occasional indications of pizzicato. The work's texture is of a roundness and fullness of sonority that can be breathtaking in an intimate concert hall. It is fitting that it closes Mozart's great period of wind writing. R.D.L.

K. 487 ***12 Duos (K⁶ 496a)***
Origin: Vienna, July 27, 1786
Scoring: 2 horns
Movements: 1. Allegro. 2. Menuetto: Allegretto. 3. Andante. 4. Polonaise. 5. Larghetto. 6. Menuetto. 7. Adagio. 8. Allegro. 9. Menuetto. 10. Andante. 11. Menuetto. 12. Allegro.

Three of the twelve duos for horn (Nos. 1, 3, and 6) are preserved in Mozart's own hand, written in separate parts. They are dated July 27, 1786, and the manuscript bears the additional note: "untern Kegelscheiben" (while playing skittles). This solves a puzzle which has long bothered many musicologists. A week and a half after the horn duos, Mozart wrote the trio for clarinet, viola, and piano, K. 498, which is sometimes called the "Kegelstatt" (skittle alley) Trio, because it was supposedly composed during a game of skittles. It is possible that these horn duos were forgotten, and, by word of mouth, the association of skittles with composing was passed on to the more important and better-known trio.

The performers must have been virtuosi, for in those days, horn playing was confined in principle to the series of natural fanfare tones, to which skilled players could add a number of in-between notes by various technical artifices. If in his orchestral horn writing, Mozart avoided these artifices, he never hesitated to require them in his solo horn parts. In these duos his demands on the players, particularly in the upper registers, verge on the incredible. D.B.

K. 522 *Ein musikalischer Spass, in F major*
Origin: Vienna, 1787
Scoring: 2 horns, 2 violins, viola, basso
Movements: Allegro. Menuetto: Maestoso. Adagio cantabile. Presto.

Mozart did little other composing during the spring months of 1787 as he was preoccupied with *Don Giovanni*. His father, who had been ailing for some time, had died in Salzburg on May 28, and the sad news must have reached Mozart in Vienna soon afterward. And on the 4th of June, the pet starling that had been a dearly loved companion for three years also died. Mozart wrote an affecting poem in its memory the same day, perhaps obliquely expressing his grief at Leopold Mozart's death.

Mozart entered *Ein musikalischer Spass* (A Musical Joke) in the catalogue of his works under the date June 14, 1787. Coming, so it seemed, so soon after his father's and pet's deaths, the *Musical Joke* has puzzled Mozart's biographers, who have struggled to offer psychological explanations: anger at his father or a primitive reassertion of life and joy. Recently, however, English musicologist Alan Tyson has demonstrated that Mozart composed most of the *Musical Joke* before he knew of his father's final illness, but he completed the Finale and some other details only in late August. (The Finale, by the way, contains a parody of a not-too-skillful fugue that Mozart's student Thomas Attwood wrote in his exercise book on August 13.) Hence, the entry in Mozart's catalogue of his works is incorrectly dated.

Nothing is known about why Mozart began this piece, put it aside, and later returned to finish it. It was presumably composed for a private musical gathering of a sort common in Vienna in the 1780s. In such circles of connoisseurs and amateurs, this wickedly pointed parody of incompetent composition and performance would have been savored.

The very start of the Allegro shows with what singular lack of invention the audience is to be entertained. The melodies and the harmonies are of the simplest variety. There are bloopers of every kind: unbalanced phrases, false leading tones, exposed parallel fifths, accompaniments meandering aimlessly along without a melody to support them, modulations that are painfully clumsy.

The Minuet, after an uneasy first half, becomes totally chaotic in the second, when the horns find themselves hopelessly out of kilter. The violins practice scales, leaps, and other technical studies in the overly extended trio.

The horns are mercifully silent in the Adagio cantabile. Basically in C major, it nevertheless discomfits us with the immediate appearance of an F sharp, a note that belongs to the key of G. There follows an orgy of non sequiturs, of sudden and unwanted loud punctuation marks. The leading violin totally loses his way in a lunatic cadenza.

The Presto is a sort of rondo, with its maddeningly perky theme reappearing whenever it is needed. A fugato passage quickly fizzles out after four measures and is followed by an episode of seemingly infinite modulation. Ill-considered deeds of contrapuntal daring are undertaken in the coda, and this odd serenade comes to a halt in a multiple and cacophonous crash of five different keys.

An interesting footnote to this amusing send up of incompetence is the fact that another supremely gifted composer once owned and treasured the manuscript of *A Musical Joke:* Franz Schubert. A.R.

K. 525 *Eine kleine Nachtmusik, in G major*

Origin: Vienna, August 10, 1787

Scoring: 2 violins, viola, violoncello and double bass

Movements: Allegro. Romanze: Andante. Menuetto: Allegretto. Rondo: Allegro.

The title *Eine kleine Nachtmusik* translates into English with deceptive ease as "A Little Night Music"; it does not actually mean "a small amount of music to be played at night" but rather "a short notturno." The eighteenth-century nocturne was essentially an instrumental serenade in several movements. In fact, when Mozart entered the piece in his catalogue as "Eine kleine Nacht-Musik" he had no intention that that should serve as its title, but merely as a convenient quick description. It would be more accurate to identify it simply as the Serenade in G Major.

Mozart's complete catalogue entry is worth quoting because it proves that K. 525 began life as a five-movement work: "Eine kleine Nacht-Musik, comprising an Allegro, Minuet and Trio, Romance, Minuet and Trio, and Finale." Obviously, somewhere along the line the first Minuet and Trio disappeared; it has never been recovered or, at any rate, identified. Whether it was Mozart or someone else who removed it, in order to change a "short notturno" into something resembling a short symphony, no one knows. But the formal balance of the work as it now stands seems so exquisite that one might be reluctant to see the first Minuet restored, even if it were found.

There is another unsolved mystery connected with this famous *Night Music*. Is it an orchestral piece or should it be played by five solo strings? In Mozart's manuscript the bass line is allotted to "violoncello e contrabasso." Although the work sounds splendid played by a string orchestra, the balance of the (admittedly ambiguous) historical evidence suggests that Mozart probably had one-on-a-part performance in mind.

A bold attention-demanding statement sets the Allegro on its cheerful way. The Romance is in four episodes. The Minuet is courtly and aristrocratic, the trio *Ländler*-like and flowing. The final Rondo shows Mozart at his most *galant,* charming and witty. A.R.

13

Chamber Music without a Keyboard Instrument

Musicians attached to the Prince de Conti. Watercolor by Louis Carrogis de Carmontelle (c. 1768).

From left to right: the singer Provers, the cellist Jean-Pierre Duport, the hornist Jean-Joseph Rodolphe, the violinist Pierre Vachon, and the oboist Vernier. Rodolphe, also an excellent violinist and composer, befriended Mozart in Paris in 1778 and was responsible for Mozart's being offered an organist's post at Versailles, which, however, he declined.

BACKGROUND AND OVERVIEW

Discussions from the second half of the eighteenth century about the nature of the audiences for music almost inevitably make use of two terms: *Kenner* and *Liebhaber* in German, connoisseur and amateur in English or French. These words permeate musical discussions of the period. Amateurs passionately love music but have little technical knowledge of it; connoisseurs not only love music, they also understand it. It was Mozart's proud claim that he could compose in a way that would satisfy both groups: a polite, entertaining surface for the amateurs along with elegant inner workings for the connoisseurs.

Mozart made this boast with regard to his piano concertos, K. 413–415. In general, however, whether a work was aimed primarily at amateurs or at connoisseurs depended on its genre. Lots of technically and conceptually easy songs and chamber music were written and published for home consumption, geared to the playing abilities and tastes of amateurs. Highly public genres—church music, opera, orchestral music—had to reach all kinds of people and, therefore, were often aimed at the same audience, although this time for the playing abilities of professionals and the tastes of amateurs. It was in the realm of "serious" chamber music, frequently in the form of sonatas, trios, quartets, and quintets, that composers most often provided more challenging fare for the connoisseurs.

Mozart's much-loved string quartets and quintets, for instance, were not concert music. They were conceived for the pleasure of their performers and a tiny circle of intimates who might be invited to listen, in someone's living room, parlor, or salon. Music-loving noblemen and -women who were connoisseurs would hire string quartets to play for their private enjoyment. (Many of them were also fully competent to play in such a group.) This is also what the musicians themselves did for recreation. For example, the Irish baritone Michael Kelly, who lived in Vienna from 1783 to 1786 and sang Basilio and Don Curzio in the premiere of *The Marriage of Figaro,* recorded such an evening in his Memoirs:

> [The English composer Stephen] Storace gave a quartet party to his friends. The players were tolerable; not one of them excelled on the instrument he played, but there was a little science among them, which I dare say will be acknowledged when I name them:
>
> The First Violin . . . . . Haydn
> " Second Violin . . . . Baron Dittersdorf
> " Violoncello . . . . . Vanhall
> " Tenor [viola] . . . . Mozart.
>
> The poet [Giovanni Battista] Casti and [the composer Giovanni] Paisiello formed part of the audience. I was there, and a greater treat, or a more remarkable one, cannot be imagined.

The four players, Joseph Haydn, Carl Ditters von Dittersdorf, Johann Baptist Vanhal, and Mozart were the four leading Viennese composers in the 1780s.

N.Z.

QUINTETS

K. 174 *String Quintet in B-flat major*
Origin: Salzburg, December 1773
Scoring: 2 violins, 2 violas, violoncello
Movements: Allegro moderato. Adagio. Menuetto ma allegretto. Allegro.

On March 13, 1773, Leopold Mozart and his son returned from their third Italian trip. It was then that Mozart must have heard the first String Quintet in C major by Michael Haydn, composed a few weeks before the Mozarts returned to Salzburg. Mozart often found in a composition by a contemporary the inspiration to write a similar work himself and, if possible, to improve on the original. Mozart's first quintet, K. 174, is believed to have been composed in the late spring of 1773. In December of that year, Michael Haydn wrote his second quintet, in G major, a work that seems to have made an equally profound impression on the young Mozart, who immediately proceeded to rewrite his own quintet, providing it with a new Trio and recasting the thematic material of the Finale.

The style of the opening Allegro moderato is a curious mixture of the old Austrian cassation, or divertimento, as practiced by Joseph Haydn in his earliest works, and the modern quartet. The older type tended to set up the violins and the violas as "choirs" and play them off against each other, whereas the newer quartet integrated the four instruments more closely. The opening of the Adagio is magical. All the upper strings are muted and the cello is marked *sempre piano* (always softly). The sturdy Minuet has something very Haydnesque about it—both the Haydn brothers liked this kind of rustic approach to the minuet, with its strong forward movement.

The Finale, in its revised version, is a much longer and more complicated movement than the original. Mozart may have been seeking to equalize the weight of the four movements. His way of increasing the Finale's importance was to pack contrapuntal weight into the development section.

Before undertaking his revision of this quintet. Mozart had paid a two-month visit to Vienna, where he had studied some of the latest music circulating in the capital city, and perhaps especially Haydn's newest and revolutionary symphonies and quartets. It seems possible that the symphonic cast of the Quintet's new Finale owes as much to these works as to the quintets of Michael Haydn.

H.C.R.L.

K. 407 *Horn Quintet in E-flat major (K⁶ 386c)*
Origin: Vienna, end of 1782
Scoring: horn, violin, 2 violas, violoncello
Movements: Allegro. Andante. Allegro.

Mozart wrote his only horn quintet for Joseph Leutgeb, a man he had known since his earliest childhood. The series of horn concertos and this quintet bear vivid testimony as much to the exhilaration they experienced in each other's company as to Mozart's great admiration for Leutgeb's abilities as a hand horn player. (The reason that the eighteenth-century orchestral horn, the ancestor of the modern French horn, is sometimes called the hand horn is that notes other than those of common fanfares could be obtained only by skillful placement of the player's hand in the instrument's bell.)

Mozart probably wrote the quintet in Vienna toward the end of 1782, but confirmation of this date is unlikely unless the autograph manuscript, lost sight of since being auctioned in London in March 1847, should resurface. It was a work for an unorthodox ensemble, like the Serenade in B flat, K. 361, which early publishers preferred to publish in arrangements rather than issuing the original. At least two versions appeared in which a second cello is substituted for the horn; yet another version is arranged for a sextet of clarinets, horns, and bassoons. Into these was interpolated a minuet-and-trio movement taken, in one instance, from the Serenade in E flat, K. 375, and, in another, from the string trio K. 563.

Many commentators have noted the *concertante* rather than the chamber-music characteristics of this quintet, particularly in its outer movements, though few would go so far as Alfred Einstein, who saw it as "a rudimentary concerto with chamber-music accompaniment." Certainly the majority of the musical argument is between horn and violin, but each movement breaks away from this routine at least once. R.H.

K. 515 *String Quintet in C major*
Origin: Vienna, April 19, 1787
Scoring: 2 violins, 2 violas, violoncello
Movements: Allegro. Menuetto: Allegretto. Andante. Allegro.

Mozart may have written the next three quintets on speculation, hoping to sell manuscript copies of them to amateurs by subscription. The three works are: K. 515, dated Vienna, April 19, 1787, in Mozart's own catalogue; K. 516, dated Vienna, May 16, 1787, and K. 406 (516b), which is Mozart's arrangement of the Wind Band Serenade, K. 388, probably made in the winter of 1787–88. Mozart played them with his friends for a while and then decided to sell them in manuscript copies. He had done the same with three new piano concertos (K. 413–415) in January 1783. But times had changed. In 1783 Mozart was the darling of the Viennese public, and his concerts were filled by the nobility. In 1788 Mozart was no longer in favor, and he was finally obliged to sell two of the quintets (K. 515 and 516) outright to the publisher Artaria and Co. at much less profit to himself. K. 515 is by far the longest of Mozart's chamber works for strings. The brilliant original opening theme uses an old device (the arpeggiated or broken chord) in a new way. The cello sweeps up two octaves on the notes of a C-major chord and is answered by the first violin in a phrase of peculiar poignancy. This formula is repeated three times before the theme comes to fruition. But hardly has Mozart completed the theme when the music comes to a dead stop. After this bar of rest, the whole process is repeated in C minor and the roles of first violin and cello are reversed.

Among the many striking innovations of the Minuet we may mention the use of a *crescendo* leading to *piano*. This would become a stylistic "fingerprint" in Beethoven. The Andante is a civilized and highly intellectual conversation between two friends, first violin and first viola. The Finale is a tribute to Haydn's famous sonata-rondo form. It is altogether a bold, assertive, and optimistic movement, as if Mozart had resolved firmly to conquer the troubles, financial and spiritual, that were beginning to darken his life.

H.C.R.L.

K. 516 *String Quintet in G minor*
Origin: Vienna, May 16, 1787
Scoring: 2 violins, 2 violas, violoncello

Movements: Allegro. Menuetto: Allegretto. Adagio ma non troppo. Adagio—Allegro.

This is the most famous of the quintets. Its very special key, its dramatic power, its combination of tragedy and tenderness have assured it a unique place in the chamber-music repertoire. Together with the great G-minor Symphony, K. 550 (completed July 25, 1788), it constitutes the most personal music, perhaps, that Mozart ever wrote. By May 1787, when he composed the quintet, it must have been obvious to Mozart that, at least with the Viennese, he had failed as a composer. Music's greatest genius was misunderstood and spurned by the only segment of society on which he could count for financial support. And even though he was engaged by Emperor Joseph II as court chamber composer, the salary, 800 gulden, was little more than a token. In fact, Joseph II, while professing admiration for Mozart, much preferred the music of Giuseppe Sarti, Giovanni Paisiello, Domenico Cimarosa, and Florian Gassmann. The success of Mozart's *Figaro* was not permanent, and he was beginning to sink into debt. To top it all, his father, Leopold, whom he loved and had rebelled against, was ill and, in fact, died less than two weeks after the Quintet was finished. The G-minor Quintet is a mirror of Mozart's personal tragedy.

The nervous desperation of the first movement's opening subject is underlined by its understatement: it is all played softly and without a real stabilizing bass. In the Minuet the angry off-beat *forte* chords are like cries of protest. The Adagio ma non troppo is couched in an extraordinary atmosphere engendered by the use of mutes on all five instruments.

Haydn sometimes begins his finales with a slow introduction, but the procedure is rarer for Mozart. This introductory Adagio is like an accompanied recitative in an opera, with the first violin acting as soprano heroine. It is an increasingly restless introduction but perfectly suited to prepare the way for the sunny conclusion, a Rondo in which Mozart's depression disappears as quickly as a single cloud in a summer sky. H.C.R.L.

K. 406 *String Quintet in C minor (K⁶ 516b)*

Origin: Vienna, winter 1787–88
Scoring: 2 violins, 2 violas, violoncello
Movements: Allegro. Andante. Menuetto in canone. Allegro.

This quintet is Mozart's own arrangement of his Serenade in C minor for Wind Octet, K. 388. (See the note for K. 388 on p. 246.) Wind-band serenades were, in the eighteenth century, among the most fragile of genres. When the occasion for which one was written had passed, the work lost its *raison d'être*. The desire to give permanence to this piece is no doubt why Mozart decided, quite against his usual practice, to reach back to an earlier work to make up the third of three quintets he was offering by subscription.

The bewildering profusion of intellectual forces with which Mozart crowds the opening theme of the Quintet in C minor is typical: there are no fewer than five separate components, all in marked dynamic and motivic contrast to each other. The Andante is in E flat. Its warmth and mellowness—so characteristic of Mozart when writing in E-flat major—are tempered with a certain nostalgic loneliness, which will become more and more an integral part of the mature Mozart's music, whether for chamber, opera house, or concert hall.

The severe canonic, or roundlike,

Minuet with its Trio *al rovescio,* or inverse canon (one in which the theme's intervals go up in one voice, then go down in the imitating voice, and vice versa), takes as its model the equally gaunt E-minor Minuet *in canone* of Haydn's Symphony No. 44 ("Mourning"), composed about a decade before the Serenade. The Finale, says American musicologist Alfred Einstein, "anticipates the spirit of the C-minor Concerto (K. 491)." Like its great successor, it is cast in the form of a theme and variations. For the last variation, in a sudden mercurial shift, there is a spring into C major, and in a hard, triumphant mood the music sweeps to an end.

H.C.R.L.

K. 581 ***Clarinet Quintet in A major***
Origin: Vienna, September 29, 1789
Scoring: clarinet, 2 violins, viola, violoncello
Movements: Allegro. Larghetto. Menuetto. Allegretto con variazioni.

Here is one of a group of masterpieces that Mozart wrote for Anton Stadler, a fellow Mason and one of several close friends among the fraternity of Viennese wind instrumentalists. The quintet seems immediately to evoke the same limpid and lyrical mood as Mozart's other late works in A major, such as the piano concerto, K. 488, and the clarinet concerto, K. 622.

The presence of a Minuet movement makes this the only one of Mozart's works for wind soloist and strings to be in four movements. The extra movement is entirely consistent with the strong chamber-music (as opposed to *concertante)* characteristics of the work, but for the composer to provide two Trios is indeed rare in any of his chamber music.

Mozart's first thoughts on a Finale petered out after 89 measures, and he replaced them with this set of five variations and coda on a not-very-remarkable theme in march rhythm. It shows unmistakable signs of Mozartean genius, however, in the delightful imitation between violin and viola in its middle section, and in the imitative second violin part, which acts as a bass to the final phrase of the theme.

R.H.

K. 593 ***String Quintet in D major***
Origin: Vienna, December 1790
Scoring: 2 violins, 2 violas, violoncello
Movements: Larghetto—Allegro. Adagio. Menuetto: Allegretto. Allegro.

Mozart composed this great work in December 1790, probably for Johann Tost, formerly the leader of the second violins in Haydn's orchestra. That Haydn was intimately involved with the first performance of Mozart's D-major Quintet is attested by their mutual friend, Abbé Maximilian Stadler, whose memories were preserved in the travel diaries of the English music publisher Vincent Novello and his wife Mary in 1829. "Mozart and Haydn frequently played together with Stadler in Mozart's Quintettos; particularly mentioned the 5th in D major, singing the Bass part, the one in C major and still more that in G minor."

Mozart opens with a typically Haydnesque slow introduction. But he has further plans in store for this Larghetto: it is destined to return just before the end of the movement, which then concludes with a superbly rhetorical flourish—a final utterance of the Allegro's main theme.

The Adagio marking for the slow movement is in itself a tribute to Haydn, whose adagios were famous. The most incredible passage in any of the quintets is in the middle of the development section, where the work's central constructive device—the use of descending thirds—

reaches a violent pitch of intensity. The Minuet, proceeding on the Adagio's motif of the downward third, introduces a strict canon on its theme in the second part.

Mozart had second thoughts about the theme of the Finale. He originally wrote it as a chromatic scale, slithering down eight notes from A above the staff to D a fifth below. He then decided on a slight reshaping of these eight notes in a diatonic pattern and painstakingly corrected the passage every time it occurred in his manuscript. In either version, the Finale is fast, intensely involved, and distinguished by its contrapuntal complexity.

H.C.R.L.

K. 614 ***String Quintet in E-flat major***

Origin: Vienna, April 12, 1791

Scoring: 2 violins, 2 violas, violoncello

Movements: Allegro di molto. Andante. Menuetto: Allegretto. Allegro.

"The Quintet in E flat, K. 614, is a tribute to Haydn," writes American pianist and writer Charles Rosen of this last piece of chamber music that Mozart ever wrote, pointing out the similarity of the Finale to that of Haydn's String Quartet, Op. 64, No. 6, which was composed for Johann Tost, who may also have commissioned K. 593 and 614. The entry of the E-flat Quintet in Mozart's catalogue is dated Vienna, April 12, 1791. Haydn had left for England and immortality, and the two friends were never to see each other again.

So this is another tribute, in absentia, to Mozart's best musical friend. "The work," continues Rosen, "which—in its outer movements—combines a detailed treatment in Haydn's fashion of the dynamic qualities of the tiniest motifs with a typically Mozartean sonorous and complex inner part-writing, makes a few musicians uncomfortable, perhaps because it lacks the expansive freedom of the other quintets, and seems to concentrate its richness."

For opening movements 6/8 is not a customary meter, and Mozart may have borrowed the idea from Haydn's Symphony No. 67 in F. The quick, nervous language is Haydn's too, as is the massive concentration of motivic relationships and expansions. The Andante is of that late-period simplicity in Mozart that astonishes in *The Magic Flute* and in passages from *La clemenza di Tito:* it is supreme art, touching, direct, and of an autumnal beauty. The Minuet contains some details of consummate subtlety. In the second part, the main theme is suddenly turned around and played against itself. In size, scope, and developmental process, the Finale, with its Haydnesque tune, completes this great and touching act of friendship, one that rounds out Mozart's tribute to the two Haydn brothers, Michael and Joseph.

H.C.R.L.

QUARTETS

A mid-eighteenth-century string quartet, Anonymous silhouette from the Öttingen-Wallerstein court.

Despite this picture's lack of detail, it clearly shows that the players' bows are not of the modern, Tourte pattern and that the cellist plays without an endpin.

K. 80 *String Quartet in G major, No. 1 (K[6] 73f)*

Origin: first three movements, Lodi, March 15, 1770; fourth movement, Salzburg or Vienna, 1773 to 1775
Scoring: 2 violins, viola, violoncello
Movements: Adagio. Allegro. Menuetto. Rondeau.

The fourteen-year-old Mozart dated this first and solitary early Quartet with unusual exactness: "Lodi, March 15, 1770, at 7 o'clock in the evening." After a long visit to Milan, Lodi was the first stop on the return trip to Parma and Modena; Wolfgang and his father were on their first trip to Italy. Mozart seems to have been especially fond of this Quartet, for eight years later he took it with him on his trip to Mannheim and Paris, where he wrote to his father on March 24, 1778: "before my departure for Mannheim, I had Herr von Gemmingen copy the Quartet that I wrote that evening at the inn in Lodi." The "Lodi" Quartet reflects clearly the musical impressions made on Mozart in Milan by Giuseppe Sammartini and his circle. The model of the trio sonata is particularly evident in the slow introductory movement. All four movements of the work are in the same key—an exceptional rarity in Mozart. W.P.

K. 136 *Divertimento in D major (K[6] 125a)*

Origin: Salzburg, early 1772
Scoring: 2 violins, viola, basso
Movements: Allegro. Andante. Presto.

K. 137 *Divertimento in B-flat major (K⁶ 125b)*
Origin: Salzburg, early 1772
Scoring: 2 violins, viola, basso
Movements: Andante. Allegro di molto. Allegro assai.

K. 138 *Divertimento in F major (K⁶ 125c)*
Origin: Salzburg, early 1772
Scoring: 2 violins, viola, basso
Movements: [Allegro.] Andante. Presto.

These three works for strings have enjoyed equal popularity as string quartets and as works for string orchestra. In both settings they sound good in modern concert halls and on recordings. The historical evidence suggests, however, that Mozart probably thought of them as composed for one player per part, and quite possibly to be played not by the normal string quartet (two violins, viola, and cello) but by the so-called "divertimento quartet" (two violins, viola, double bass). A performance by a "divertimento quartet" plus two horns was portrayed on the title page of the first edition of Mozart's *Musical Joke*, K. 522, which is reproduced on p. 238. N.Z.

The first movement of K. 136 assigns the first violin a self-sufficient, almost prima-donna-like role; the second movement is filled with tender, Italianate charm; the last, in sonata form, varies the ideas of the opening movement in its main theme, and displays an element of seriousness in the contrapuntal efforts of the development section. K. 137 puts its slow movement at the beginning, and stresses an alfresco mood in the following Allegro di molto, a mood that also characterizes the *buffonesque* final movement. The first and last movements of K. 138 also show a *concertante* simplicity: only the Andante with its pointed motives and independent countermelodies suggests something of the technique of an individual string quartet movement. The finale, with a minor episode *à la* Johann Christian Bach, looks forward—but it is surely a spot of tonal color, rather than a first step toward that curious melancholy that emerges ever more strongly in Mozart's later works. U.K.

K. 155 *String Quartet in D major, No. 2 (K⁶ 134a)*
Origin: Bozen and Verona, October to November 1772
Scoring: 2 violins, viola, violoncello
Movements: [Allegro.] Andante. Allegro molto.

K. 156 *String Quartet in G major, No. 3 (K⁶ 134b)*
Origin: Milan, end of 1772
Scoring: 2 violins, viola, violoncello
Movements: Presto. Adagio. Tempo di Menuetto.

K. 157 *String Quartet in C major, No. 4*
Origin: Milan, late 1772 or early 1773
Scoring: 2 violins, viola, violoncello
Movements: [Allegro.] Andante. Presto.

K. 158 *String Quartet in F major, No. 5*
Origin: Milan, late 1772 or early 1773
Scoring: 2 violins, viola, violoncello
Movements: Allegro. Andante un poco allegretto. Tempo di Menuetto.

K. 159 *String Quartet in B-flat major, No. 6*
Origin: Milan, early 1773
Scoring: 2 violins, viola, violoncello
Movements: Andante. Allegro. Rondo: Allegro grazioso.

K. 160 *String Quartet in E-flat major, No. 7 (K⁶ 159a)*
Origin: Milan, early 1773
Scoring: 2 violins, viola, violoncello
Movements: Allegro. Un poco adagio. Presto.

The six works in this cycle are arranged according to the circle of fifths (D–G–

C–F–B♭–E♭). The original manuscripts bear no dates, but from certain remarks in Leopold Mozart's correspondence, and from an examination of the handwriting itself, one may deduce the origin with reasonable certainty: it was the period of the third trip to Italy, from late autumn 1772 to the beginning of 1773, the same time that Mozart composed the opera *Lucio Silla* for Milan.

All of these quartets have in common a three-movement format, in which the final movement is always either a rondo (though not so titled) or a *tempo di menuetto*. Only the first and last works of the cycle (K. 155 and 160) are completely in a major key; the four middle quartets outdo each other, in fact, in their emphasis of minor-key contrasts. Their middle movements, all in minor keys, are among the most extraordinary movements to be found in all of Mozart's youthful works. From the novel give-and-take of the four strings, treated in principal on an equal basis, come musical panoramas of entirely original design and color, and with an expressive power that touches on highly personal, even remote feelings. Some have seen an indication of a "romantic crisis" for the young Mozart here; it is probably more accurate to speak of a protest against convention—a protest that is so very clearly articulated in so many other inner movements and minuets of Mozart's symphonies of 1772–73, that German musicologist Hermann Abert calls it a "tendency toward the eccentric." At any rate, one may surely call the B-flat Quartet "eccentric": instead of a slow middle movement, the work has a second main movement in the relative minor (G minor), an oversized structure full of aggressive energy that threatens to overthrow the tonal and structural coherence of the work as a whole. Next to the concentrated strength of such a monster of a movement, all the refinements of the opening movement pale—such as the playful use of a model Baroque bass line at the opening, where the listener waits in vain for a concluding cadence after the deceptive one in measure 4, or (one of the most striking effects in early Mozart) the provocative "wrong"—or seemingly premature—entrance of the first violin in measure 9. W.P.

K. 168 *String Quartet in F major, No. 8*
Origin: Vienna, August 1773
Scoring: 2 violins, viola, violoncello
Movements: Allegro. Andante. Menuetto. Allegro.

K. 169 *String Quartet in A major, No. 9*
Origin: Vienna, August 1773
Scoring: 2 violins, viola, violoncello
Movements: Molto allegro. Andante. Menuetto. Rondeaux: Allegro.

K. 170 *String Quartet in C major, No. 10*
Origin: Vienna, August 1773
Scoring: 2 violins, viola, violoncello
Movements: Andante. Menuetto. Un poco adagio. Rondo: Allegro.

K. 171 *String Quartet in E-flat major, No. 11*
Origin: Vienna, August 1773
Scoring: 2 violins, viola, violoncello
Movements: Adagio—Allegro assai. Menuetto. Andante. Allegro assai.

K. 172 *String Quartet in B-flat major, No. 12*
Origin: Vienna, September? 1773
Scoring: 2 violins, viola, violoncello
Movements: Allegro spiritoso. Adagio. Menuetto. Allegro assai.

K. 173 *String Quartet in D minor, No. 13*
Origin: Vienna, September 1773
Scoring: 2 violins, viola, violoncello
Movements: Allegro, ma molto moderato. [Andante grazioso.] Menuetto. [Allegro.]

This second cycle of six quartets is likewise arranged in an orderly fashion, following a complicated scheme of third-related keys, mainly in ascending order: F–A–C–E♭–B♭–D. The works were composed in the summer and autumn of 1773 during Mozart's visit to Vienna (from mid-July to the end of September), thus about nine months after his first series of quartets. Nevertheless one can see differences, and observe a further step along the path of progress. The quartets of the new series all have four movements, i.e., they have attained and established the regular form of the "Classical" string quartet. And their central concern is—simply speaking—no longer the exploration of new emotive and expressive regions in minor territory, far from the beaten path of convention, but consolidation of quartet writing in the no-man's-land between *"galant"* and "academic" styles, i.e., between melodic and contrapuntal techniques. In this period Mozart came under the two-fold influence of Joseph Haydn, whose Quartets Op. 9, 17, and 20 he must have come to know in Vienna. The closing Fugues of the F-major and D-minor Quartets, which form the programmatic-schematic frame of Mozart's cycle, are certainly unthinkable without Haydn's model—and likewise so many other details, such as the theme of the variation movement of the C-major Quartet, K. 170. But however one assesses the significance of such influences, one must fundamentally admit that in his compositional style Mozart let himself get sidetracked by Haydn to an amazingly small degree.

The closing Fugues of the first and last quartet of the cycle, showpieces of proper academic artfulness, mark only one extreme; the other—flowing melody with more or less simplified chordal accompaniment—is found in the slow movements of K. 170 and 172. Between these two extremes Mozart discloses an astonishing abundance of possibilities. He composes the F-minor Andante of K. 168 "in the style of a canon," the C-minor Andante of K. 171 "in the style of a double fugue"; in the B-flat Quartet, K. 172, he even carries the principle of canonic imitation to the Minuet movement. But the game of counterpoint, the "contrapuntal" style, is only one possibility in quartet writing. In the Andante of the A-major Quartet, K. 169, Mozart created—probably for the first time in his music—a formal type that would occupy him up to his late Viennese period; one may compare the Andante of the Piano Concerto in C Major, K. 467. No less prophetic is the opening movement of K. 173 (D minor). And the Minuet of this quartet—one of the grandest movements of the whole series—must surely be reckoned among the wonders of 1773. W.P.

K. 285 *Flute Quartet in D major, No. 1*
Origin: Mannheim, December 25, 1777
Scoring: flute, violin, viola, violoncello
Movements: Allegro. Adagio. Rondo: Allegretto.

Mozart wrote his first three flute quartets while in Mannheim in the winter of 1777–78. His patron was a Dutchman, nicknamed "the Indian" by Mozart, who spelled his name phonetically, "de Jean" or "Deschamps." It has recently been demonstrated that this was Ferdinand de Jean (1731–97) a wealthy amateur flutist who worked for the Dutch East India Company. Mozart first referred to de Jean's commission on December 10, 1977, as "three short, simple concertos and a couple of quartets for flute," required within two months for a fee of 200 gulden. He evidently set about this work promptly and a week later was telling his father: "I shall soon have finished one quartet for the Indian Dutchman, that true friend of humanity." But by the end of January 1778 Mozart was evidently far behind schedule and temporizing over a commission that was bigger than he first admitted. On the 15th of February, de Jean left for Paris, and Mozart was obviously somewhat hurt to receive only 96 gulden for the two concertos and three quartets he had finished by that date. He was in fact lucky to receive that much, since one of the concertos was merely a transcription of his earlier oboe concerto, and of the quartets one was only two movements, and another probably unfinished.

The opening allegro movement of the first flute quartet finds Mozart in a highly ebullient mood as he reveals a seemingly unending stream of melodies. Musicologist Alfred Einstein admires the "sweet melancholy" of the second movement, an Adagio in B minor, which he calls "perhaps the most beautiful accompanied solo ever written for the flute." Mozart turns his second movement into an introduction to the Finale simply by interrupting the logical progress of its final cadence in a way that leaves the return to D major all but inevitable. R.H.

K³ 285a ***Flute Quartet in G major, No. 2***
Origin: Mannheim, January or February 1777
Scoring: flute, violin, viola, violoncello
Movements: Andante. Menuetto.

This little quartet, being in two movements only, follows a pattern created by Johann Christian Bach, one of the composers Mozart most admired during his formative years. The quartet opens with a quietly relaxed and languorous Andante movement, its themes reflecting the gentle coloring of the instrumentation. The finale is a Minuet without a Trio, in simple ternary, or **A–B–A** form. It ends with a short codetta—quiet, simple, and utterly effective. R.H.

K³ 285b ***Flute Quartet in C major, No. 3 (K¹ Anh 171)***
Origin: Vienna? 1781 to 1782
Scoring: flute, violin, viola, violoncello
Movements: Allegro. Andantino.

The authenticity of this work has still not been entirely proved. Long-held doubts about the first movement were recently resolved by the discovery of a sketch of part of it in Mozart's handwriting. The second movement, a theme and variations, is virtually identical with the sixth movement of the great Serenade in B flat, K. 361, but experts now believe that the version for flute and strings is not the prototype of the serenade but rather an anonymous arrangement probably commissioned by Heinrich Philipp Carl Bossler, who first published the Quartet in 1788. According to this theory, an otherwise incomplete quartet was turned into a saleable work. If the movement is an arrangement and if the arranger was not Mozart himself, the job was nonetheless expertly carried out. Given the simpler instrumentation, the six variations of the second movement are identical with those in the serenade, except that each half of the third is repeated conventionally, whereas in the serenade this is a double variation without repeats. R.H.

K. 298 ***Flute Quartet in A major, No. 4***
Origin: Vienna, 1786 to 1787
Scoring: flute, violin, viola, violoncello
Movements: [Andantino.] [Menuetto.] Rondeaux: Allegretto grazioso.

This flute quartet is a much later piece than the first three. It was written by

Mozart in Vienna in 1786 or 1787, perhaps for performance in the musical circle of Mozart's Viennese friend Gottfried von Jacquin.

Mozart used as the principal theme of the Finale an aria by the enormously popular Italian composer Giovanni Paisiello from his opera *Le gare generose* (The Generous Rivals), first performed in Vienna on September 1, 1786, and in Naples only a few months earlier. In fact, Mozart seems also to have based the opening movements on themes by other composers: the first movement is a set of variations based on a song by Franz Anton Hoffmeister, to Wilhelm Gottfried Becker's poem *An die Natur* (To Nature), and the underlying theme of the second is an old French rondo, "Il a des bottes, des bottes Bastien" (He has some boots, has Bastien). This use of contemporary tunes supports Alfred Einstein's suggestion that the quartet is a good-natured parody of the vacuous and perfunctory style characteristic of the many "quartets on popular airs" of that time.

Mozart reveals his jocular intent unmistakably in the last movement, which bears the *Alice in Wonderland* heading: "Rondieaoux/Allegretto grazioso, mà non troppo presto, però non troppo adagio. Così—così—con molto garbo ed espressione" (Rondo-meow/Allegretto grazioso but not too presto, but not too adagio, either. So-so—with much charm and expression). What follows is Paisiello's perfunctory little theme, which in spite of its threadbare invention, dominates a movement of rather lavish proportions. R.H.

K. 370 *Oboe Quartet in F major (K⁶ 368b)*
Origin: Munich, early 1781
Scoring: oboe, violin, viola, violoncello
Movements: Allegro. Adagio. Rondeau: Allegro.

Friedrich Ramm was unquestionably one of the great oboists of his age. He was about thirty-three when Mozart first met him in Mannheim in 1777, and had by then already been principal oboist there for fourteen years. He had joined the orchestra at the amazingly early age of fourteen and was soon placed above a senior colleague, the oboist Ludwig August Lebrun, because of the size and quality of his tone. He moved with the orchestra to Munich in 1778 when his patron, Karl Theodor, Elector of the Palatine, became also Elector of Bavaria, and was still performing there in 1806 and probably later. Ramm was permitted by the elector the luxury of pursing an active international career as a soloist, visiting places as far apart as Vienna, London, and Berlin.

Mozart could scarcely contain his enthusiasm for what he called Ramm's "delightfully pure tone." He presented him with the Oboe Concerto (K. 271k) he had earlier written for Giuseppe Ferlendis and reported that Ramm was "quite crazy with delight" with it and had adopted it as his *cheval de bataille* (war horse). It was for Ramm that Mozart wrote the oboe part in his (lost) Sinfonia Concertante for flute, oboe, bassoon, and horn (K. 297B). He also wrote at least two arias with obbligato oboe parts for him. And when he went to Munich in the winter of 1780–81 for the opening of his opera *Idomeneo,* he composed the present oboe quartet for the great player, though whether it was intended as a gift or written on commission we are not informed. The work is a masterpiece; its range of technical and musical demands reflect the utmost credit on Ramm's artistry.

An aura of gentle intimacy pervades

this quartet—the intimacy that resides supremely in chamber music. It is inevitable that the oboe plays the dominant part, inevitable too that Mozart should not even attempt to blend the accompanying string chords with an instrument so individual in tone. R.H.

The "Haydn" Quartets

The six "Haydn" Quartets memorialize in tones an altogether extraordinary artistic friendship. In 1785, before the set had been published, Haydn paid a visit to Vienna and heard several of the new quartets performed by Mozart himself, with his father Leopold, and two friends. In a famous letter, Leopold reported Haydn's comments to him afterward: "I tell you before God as an honest man that your son is the greatest composer known to me either in person or by reputation. He has taste, and what is more, the most profound knowledge of composition." The other side of the coin, so to speak, is Mozart's dedicatory address to Haydn, which was printed with the six quartets and is worth quoting in full:

To my dear friend Haydn

A father who had decided to send his children into the world at large thought best to entrust them to the protection and guidance of a famous man who fortunately happened to be his best friend as well. Behold here, famous man and dearest friend, my six children. They are, to be sure, the fruit of long and arduous work, yet some friends have encouraged me to assume that I shall see this work rewarded to some extent at least, and this flatters me into believing that these children shall one day offer me some comfort. You yourself, dearest friend, have shown me your approval of them during your last sojourn in this capital. Your praise, above all, encourages me to recommend them to you, and makes me hope that they shall not be entirely unworthy of your good will. May it please you, therefore, to receive them kindly and to be their father, their guide, and their friend. From this moment I surrender to you all my rights in them, but beg you to regard with leniency the faults that may have remained hidden to the partial eye of their father, and notwithstanding their shortcomings to preserve your noble friendship for him who loves you so dearly. Meanwhile I am, with all my heart, etc.,

W. A. Mozart.

Mozart had begun to work on the "Haydn" Quartets the year following his move from Salzburg to Vienna. It was during this time that he came to know the music of Bach and Handel through Baron van Swieten's musicales, an experience that had the force of revelation for him and had profound effects upon the manner of his polyphonic writing. Moreover, in 1781 Haydn brought out his six "Russian" Quartets, Op. 33, written, as the composer put it, "in an entirely new and special manner." The crux of the new manner was a greatly increased democratization in part-writing; all the instruments of the quartet were now to participate in the thematic elaboration, and furthermore, that elaboration was no longer to be confined only to development sections, but would permeate the whole texture of an opus.

Mozart transplanted these principles to his own six new "children" in tribute to Haydn. As ever with Mozart in his inspired creations, the effort is transmuted in the final product into a surface of seemingly spontaneous fluency and grace. A.M.K.

K. 387 *String Quartet in G major, "First Haydn," No. 14*

Origin: Vienna, December 31, 1782
Scoring: 2 violins, viola, violoncello
Movements: Allegro vivace assai. Menuetto: Allegretto. Andante cantabile. Molto allegro.

The first quartet in the series is a boundlessly effusive creation that, for all its spill of emotion, is yet contained within absolutely ideal proportions. The opening movement envelops one instantly in Mozart's outpouring in its very first phrase, an octave-spanning upward spring, bold and memorable in outline. The Menuetto reverses the upsweep of the first movement's initial theme in the gently falling phrases of its opening measures. The Andante is a fine outpouring of four successive themes. The melodies are not in themselves memorable, perhaps, but their setting is gemlike and the entire movement gives off a golden C-major radiance all its own.

The four-note theme at the beginning of the Finale, and indeed, the whole movement, is celebrated because of its close resemblance to the finale of the "Jupiter" Symphony. The movement sounds like a fugue because of the way the string instruments imitate each other in close succession, but Mozart shuttles between the "learned" style (i.e., strictly contrapuntal) and the *"galant"* (i.e., prevailingly melodic) with quicksilver ease. In a final Haydnesque touch, after giving us a false ending of loud, declarative chords, Mozart makes his concluding cadence a quiet one—but it is still the same four-note germ that has dominated the whole movement. A.M.K.

K. 421 *String Quartet in D minor, "Second Haydn," No. 15 (K^6 417b)*

Origin: Vienna, June 1783
Scoring: 2 violins, viola, violoncello
Movements: Allegro. Andante. Menuetto. Allegretto ma non troppo.

If the fundamental progression of the preceding G-major Quartet was a proud, upward burst, here it is descent, to the nether regions of austere pathos. The key is D minor—the key of the brooding Piano Concerto No. 20, K. 466; the death-interrupted Requiem, K. 626; and the fateful element in *Don Giovanni*.

The very first move in the opening Allegro moderato is the first violin's blunt downward plunge of an octave, the lower D nailed home with a sixfold reiteration. The second theme, its pleading lyricism (despite the major key) reinforced by a palpitating accompaniment, accelerates on repetition into a nervous triplet figure that becomes almost a signature motive for the opus.

The Andante is, on the surface, more serene than the first movement. But beneath that surface are deep currents of sorrow and unrest. The theme has a stately 6/8 dance motion, almost like a slow minuet; it also has something of the cut of Austrian folksong—like those that Haydn often favored in his slow movements.

A slow, pained descent characterizes the Menuetto (how far Mozart has come from the rococo ballroom!).

The theme of the concluding variation movement commences with a taut siciliano tune, immediately followed in the first violin by a brusque little repeated-note figure. The coda has new tempo marking; *più* Allegro (faster). It is here that the repeated-note figure of the theme is transformed, by the addition of one note and a quickening of pulse, into the triplet motive of the first movement.

A.M.K.

K. 428 *String Quartet in E-flat major, "Third Haydn," No. 16 (K⁶ 421b)*
Origin: Vienna, June or July 1783
Scoring: 2 violins, viola, violoncello
Movements: Allegro ma non troppo. Andante con moto. Menuetto: Allegro. Allegro vivace.

This is the least troubled of the "Haydn" Quartets, and the one most closely approximating Haydn in its naïve affability of tone. The wonderful opening melody, announced in soft unison by all four instruments at the start of the Allegro ma non troppo, again covers the interval of an octave that we have seen play such a key role in both of the preceding quartets. But lyricism, rather than drama, pervades the exposition.

The lovely and remarkable Andante con moto is a one-of-a-kind movement. Though there is a long-drawn-out tender melody in the first violin at the start, it is the whole four-part texture supporting this melody with gently rocking triplets that is the "theme" of the movement. The sensuousness of this texture, its exquisite, hymnic quality, and its harmonic nuances evoke the spirit of Franz Schubert. The movement, moreover, is in one long, celestially sustained line. The form is sonata form, complete with genuine, if short, development section.

The rollicking Menuetto brings us to the Haydnesque realm of peasant merrymaking. The final Allegro vivace, though it is a truncated sonata form (minus development section) rather than a rondo, is the most obvious instance of a Haydn-inspired movement in the six quartets. Arrogant jollity, tricky pauses, abrupt dynamic shifts, and a backslapping ending are among its genial and beautifully crafted features. A.M.K.

K. 458 *String Quartet in B-flat major, "Fourth Haydn," "Hunt," No. 17*
Origin: Vienna, September 9, 1784
Scoring: 2 violins, viola, violoncello
Movements: Allegro vivace assai. Menuetto moderato. Adagio. Allegro assai.

Chronologically, the last three quartets form a kind of subset within the six. They are distinguished from their predecessors by an even more stringent economy of means, a greater application of contrapuntal techniques, a more intensified pursuit of the developmental principle and, in two of the slow movements (K. 458 and 465) at any rate, an emotional profundity that has been encountered heretofore only in the Andante con moto of the third "Haydn" Quartet, K. 428. These differences are at once in evidence in the B-flat major Quartet, which bears the sobriquet "Hunt" from the horn-call character of its opening theme. All the subsequent material of the movement is derived directly from the thematic statement of the first twelve measures. Moreover, within those twelve measures, all the melodic and rhythmic gestures proceed from a much smaller number of brief motivic cells.

There is a seriousness, an earnest and even impassioned quality to the Minuet that was by now becoming the norm for Mozart in this genre. But for the seriousness and passion, nothing in the "Haydn" set quite matches the extraordinary movement that follows. It is marked Adagio—the only slow movement of six that is so labeled—and the designation, to Mozart as to all eighteenth-century composers, was as much an indication of expressive intent as of tempo. Portions of this great Adagio do not so much emulate Haydn as they forecast the mature Beethoven. The breakneck Finale is once more in the Haydn mold, a sonata with a rondo-like insistence on its opening tune that has, despite the Haydn overtones, an urgency and moments of lyrical expansiveness that are pure Mozart. A.M.K.

K. 464 *String Quartet in A major, "Fifth Haydn," No. 18*

Origin: Vienna, January 10, 1785
Scoring: 2 violins, viola, violoncello
Movements: Allegro. Menuetto. Andante. Allegro.

In many respects the A-major Quartet is the most stunning example of musical craftsmanship among the six "Haydn" Quartets. Mozart's compositional technique has become refined here to a point of intellectual brilliance in almost every measure of the opus. No less ahead of its time is the prevalence of chromaticism. In the opening Allegro, the principal theme itself already betrays chromatic inflections, and the movement as a whole is drenched in them. It is also a highly polyphonic movement: both the first and second themes are immediately developed in contrapuntal fashion as soon as they are announced.

The same is only slightly less true of the Minuet movement, where the successive and contrasting motifs of the opening theme are immediately thereafter combined contrapuntally. Another noteworthy feature of this Minuet is the dramatic and structural use of silence. The Andante is a splendid set of variations on one of those utterly natural-sounding arietta themes so typical of Mozart.

The concluding Allegro, whose main subject is a chromatically transformed version of the principal theme of the first movement, is the contrapuntal *ne plus ultra* of the "Haydn" Quartets, and one of the most consummate examples of the "learned" style in all of chamber music. With the exception of a sunny closing tune to round off the exposition, and one other surprising intrusion, the entire movement evolves with invincible contrapuntal logic from the opening motive of the principal theme and its answering phrase—a mere handful of notes, but what Mozart makes of them! A.M.K.

K. 465 *String Quartet in C major, "Sixth Haydn," "Dissonance," No. 19*

Origin: Vienna, January 14, 1785
Scoring: 2 violins, viola, violoncello
Movements: Adagio—Allegro. Andante cantabile. Menuetto: Allegro. Allegro.

The C-major Quartet is not only the last of the "Haydn" Quartets but also in large measure a summation of the artistic evolution that had taken place in the set. There is, moreover, an instrumental brilliance about K. 465, a kind of concert-hall grandeur, that exceeds anything in this direction among its predecessors.

This quartet has come to be known as the "Dissonance" because of its daring slow introduction, filled with startling cross-relations (A natural against A flat, for example, in the second measure), insistently chromatic voice-leading that presages much to come later in the quartet, and a disturbing harmonic ambiguity (what key are we actually in, for the first dozen measures?). By the end of the Adagio the ambiguity has been fully resolved, but after all the disorientation of the opening measures, it still comes as a sort of relief to land squarely in bright, unclouded C major with the start of the Allegro. The profile of the forward-thrusting first theme implies a self-perpetuating, restless momentum. The steady drive of this first movement relents only with the final, surprisingly quiet measures of the coda, in itself a variant of the Allegro's opening theme.

The endearing Andante cantabile begins with a sustained, ardent *cantilena* of operatic character, worthy of *Figaro*'s Countess. The movement is on a par in poignant eloquence with the comparable movements of the E-flat and B-flat Quartets. The brusque energy of the Minuet suggests almost the roughhewn tumble of a Beethoven scherzo. The Finale, marked Allegro molto, returns to a Haydnesque vein, as befits the last movement of the last quartet in the set, except that there is a sort of rhapsodic frenzy and melodic profusion here that are peculiar to Mozart. A.M.K.

K. 499 ***String Quartet in D major, "Hoffmeister," No. 20***
Origin: Vienna, August 19, 1786
Scoring: 2 violins, viola, violoncello
Movements: Allegretto. Menuetto: Allegretto. Adagio. Allegro.

Mozart composed this piece for Franz Anton Hoffmeister (1754–1812), a minor composer who early in 1785, founded a music publishing shop that specialized in providing the music-loving Viennese with chamber music. Almost immediately he asked Mozart to provide him with three piano quartets. Mozart eventually produced the emotionally charged Piano Quartet in G minor, K. 478, in November 1785. Hoffmeister later complained "the public found the work too difficult and would not buy it." After launching *The Marriage of Figaro* in 1786, Mozart wrote his second, and last, piano quartet (K. 493). Although it is somewhat easier than the first to perform, Hoffmeister did not publish it. Then, in August 1786, Mozart composed the string quartet, K. 499, which must have pleased Hoffmeister, since he published it soon thereafter.

The opening Allegretto follows sonata form and is monothematic: instead of presenting contrasting themes, it gives the same theme in contrasting ways. The quartet's bid for popularity shows most clearly in the Minuet, a lusty movement that verges on a German dance like those Mozart wrote for the Redoutensaal, Vienna's famous ballroom. Canonic imitations enter right after the theme, but are so brief they may be difficult for the listener to detect.

The Adagio provides a marked change of mood, as well as pace. Mozart never takes the term "adagio" lightly. This is a discursive, introspective interlude spinning out its melody fragment by fragment. Mozart returns to a brightly sunlit Vienna in the Finale. The violin takes the lead throughout, opening with running, detached phrases that hark back to the Minuet's Trio. A brief, lightly scored coda closes the quartet. C.S.

K. 546 ***Adagio and Fugue in C minor***
Origin: Vienna, June 26, 1788
Scoring: 2 violins, viola, basso

Mozart transcribed the Fugue in this work from the two-piano fugue, K. 426. To it he added a short Adagio introduction in dotted rhythms, in which, as the American pianist and writer Robert D. Levin put it, "angular outbursts alternate with unearthly hush; its suggestions of violence and mysticism make the ensuing geometry of the fugue seem a relief." The occasion for the arrangement is unknown, but perhaps it was at the suggestion of F. A. Hoffmeister, who published the work. Moreover, Mozart made it at a time when he was immersed in the composition of his final three symphonies, K. 543, 550, and 551, the last of which concludes with an elaborate fugue in C major.

The original manuscript of the Adagio is not extant, but that of the Fugue has a divided bass line for "Violoncelli" (plural) and "Contra Basso," implying an orchestral conception rather than one for chamber forces. The work is more frequently played today as a string quartet, however, than an orchestral piece.

W.C.

The "Prussian" Quartets

Like his pianist-composer cousin, Prince Louis Ferdinand, and his flutist-composer uncle, Frederick the Great, whom he followed to the Prussian throne, King Frederick William II (1744–97) was a well-trained practicing musician. His instrument was the cello. He also was an enthusiastic patron of music, with the power and the purse to attract the leading composers of his age.

Mozart was constantly dogged by financial worries. His pupil, Prince Karl Lichnowsky, later to become one of Beethoven's patrons, offered to take him to meet Frederick William, and on April 8, 1789, the prince and the pauper left Vienna for the royal seat at Potsdam. Mozart's stay there was a very disheartening time. On May 26 he played at the Prussian Court and returned to Vienna. All told, the journey netted Mozart a modest 500 gulden and a commission to compose "six easy clavier sonatas for Princess Frederike and six quartets for the King."

Once home, he composed the quartet, K. 575, and the Piano Sonata in D Major, K. 576. His wife Constanze fell seriously ill, however, and he postponed further work on the "Prussian" Quartets for eleven months, and even then managed to add only two more to the projected six. (Mozart never completed the set of sonatas for the Princess, either.)

Since it would not do to have a chamber music-loving king inconspicuously hew to a modest bass line, composing for the royal cellist presented a problem. Mozart's solution was resourceful, especially in K. 575. Instead of just highlighting the cello, he gave all four instruments featured roles; they shift constantly between playing the melody and collaborating in the accompaniment. His complete rethinking of a quartet's instrumental balance has led some critics to call these works the "Solo Quartets."

C.S.

K. 575 ***String Quartet in D major, "First Prussian," No. 21***

Origin: Vienna, April 1790
Scoring: 2 violins, viola, violoncello
Movements: Allegretto. Andante. Menuetto: Allegretto. Allegretto.

Mozart's new approach and the richly varied sound it produces comes through right at the start of the first "Prussian" Quartet. The first violin sings the expansive main theme; then the viola repeats the theme. In the second theme the cello takes the spotlight, playing high in its register.

The lovely, tranquil Andante recalls the melody of *Das Veilchen* (The Violet), K. 476, a song Mozart wrote in 1785, and the quartet itself is sometimes known by that title. The Minuet hovers between traditional dance music and the fanciful scherzos of later composers such as Beethoven and Mendelssohn. The Finale is a monothematic sonata-rondo. The spacious theme resembles the first movement's principal theme so strongly that the Finale becomes, in effect, an eighteenth-century anticipation of the nineteenth-century cyclic principle of returning themes.

C.S.

K. 589 *String Quartet in B-flat major, "Second Prussian," No. 22*

Origin: Vienna, May 1790
Scoring: 2 violins, viola, violoncello
Movements: Allegro. Larghetto. Menuetto: Moderato. Allegro assai.

In the first movement of the B-flat Quartet, the triple meter and the elegant contours of the principal theme set an especially lyric tone for the opening Allegro. The lead violin, backed by viola, muses over the theme and the cello repeats it. Eventually the cello sounds an arching, sinuous second theme and the violin extends it. With the return of the opening, the themes pass in review but, as in the earlier quartets, changes in instrumentation impart new color to them.

The Larghetto presents a simple yet shapely instrumental song. To the accompaniment of the middle strings, the cello opens in its rich upper register with a sensuous theme beautifully suited to the instrument. Having spotlighted the cello in the Larghetto, Mozart gives it a more modest role as an ensemble instrument in the Minuet, which—like the Minuet in K. 575—suggests a scherzo in its contrast between brief bold gestures and equally short running phrases. A brief and ebullient sonata-rondo, the Finale bubbles along in 6/8 meter. C.S.

K. 590 *String Quartet in F major, "Third Prussian," No. 23*

Origin: Vienna, June 1790
Scoring: 2 violins, viola, violoncello
Movements: Allegro moderato. Andante. Menuetto: Allegretto. Allegro.

The last "Prussian" Quartet is the most extroverted and brilliant of the three. The cello reassumes a featured role, but only in the first movement. As in K. 499, all the strings in unison anticipate the principal theme of the opening movement—a sonata form with matched rather than contrasting themes. The first violin states the arched opening theme. Swooping up almost three octaves, the cello then sounds a second theme that closely resembles the opening. In the recapitulation the viola takes over the solo passages the cello had played earlier.

As Mozart scholar Alec Hyatt King has observed, "The Andante is a meditation on a simple rhythmical phrase." Heard at the start, the phrase recurs over and over again with a tenacity that is quite unusual for Mozart. The Minuet's exceptionally light and transparent scoring focuses on the first violin playing high in its register.

In the Finale, Mozart takes a different approach to a problem that underlay much of the Classical period: that of shifting the emotional weight of a piece from the first movement to the last. Here, he caps the work with a perpetual motion, in contrapuntal style, that combines rondo and sonata form. The Finale's ebullient theme anticipates the popular "Gypsy" Rondo from Haydn's Piano Trio in G Major, written a few years later. C.S.

DUOS AND TRIOS

K³ 46d *Sonata in C major*
Origin: Vienna, September 1, 1768
Scoring: violin, basso (or solo keyboard)
Movements: Allegro. Menuet 1. Menuet 2.

K³ 46e *Sonata in F major*
Origin: Vienna, September 1, 1768
Scoring: violin, basso (or solo keyboard)
Movements: Allegro. Menuet 1. Menuet 2.

In September 1768 Leopold Mozart drew up a document which he entitled "List of everything that this twelve-year-old boy has composed since his seventh year, and can be exhibited in the originals." On this impressive list of dozens of works there appears an entry that has long puzzled music historians: "Various solos . . . for the violin." In the mid-eighteenth century "solo" meant a multi-movement work for a melody instrument and figured or unfigured bass; in this kind of music, "solo" was interchangeable with "sonata" on title pages. Certainly among the works Leopold had in mind were these two tiny sonatas, K. 46d and 47e.

Both works are brief (two-movement) works for violin and unfigured bass: a binary sonata movement followed by a pair of minuets. They are found together in an autograph manuscript dated September 1, 1768, or just a few days before Leopold Mozart drew up his "List." They represent that kind of charming, slight music much in demand for domestic music-making. We should probably imagine Nannerl realizing the unfigured bass at the harpsichord and Wolfgangl playing the melody on his violin, to admiring friends and relatives. N.Z.

K. 292 *Sonata in B-flat major (K⁶ 196c)*
Origin: Munich? early 1775?
Scoring: bassoon, violoncello
Movements: Allegro. Andante. Rondo: Allegro.

Mozart is reported to have composed this sonata, along with three bassoon concertos (not including K. 191), for a certain Munich bassoon enthusiast, Baron Thaddäus von Dürnitz, who commissioned bassoon works from various composers. Presumably Mozart wrote these pieces in early 1775 while he was staying in Munich for the production of *La finta giardiniera,* but no concrete proof of this exists, nor does the original manuscript survive. The *Neue Mozart-Ausgabe* has suggested that the violoncello part may have originally been intended as a second bassoon part, to judge from the style of the voice-leading.

The attractive and generously proportioned composition gives more weight to the bassoon (the upper part) than to the cello, which plays a relatively accompanimental role. Indeed, the demands on the upper part approach the virtuosic in terms of range, agility, and, in the Andante, expressivity. Several opportunities arise for *Eingänge,* or ornamental passages improvised to decorate pauses at half-cadences; these would presumably be supplied by the upper part. Despite the work's unusual scoring, it is rich in melodic and rhetorical character. W.C.

K. 266 *Adagio and Menuetto in B-flat major (K⁶ 271f)*
Origin: Salzburg, early 1777?
Scoring: 2 violins, basso

This endearing little work has been dated solely on the basis of the handwriting and paper-type of the original manuscript. No occasion for its composition is known. Although Leopold Mozart composed and published many trio sonatas for two violins and violoncello, this is the only such work of Wolfgang's extant (except for a very brief sketch from his Viennese years).

Notably, Mozart endows the two upper parts with equal importance, with the first violin dominant in the Adagio, and the second in the Menuetto. The Adagio opens with a prefatory announcement, then continues with a binary-form movement in a warmly lyrical vein; the music unfolds continuously without the expected recapitulation of the opening themes. The Minuet moves robustly in a dotted rhythm; its trio imitates horn calls with double-stopped chords. W.C.

K. 423 ***Duo in G major***
Origin: Salzburg? summer 1783
Scoring: violin, viola
Movements: Allegro. Adagio. Rondeau: Allegro.

In 1806, Joseph Haydn's brother, Johann Michael, died in Salzburg, where he had been in the service of the prince-archbishop since 1763. Two years later a *Biographical Sketch of Haydn* was issued in Salzburg "for the benefit of his widow." Written by two of Michael's pupils and published anonymously, this interesting little book relates that Michael Haydn was ordered by high authority (i.e., Archbishop Hieronymus Colloredo)

to compose duets for violin and viola. He could not, however, deliver them at the appointed time because he became seriously ill and the convalescence lasted longer than had been expected, rendering him incapable of doing any work at all; the great man was unable to find a *quid pro quo*. He was threatened with the cancellation of his salary on account of the delay, probably because his patron was too little informed about Haydn's circumstances, or had been deliberately misinformed.

Mozart, who visited him daily, found out about this, sat down and wrote for his upset friend with such uninterrupted speed that in a few days the duets were finished and delivered under Michael's name. In later years, we reminded ourselves with delight of this wonderful example of brotherly love; our master kept the original manuscripts as a sacred relic, honorable to the memory of the immortal Mozart.

Writing these two works for his Salzburg colleague was not only a deed of kindness but an act of homage. Mozart thought highly of Michael Haydn's music, which is just now, in the latter part of the twentieth century, beginning to receive its due; he studied and performed a number of Haydn's symphonies and church works, even composing a slow introduction (K. 444) for one of Haydn's G-major symphonies.

Michael Haydn had apparently intended to compose a series of six violin and viola duets for the archbishop; the Berlin State Library owns copies of four such duets (in C, D, E, and F major). When we examine these four works it seems possible that Mozart's two, in G and B flat, were carefully designed to complete the set by the choice of two keys not employed in the four already composed by Michael Haydn. Mozart also apparently took pains to compose in Michael Haydn's style, since he did not want to compromise Haydn by possible detection. Among the devices Mozart uses to camouflage his authorship are the chirping grace notes and trills in the opening movement of K. 424 and the popular tunes in the Finale of K. 423.

The opening Allegro of K. 423 is a densely packed movement in the usual sonata form. The songful Adagio is, by its very use of a genuinely slow tempo, another of Mozart's camouflaging tactics. He usually wrote andantes rather than adagios as slow movements, whereas in the bona fide Michael Haydn duets, three of the slow movements are marked "adagio" and the fourth "adagietto."

H.C.R.L.

K. 424 *Duo in B-flat major*
Origin: Salzburg? summer 1783
Scoring: violin, viola
Movements: Adagio—Allegro. Andante cantabile. Thema con variazioni: Andante grazioso.

The Mozartean chromaticism of the introductory Adagio of the second of these Michael Haydn "forgeries" (see the previous note) gives way to the opening theme of the following Allegro, equally Mozartean in its great poise and in the seamless flow of the music. It is quite possible that Mozart also knew and had carefully studied Joseph Haydn's six duets for violin and viola—they were called "Sonatas"—which had started to circulate within Austria in the 1770s. Some of Haydn's learned developmental technique, the closely packed working with small motivic fragments, can be heard in the first movement of K. 424.

The yearning aspirations of the Andante cantabile again seem to be close to the Mozartean spirit. Despite its eloquent late-Classical expression, the movement is cast in the form of an antique siciliano, a slow dance in 6/8 time popular throughout the eighteenth century. The Finale is a theme and variations of the type brought to a rare perfection by Joseph Haydn in his 1770s chamber music; the form was also used in his duets. Noticeable in these vivacious Mozart variations is the difficulty of the viola part, which requires a real virtuoso. H.C.R.L.

K. 563 *Divertimento in E-flat major*
Origin: Vienna, September 27, 1788
Scoring: violin, viola, violoncello
Movements: Allegro. Adagio. Menuetto: Allegro. Andante. Menuetto: Allegretto. Allegro.

Mozart wrote this divertimento in the summer of 1788, shortly after the composition of his last three great symphonies. It was written for his friend the Viennese merchant Michael Puchberg, the man who so often helped Mozart when he was in desperate need of money during the last years of his life. This work was probably intended for private musical evenings at Puchberg's house. Mozart's use here of the description "Divertimento" is explained by the sequence of movements, which is typical of works of that nature: two rapid outer movements, and two slow movements alternating with two minuets.

It is Mozart's only string trio for violin, viola, and cello, and indeed the first ever written, viewed from the standpoint of the concept of mature Classical chamber music. With incredible assurance Mozart at once exploited all the possibilities inherent in the scoring for these three strings: he treated the instruments as absolute equals, even sometimes writing for them in strict counterpoint, as in the minor variation of the Andante; the viola, especially, joins the violin as a melody instrument, for example in the first Trio of the second Minuet. Within its class this work could scarcely be excelled, and it belongs, with Mozart's string quintets, among his most mature chamber works.

The first movement (Allegro), which is in the customary sonata form, opens with a descending triad figure. The two themes and a concluding motif are not merely presented in the exposition, but are already treated there as in a development section, the concluding motif with its countermelody being passed between cello and violin in double counterpoint. The development of this movement is notable for its bold modulations.

The descending triad figure of the first movement recurs in ascending form in the second movement (Adagio), thus creating a certain thematic connection between the first two movements. The Adagio is also written in sonata form, but instead of a second subject appearing, the violin transforms the cello's triad motive, and the recapitulation is a variant of the exposition.

In the four variations which make up the fourth movement (Andante), Mozart, unusually, varied even the repetitions of the individual sections. He treated the simple melody on which the variations are based with such freedom—especially in the third, minor variation—that the effect is of hearing completely different melodies. Two Minuets frame this Andante; the second of them has two trios (as was customary in serenades).

The Finale is a freely constructed rondo on a folklike theme; at the center of this rondo, as in the first movement, Mozart introduced audacious modulations in the minor. H-C.M.

14

Chamber Music with a Keyboard Instrument

Title-page vignette for the first edition of Joseph Haydn's Trio for harpsichord or pianoforte with the accompaniment of a violin and a violoncello, Hob. XV:10 (Vienna, Artaria, 1798).

As usual with eighteenth-century pictures of amateur music making, the keyboard player is a woman, the string players men.

BACKGROUND AND OVERVIEW

Mozart's earliest recorded musical experience was with the clavichord or harpsichord. The following anecdote, related by his sister Nannerl after his death, is well known:

> The son was three years old when the father began to instruct his seven-year-old daughter in the clavier. The boy at once showed his God-given, extraordinary talent. He often spent much time at the keyboard, picking out thirds, which he was always striking, and his pleasure showed that it sounded good. In the fourth year of his age his father, for a game as it were, began to teach him a few minuets and pieces at the keyboard. It was so easy for this child and for his father that he learned a piece in an hour and a minuet in half an hour, so that he could play it faultlessly and with the greatest delicacy, keeping exactly in time. He made such progress that at the age of five he was already composing little pieces, which he played to his father who wrote them down.

Reports from many corners of Europe during Mozart's childhood tours tell of his extraordinary technical accomplishments—that at an early age he could sight-read, improvise, and play with a brilliance perhaps unsurpassed by any other keyboard player of his time. But what kind of performer was he in his maturity? Some idea of what Mozart valued can be gleaned from letters in which he criticized performers who grimaced while playing, whose rhythm was weak, who rushed, who played in a choppy or heavy manner, or whose use of rubato destroyed rather than affirmed the tempo. When he felt a performance had gone well, he wrote that it "flowed forth like oil," and he once urged his sister to play with "plenty of expression, taste, and fire." Unfortunately, however, descriptions of Mozart's playing from the last decade of his life, while making clear that it was unsurpassed, generally either are vague or lapse into hagiology.

Mozart composed keyboard music in all periods of his life. He wrote for himself and his sister, for his own, his sister's, and his father's pupils, for friends who were amateur or professional musicians, and for the commercial market of amateur keyboard players. Mozart's organ compositions were apparently improvised, and virtually nothing remains, aside from a few tantalizing descriptions. His early keyboard music reckoned with the harpsichord and the clavichord. (The Mozarts owned a folding clavichord, which they took with them on journeys for practice purposes.) Then, at some unknown point in the 1770s the fortepiano, ancestor of the modern piano, entered the picture, becoming Mozart's favorite instrument, even though in the homes of many of his friends, colleagues, and patrons only a harpsichord could be counted on.

The large harpsichords and the fortepianos for which Mozart composed had a range of five octaves, from F to f‴. Many of his early pieces use a narrower range, suitable for clavichords and smaller harpsichords.

Accompanied Keyboard Music

In Mozart's time the works now called violin sonatas, cello sonatas, and piano trios, quartets, or quintets were conceived as domestic music for keyboard, accompanied by one or more (usually) stringed instruments. The origin of this practice lies in certain social circumstances: in middle- and upper-class families, the daughters were frequently keyboard players and the sons violinists or cellists. The daughters, whose musical skills helped to snare a husband, were commonly more accomplished than the sons, who were also expected to advance further in their formal education and to master such manly arts as fencing and horsemanship. Hence, for an evening's private music-making, a repertory was required that assigned greater responsibility to the women.

In Mozart's earliest such works, the juvenile Opuses 1–4 from 1763–65, the technical and conceptual demands on both players are modest. But from recurring remarks in the press during the second half of the 1780s, it seems that later on Mozart showed blithe disregard for the limitations of many musical amateurs. In an essay entitled "Concerning the Latest Favorite Music at Grand Concerts, especially in regard to Ladies' Predilections in Pianoforte Dilettantism," for instance, a piano quartet is discussed:

> Some time ago, a single quartet by [Mozart] (for fortepiano, one violin, one viola, and violoncello) was engraved and published, which is very artistically composed and in performance needs the utmost precision in all the four parts, but even when well played, or so it seems, is able and intended to delight only connoisseurs of music in a *musica di camera*. The cry soon made itself heard: "Mozart has written a very special new quartet, and such-and-such a princess or countess possesses and plays it!," and this excited curiosity and led to the rash resolve to produce this original composition at grand and noisy concerts and to make a parade with it *invita Minerva*. Many another piece keeps some countenance, even when indifferently performed; but in truth one can hardly bear listening to this product of Mozart's when it falls into mediocre amateurish hands and is negligently played.
>
> Now this is what happened innumerable times last winter; at nearly every place to which my travels led me and where I was taken to a concert, some young lady or pretentious middle-class *demoiselle,* or some other pert dilettante in a noisy gathering, came up with this engraved quartet and fancied that it would be enjoyed. But it *could* not please: everybody yawned with boredom over the incomprehensible *tintamarre* of four instruments which did not keep together for four bars on end, and whose senseless *concentus* never allowed any unity of feeling; but it *had* to please, it *had* to be praised! It is difficult for me to describe to you the persistence with which attempts were nearly everywhere made to enforce this. It were too little merely to rail at an ephemeral *manie du jour,* for it went on almost throughout a whole winter. . . .
>
> What a difference when this much-advertised work of art is performed with the highest degree of accuracy by four skilled musicians who have studied it carefully, in a quiet room where the sound of every note cannot escape the listening ear, and in the presence of only two or three attentive persons! But, of course, in this case no *éclat,* no brilliant, modish success is to be thought of, nor is conventional praise to be obtained! Here political ambition can have no part to play, nothing to gain, nothing to bestow, nothing to give and nothing to take—in contrast to *public* concerts of the modern kind, where such factors exert an almost constant influence *(Journal des Luxus und der Moden,* June 1788; translation by E. Blom, P. Branscombe, J. Noble).

Our anonymous critic makes a number of points: Mozart's late accompanied keyboard music is technically and conceptually difficult compared to the repertory most amateurs played; music of such difficulty could not be adequately performed in the salons, as long as playing at sight was the norm. Even if the music were properly prepared, any noise and lack of seriousness would make comprehension difficult; and in any case, this is music for connoisseurs, not the general public.

Certainly Mozart never lowered his standards, despite his father's urging him in 1778 to mimic J. C. Bach by writing something short and easy, and despite Mozart's own assertion in 1782 that his music was designed to please both learned and naive listeners. In the later 1780s, however, for all his considerable fame and his declarations of moderation and accessibility, Mozart's career went seriously wrong; the reception of his piano quartets is just one symptom of this. And although it took only a few more years for professional musicians, patrons, and audiences generally to catch up with Mozart's conceptual and technical complexities and his flights of genius (his "speculations," Leopold would have called them), by then it was too late for him to benefit financially or emotionally. N.Z.

QUINTETS, QUARTETS, AND TRIOS

A late-eighteenth-century house concert. Watercolor by Nicholas Aertmann (Rijksmuseum, Amsterdam).

The ensemble consists of two violins, two oboes, cello, and a square piano. The first violinist, center, with his back to us, is conducting with his bow.

K. 254 *Divertimento in B-flat, (Piano Trio) No. 1*

Origin: Salzburg, August, 1776
Scoring: violin, violoncello, piano
Movements: Allegro assai. Adagio. Rondeaux: Tempo di menuetto.

Mozart saw the piano trio medium essentially as an accompanied piano sonata (the view taken by Haydn and other contemporaries). Nonetheless, in his six works in the genre (as well as a seventh, K. 442, which was completed by Maximilian Stadler), piano and violin share in melody and accompaniment as almost equal partners, and the cello serves both as bass, and, more rarely, as a melodist of some significance. And increasingly in his trios, from the development of the first movement of K. 496 onward, Mozart uses what the musicologist Karl Geiringer has termed a new "quartet-style," in which he writes four equally weighted contrapuntal lines for the violin, the cello, and the treble and bass of the piano. But for all that, the piano, with its ability to sustain both melody and accompaniment, remains first among equals in these works. We are even visually reminded of the piano's centrality in the trios as we look at Mozart's autograph manuscripts: the violin is written above and the cello below the piano staves.

The first piano trio is modestly entitled "divertimento." The first movement is a fast-moving and high-spirited Allegro, full of strong, dynamic contrasts. The string parts are merely supplementary and could be eliminated without serious musical loss. For the Finale Mozart chooses a type of movement to which he constantly returned in his early years, a Rondo in the style of a graceful minuet. Its leisurely pace and abundance of melodic invention belie its formal strength.

R.H.

K. 452 *Quintet for Piano and Winds in E-flat major*

Origin: Vienna, March 30, 1784
Scoring: oboe, clarinet, bassoon, horn, piano
Movements: Largo—Allegro moderato. [Larghetto.] Rondo: Allegretto.

Although Mozart entered this quintet into his personal catalogue on March 30, 1784, he may in fact have completed it nearly two weeks earlier, since he originally planned its first performance at his benefit concert in the Burgtheater in Vienna on March 21. But Prince Alois Liechtenstein had chosen that night to give an opera performance at his palace, which would perforce have lured Mozart's noble patrons away from his concert, so he postponed it until April 1. Writing to his father nine days later he reported that the new quintet "called forth the very greatest applause."

The quintet is unique in the corpus of Mozart's concerted writing for wind instruments in that he was here dealing with a group of four dissimilar voices pitted against a common background, the piano. He realized that there was a world of difference between composing *Harmoniemusik,* involving pairs of wind instruments, and this quintet, with only one of each type. Therefore he kept brief chord passages unsupported by the piano and contrasted the instruments in various permutations against the piano, endeavoring never to make any one of them disproportionately prominent.

The composer was delighted with the results: "I myself consider it to be the best work I have ever composed," he told his father in an excess of enthusiasm. "How I wish you could have heard it! And how beautifully it was performed!" In this quintet Mozart decided to build up fairly long themes by a sort of patchwork method—that is, by stitching together short motifs. The constantly changing instrumentation suggests a superficial instability. But as the quintet unfolds before us, its fundamental unity becomes clear. R.H.

K. 478 ***Piano Quartet in G minor***
Origin: Vienna, October 16, 1785
Scoring: violin, viola, violoncello, piano
Movements: Allegro. Andante. Rondo.

K. 493 ***Piano Quartet in E-flat major***
Origin: Vienna, June 3, 1786
Scoring: violin, viola, violoncello, piano
Movements: Allegro. Larghetto. Allegretto.

Mozart seems virtually to have invented the piano quartet. His interest in it may have arisen from a preference in his Viennese years for participating in chamber music as a violist: thus we have the so-called "Kegelstatt" Trio for piano, clarinet, and viola, K. 498; the string quintets with two violas, rather than Luigi Boccherini's familiar configuration involving two cellos; and we have also, perhaps, the addition of a viola to the ubiquitous piano trio to form a piano quartet.

Although never as popular a genre as the piano trio or string quartet, the piano quartet was later taken up by Beethoven, Schubert, Mendelssohn, Schumann, Dvořák, Brahms, and others. By the time of Dvořák and Brahms, piano quartets were intended for four equally virtuosic partners in a concert hall.

In Mozart's catalogue of his own works the Piano Quartet in G minor, K. 478, is assigned to July 1785, about the same time as the first version of the Masonic Funeral Music, K. 477. The completion of the quartet is usually given as October 16, 1785, however, because that date is found on the autograph manuscript (now in Warsaw). Perhaps these dates mark off the period from Mozart's first draft of the piece to his putting the final touches on the manuscript. On December 1, in any case, Leopold Mozart received a packet from his son which contained, among other music, a manuscript score of K. 478 (perhaps the autograph) and the engraved violin and viola parts from the first edition by the Viennese publisher Franz Anton Hoffmeister.

According to Georg Nikolaus Nissen (Constanze Mozart's second husband), the G-minor Piano Quartet was the first of three piano quartets commissioned from Mozart by Hoffmeister, but as the public found the work too difficult, the publisher withdrew from the venture. Before that, Mozart had entered a second (and final) piano quartet, in E-flat major (K. 493), in his catalogue, under the date June 3, 1786. This quartet was issued in 1787 by Artaria and Co., who purchased the engraved but subsequently abandoned plates for the piano, viola, and cello parts from Hoffmeister. Apparently, the autograph for K. 493 was already missing in Mozart's lifetime, although two sketches for the Finale do survive.

Both piano quartets are in three movements: a large-scale sonata form first movement with coda; a lyrical, slower movement in sonatina form (K. 478) or in full-blown sonata form (K. 493); and a rondo-finale, in which high spirits abound. In Mozart's piano trios the most common textures arise either from the strings accompanying or doubling the piano, or from the thematic material being passed among the three participants. Antiphonal exchanges between the strings as a group and the piano are infrequent, and rarer still is "piano-concerto" writing with the two strings acting as the "orchestra." In the piano quartets, on the contrary, the weight that the addition of a viola imparts to the strings seems to have influenced Mozart's general artistic conception: sonorous antiphonal exchanges and (especially in K. 493) brilliant "concerto" writing are much in evidence. N.Z.

K. 442 *Piano Trio in D minor (completed by Maximilian Stadler)*
Origin: Vienna, 1785 to 1788?
Scoring: violin, violoncello, piano
Movements: Allegro. Andantino. Allegro.

This work incorporates three fragmentary movements of independent origin, completed and assembled after Mozart's death by the Abbé Maximilian Stadler. Stadler also completed several fragmentary works for piano and violin (K. 372, 403, 402, and 396), all perhaps at the request of Mozart's widow Constanze. Approximately the first quarter of movement one, and slightly more than half each of movements two and three are original.

The usual dating of 1783 for all three fragments has been recently contested by German musicologists Wolfgang Plath and Wolfgang Rehm in the *Neue Mozart-Ausgabe*. According to them, the first movement appears to date from 1785 or 1786, about the time Mozart commenced work on a sequence of completed piano trios, K. 496, 502, 542, 548, and 564. The second movement, originally entitled "Tempo di Menuetto," appears to come from about the same time, and may originally have been intended as a finale rather than a middle movement. The third movement appears to date from 1788 or later, and was most likely intended as an opening movement rather than a finale; it is presumably Mozart's last extant essay in the piano trio genre. W.C.

K. 496 *Piano Trio in G major, No. 2*
Origin: Vienna, July 8, 1786
Scoring: violin, violoncello, piano
Movements: Allegro. Andante. Allegretto.

After K. 254 Mozart did not complete another piano trio for ten years. Then, between 1786 and 1788, he composed five more, probably for his own use. Such was the growing popularity of the genre, particularly among amateur music makers, that the first four were very soon published—K. 496 in 1786 by Franz Anton Hoffmeister, and K. 502, 542, and 548 as a set in 1788 by Artaria and Co. Mozart was still somewhat unsure as to what to call K. 496: he wrote "Sonata" on the title page, but entered "Terzett" into his personal catalogue of compositions on July 8, 1786. By the time K. 502 was completed on November 18, 1786, "Terzett" had become the standard title.

For seventeen long measures at the start of K. 496, the piano alone unravels one of Mozart's most sinuous opening themes. It constantly seems to turn away from any conclusion. The second movement is one of Mozart's great slow movements, intricate, refined, and majestic. His genius for counterpoint blossoms throughout. The theme and six variations that constitute the Finale are in general a lighthearted relief after the intensity of the slow movement. R.H.

K. 498 *Clarinet Trio in E-flat major, "Kegelstatt"*
Origin: Vienna, August 5, 1786
Scoring: clarinet, viola, piano
Movements: Andante. Menuetto. Rondeaux: Allegretto.

For this trio Mozart chose the members of the keyboard, string, and wind instrument families that he loved best, and one can well visualize his savoring their qualities and potential.

History has awarded the clarinet trio

the nickname "Kegelstatt" (which, loosely translated, means "bowling alley"). According to a questionable tale, it was written during a game of skittles. (See also the discussion of the twelve Duos for two horns on p. 248.) He entered the work into his personal catalogue on August 5, 1786, and, according to his friend Caroline Pichler, he wrote it for Franziska von Jacquin, one of the best of his piano pupils. It was probably originally played in the intimacy of the Jacquin family circle by Franziska, with Mozart himself playing viola and Anton Stadler, clarinet.

The first slow movement offers totally new evidence of Mozart's uncanny mastery of sonata form. Its unity arises from one principal source, namely the *gruppetto* (or ornamental turn in fast notes), which dominates every musical idea in the movement from the first measure on. With the Minuet and Trio that follows, Mozart shows how far behind he has left the simple dance structure. The Minuet has a grandeur that would do no disservice to a symphony. The Finale is a spacious, timeless Rondo that sings from beginning to end. R.H.

K. 502 ***Piano Trio in B-flat major, No. 3***
Origin: Vienna, November 18, 1786
Scoring: violin, violoncello, piano
Movements: Allegro. Larghetto. Allegretto.

Almost all the material in the first movement of this masterly trio evolves from a single theme. Even the codetta theme, which completes both the exposition and the movement, where one would normally expect Mozart to write a new and germinal motive, is in fact a further development of this principal idea, this time demonstrating the imitative potential of his new quartet style.

The glorious beauties of the Larghetto betray that Mozart was a true romantic at heart. Its radiant melody, as long and as spacious as some of Schubert's, would not be out of place in one of the late piano concertos.

The Finale vividly shows Mozart's eagerness for developing his material at every available opportunity. In the coda Mozart's contrapuntal genius takes over and sets motive against motive in a dazzling display of virtuosity. This is a Finale of impressive unity and strength and one of Mozart's greatest achievements in the sonata-rondo form that he had virtually invented and made so much his own.

R.H.

K. 542 ***Piano Trio in E major, No. 4***
Origin: Vienna, June 22, 1788
Scoring: violin, violoncello, piano
Movements: Allegro. Andante grazioso. Finale: Allegro.

The last three trios were composed over a four-month period in 1788. Mozart entered K. 542 in his catalogue on June 22, having announced its completion a few days earlier in a letter to his fellow Mason and benefactor Michael Puchberg, suggesting at the same time that they try it out at a musical party at Puchberg's house in the near future. He also sent a copy of the Trio to his sister, Nannerl, urging her to play it to Michael Haydn, who he was certain would enjoy it.

As with other opening statements in these piano trios, the principal theme is offered here by piano alone before being enriched and enlarged by all three instruments. The somewhat melancholy Rondo that is the second movement is dominated by its principal theme, which is one of those transparently simple Mozartean melodies that can have such uncannily moving properties. Mozart's original Finale for this work grew to sixty-five measures before he finally rejected it in favor of the present one, a Rondo of almost concerto-like glitter, with episodic passages of considerable virtuosity for both violin and piano.

R.H.

K. 548 ***Piano Trio in C major, No. 5***
Origin: Vienna, July 14, 1788
Scoring: violin, violoncello, piano
Movements: Allegro. Andante cantabile. Allegro.

Musicologist Alfred Einstein considers this trio "classic in its mastery." One can perhaps see what he means in the simplicity of its structure; in the triadic nature of its principal theme, employing for once all three instruments in unison; and in its classical diatonic harmony, in stark contrast to the rich romantic hues that so often imbued its E major predecessor. For the slow movement Mozart finds a much more relaxed mood with a succession of beautiful, warm melodies enlivened by an occasional measure of sixteenth notes from the piano. Mozart is irrepressibly abandoned in the Rondo Finale, adroitly interweaving his many closely related themes into a virtual nonstop welter of activity. The Finale ends as the trio began, with all three instruments in unison voicing the chord of C major.

R.H.

K. 564 ***Piano Trio in G major, No. 6***
Origin: Vienna, October 27, 1788
Scoring: violin, violoncello, piano
Movements: Allegro. Andante. Allegretto.

It was Otto Jahn, Mozart's great nineteenth-century biographer, who first suggested that the last trio may have started life as a piano sonata, and that the trio version was hastily assembled, perhaps to fulfill some now-unknown commission. While this opinion is no longer given much credence, the peculiar state of the autograph manuscript (which has been examined and described by Alfred Einstein) does seem to bear out Jahn's contention. Only the string parts were in Mozart's handwriting, the keyboard part having been copied out by someone else. There was also a solo keyboard part in Mozart's hand, which survives as a fragment only. Whatever the reason for this odd situation, it is a fact that this trio seems but a pale imitation of its great predecessors. There is little conversation between the three instruments; the violin and cello play together in parallel motion for much of the time, with little imitation or use of the new quartet style that had become a feature of Mozart's language. But for all that, it is a work of considerable skill and many beauties. The Andante is an uncomplicated theme-and-variations movement with a theme of charming simplicity that is played in turn by piano, violin, and cello. The Finale is as usual a Rondo.

R.H.

K. 617 ***Adagio in C minor and Rondo in C major (Glass Harmonica Quintet)***
Origin: Vienna, May 23, 1791
Scoring: flute, oboe, viola, violoncello, glass harmonica
Movements: Adagio—Rondo: Allegretto.

In 1761 Benjamin Franklin devised a primitive "musical glasses" instrument, called a (h)armonica, consisting of a series of tuned glass bowls or discs mounted concentrically on a horizontal axle that is rotated by a treadle. As the bowls rotate, they are moistened in a trough of water placed below, and played by one's fingers from above, just as one induces vibrations in a crystal dinner glass. The invention was improved in Europe by Joseph Aloys Schmittbaur, who expanded its range to four octaves, from tenor c to high c‴. The instrument enjoyed a modicum of domestic popularity in the late eighteenth and early nineteenth centuries.

Mozart composed this work, along with the solo Adagio, K. 356, for Marianne Kirchgessner who, blind from early youth, had studied with Schmittbaur and attained a noted level of virtuosity. Kirchgessner premiered K. 617 in a recital at the Kärntnerthor Theater, Vienna, on August 19, 1791. It was to be Mozart's last piece of chamber music.

The quintet possesses a hauntingly attractive quality that results from its uncanny combination of timbres: the harmonica and winds engage in colorful melodic dialogue, while the low strings provide a soft accompanimental cushion. As in the contemporaneous works for mechanical organ, the sheer simplicity of formal and harmonic procedures gives the work an aspect of piercing clarity, free of extraneous decoration. A product of Mozart's most mature style, the quintet is a thoroughly distilled, captivating creation.

W.C.

SONATAS, SONATA MOVEMENTS, AND VARIATIONS WITH VIOLIN

Amateur music making at home. Engraving by Denis Née, 1773.

Sonatas for harpsichord or fortepiano with violin accompaniment were sometimes published only in score, so the violinist had to look over the keyboard player's shoulder to follow his part.

K. 6 ***Sonata in C major***
Origin: Salzburg or Paris, 1762 to 1764
Movements: Allegro. Andante. Menuetto I / Menuetto II. Allegro molto.

K. 7 ***Sonata in D major***
Origin: Salzburg or Paris, 1762 to 1764
Movements: Allegro molto. Adagio. Menuetto I / Menuetto II.

K. 8 ***Sonata in B-flat major***
Origin: Paris, 1763 or 1764
Movements: Allegro. Andante grazioso. Menuetto I / Menuetto II.

K. 9 ***Sonata in G major***
Origin: Salzburg or Paris, 1763 or 1764
Movements: Allegro spiritoso. Andante. Menuetto I / Menuetto II.

K. 10 ***Sonata in B-flat major***
Origin: London, 1764
Movements: Allegro. Andante. Menuetto I / Menuetto II.

K. 11 ***Sonata in G major***
Origin: London, 1764
Movements: Andante. Allegro. Menuetto.

K. 12 ***Sonata in A major***
Origin: London, 1764
Movements: Andante. Allegro.

K. 13 ***Sonata in F major***
Origin: London, 1764
Movements: Allegro. Andante. Menuetto I / Menuetto II.

K. 14 ***Sonata in C major***
Origin: London, 1764
Movements: Allegro. Allegro. Menuetto I / Menuetto II (en carillon).

K. 15 ***Sonata in B-flat major***
Origin: London, 1764
Movements: Andante maestoso. Allegro grazioso.

K. 26 ***Sonata in E-flat major***
Origin: The Hague, February 1765
Movements: Molto allegro. Adagio poco andante. Rondo: Allegro.

K. 27 ***Sonata in G major***
Origin: The Hague, February 1765
Movements: Andante poco adagio. Allegro.

K. 28 ***Sonata in C major***
Origin: The Hague, 1765
Movements: Allegro maestoso. Allegro grazioso.

K. 29 ***Sonata in D major***
Origin: The Hague, 1765
Movements: Allegro molto. Menuetto.

K. 30 ***Sonata in F major***
Origin: The Hague, 1765
Movements: Adagio. Rondo: Tempo di menuetto.

K. 31 ***Sonata in B-flat major***
Origin: The Hague, 1765
Movements: Allegro. Tempo di menuetto.

For three-and-a-half years—from June 9, 1763, to November 29, 1766—Leopold Mozart took a leave of absence from his post as vice kapellmeister in Salzburg, and, accompanied by Wolfgang, Nannerl, and his wife, traveled around western Europe. The goals of this extraordinary journey were to make money by buying and selling music and other items and by giving private and public concerts with his two child prodigies, to publicize the miracle of Wolfgang's precocious talents, and to educate his son by exposing him at first hand to the music and opinions of some of Europe's distinguished musicians. The three principal stopping points were Paris (November 18, 1763–April 19, 1764; May 10–July 9, 1766), London (April 23, 1764–July 24, 1765), and the Low Countries (September 4, 1765–May 9, 1766). In each of these places, Leopold Mozart contrived to publish his son's first sonatas.

Acting as Wolfgang's teacher, amanuensis, editor, and business manager, Leopold observed that in Paris, London, and Holland (unlike in central Europe) there was a large amateur market for engraved editions of sonatas for keyboard accompanied by violin. Hundreds of such volumes were published in the mid-eighteenth century. He therefore supervised Wolfgang's creation of sixteen diminutive sonatas, found the necessary noble patrons to whom to dedicate each volume, and saw the works through the press. He also sent and carried copies to Salzburg, later on selling them himself and through the firm of Johann Gottlob Immanuel Breitkopf in Leipzig.

The sonatas were assembled as follows. Some of the single-movement keyboard pieces that Wolfgang had composed in his study notebooks (for instance, Nannerl's Notebook, K. 1a–5b, and the London Notebook, K. 15a–ss) were grouped in twos, threes, fours, or fives, according to keys and tempos, to form "sonatas." Where necessary, new movements were created, and at least one of the little "source" pieces was probably by Leopold himself. These movements were then reworked to improve them, and the optional violin (or flute) and (in the case of Op. 3) cello parts were created to accompany them. The results are entirely acceptable *galant* sonatas, not very different in style, length, or difficulty from many others published in the same cities around that time. The title pages of the four publications read in part as follows.

(K. 6–7)

Sonatas for Harpsichord, Which can be Played with Violin Accompaniment. Dedicated to Louise-Marie-Thérèse de Bourbon, Madame Victoire de France [Louis XV's second daughter]. Opus 1. [Published in Paris, February 1764.]

(K. 8–9)

Sonatas for Harpsichord, Which can be Played with Violin Accompaniment. Dedicated to Madame la Comtesse de Tesse, [Lady-in-Waiting to the wife of the Dauphin]. Opus 2. [Published in Paris, April 1764.]

(K. 10–15)

Six Sonatas for the Harpsichord, Which can be Played with the Accompaniment of a Violin or Transverse Flute, and a Violoncello. Dedicated to her Majesty Queen [Sophie] Charlotte of Great Britain. Opus 3. [Published in London, January 1765.]

(K. 26–31)

Six Sonatas for the Harpsichord with the Accompaniment of a Violin. Dedicated to the Princess [Caroline] of Nassau-Weilburg, *née* Princess of Orange. Opus 4. [Published in The Hague, March 1766.] N.Z.

The "Palatine" Sonatas

From Mannheim on October 6, 1777, Mozart wrote to his father, "I send my sister herewith six duets for *clavicembalo* and violin by [Joseph] Schuster, which I have often played here. They are not bad. If I stay on I shall write six myself in the same style, as they are very popular here."

Mozart carried out his intention of rivaling these works by composing four violin sonatas in Mannheim and another three when he reached Paris. One of the Mannheim group (K. 296) was saved for later publication in 1781. The remaining six were brought out by the Paris firm of Jean-Georges Sieber in November of 1778 with a meaningless "Opus 1" designation and a dedication to the Electress of the Palatine. Their published sequence is the same as their order in the first Köchel catalogue: 301–306.

With these "Palatine" Sonatas Mozart reached the first stage on the way to equal partnership of the two instruments as it was to be supremely achieved in the sonatas K. 454, 481, and 526. The accent is still on the keyboard, but there is no movement that could dispense with the cooperation of the violin. Besides the influence of Schuster, the sonatas for clavier with violin accompaniment by Johann Schobert also proved helpful models; and finally there was the inspiration of Johann Christian Bach, whom Mozart esteemed highly and had met again in Paris for the first time since his childhood visit to London. Five out of the six "Palatine" Sonatas consist of only two movements, a structure found fairly frequently in J. C. Bach and Joseph Haydn, but rarely in Mozart. M.F.

K. 301 ***Violin Sonata in G major (K^6 293a)***
Origin: Mannheim, early 1778
Movements: Allegro con spirito. Allegro.

Although the first movement of K. 301 is in a regular sonata form, there is no true development of the exposition's thematic material. The movement is held together in a very peculiar way, by a kind of ritornello, or refrain, which appears frequently in various guises. The second movement, thematically related to the first, is in gentle 3/8 rhythm despite its Allegro designation. It is an amalgamation of French formal principles with the rhythm of the German dance and consists of three sections, the third of which is an exact repeat of the first, whereas the contrasting second is in the minor key. The three sections have basically the same structure; a short coda concludes the movement. M.F.

K. 302 ***Violin Sonata in E-flat major (K^6 293b)***
Origin: Mannheim, early 1778
Movements: Allegro. Rondo: Andante grazioso.

Unlike the G-Major Sonata, K. 301, which begins so lyrically, the second "Palatine" Sonata starts in a more typically Mozartean way, an example of which can be found as early as the Symphony in E flat, K. 16: the main theme begins with a sounding of the chord of E-flat major, followed by an enthusiastic downward progression on each of the separate notes of that chord. The development section is powerful and largely in minor tonalities. It is also entirely thematic—an important step forward, as compared with the "fantasy" development in K. 301.

Once more, Johann Christian Bach has put his mark on a Mozart work: the rondo is inscribed Andante grazioso and recalls several movements in the same vein in the piano sonatas by the London master. It does not mean, however, that this movement is impersonal or merely derivative. It has, in fact, an affecting, almost hymnlike solemnity. M.F.

K. 303 ***Violin Sonata in C major (K^6 293c)***
Origin: Mannheim, early 1778
Movements: Adagio—Allegro molto. Tempo di menuetto.

This, the third of the "Palatine" Sonatas, is certainly one of the most unusual sonatas Mozart ever wrote. It begins with a leisurely Adagio, followed by a glowing and passionate Allegro. The Adagio is actually the main theme and the Allegro the second theme (it even begins in the dominant key, a sure sign of a second theme). However, the movement is not really in sonata form, or is at best only an aborted sonata. After the Allegro, the Adagio returns in an elaborately decorated form that shows Mozart's art of expressive ornamentation at its highest level. Then the Allegro "resumes its heroic ride" (to quote Alfred Einstein), bringing this strange movement to a close.

The second, and last, movement, although it is inscribed Tempo di Menuetto, is really not in minuet form but in sonata form—perhaps to make up for the abortive sonata of the first movement. But the term "minuet" is amply justified by the dignified dance rhythm and charming grace of the piece. M.F.

K. 305 *Violin Sonata in A major (K^6 293d)*
Origin: Mannheim, early 1778
Movements: Allegro molto. Tema con variazioni: Andante grazioso.

A piece of music in the key of A major sounds particularly brilliant when it is played on a stringed instrument, and this A-major Sonata is certainly brilliant, if a little superficial. More than any of the other sonatas in the Palatine set this one betrays its Mannheim background in the frequency of its crescendos and in the unison writing for both instruments.

Despite its *galant* leanings, however, the first movement has a strikingly ingenious development section. The concluding movement is a set of variations, the first of its kind since the variations Mozart wrote in his early Violin Sonata, K. 31. M.F.

K. 296 *Violin Sonata in C major*
Origin: Mannheim, March 11, 1778
Movements: Allegro vivace. Andante sostenuto. Rondo: Allegro.

Mozart composed this sonata as a parting thank-you gift for Therese Pierron Serrarius, the fifteen-year-old daughter of a court chamberlain in Mannheim; Mozart and his mother stayed in the Serrarius household free of charge during the latter part of their visit to the city. Therese, whom Mozart referred to as the "house nymph," was a pianist of modest endowments; he probably gave her a few piano lessons as well as a copy of this Violin Sonata, which he completed on March 11, 1778. The work was published late in 1781 as the second of the Auernhammer group (see p. 291), and may well be looked upon as the link between those works and the Palatine set, most of which were slightly earlier in date of composition.

The first movement opens with vigor and *élan*, very much in keeping with its bright C-major tonality, and retains that mood throughout. The Andante is tender and dreamlike.

The final Rondo contains a wealth of themes arranged in a highly original way: instead of the more usual three appearances of the Rondo theme, with two contrasting episodes sandwiched between them—schematized as **A-B-A-C-A**—the final repeat of the Rondo theme is delayed while the C-major episode is greatly expanded, with a central episode of its own. When the rondo tune at last reappears, it is only to serve as a brief coda or leave-taking. This lively movement was to form the starting point for the Finale of the Concerto for Flute and Harp, K. 299, written a few weeks later in Paris. M.F.

K. 304 *Violin Sonata in E minor (K^6 300c)*
Origin: Paris, early summer 1778
Movements: Allegro. Tempo di menuetto.

Generally considered the greatest of the "Palatine" Sonatas, K. 304, in the very unusual key (for Mozart) of E minor, was composed in Paris in May 1778, immediately before the similarly intense Piano Sonata in A minor, K. 310. Mozart's loneliness, indeed his feelings of despair in the great city, where he was largely neglected and where his mother fell ill and died, leave their mark on this work. "It springs from the most profound depths of emotion," remarks Alfred Einstein, "and goes beyond the alternating dialogue style to knock at those gates of the great world of drama that Beethoven was to fling wide open."

The first movement is one of the most dramatic Mozart ever wrote and certainly the first of its kind in his whole output. Every note counts in this superbly organized movement; each theme is related to all the others. The second movement, like that of K. 303, is in the rhythm of a minuet, but this time it takes the form of a rondo. The main theme, which is never repeated literally, is based on the descending bass line, a procedure characteristic of the Baroque era. This theme imparts an elegaic mood to the entire movement. Only at the end, when the coda brings us back to the drama of the first movement, do we become aware that this elegy is indeed a song of lamentation for the dead. M.F.

K. 306 *Violin Sonata in D major (K^6 300l)*
Origin: Paris, summer 1778
Movements: Allegro con spirito. Andante cantabile. Allegretto.

This is the last of the "Palatine" Sonatas. The words with which Beethoven characterized his "Kreutzer" Sonata, Op. 47, "written in a *concertante* style," would apply just as well to this work, the most brilliant of the whole set and a worthy crowning of the cycle. It is the only one in three movements and the only one with a true slow movement.

The playfulness of this sonata makes it understandable that the development section in the first movement is of the "fantasy" type—that is, it is connected with the exposition not by the themes but only by a secondary motif. The second movement maintains the normal organization of the sonata form; the development section brings a logical continuation of the ideas of the exposition without ever quoting them literally. The extensive cadenza in the Finale certainly stresses the *concertante* character of the entire work, and the continuous alternation of a French-sounding Allegretto in 2/4 time and an Italian Allegro in 6/8 time brings to mind Mozart's own Violin Concerto in D major, K. 218, written only a few years before. M.F.

K. 378 *Violin Sonata in B-flat major (K^6 317d)*
Origin: Salzburg or Vienna, early 1779 or 1781
Movements: Allegro moderato. Andantino sostenuto e cantabile. Rondeau: Allegro.

Mozart included this work among the six "Auernhammer" Sonatas, published in 1781 (see below). Although musicologists are divided in their dating of this work, it must have been written earlier than the other works in the Auernhammer set, except for K. 296, since Mozart, in sending the complete set of six sonatas to his sister, remarked that she was already familiar with those in C major (K. 296) and in B flat (K. 378). Probably it was Mozart's first composition on his return to Salzburg from his Paris journey in the early days of 1779.

With the first movement, a new world opens up. The brilliance of the D-major Sonata (K. 306) is here combined with thematic material of great melodic intensity. Besides, it is one of the early instances of a sonata form with three themes—a device that is more characteristic of Anton Bruckner than of Mozart.

The deeply expressive slow movement has struck more than one critic as a blood relative to the more lyrical passages in the soon-to-be-written opera, *The Abduction from the Seraglio,* although it also looks backward to the mellifluous slow movements of Johann Christian Bach.

The concluding Rondeau uses the lively dance rhythm (3/8) we know from the G-Major Sonata, K. 301, but with more brillance; as a great surprise, Mozart brings in a second episode in the main key but in a new meter, 4/4. Almost every work of the Auernhammer set has surprises—they are indeed "rich in new ideas," as the anonymous Hamburg reviewer of 1783 said. M.F.

K. 372 *Allegro in B-flat major (completed by Maximilian Stadler)*

Origin: Vienna, March 24, 1781

This fragmentary movement would appear to be an abandoned forerunner of Mozart's series of completed violin sonatas from 1781. The autograph manuscript bears the inscription, "Sonata I. Vienna li 24 di Marzo 1781." Thus the work is Mozart's first known piece of chamber music composed after his move to Vienna, albeit still during his service to Archbishop Colloredo. The heading suggests that he had already decided to bring out a series of piano and violin sonatas. Perhaps, as in the case of K. 379 (see below), Mozart planned to perform the work with the archbishop's concertmaster Antonio Brunetti, who had come with him to Vienna in the court's entourage. Like several of Mozart's later violin sonata fragments (see K. 403, 402, and 396 below), K. 372 was completed after his death by Maximilian Stadler. W.C.

The "Auernhammer" Sonatas

In the summer of 1781, more than two years after the publication of the six "Palatine" Sonatas, Mozart gathered together a second series of six, the so-called Auernhammer set. Two of them, K. 296 and 378, had already been completed—the first in Mannheim, the second in Salzburg. Now, taking up residence permanently in Vienna, he quickly wrote four more: K. 379, 376, 377, and 380. All six were published as "Opus 2" by Artaria and Co.

Although Josepha von Auernhammer (1758–1820), the dedicatee of this set of violin sonatas, was something more than a gifted amateur, she would nowadays probably be forgotten had she not been closely associated with Mozart. In spite of sarcastic remarks Mozart made about her, he must have appreciated her talent: he entrusted her with one of the parts of his brilliant Sonata for Two Pianos in D, K. 448, and asked his father to send him the parts of his two concertos for two pianos, which he wanted to play with her. It should not be overlooked that the dedication of this second set of six sonatas is not to a violinist but to a pianist; and also that it is no longer to a noble patron but to a musician and a burgher, just as, three years later, Mozart was to dedicate six string quartets to his colleague Joseph Haydn.

K. 379, 376, 377, and 380 are works of great historic significance: They are the first important chamber works Mozart wrote after his decision to stay in Vienna as a free artist; they constitute his visiting card as a composer. The grand style of *Idomeneo* is still ringing in them, and at other moments they foreshadow *The Abduction from the Seraglio,* the first act of which was completed by August 22, 1781.

An astute, anonymous review of the "Auernhammer" Sonatas appeared in a Hamburg publication, *Magazin der Musik,* (edited by Carl Friedrich Cramer), on April 4, 1783: "These sonatas are the only ones of their kind. They are rich in new ideas, showing traces of the great musical genius of their author. Very brilliant, and well suited to the instrument. Moreover, the violin accompaniment is so ingeniously combined with the piano part that both instruments are continuously employed; and thus these sonatas demand a violinist as accomplished as the pianist." M.F.

K. 379 ***Violin Sonata in G major (K^6 373a)***
Origin: Vienna, April 1781
Movements: Adagio—Allegro. Andantino cantabile.

The creation of this work is documented in Mozart's letter of April 8, 1781, to his father. Mozart and a few other Salzburg court musicians had been abruptly summoned to Vienna in the entourage of the archbishop. A chamber music concert was ordered on short notice. Mozart had brought little music with him, so he quickly wrote a concerto movement for the violinist Antonio Brunetti, an aria for the castrato Francesco Ceccarelli, and for himself and Brunetti "a sonata with accompaniment for a violin, which I composed last night between 11 o'clock and midnight, but to be ready in time, I wrote out only Brunetti's accompanying part, keeping my own part in my head." The condition of the autograph manuscript, in the Library of Congress in Washington, D.C., confirms Mozart's claims about the work's genesis. N.Z.

Musicologist Hermann Abert's classic appreciation of this G-major Violin Sonata, which appeared in Walter Willson Cobbett's *Cyclopaedia of Chamber Music,* deserves quotation in full:

The G-major Sonata, K. 379, is a masterpiece of its kind. Here two G-major movements enclose one in G minor which is spiritually the essence of the whole. It is like a thunderstorm sweeping suddenly over a smiling landscape. The Adagio, of the type of the older Italian sonata, is nothing but one continuous song, full of peace and bliss—undimmed until the very last bars. The close on the dominant is of thrilling effect. Then, in the Allegro the storm of passion bursts forth with its grinding mordents and its questioning close—which pulls up suddenly in the Beethoven way before a grand pause. There is no tarrying; even the development is taken at a stride with a few pregnant bars of sequence, and we are hurried breathless through the recapitulation, in which the expression is heightened by the retention of the key of G minor throughout, in Mozart's typical manner, and by certain striking alterations.

But the storm vanishes as quickly as it came, and the childlike theme of the variations brings us once more into brightest sunlight. Not until the variations begin do we learn that the spirit of agitation is not yet expelled. Regard, for instance, the modulation to D minor at the beginning of the second part; it was not there in the theme itself. Here too there is growing agitation up to the G-minor variation, but the tide turns in the fifth with its gorgeous, elaborated melody, and at the end the theme returns in its original form followed by a sentimental and soothing coda. M.F.

K. 359 *12 Variations on "La Bergère Célimène" in G major (K⁶ 374a)*
Origin: Vienna, June 1781

Mozart probably wrote this set of variations, along with a second set (K. 360) for one of his aristocratic piano pupils, Countess Maria Karoline Thiennes de Rumbeke. Both are in a popular, easy vein that the countess and her violin partner could master without difficulty. K. 359 was brought out by no fewer than three music publishers in Mozart's lifetime.

The theme of the variations is an anonymous French chanson. Its words, as naive as its music, can be translated thus: "The shepherdess Célimène goes singing through the woods, 'Gods! What pain one suffers with an inconstant lover! If he wants to break his vows, I can do nothing to prevent it.' " M.F.

K. 360 *6 Variations on "Hélas, j'ai perdu mon amant" (K⁶ 374b)*
Origin: Vienna, June 1781

Like K. 359, this set of variations was probably written for Mozart's piano student Countess Thiennes de Rumbeke, and employs another eighteenth-century French tune as its theme. The author of the tune (whose title translates "Alas, I have lost my lover") is Egidio Giuseppe Ignazio Antonio Albanese, an Italian-born singer and composer who made his career in Versailles and Paris, as a musician at the French court, and a popular soloist at the Concert spirituel. The theme has the sophisticated design of a French operatic air. M.F.

K. 376 *Violin Sonata in F major (K⁶ 374d)*
Origin: Vienna, summer 1781
Movements: Allegro. Andante. Rondo: Allegro grazioso.

K. 376 is the first "Auernhammer" Sonata in the published sequence. Its lively, energetic, and concise first movement seems very close to Joseph Haydn; the development section uses material that is only very loosely connected with the preceding exposition. The second movement too is Haydnesque: it is a very simple three-part form, with a middle section that is thematically only a variant of the first. This deliberate absence of contrasts creates an almost idyllic atmosphere, heightened by the dialogue-like give-and-take of the two instruments.

The full weight of the sonata is contained in the extensive Rondo. A typical Mozartean feature, which he was to work out even more ingeniously in later compositions, is the juxtaposition of elements from the main theme and from the first episode in the coda: a kind of summing up of what we have heard previously. M.F.

K. 377 *Violin Sonata in F major (K⁶ 374e)*
Origin: Vienna, summer 1781
Movements: Allegro. [Andante.] Tempo di menuetto.

This work was published as No. 3 of the six violin sonatas brought out in Vienna by Artaria and Co. in November of 1781. Since Mozart produced two F-major sonatas in close succession (K. 376 and 377), he or his publisher decided to separate them in the printed edition by placing the considerably earlier C-major Sonata, K. 296, between them.

Although it shares the same key, K. 377 is a strikingly different work from

K. 376. Its first movement overflows with energy. The continuous rush of triplets so dominates the discourse that the second theme, shapely and memorable though it is, hardly has a chance to make itself felt. The recapitulation is full of surprises, including some recall of the preceding development section.

The slow movement is a set of six variations in D minor, foreshadowing the Finale of the great String Quartet in D minor, K. 421. For Hermann Abert these variations "suggest gloomy resignation; and the development of a syncopated figure has a goading effect."

Whenever we see Tempo di Menuetto as the title of a final movement, we expect either a rondo or a rather extended minuet with trio. Here, two sections of the Minuet have repeats that are written out, as they are slightly varied, and the violin joins in only at these repeats. At the end this whole complex is repeated and followed by a coda. In between, we hear two different sections—one might say two trios, but the traditional repeat of the minuet after the first trio is left out.

M.F.

K. 380 *Violin Sonata in E-flat major (K⁶ 374f)*

Origin: Vienna, summer 1781

Movements: Allegro. Andante [con moto]. Rondeau: [Allegro.]

As in the "Palatine" Sonatas, Mozart places the most interesting and most brilliant work at the end of the Auernhammer set. Here also we notice the broad, theatrical gestures of *Idomeneo,* especially in the powerful first movements of K. 380. Its development section is partly "fantasy" (it begins and ends with an entirely new subject), partly thematic; the manner in which these two principles are freely combined once more shows Mozart's growing mastery.

The second movement is in Mozart's grandly tragic key of G minor, a third above the key of the first movement. This "thirds-relationship" *(Terzverwandtschaft),* so typical of High Romanticism, was still rather rare in Mozart's time. This chromatic and highly expressive slow movement is Haydnesque insofar as it is almost entirely built upon one theme.

The final Rondo starts with an ingenuous melody, sounding almost like a folk tune. But its second episode, in C minor, is, for that reason, all the more impressive: it introduces a kind of drama that counterbalances the weight of the first movement. The whole Rondo resembles the Finale of the Concerto for Two Pianos (K. 365), but in its fine balance between the two instruments it respects the criteria of true chamber music—a worthy conclusion of a most exciting series of sonatas.

M.F.

K. 403 *Violin Sonata in C major (K⁶ 385c) (completed by Maximilian Stadler)*

Origin: Vienna, c. 1784?

Movements: Allegro moderato. Andante. Allegretto.

This is one of a series of incomplete sonatas for piano and violin, K. 403, 402, 396, and 404. Three of the fragments, K. 403, 402, and 396, were completed after Mozart's death by the Abbé Maximilian Stadler, perhaps at Constanze's request.

Mozart's manuscript of K. 403 bears the inscription, "Sonata Premiere. Par moi W. A. Mozart pour ma très chère Epouse" (Sonata No. 1, by myself, W. A. Mozart, for my dearest wife). From this one may deduce that Mozart intended to compose a series of sonatas, perhaps three or six in all, of which this was to be the first. One may also conclude that Mozart began the sonata sometime after August 4, 1782, the date of his marriage. The manuscript is written on a kind of paper used by Mozart almost exclusively in 1784. Of the work's three movements, the first two were completed by Mozart, while the last was only begun with a passage of twenty measures. W.C.

K. 402 ***Violin Sonata in A major (K^6 385e) (completed by Maximilian Stadler)***

Origin: Vienna, c. 1784?

Movements: Andante, ma un poco adagio. Fuga: Allegro moderato.

Like K. 403 (see above), this sonata was left unfinished by Mozart, and was later completed by Stadler. The manuscript bears the inscription, "Sonata IIda," referring apparently to the series of sonatas that Mozart had begun with K. 403. The opening Andante is complete in Mozart's manuscript but approximately the second half of the Fugue was appended by Stadler.

The theme of the opening Andante is strikingly similar to the famous Minuet in the Act I Finale of *Don Giovanni*. While this fact might suggest a later date, the presence of a fugue strongly supports a date closer to 1782, the year in which Mozart and his wife discovered the fugues of J. S. Bach and G. F. Handel. On April 20 Wolfgang wrote to his sister, "Baron van Swieten, whom I visit every Sunday, gave me all the works of Handel and Bach to take home . . . when Constanze heard the fugues she was completely enraptured. . . . She would listen to nothing but fugues, and for that matter none but those specifically by Handel and Bach;—and then whenever she heard me playing fugues off the cuff, she would ask whether I had written any of them down—and when I answered 'no'—she would accuse me bitterly of not wanting to compose the things that are the most beautiful and artful in music; and she would not stop begging until I wrote her a fugue. . . ." Indeed, in the following months a stream of fugues poured forth, including several arrangements of works by J. S. Bach and W. F. Bach (K. 404a, 405), several fragments (K. Anh 45, 401, 153, Anh 41, Anh 40, Anh 39, 154, 443, Anh 77), and one completed original work (K. 394).

There exists a thirty-four measure fragment of a sonato-allegro movement for piano and violin in A major, K. Anh 48 (K^3 480, K^6 385E), which could conceivably have arisen in connection with K. 402—perhaps as a projected opening movement for the sonata. W.C.

K. 396 ***Sonata Movement in C minor (K^6 385f) (completed by Maximilian Stadler)***

Origin: Vienna, c. 1784?

This astonishing fragment appears to constitute the complete exposition of a sonata movement in the *stylus fantasticus* ("fantastic style," that is, freely improvisatory) of C. P. E. Bach, to whose C-minor Fantasia in the *Versuch über die wahre Art das Clavier zu spielen* (Essay on the True Art of Keyboard Playing) it bears a certain resemblance. Unfortunately, Mozart's manuscript contains a violin part only for the last few measures. Perhaps it is for this reason that Stadler "completed" K. 396 as a piano solo; he also gave it the unauthentic title "Fantasia" and tempo marking of "adagio." (See the note on p. 323.)

A copy of this work in Stadler's hand bears a dedication to Constanze Mozart. Assuming this is not of Stadler's own invention, it would appear that Mozart intended K. 396 as part of the sonata series that he had begun with K. 403 and 402. As in the case of K. 402, it seems likely that Wolfgang and Constanze's recent discovery of the music of the Bach family, at the hands of the Baron van Swieten, might have played a role in determining the musical substance of the piece. W.C.

K. 404 ***Andante and Allegretto in C major (K⁶ 385d) (incomplete)***
Origin: Vienna, c. 1784?
Movements: Andante. Allegretto.

These two miniature movements may have arisen either together or independently. They were published posthumously by J. A. André as 'Andante et Allegretto faciles." The manuscript of the Andante yields no clue as to its origin; that of the Allegretto is not extant.

The last few measures of the eighteen-measure Andante were reportedly appended by André himself. The Allegretto is a self-sufficient twenty-four measure piece in binary form, and was perhaps originally conceived as a theme for a set of variations. It is tempting to wonder whether these fragments might have been the beginnings of projected second and third movements of a sonata whose first movement was to have been K. 396 (see above). W.C.

K. 454 ***Violin Sonata in B-flat major, "Strinasacchi"***
Origin: Vienna, April 21, 1784
Movements: Largo—Andante. Allegretto.

The four final violin sonatas (K. 454, 481, 526, and 547), dating from the years 1784 to 1788, do not form a set but have in common that they were composed in Vienna in the period of Mozart's greatest mastery. The first, K. 454, in B-flat major, was published by Christoph Torricella of Vienna in a group of three sonatas, two of which were for piano alone (K. 284 and 333).

The first of these four works constituting Mozart's final thoughts on the subject of the sonata for violin and piano was written for a violin virtuoso, Regina Strinasacchi of Mantua. Mozart was not alone in admiring the art of this remarkable performer. When his father, Leopold, heard her in Salzburg, he described her playing enthusiastically in a letter to his daughter, adding "In general, I think that a woman who has talent plays with more expression than a man." High praise indeed, coming from a man who was the leading authority on violin playing. Strinasacchi was twenty-three when Mozart composed the B-flat Sonata, K. 454, to be performed by them jointly at a concert in the Kärntnerthor Theater in Vienna on April 29, 1784.

As with the sonata (K. 379) that he had written for a concert with the violinist Antonio Brunetti, Mozart did not give himself enough time to write out his piano part, although he had it pretty securely in his head. He performed with a sheet of blank music open before him to fool the audience, but—according to a story told by his widow—the Emperor Joseph II, who was attending the performance, saw the empty sheet through his opera glasses and summoned the composer and his manuscript. Mozart had to confess his ruse, which surely must have amused and impressed the monarch rather than annoying him. The story is well substantiated by the state of the finished autograph manuscript. The piano part is written in ink of a different color, and Mozart, miscalculating his space, has a difficult time squeezing it all in.

The B-flat Sonata was composed in the midst of an intense period of creativity. Immediately preceding it were the piano concertos K. 449, 450, 451, and 453, as well as the piano quintet K. 452; immediately following it were two further Piano Concertos, K. 456 and 459. Little wonder, then, that this violin sonata at times takes on a concerto-like brilliance. It differs from all the other violin sonatas in that is has an extremely slow introduction, which immediately stresses the equality of the two instruments, an equality that does not change throughout the whole sonata. The middle movement, marked Andante but with the melodic intensity of an adagio (this was the tempo indication Mozart wrote down at first but then crossed out), is certainly the peak of the work. Mozart uses his boldest chromatic modulations in the development section. The concluding movement returns to the playful mood of the first. It is an extremely elaborate Rondo. M.F.

K. 481 *Violin Sonata in E-flat major*
Origin: Vienna, December 12, 1785
Movements: Molto allegro. Adagio. Allegretto.

We do not know much about the history of this work apart from the bare facts as they appear in Mozart's own catalogue, in which he listed it under December 12, 1785. It was published separately by Franz Anton Hoffmeister, just like the Sonata in A major, K. 526, and the String Quartet in D major, K. 499.

The Sonata in E-flat major is certainly one of the most mature works in Mozart's whole chamber music output. The three movements are in complete balance with one another, each having its own structural principle and each starting with an individual interpretation of one of the oldest and commonest thematic principles: the major triad. The exposition of the first movement contains three clearly outlined subjects.

The Adagio, in A-flat major, is a rondo with two episodes and varied repeats of the principal subject; it is full of romantic modulations. The Finale, a set of variations on a leisurely theme twenty measures in length, brings the desirable relaxation after the emotional tension of the Adagio. M.F.

K. 526 *Violin Sonata in A major*
Origin: Vienna, August 24, 1787
Movements: Molto allegro. Andante. Presto.

A number of critics consider this work to be the greatest of the Mozart violin sonatas. It was finished while Mozart was in the midst of composing *Don Giovanni.* But the work to which it is more spiritually akin is the Piano Concerto in A major, K. 488. Both of them have quick finales in *alla breve,* or cut time, and both have a marvelous richness of texture and generosity of melody. Throughout the sonata an easy and fluent use of counterpoint recalls the mastery of J. S. Bach, although the musical language is unmistakably that of Mozart.

The brilliant opening Molto Allegro is in 6 / 8, a prancing meter Mozart usually reserved for finales. The exposition impresses one by its straightforward concision, although it contains no fewer than five melodic or thematic ideas. Like the first movement, the Andante is in sonata form. It is dominated by a very regular, very solemn bass theme, first heard in the piano. Sudden alternations of major and minor characterize the entire movement, giving us a strong foretaste of the world of Franz Schubert.

The *alla breve* Finale is one of the longest rondos that Mozart ever wrote in a chamber work; its wealth of themes is handled with that combination of freedom and logic that is the mark of true mastery. Its high spirits go a long way toward assuaging the tragic implications of the Andante. M.F.

Mozart's Finale is based upon that of Carl Friedrich Abel's Violin Sonata in A major, Op. 5, No. 5—perhaps as a memorial tribute, since Abel died on June 20, 1787. N.Z.

K. 547 *Violin Sonata in F major, "For Beginners"*

Origin: Vienna, July 10, 1788
Movements: Andante cantabile. Allegro. Andante con variazioni.

Mozart called his last violin sonata, finished on July 10, 1788, "a small piano sonata for beginners, with a violin." Both this sonata and the famous "little" Piano Sonata in C major, K. 545, which was composed just two weeks earlier, came into being while Mozart was creating his last three symphonies and must have served him as pure relaxation amid those mighty works. Except for the first movement, where the two instruments engage in genuine give-and-take, the violin plays an almost humiliatingly supernumerary role. This throwback to Mozart's earliest compositional procedures is further emphasized by the fact that all three movements are in the same key.

Despite these drawbacks, there is much to admire and love in this sonata. First, Mozart's sense of effective sequencing is evident in his reversing the order of the first two movements, so that the work begins with a rather terse slow movement and continues with a more expansive fast movement. "Slow" is perhaps an overstatement in describing the opening Andante cantabile (in rondo form), which moves at a fairly lively clip. Humor and tenderness predominate.

The Allegro (in sonata form) is by no means an easy piece, even if it was designed for beginners: it requires clean, fleet fingerwork by both hands. The Finale is a set of six variations on a theme of childlike simplicity. Until Variation Four arrives, the violin is virtually undetectable (it plays a total of ten notes in each half of Variation Two, for instance). Variation Five, in F minor, is for piano alone and lightly flirts with the possibilities of counterpoint. An exquisite coda bids us adieu. Mozart himself made a solo piano arrangement of these variations. (See note for K. 54 on p. 320). M.F.

SONATAS, SONATA MOVEMENTS, AND VARIATIONS FOR PIANO DUET

Domestic music making, 1781. Engraving by Johann August Rosmaesler.

The Mozarts popularized four-hand playing by their European tours of the 1760s, during which Mozart and his sister frequently performed together (see frontispiece). In the preface to the first published four-hand music (London, 1777), Charles Burney requested that a lady who wished to play four-hands remove the hoops from her skirt and urged her not to be embarrassed should her left hand occasionally graze the gentleman's right hand. The instrument here is a north German square piano.

K³ 19d ***Sonata in C major***
Origin: London, May 1765
Scoring: piano four-hands
Movements: [Allegro moderato.] Menuetto. Rondeau: Allegretto.

This work of questionable authenticity is first found in two published editions that were brought out independently in London and Paris, both *c.* 1789. Its relative naïveté suggests that if it is indeed by Mozart, it might be a very early work. The fact that it was published in London and Paris suggests that its origin might date from Mozart's youthful tour to those cities from 1763 to 1765, but why such a work would have lain dormant for a quarter of a century, suddenly to be published in both cities, is yet to be explained.

To be sure, Mozart is known to have

performed four-hand music with his sister Nannerl in London during the last few months of their stay there. On May 13, 1765, they reportedly performed an original composition of Wolfgang's together on a two-manual harpsichord in Hickford's Great Room, Brewer Street. On July 11 a notice in the *Public Advertiser* mentioned that "The two children will play also together upon the same harpsichord . . . ." Moreover, in a letter of Leopold Mozart's dated July 9 (as published in the biography of Mozart by Constanze Mozart and her second husband G. N. Nissen) a sentence was inserted that is not in the original manuscript of that letter (in the Internationale Stiftung Mozarteum, Salzburg): "Wolfgang composed his first piece for four hands in London. No such four-hand sonata had ever been composed before that time." This information, which could have come from Mozart's sister Nannerl, may in fact be correct, but the attempt to predate it to Leopold's letter of 1765 was blatant forgery.

An interesting feature of K. 19d is an occasional colliding of the left hand of the *primo* with the right hand of the *secondo*. This suggests an original conception for a two-manual harpsichord such as the London reports mention. Both of the original editions alike state that the work is for either "Piano Forte or Harpsichord" ("Pour le Piano Forte, ou le Clavecin"). W.C.

K. 381 ***Sonata in D major (K^6 123a)***
Origin: Salzburg, mid-1772
Scoring: piano four-hands
Movements: Allegro. Andante. Allegro molto.

The date of composition of K. 381 is uncertain. (The individual pages of the autograph have long been separated and some of them have been lost.) In the sixth edition of the Köchel catalogue of Mozart's works, the sonata is dated the beginning of 1772. But Wolfgang Plath, the world's leading authority on Mozart's handwriting, dates the sonata a half-year later. It is orchestral in texture, rhetoric, and character, and evokes the Italian symphonies and opera overtures of this period. The outer movements are typically boisterous, while the slow movement presents another Italian set piece, the uninterrupted *cantilena* with graceful accompaniment. The sixteen-year-old Mozart adapts these to the keyboard with aplomb, and the work sounds equally effective on fortepiano and harpsichord. R.D.L.

K. 358 ***Sonata in B-flat major (K^6 186c)***
Origin: Salzburg, late 1773 to early 1774
Scoring: piano four-hands
Movements: [Allegro.] [Adagio.] Molto presto.

In many ways K. 358 is a sister sonata to K. 381 (see above), with which it shares the orchestral vigor of the Italian sinfonia. Both works use sonata form for all three movements, although in K. 358 each movement has a short coda. Also, K. 358 goes considerably beyond the earlier work both in the amount of dialogue between *primo* and *secondo,* and in the richness of counterpoint and motivic structure. Curiously, the second movement uses the opening theme of Mozart's last Milan quartet, K. 160, recast in triple meter rather than duple.

Mozart's manuscript was preserved in the estate of his sister Nannerl, for whom he presumably composed the work. It seems to have been a favorite of his, for he mentions it several times in his correspondence. He had his father send him copies of it both at Mannheim in 1777, for two of his students, and at Vienna in 1781, perhaps to play with Josepha von Auernhammer, for whom he was soon to compose the two-piano sonata, K. 448. W.C.

K. 448 ***Sonata in D major (K⁶ 375a)***
Origin: Vienna, September 1781
Scoring: 2 pianos
Movements: Allegro con spirito. Andante. Allegro molto.

Mozart met Josepha von Auernhammer in 1781. He started teaching her that summer and reported his impressions of her with characteristic mercilessness:

> I dine almost daily at Herr von Auernhammer's. The young lady is a monster! But plays enchantingly; only the true, fine, singing taste in *cantabile* [passages] is missing; she chops up everything. She revealed to me (as a secret) her plan, which is to study righteously for two or three more years, and then go to Paris and pursue her career. "For," she says, "I am not beautiful," *au contraire,* [she is] ugly. . . .

In the early 1780s she and Mozart played as many as six times together in public. Mozart dedicated his six Violin Sonatas, K. 296 and 376–380, to her and she supervised the engraving of a number of Mozart's works for publication. He reported the performance of his new "Sonata for Two" (K. 448) at a concert ("accademie") at the Auernhammer residence on November 23, 1781, and refers to the work in his letters numerous times over the ensuing six weeks.

The music is a tour de force in every way. Its outer movements are audaciously virtuosic within a structure of remarkable economy: flamboyance is never allowed to triumph over musical substance. The Andante presents a seamless dialogue between the players; while the first piano presents the principal theme, the second player opens the second half with an eight-measure solo passage. Beyond the undeniable exhilaration the work affords to performers and listeners alike, it displays a rhetorical suavity and a perfect equilibrium of content and form that the twenty-five-year-old Mozart had long since made his hallmark.

Mozart wrote the first piano part for Fräulein von Auernhammer and the second for himself; we know this because he said so in a letter dated January 9, 1782. Moreover, the first piano part contains a high F sharp in the third movement—a note otherwise *never* used by Mozart in a keyboard work. The normal range of the fortepiano at that time was the five octaves from low F to high f‴. It would appear that she had a newer instrument that had the high F sharp on it (and thus a high G as well) and Mozart amused himself by writing one for her. R.D.L.

K. deest ***Larghetto and Allegro in E-flat major (completed by Maximilian Sadler)***
Origin: Vienna? 1782 to 1783
Scoring: 2 pianos
Movements: Larghetto; Allegro.

This work was discovered in the early 1960s, in the castle of Kroměříž in South Moravia (Czechoslovakia). It therefore does not appear in any edition of the Köchel catalogue. Kroměříž was a residence of the Archduke Johann Joseph Ranier Rudolf of Austria, to whom Beethoven dedicated several of his most important works. Mozart's manuscript was found in Rudolf's archives there. Its existence had long been ignored due to a misidentification: a penciled note, in Rudolf's own hand, attributed the work to Christoph Willibald Gluck.

The Kroměříž autograph consists of

an incomplete score, together with a carefully copied first page of the first piano part. (It would seem unprecedented for Mozart to have started copying out parts for a work he had not yet completed.) Perhaps the last pages of the sketch once existed and were lost. In any case, Constanze Mozart seems to have given the fragment to Maximilian Stadler, who completed it as he did many other unfinished Mozart pieces.

The work consists of a completed thirty-five-measure introductory Larghetto, which leads directly into an Allegro in sonata form. The first piano part is indicated for the entire exposition, whereas the second part appears only from time to time. The movement breaks off just after the exposition ends. Stadler's completion is extremely mechanical, quite inferior to his excellent completion of the Fantasy in C Minor for piano, K. 396. In modern times, other completions have been composed by pianists Paul Badura-Skoda and Robert Levin. R.D.L.

K. 426 *Fugue in C minor*
Origin: Vienna, December 29, 1782 or 1783
Scoring: 2 pianos

This work has a precise dating in Mozart's hand (December 29, 1783), but the "3" has been changed from a "2." Were the Fugue composed in 1782, it would be appropriate to link its composition with Josepha von Auernhammer, for whom Mozart wrote the two-piano sonata, K. 448. A 1783 dating suggests a different instigation—Mozart's contact with Baron Gottfried van Swieten. Van Swieten introduced Mozart to the music of Bach and Handel and provoked Mozart's "Bach crisis." During that time Mozart instrumented a number of Bach's fugues, providing preludes of his own composition for some of them. He wrote several fugues and many more fugal fragments in an attempt to reconcile Bach's powerfully expressive counterpoint with his own abilities.

The C-minor Fugue is as different from Mozart's other piano duet music as one could imagine. Instead of brilliance and wit contrasted with *cantabile* passages, we are here confronted with obsessive counterpoint of a relentless willfulness rare in Mozart's oeuvre. His decision to write such a piece for two pianos may have been made in order to allow each voice maximum freedom without creating any resultant physical problems in performance. The Fugue subject is systematically worked out, with canon, stretto, and inversion. Only at the very end does Mozart momentarily allow the Alberti bass of the Classical period to give this otherwise archaic work a hint of his normal language. R.D.L.

K. 497 *Sonata in F major*
Origin: Vienna, August 1, 1786
Scoring: piano four-hands
Movements: Adagio—Allegro di molto. Andante. [Allegro.]

The Sonata in F major is Mozart's most serious work for piano four-hands. In its inspiration, imagination, and dramatic intensity it is on a level with the string quintets, the "Haydn" Quartets, and the piano concertos. The very presence of a slow introduction to the first movement, brooding and turbulent, announces at once the scale of Mozart's undertaking. The development of the first movement is unusually spacious. The second movement is a veritable operatic scene featuring a dialogue between the registers of the keyboard, and the Finale combines irresistible cheerfulness with fiery outbursts that remind us again of the overall seriousness of the work. R.D.L.

K. 501 ***5 Variations on an Original Andante in G major***
Origin: Vienna, November 4, 1786
Scoring: Piano four-hands

This brief but wonderful set of variations dates from late 1786 and was published within a year by Franz Anton Hoffmeister of Vienna. Hoffmeister had previously invited Mozart to compose various chamber works for his publishing house, beginning with the G-minor Piano Quartet, K. 478, of October 1785. It seems likely that these variations might have resulted from a similar invitation.

The work overflows with intricate imitative dialogue for the two performers. In the final variation the *primo* and *secondo* take turns embellishing the repeated phrases with ever fleeter figuration. All subsides into a graceful return of the opening theme at the conclusion.

Mozart abandoned another four-hand work based on nearly the same theme: a rather perfunctory rondo fragment, K. 500a, that his widow Constanze mistook for an extra variation to K. 501. The rondo might, however, have arisen in connection with a very fine four-hand sonata movement in G major, K. 497a, that was also unfortunately abandoned just after the beginning of the development section was composed. Perhaps K. 497a and 500a constituted Mozart's first thoughts on a four-hand project for Hoffmeister that he eventually fulfilled with the present variations. W.C.

K. 521 ***Sonata in C major***
Origin: Vienna, May 29, 1787
Scoring: piano four-hands
Movements: Allegro. Andante. Allegretto.

Mozart composed this work during the period of the great quintets, K. 515 and 516, a period overshadowed by the impending death of his father; in fact, news of Leopold's death reached Wolfgang on the day he completed the sonata. On the same day, he sent the piece off to his close friend and student Gottfried von Jacquin, instructing him to "have the goodness to give the sonata to my lady, your sister, with my compliments—but she might have a go at it immediately, for it is a bit difficult."

Its difficulty lies perhaps less in its technical demands than in its character, which is subtle and elusive, especially in comparison with Mozart's flamboyantly dramatic previous four-hand sonata, K. 497, which was composed only ten months earlier (see above). Its affinities, both structural and thematic, lie rather in the direction of *Eine kleine Nachtmusik,* K. 525, of two months later, a work that shares the sonata's grace and understatement. Particularly the last movement, a Rondo with a bagpipe-like theme, maintains a self-effacing shyness in the face of much flattering technical display, and thereby achieves a complexity and depth of character rarely matched in Mozart's keyboard works.

When Mozart published the sonata about a year later, he dedicated the work not to Franziska von Jacquin, but rather to two gifted young Viennese sisters, Babette and Nanette Natorp, friends of the Jacquins. Babette (Maria Barbara) was later to marry Gottfried's older brother, Josef Franz von Jacquin, and in time to become a reknowned pianist in Viennese circles. For Miss Jacquin Mozart is believed to have composed one of his finest chamber works, the "Kegelstatt" Trio, K. 498 (see the note on p. 281).

W.C.

15

Solo Keyboard Music

Joseph Haydn. Engraving of 1792 by Luigi Schiavonetti after an oil painting by Ludwig Guttenbrunn.

Seated at a spinet (a small harpsichord) or clavichord, quill in hand, Haydn is shown trying an idea with his left hand, and, staring into the middle distance, trying to decide whether or not to write it down. The friendship and artistic interchanges between Mozart and Haydn in the 1780s constitute one of the happiest chapters of Mozart's last decade.

BACKGROUND AND OVERVIEW

Pianists who love Mozart's music spend endless hours trying to divine the secrets of making it sound as beautiful coming from their instruments as it sounds to them in their imagination. There is no consensus about how Mozart's music should be played. Modern ideas about his piano music range from lushly romantic approaches to austerely restrained ones, from commitment to large modern Steinways to preference for the smaller, leaner pianos of Mozart's time.

What wouldn't we give to be able to hear how Mozart played? If only one could visit him in heaven, or bring him back to life, or find a time machine to travel to the 1780s, or discover lost tape recordings made at the time by a prescient inventor. In the absence of these improbable events, however, all we have to fall back on are some eyewitness accounts of his playing. These are edifyingly enthusiastic but disappointingly short on telling details:

> *March 22, 1783:* . . . the two new concertos and additional fantasies which Mr. Mozart played on the fortepiano were received with the loudest applause. . . . the entire audience accorded him such unanimous applause as has never been heard of here [in Vienna].
>
> *April 1, 1784:* I have heard Mozart, . . . great and original in his compositions, and a master when seated at the keyboard. His concerto on the fortepiano, how excellent that was! And his improvisations, what a wealth of ideas! what variety! what contrasts in passionate sounds! One is washed away unresistingly on the stream of one's own emotions.
>
> *January 19, 1787:* By general request [Mozart] then performed on the fortepiano at a great concert in the opera house [in Prague]. Never had the theater been so full of people as it was on this occasion; never had there been greater or more unanimous delight that his divine playing aroused. Indeed, we did not know what to admire more—the extraordinary composition, or the extraordinary playing; both together made a total impression on our souls that could only be compared to sweet enchantment! But at the end of the concert, when Mozart extemporized alone for more than half an hour at the fortepiano, raising our delight to the highest degree, our enchantment dissolved into loud, overwhelming applause. And indeed, this extemporization exceeded anything normally understood by fortepiano playing, as the highest excellence in the art of composition was combined with the most perfect accomplishment in execution.
>
> *January 29, 1787:* . . . Mozart is the most skillful and best keyboard scholar I have ever heard. . . .
>
> *August 24, 1788:* . . . to Kapellmeister Mozart's. There I had the happiest hour of music that has ever fallen to my lot. This small man and great master twice extemporized on a pedal fortepiano, so wonderfully—so wonderfully that I quite lost myself! He intertwined the most difficult passages with the most lovely themes. . . . His pedal in the second improvisation in particular made the most agreeable impression. [I was] happy and quite overcome at having heard Mozart.
>
> *November 12, 1788:*
> When Mozart masterly music plays,
> And gathers undivided praise,
> The choir of Muses stays to hear,
> Apollo is himself all ear.
>
> *April 14, 1789:* . . . his agility on the harpsichord and on the fortepiano is quite inexpressible—and to this is added an extraordinary ability to read at sight, which truly borders on the incredible—for he himself is hardly able to play a thing better after practice than he does the very first time. On the organ too he showed his great skill in the strict style.
>
> *March 4, 1791:* Kapellmeister Mozart played a concerto on the fortepiano, and everyone

admired his art, in composition as well as in performance. . . .

Brilliance, fluency, lyricism, clarity, and extraordinary communicative powers—Mozart seemed to have had them all. Small wonder he was considered the finest pianist of his generation. N.Z.

SONATAS AND SONATA MOVEMENTS

An engraving by Daniel Chodowiecki entitled "La Musique" from a series called *Occupations des dames* (Berlin, 1780)

A young woman plays a square piano while a male admirer (or perhaps her music teacher) watches her closely.

BACKGROUND AND OVERVIEW

Given that Mozart's training and career were so closely linked to the keyboard, it seems surprising that the earliest work in this section is the Sonata in C major, K. 279, which dates from 1775. Why don't we have any solo keyboard sonatas from Mozart's decade of active composing leading up to 1775? There are two answers to this question: in the 1760s and 1770s keyboard sonatas with violin accompaniment were all the rage, and Mozart published sixteen of these as his Opp. 1–4 (K. 6–15 and 26–31). Then it seems that there probably were some earlier solo sonatas, which have been lost.

Five such works are documented. Three of them were in the possession of Mozart's sister Nannerl until the beginning of the nineteenth century, when she sent them to the Leipzig music publishers Breitkopf

& Härtel. The latter never published them and eventually they were irretrievably lost. All that survives of them are the opening measures of the first movement of each sonata, as recorded in a catalogue kept by Breitkopf & Härtel. These "incipits" may be seen in the Köchel Catalogue, listed under the arbitrarily assigned numbers K. 33d–f. Nannerl described these as "among my brother's first compositions." The same Breitkopf & Härtel catalogue shows the incipit of a fourth lost sonata in an apparently similar style, which is now known as K. 33g.

Knowledge of a fifth sonata comes to us from quite a different source. When Mozart and his father were in Verona in January 1770, the nearly fourteen-year-old Mozart's portrait was painted by Saverio dalla Rosa. Mozart is shown seated at the keyboard and on the music desk there is a sonata, which is so clearly painted that one can transcribe the first thirty-four measures of a movement marked Molto Allegro. Although we cannot be certain that this was a work by Mozart, the presumption that it is is a reasonable one. This fragment will be found in the Köchel Catalogue as K. 72a. N.Z.

K. 279 *Piano Sonata in C major, No. 1* *(K⁶ 189f)*

Origin: Munich, between January 14 and March 6, 1775

Movements: Allegro. Andante. Allegro.

In 1774 Mozart received an opera commission from Maximilian III Joseph, Elector of Bavaria for the 1775 carnival season. Composing *La finta giardiniera*, K. 196, however, also meant traveling to Munich to supervise its production. After directing the successful premier Mozart lingered several months in Munich, keeping busy by composing several divertimentos for winds and a set of six piano sonatas (K. 279–284), the first of his works in that genre to have come down to us. As with his later sonatas (as well as his piano concertos) these were repertoire pieces designed to display his gifts as a composer and performer. He played them not only in Munich but during his later visits to Augsburg, Mannheim, and Paris.

As a group, these first sonatas show Mozart experimenting to some extent, testing both the form and the instrument to find his authentic voice. They show an extraordinary range of styles, even from movement to movement within a single work, and one can rarely guess what the next sonata will be like by studying its predecessor.

Reflecting Mozart's move from harpsichord to piano, this first sonata clearly spans both instruments: the dynamic changes, such as loud to soft, belong to the piano, while the strummed chords and light-fingered, tart staccatos are distinct remnants of harpsichord style.

The opening Allegro is in sonata form. The Andante mirrors the understated simplicity characteristic of the *galant* style prevalent in Mozart's youth. The influence of Italian melody is palpable in this movement. The lively closing Allegro crowns the sonata. It, too, is in sonata form. C.S.

K. 280 *Piano Sonata in F major, No. 2* *(K⁶ 189c)*

Origin: Munich, between January 14 and March 6, 1775

Movements: Allegro assai. Adagio. Presto.

The second sonata opens the door to a new era. Mozart writes with the piano plainly in mind—and in doing so he evidently turns to Joseph Haydn for guidance: this work is modeled after a sonata, also in F major, that Haydn composed in

1773 and published as Op. 13, No. 3.

Clarity, restraint, and an air of nobility characterize the opening Allegro as it strides confidently along in classic minuet rhythm.

In the Adagio Mozart makes such effective use of a minor key that one critic felt impelled to ask: "Has anyone ever heard a more soul-stirring lament by an eighteen-year old?"

All traces of sadness vanish in the ebullient Presto. In 3/8 time, its rhythm ties back to the earlier movements and makes this Mozart's only sonata in triple time from start to finish. C.S.

K. 281 *Piano Sonata in B-flat major, No. 3 (K⁶ 189e)*

Origin: Munich, between January 14 and March 6, 1775

Movements: Allegro. Andante amoroso. Rondeau: Allegro.

Haydn's influence continues in the third sonata. Alfred Einstein even goes so far as to say that "the first two movements seem more like Haydn than Haydn himself." There is still much Mozart to be heard in these movements, however—albeit a Mozart who is still maturing and testing out his efforts in sophisticated Munich by adhering to the style of a recognized composer. Haydn was forty-two at the time, Mozart just nineteen.

In the Allegro, Haydn's hand shows most plainly in the clarity of its form, the mosaic of small melodic thoughts, often breaking into triplet patterns, and in the well-contrived development section.

In sonata form, the Andante amoroso opens with a limpid introduction. If there is anything "amorous" about this Andante, it is couched in the language of light flirtation and gallantry.

From this early Haydnesque style, Mozart leaps years ahead in the masterly closing Allegro. Using fashionable French, Mozart calls it a "rondeau," a form that was to become a favorite in both his sonatas and piano concertos. C.S.

K. 282 *Piano Sonata in E-flat major, No. 4 (K⁶ 189g)*

Origin: Munich, between January 14 and March 6, 1775

Movements: Adagio. Menuetto I / Menuetto II. Allegro.

If these first sonatas show Mozart feeling his way—experimenting, as it were—then the fourth sonata is the least conventional of all, the only one, except for K. 331, that begins with a movement in slow tempo instead of an allegro.

In this opening Adagio Mozart has written a youthful essay on melodymaking. It begins with a rather melancholy introductory idea that also brings the movement to a close. The second movement is the standard Minuet with Trio. The procedure here is typically Classical: Minuet I has a slightly percussive, detached melodic line, and Minuet II provides a more lyrical and flowing contrast before the first Minuet returns.

The sonata ends with a dashing Allegro, as clear and sparkling as cut crystal. All is worked out in miniature, including a tiny development section. C.S.

K. 283 *Piano Sonata in G major, No. 5 (K⁶ 189h)*

Origin: Munich, between January 14 and March 6, 1775

Movements: Allegro. Andante. Presto.

No questions of influence or sequence trouble the G-major Sonata, the fifth of the six sonatas written in the first quarter of 1775. It has long been a favorite with pianists. Bright Italian sunshine and tunefulness suffuse its every measure, as at the start of the Allegro, where the airy principal theme suggests both a minuet and a *galant* duo with voice replying to voice. The Andante continues in a more thoughtful but still happy vein.

In 3/8 time, the closing Presto moves like a gossamer whirlwind, suggesting both a dance and a scherzo. Yet throughout the insubstantial fabric, Mozart has woven solid craftsmanship: form, balance, and brief flashes of counterpoint.

C.S.

K. 284 *Piano Sonata in D major, "Dürnitz," No. 6 (K⁶ 205b)*

Origin: Munich, between January 14 and March 6, 1775

Movements: Allegro. Rondeau en Polonaise [Andante]. Thema con dodieci variazioni.

Mozart composed this work, the last of his six Munich sonatas, for a well-known music patron, Baron Thaddäus von Dürnitz. Alfred Einstein speculates that "Mozart must have had a personal or musical experience that suddenly lifted him to a new and higher level." We cannot even guess what that experience might have been or what took place deep within his creative psyche, but its results are plain: assurance, a style that utilizes all the piano's resources and, again, an uncommon succession of movements.

He made two attempts at composing the opening Allegro. The first, similar in manner to the foregoing sonatas, breaks off after seventy-one measures. Then, using some of the same thematic material, he began afresh, in a more brilliant style, and brought the movement to a conclusion. The whole movement, including the harmonically pungent development, seems to be a virile symphonic overture scored for piano. Mozart calls the Andante that follows a "Polonaise en Rondeau." The rondo refrain takes on new and progressively richer figuration each time it returns, creating a kind of hybrid variation-rondo. Having hit upon the idea of variations, Mozart uses it for the extended Finale—a movement more than twice as long as the first two combined and longer than some complete sonatas.

This sonata evidently pleased Mozart, since he did not hesitate to publish it fully a decade later—in 1784, when he was the musical darling of Vienna—in a triple publication that included the piano sonata, K. 333, and the violin sonata, K. 454. (The first five Munich sonatas remained in manuscript until eight years after his death.)

C.S.

K. 309 *Piano Sonata in C major, No. 7 (K⁶ 284b)*

Origin: Mannheim, between October 22 and November 13, 1777

Movements: Allegro con spirito. Andante un poco adagio. Rondeau: Allegretto grazioso.

After stretching out his Munich stay as long as he dared, Mozart returned to Salzburg, where he remained for two and a half more years providing music for Archbishop Colloredo and his court. Inevitably, though, he realized that Salzburg held no future for him. It was time to go job hunting and, with his mother along as combined chaperone and cashier, he departed on September 23, 1777, on a fateful journey to Paris that was to hold bitter disappointments.

This trip, to Munich, Augsburg, Mannheim, Paris, and back to Salzburg, lasted more than a year and produced three piano sonatas (K. 309, 311, and 310). At Mannheim, Mozart met Christian Cannabich, director of the famed court orchestra. "I am with Cannabich every day," he wrote to Leopold. "He has a daughter who plays the keyboard quite nicely and in order to make a real friend of him, I am now working on a sonata for her, which is almost finished, save for the Rondo." Four days later, on November 8, 1777, the Rondo was finished, the sonata for fifteen-year-old Mlle. Rosa Cannabich complete. Along with sonatas K. 311 and 310, it was published in Paris the following year.

The Allegro opens boldly with a unison motif that acts as a motto for this lucid sonata-form movement. Mozart included a local musical specialty for his hosts: the bright ascending staccatos in the transition to the second theme, known as the "Mannheim rocket."

Asked what he was thinking while composing the Andante un poco Adagio, Mozart replied: "I would make it fit closely the character of Mlle Rosa. . . . She is exactly like the Andante." The Rondo perfectly matches the graciousness of its tempo marking. It is brilliant yet not taxing, ideally tailored to display Rosa's abilities. Her playing of the sonata delighted the twenty-one-year-old composer. C.S.

K. 311 ***Piano Sonata in D major, No. 9 (K⁶ 284c)***

Origin: Mannheim, mid-December 1777

Movements: Allegro con spirito. Andante con espressione. Rondeau: Allegro.

The D-major Sonata, K. 311, was written during Mozart's stay in Mannheim or, quite possibly, even earlier in Munich, where he had met a Josepha Freysinger, daughter of one of his father's friends, and promised her a sonata. This may be that sonata.

German writer Hans Dennerlein calls the Allegro con spirito "a fire-work of good spirits, bustling and crackling with life." Yet beneath this glittering surface lies a deeper life. Mozart is still reshaping the sonata form to suit his inspiration. Themes are connected: the main subject's rising staccato motif becomes a descending legato melody in the lyric second theme. The little descending motive at the exposition's close seems to be an afterthought, but becomes the only material dealt with in the development. This trick became a hallmark of Mozart's mature style and shows up again in the piano sonatas K. 545 and K. 576, as well as in many other works.

The form of the Andante con espressione defies strict classification but comes closest to what the Germans call *bar form,* which consists of two strophes—each one here opening and closing with a version of the refrain and followed by a shorter "after-song." But because of the frequent return to the opening melody, simple or decorated, one tends to hear the movement as a rondo in a slow tempo.

The Allegro Finale includes the roominess and *élan* characteristic of the Rondo in K. 309, along with more substantial musical ideas, all presented in a lilting 6/8 rhythm that anticipates the concerto finales. The Finale even includes a brief cadenza to enhance the concerto-like flavor. C.S.

K. 310 ***Piano Sonata in A minor, No. 8 (K⁶ 300d)***

Origin: Paris, between March 23 and July 20, 1778

Movements: Allegro maestoso. Andante cantabile con espressione. Presto.

Compositions in minor keys are rare in Mozart's works: only two each among the piano sonatas, concertos, and symphonies, just one each among the mature string quintets, quartets, and violin sonatas—barely a dozen pieces out of scores of instrumental compositions. This sonata is one such work. It moves us ahead to Paris, where Mozart arrived toward the end of March 1778 for a six-month stay. While in Paris (no one knows just when) he composed the A-minor Sonata and a companion work, the Violin Sonata in E minor, K. 304. Among the several explanations that have been suggested, the most prevalent perhaps is that the death of Mozart's mother on July 3, 1778, after a short, unforeseen illness, gave rise to a deep sense of loss that is reflected in these sonatas. Or perhaps it was the enforced absence from Aloysia Weber, the young Mannheim soprano with whom he had recently fallen in love, that drove him toward a more turbulent minor-keyed creativity.

This A-minor work ushers into the sonatas a vibrant emotional intensity. The Allegro, despite its qualifier "maestoso" (stately), has a persistent querulousness, a mood, compounded of angular melody, repeated left-hand chords, and dotted rhythms, that will not be placated. Also in sonata form, the Andante, marked "cantabile con espressione," offers solace in its spacious opening melody, but the development casts a long shadow that obscures the consolation promised at the beginning.

Once its dotted-rhythm refrain starts, the concluding Presto, again in the minor, moves like a wraith spinning about without ever coming to rest. "It is a most personal expression," writes Alfred Einstein. "One may look in vain in all the works of other composers of the period for anything similar." C.S.

K. 400 ***Allegro in B-flat major (K⁶ 372a) (completed by Maximilian Stadler)***

Origin: Vienna, 1781

Between 1778 and 1783 Mozart did not write a single pianoforte sonata; but he did leave us this movement in B flat as a perfect example of his "early Viennese" style, in which brilliance and tenderness battle for supremacy but without either of them gaining the upper hand. During the summer of 1781 Mozart stayed with the Weber family in Vienna, "fooled about and had fun," as he told his father in a letter of July 25, and became particularly fond of two of Frau Weber's daughters: Constanze, whom he married in 1782, and her younger sister Sophie, who remained always devoted to him. Soon after the beginning of the development, there are two successive phrases of a soulful character, and over one of these phrases Mozart has written the name "Sophie," over the other, "Constanze."

Mozart did not finish the movement. He got only as far as the end of the development, and years later Abbé Stadler added the reprise with quite convincing effect. W.G.

K. 330 ***Piano Sonata in C major, No. 10 (K^6 300h)***

Origin: Salzburg, between late July and late November 1783

Movements: Allegro moderato. Andante cantabile. Allegretto.

The group of three sonatas K. 330–332 was published by Artaria and Co. in Vienna in 1784. Each is quite distinct from the others, with its own felicities and idiosyncrasies. Along with the slightly later B-Flat Sonata, K. 333, they form the most gratifying group he composed for the piano.

Alfred Einstein described the C-major Sonata as "one of the most lovable works Mozart ever wrote." Indeed, it is difficult to resist its Classical symmetry and ingratiating piano style. The opening Allegro moderato maintains such a light, feathery touch that it is almost an imposition on the music to attempt to explain how it is achieved.

The Andante cantabile, in **A-B-A** form with a brief coda based on the **B** section, is the most striking part of the sonata. The spare style at the beginning suggests emotion deeply felt but restrained.

Balancing off the sonata, the Allegretto returns to the Allegro's relaxed ebullience. But in place of the standard development, Mozart surprises us once more, as he had in the opening movement, by substituting a little interlude inspired by folksong. C.S.

K. 331 *Piano Sonata in A major, No. 11 (K⁶ 300i)*

Origin: Salzburg, between late July and late November 1783

Movements: Andante grazioso. Menuetto. Alla turca: Allegretto.

With its unusual sequence of movements—a set of variations, a minuet, and a march-rondo—the A-major Sonata resembles a four-movement sonata lacking its opening (sonata form, allegro) movement. Generations of music lovers have made the work, with its famed "Turkish" Rondo, a great favorite.

The sonata opens with a lilting set of variations in 6/8 meter, Andante grazioso. Its theme is the Czech folksong "Hořela líps, hořela," also sung to the German words "Freu dich, mein Herz, denk' an kein." In some ways, the Minuet is the most extraordinary movement of the sonata, quite unlike anything else Mozart wrote at this point in his career. With its short yearning phrases, chromatically altered harmonies, and nocturne-like accompaniment, it strains our concept of a minuet. The sonata ends with the rondo Alla turca, that wonderful evocation of janissary music (the jangling percussion instruments of a Turkish marching band). Delightfully brash and replete with imaginary drums and cymbals, here is Mozart's vision of extravagantly clad, mustachioed Turkish soldiers parading down a European city boulevard. C.S.

K. 332 *Piano Sonata in F major, No. 12 (K⁶ 300k)*

Origin: Salzburg, between late July and late November 1783

Movements: Allegro. Adagio. Allegro assai.

A remarkable aspect of Mozart's genius was his ability to compose works such as these early Viennese sonatas within a short space of time and stamp each with a unique character: the C-major Sonata with its intimacy and formal balance, the almost bizarre juxtapositions of the A-major Sonata and now this F-major Sonata—expansive, extroverted, and dramatic. In K. 332, melodic ideas abound, contrasts are highlighted by abrupt changes between major and minor keys, and vigorously sonorous style prevails throughout.

The opening Allegro presents no fewer than seven distinct melodic ideas. Diversified and varied, they reveal unexpected happenings at every turn.

The English critic Arthur Hutchings called the Adagio "the summit of expression Mozart reached without departing from the formality and reticence of his epoch." In Mozart's manuscript, the second half of the movement is a simple repeat of the first half, with slight key adjustments; but the first edition of the sonata (1784) included a beautifully embellished version of this repeat, which was almost certainly supplied by Mozart.

In purely pianistic terms the concluding Allegro assai is a brilliant showpiece—a kind of eighteenth-century anticipation of the Lisztian concert étude. Like the first movement, this simple sonata-form Finale presents a wealth of contrasting ideas—six at least—and shifts constantly between major and minor. At the end, though, Mozart lets the bravura fireworks play themselves out and brings the movement to a quiet close. C.S.

K. 333 *Piano Sonata in B-flat major, "Linz," No. 13 (K⁶ 315c)*

Origin: Linz and Vienna, mid-November 1783

Movements: Allegro. Andante cantabile. Allegretto grazioso.

A distinct similarity between this sonata and the sonata, Op. 17, No. 4, of J. C. Bach has misled generations of scholars into thinking that Mozart composed K. 333 soon after meeting Bach—and presumably seeing his Sonata—in Paris in 1778. However, recent investigation of the manuscript's handwriting and watermarks (by Wolfgang Plath and Alan Tyson) suggests that Mozart composed it in late 1783 on his return to Vienna, via Linz, from his extended stay in Salzburg that autumn. During this time he was busily preparing new music for the coming winter concert season in Vienna, including the "Linz" Symphony (K. 425), two aborted comic operas *(L'oca del Cairo* and *Lo sposo deluso*), and some ballroom dances (K. 363, 463, and 610). After Mozart had presumably made ample use of the sonata as a concert piece he released it, together with the "Dürnitz" and "Strinasacchi" Sonatas (K. 284 and 454, the latter with violin), for publication as Op. 7 by Christoph Torricella of Vienna in the summer of 1784.

The B-flat sonata was clearly written as a showpiece. All three movements begin unassumingly, even self-effacingly, but each one unfolds into a tapestry of masterful design, rich in melody and broad in scope. Both of the first two movements are in full sonata form. The first opens with the forementioned *galant* reference to J. C. Bach—if it is one; by contrast the development is surprisingly stormy. The second movement is in a very tender and lyrical vein, but it gives way to unusual chromaticisms in the development section. The last movement, the *pièce de résistance,* is a rondo with three generous episodes. The last episode suddenly blossoms forth into a full-fledged cadenza, quite stunning in effect. In its skillful and humorous balance of sentimentality and showmanship, the sonata prophesies the great piano concertos of 1784 to 1786. W.C.

K. 457 *Piano Sonata in C minor, No. 14*

Origin: Vienna, October 14, 1784

Movements: Allegro. Adagio. Allegro assai.

Mozart's masterly C-minor Sonata bears this handwritten dedication: "Sonata. For Piano Solo. Composed for Mrs. Theresa von Trattner by her most humble servant Wolfgang Amadeus Mozart. Vienna, 14 October 1784." It remains a generous tribute to his talented twenty-six-year-old pupil, the wife of a Viennese book publisher and entrepreneur. To add to its power, Mozart himself prefaced it with a fantasia in the same key, completed seven months later, in May 1785 (K. 475).

A deep emotional drive permeates the opening Allegro with its portentous octaves forming a defiant rising motif that dominates all parts of the movement. The Adagio provides a restful interlude in this troubled work. It is in **A-B-A** form with rondo elements added, since the refrain-like opening melody recurs several times with ever more elaborate embellishments.

The concluding rondo, Allegro assai, returns to the troubled atmosphere of the first movement. Mozart also introduces a new and powerful dramatic device—silence. Time after time the music builds to a climax only to be followed by a void, a deadly pause of frustration.

The Beethoven-like passion and power of this sonata are unmistakable. *"Beethovenisme d'avant la lettre"* (Beethovenism before the fact) is how a French critic expressed it. Alfred Einstein, quoting the remark, went beyond it to claim that "this very sonata contributed a great deal to making Beethovenism possible."

C.S.

K. 533 ***Piano Sonata in F major, No. 18***
Origin: Vienna, January 3, 1788
Movements: Allegro. Andante. Rondo: Allegretto

Sometime in 1790 the Viennese publisher Franz Anton Hoffmeister issued Mozart's Sonata in F major. Although the public did not know it at the time and willingly accepted the work, Mozart cheated a bit in creating this sonata. He included an Allegro and Andante he wrote in January 1788 as the first two movements and completed the work with a "little" Rondo, (K. 494), he had written earlier, in June 1786, revising and beefing it up for its new role. Nevertheless, the F-major Sonata is as proper a sonata as any and a masterpiece by any standard.

Alfred Einstein hears in the two movements "a grandeur of harmonic and polyphonic conception, a depth of feeling, and a harmonic daring such as we find only in his last works; indeed they are conceived for an entirely different and more powerful instrument than the innocent Rondo, which is written mostly for the middle register." But even this earlier Rondo, writes Einstein, "is so rich and perfect that no uninitiated listener would observe any break in style."

The opening Allegro finds Mozart fascinated with contrapuntal textures, as in his other late piano sonatas (K. 570 and 576) and in the great "Jupiter" Symphony, composed in the same year, 1788. The Andante is one of the most daring and disturbing movements in all of Mozart's music. Ostensibly written in sonata form, it strikes the ear more like a free-floating slow fantasia.

After two such movements it is a distinct relief to enter the world of the Rondo, K. 494. Both hands play high up on the keyboard during much of this charming movement, giving it a delicate, almost glass harmonica aura. But a quickening sense of drama builds throughout, culminating in a twenty-seven measure cadenza ending with a trill—a concerto-like feature that Mozart added in 1788 when he revised the Rondo.

C.S.

K. 545 ***Piano Sonata in C major, "For Beginners," No. 15***
Origin: Vienna, June 26, 1788
Movements: Allegro. Andante. Rondo: Allegretto.

On June 26, 1788, he listed in his catalogue "eine kleine Klavier Sonate für Anfänger" (a little piano sonata for beginners). It is the delightful and immensely popular C-major Sonata, K. 545, known to generations of piano students as the epitome of Mozartean elegance.

Mozart must have been thinking about a series of children's works at the time; he completed a companion piece for beginners, the violin sonata, K. 547, two weeks later. Yet genius works in unfathomable ways: on one hand Mozart was busy simplifying and distilling his art for youngsters while on the other he was busy writing the monumental triptych of his last three symphonies. The very day he completed this C-major Sonata he finished the Symphony No. 39 in E flat, K. 543, and the last movements of both works have similar thematic ideas.

The texture of the first movement is as fresh and transparent as spring water: Mozart's beginner must learn to play scales with perfect evenness and control. While the Andante makes no attempt at profundity, it shows Mozart spinning out seamless melodic transformations of the gently contoured opening phrase, which somewhat resembles the aria "Dalla sua pace," written the same year for the Viennese production of *Don Giovanni*. The Allegretto ends with a bouncy little rondo, rounding out this sonata "for beginners" in merry fashion. C.S.

K. 570 ***Piano Sonata in B-flat major, No. 16***
Origin: Vienna, February 1789
Movements: Allegro. Adagio. Allegretto.

Mozart's penultimate sonata was composed in February 1789 and reached the public in 1796, five years after his death, tricked out with a completely spurious and inane violin part. The piano style, to be sure, is modest and recalls the sonata "for beginners," K. 545. But, for the rest—form, melody, scope—the work moves in the mainstream of Mozart's sonata production.

The opening Allegro is all of a piece since its thematic ideas are related. The Adagio, the centerpiece of the sonata, serves to remind us how restrictive it can be to label Mozart, as some do, strictly a Classicist: the movement is quite Romantic in its luxuriant harmonies and supple, vocally conceived melodies. It is, in fact, one of the most singable movements in all of Mozart's compositions. Structured as a rondo, the Adagio opens with its refrain—eloquent, yet with a grave, almost ceremonial air about it.

An airy rondo, the Allegretto Finale has a refrain alive with motion. With it, Mozart has written a well-nigh perfect foil for what has gone before in a sonata that Alfred Einstein considered "perhaps the most completely rounded of them all, the ideal of his piano sonata." C.S.

K. 576 ***Piano Sonata in D major, No. 17***
Origin: Vienna, July 1789
Movements: Allegro. Adagio. Allegretto.

In July 1789 Mozart composed his last piano sonata. That spring his fortunes had reached one of their periodic low points, so low that a noble pupil, Prince Karl Lichnowsky, took him north to Berlin in hopes that King Frederick William II of Prussia would find some use for his talents. A good cellist, the king frequently commissioned pieces for himself; Luigi Boccherini, Joseph Haydn, and Beethoven, among others, provided them. In Mozart's case, however, the journey seems not to have produced all he had hoped for. He returned to Vienna with an assignment to compose "six easy clavier sonatas for Princess Frederike and six quartets for the King," a commission he never completed.

He did, in time, finish three of the six quartets, the "Prussian" Quartets. But, as for the sonatas, he wrote only one, which, as it turned out, never reached the Princess. This is probably just as well, for it is not suitable for a royal amateur but is one of the most difficult and demanding sonatas of them all. Mozart had been profoundly impressed with Bach's motets, which he encountered in northern Germany. He had written his Bach-oriented Gigue, K. 574, in Bach's own city of Leipzig. Little wonder that the last piano sonata is permeated with masterly contrapuntal display.

The Allegro opens with a jaunty, trumpet-like fanfare in 6/8 rhythm. In one form or another the fanfare permeates the whole movement. The lovely Adagio is full of yearning couched in subtle melodic and harmonic turns. We are back in the contrapuntal world of J. S. Bach—brought up to date by Mozart's distinctive voice—in the rondo Finale, a tour de force both as composition and as a pianistic showpiece. C.S.

VARIATIONS

The Harpsichord Lesson. Engraving by Sigmund Freudenberger (1795–1801) Paris, c. 1770.

Much of Mozart's keyboard music was conceived for just such bourgeois circumstances as portrayed in this scene. The representation of a male teacher or admirer standing over a female keyboard player is a topos of seventeenth- and eighteenth-century art, found in dozens of paintings, drawings, and engravings. It captures salient social, political, and gender-related attitudes of the era. (The Bettmann Archive)

K. 24 *8 Variations on "Laat ons Juichen" in G major*
Origin: The Hague, January 1766

K. 25 *7 Variations on "Willem van Nassau" in D major*
Origin: Amsterdam, February 1766

Mozart composed these two sets of variations while visiting the Netherlands as part of his grand tour of 1763–66. The theme of K. 24 had just been composed by Christian Ernst Graaf, the kapellmeister at The Hague, for the celebrations marking the twenty-first birthday of Prince William V of Orange. The theme of K. 25, very noble and deliberate, is the old Netherlands national anthem which seems to have been printed as early as 1603. K. 25 was immediately engraved in The Hague, and is thus one of Mozart's first published works.

Both works are fairly primitive, although there is an attempt in K. 25 to give each variation an individual character, whereas in K. 24 the earlier variations are merely stages in a progress toward shorter and shorter note values. W.G.

K. 180 *6 Variations on "Mio caro Adone" in G major (K⁶ 173c)*
Origin: Vienna, autumn 1773

The theme of these variations is an air (My dear Adonis) from Salieri's opera *La fiera di Venezia,* first performed in 1772 and probably heard by Mozart during his visit to Vienna in 1773. The variations follow the Viennese practice of "transforming" the theme, rather than the Italian practice of embellishing it as a singer embellishes the outlines of an aria. They are remarkable for their wealth of expressive nuance. W.G.

K. 179 *12 Variations on a Minuet by Johann Christian Fischer in C major (K⁶ 189a)*
Origin: Salzburg, summer 1774

Mozart played these variations as a show piece, and often mentioned them in his letters. The theme comes from the last movement of an oboe concerto by Johann Christian Fischer (1733–1800), a famous oboist who settled in London and married the painter Thomas Gainsborough's daughter.

Mozart's twelve variations are worldly and in no sense profound, yet there is every sign that he wrote them with great interest. W.G.

K. 354 *12 Variations on "Je suis Lindor" in E-flat major (K⁶ 299a)*
Origin: Paris, early 1778

When Mozart went to Paris in 1788, he found the variation form to be very much *à la mode.* Mozart wrote two works in this form, choosing French melodies for his themes; indeed in the present instance he chose one of the most popular melodies of the day, the serenade sung by Count Almaviva in the first act of Beaumarchais's *Le barbier de Séville,* in which he declares quite untruthfully to Rosina: "Je suis Lindor, ma naissance est commune" (I am Lindor, born a commoner). The music was by composer Nicolas Dezède, as was the tune on which K. 264 is based (see below).

It would be difficult to name another piano work of Mozart's that has such richness of texture and such an extraordinary tenderness of expression. The work ends curiously, with a short cadenza marked "Caprice." W.G.

K. 264 *9 Variations on "Lison dormait" in C major (K[6] 315d)*
Origin: Paris, late summer 1778

The theme of these variations is also an air (Lison slept) by Nicolas Dezède, a remarkable composer born in Croatia in the 1740s and already at the height of his fame when Mozart visited Paris. Mozart evidently liked his music for he set another of his airs as K. 354 (see above). Those are the more poetical variations, these are the more brilliant and daring. K. 264 is also very daring in it harmonies; for C major is a key in which Mozart liked to confront us with the last word in modernism. W.G.

K. 352 *8 Variations on "Dieu d'amour" in F major (K[6] 374c)*
Origin: Vienna, June 1781

André-Ernest-Modeste Grétry wrote this march (God of Love) in E major, but Mozart raised it to F, the key of the March of the Priests in *Die Zauberflöte*. It makes a noble theme, whose most dramatic detail is an ascending scale toward the end. Mozart's treatment is serious throughout; even the final Allegro variation is cut off the moment it has run the course of the theme, and so the work has no concluding flourish. W.G.

K. 265 *12 Variations on "Ah vous dirai-je, Maman" in C major (K[6] 300e)*
Origin: Vienna, 1781 or 1782

These C-major Variations are so much like a series of exercises for mastering the various kinds of touch, and in playing scales, arpeggios, and ornaments, that Mozart must surely have written them for one of his pupils. Even so, this technical aspect is the least interesting; for, in listening to the music, we are aware far more of the delicate ordering of the variations and of their individual beauty. The theme was a popular French air entitled "Les amours de Silvandre" (Silvandre's loves). This tune is known to Americans as the children's song "Twinkle, twinkle little star." W.G.

K. 353 *12 Variations on "La belle Françoise" in E-flat major (K[6] 300f)*
Origin: Vienna, 1781 or 1782

These variations are among the finest of all those written by Mozart. Why "La belle Françoise" (the beautiful French woman)? In the 1930s Georges Saint-Foix came across a potpourri (by a certain Mme Kamermann) "sur le Départ, et la Mort de M. Malbrough. . . ." (on the departure and death of the Duke of Marlborough). Page 4 of this potpourri has the title: "Les Adieux de M. à Mme Malbrough" (the Duke's farewells to his wife); and there the illustrious English soldier says to his companion: "Adieu donc, Dame française" (Goodbye, then, my French lady)—to the same melody as the theme of K. 353. W.G.

K. 398 *6 Variations on "Salve tu, Domine" in F major (K[6] 416e)*
Origin: Vienna, March 1783

Mozart tells his father (March 29, 1783) that at his last concert he had improvised "variations on an air from [Giovanni Paisiello's] opera called *Die Philosophen [I Filosofi immaginarii]*, which were encored." These have come down to us as K. 398. They are extraordinarily free, and some of the patterns (Variations 2 and 6) still preserve the theatrical excitement of a great occasion. The theme is quite complex; it runs on without any repeats, and falls into two main sections, with a pause toward the end, which Mozart observes whenever he reaches it. The fact is, however, that after Variation 3 he never does reach it; indeed Variation 5 and 6 never even get as far as the second half of the theme. W.G.

K. 460 ***8 Variations on "Come un agnello" in A major (K^6 454a)***
Origin: Vienna, June 1784?

In the early summer of 1784 both Giovanni Paisiello and Giuseppe Sarti came to Vienna. Mozart wrote to his father about Sarti: "He is a good honest fellow! I have played a great deal to him and have composed variations on an air of his, which pleased him tremendously." The variations are on an air ("Like a lamb") from Sarti's opera *Fra i due litiganti.* The same air reappears in the second finale of *Don Giovanni,* as one of the popular hits of the day. Mozart's autograph manuscript contains only the tune and two variations; the authenticity of the other six variations; found in the first edition of 1803, are hotly debated among Mozart experts. W.G.

K. 455 ***10 Variations on "Unser dummer Pöbel meint" in G major***
Origin: Vienna, August 25, 1784

The theme of these variations is an air from Christoph Willibald Gluck's comic opera *La rencontre imprévue.* It is sung by the Calender Monk, who in his wisdom feasts on wine and delicatessen while the "stupid man in the street" ("Der dummer Pöbel") imagines him living on fruit and milk. Mozart reflects this buffoonery once or twice. Otherwise, however, he takes Gluck's air simply as the starting point for some of his finest variations. W.G.

K. 500 ***12 Variations on an Original Allegretto in B-flat major***
Origin: Vienna, October 12, 1786

This seems to be one of those works in which unusual elements meet and interact for a moment, leaving a flavor that is quite unique. Certain new techniques come from Muzio Clementi: the triplet figuration in Variations 1 and 2, for example; the bass pattern in Variation 4; and most striking of all, the successions of chords placed in a high register in Variation 8. It is not known who wrote the theme of K. 500—possibly Mozart himself. W.G.

K. 54 ***6 Variations on an Original Andante in F major (K^2 Anh 138a, K^6 547b)***
Origin: Vienna, July 1788

These variations appear both as the last movement of the Sonata in F for Piano and Violin, K. 547 ("for beginners"); and also, with a new Variation 4 and the coda to Variation 6 rewritten, as a keyboard piece. It is an indication of their quality that Variation 5 (in the minor) and Variation 6, with its brilliant flow of thirty-second notes, are reminiscent of the last two variations in the Andante of the great String Trio (Divertimento), K. 563. W.G.

K. 573 ***9 Variations on a Minuet by Jean-Pierre Duport in D major***
Origin: Potsdam, April 29, 1789

Duport was a famous cellist who worked for Frederick the Great at the Prussian court, which Mozart visited in 1789 seeking patronage. Duport's dull Minuet (a well-worn formula that Mozart himself had turned into poetry in "Deh vieni, non tardar" in *The Marriage of Figaro*) evidently did not incite Mozart to compose anything of great quality; only the keyboard style, one or two variations, and the coda suggest that K. 573 is a work of his last years. Mozart's autograph manuscript is lost. Since his catalogue of his own works and advertisements for manuscript copies in a Viennese newspaper in 1791 both refer to K. 573 as having only six variations, three of the variations may be spurious. W.G.

K. 613 ***8 Variations on "Ein Weib ist das herrlichste Ding" in F major***
Origin: Vienna, March 1791

Mozart wrote these variations on "A wife is the most splendid thing" in March 1791. The theme is a song from the second part of an operetta called *Der dumme Gärtner aus dem Gebirge* (The Dumb Gardener from the Highlands), by Benedikt Schack and Franz Xaver Gerl, which Emanuel Schikaneder (of *Magic Flute* fame) produced in Vienna with great success in 1789. The first eight measures of the theme remain, in a sense, separate from the rest. In no single instance does Mozart set the distinctive pattern of each new variation until the first eight measures are over. The explanation must be that these first eight measures are an instrumental introduction to the song, and Mozart evidently thought of them as such. W.G.

FANTASIAS, FUGUES, AND INDEPENDENT MOVEMENTS

Mozart improvising at the fortepiano. Engraving by Giovanni Antonio Sasso (Milan, c. 1815), allegedly after a lost painting by G. B. Bosio, c. 1785.

The persistent myth that Mozart composed only in his head is contradicted both by numerous surviving sketches and by two letters, one by his mother and one by himself, stating that he used a keyboard instrument while composing. He was famous for his skilled improvisations, of which the few written-down fantasies must preserve only a faint idea. The romanticizing tendencies of the present engraving suggest that it may be an early 19th-century forgery.

K^2 154a *Two Little Fugues (Versets) (K^3 Anh. 109^{VIII}, K^6 Anh. A61 and A62)*

Origin: Salzburg? c. 1772 to 1773
Scoring: organ?

These two fugues, of twelve and thirteen measures respectively, have the look of miniature exercises in seventeenth-century keyboard counterpoint, although they are well polished. Mozart wrote them on two sides of a single sheet. Each consists of an exposition in four voices and a concluding cadential passage.

The fugues are easily playable by two hands. Since in 1773 Mozart had not yet been appointed organist at Salzburg, the occasion for these works and the following Fugue, K. 401, is unclear. They may prove to be Mozart's copies of works by an earlier Salzburg composer. W.C.

K. 401 *Fugue in G minor (completed by Maximilian Stadler) (K^6 375e)*
Origin: Salzburg? 1772 or 1773?
Scoring: organ?

This lengthy fugue is in many ways a precursor of the great C-minor Fugue for Two Pianos, K. 426. The subject prominently features the interval of a diminished seventh (which reappears in both K. 426 and the Kyrie of the Requiem). It is developed exhaustively in inversion and stretto (closely overlapping entries of the theme), with much chromaticism and excursions into keys as distant as E minor. Like a few of J. S. Bach's early fugues, the final cadence is left uncomposed, to allow for an improvised conclusion. Stadler's completion proceeds directly to a pedal point and a final canonic statement of the subject.

Despite its notation in piano score, the piece is unplayable by two hands; it is usually performed on the organ or as a piano duet. W.C.

K. 395 *Capriccio in C major (K^3 284a, K^6 300g)*
Origin: Munich, October 1777
Scoring: piano

This extraordinary piece shows the influence both of J. S. and of C. P. E. Bach. J. S. Bach's influence is seen in the imitations of the first part and in certain figurative patterns in the Allegro assai (Prelude No. 2 of the *Well-Tempered Clavier*). C. P. E. Bach's influence is apparent in the sudden changes of mood, in the great use of diminished chords (measure 7, which lasts for a whole page, is more or less a fantasia on the diminished seventh), and above all, in the design (Allegretto—Andantino—Capriccio: Allegro assai) with the slow section in the middle. W.G.

K. 394 *Prelude and Fugue in C major (K^6 383a)*
Origin: Vienna, early 1782
Scoring: piano

It was in 1782 that Mozart was first introduced by Baron van Swieten to the works of Bach. Köchel's catalogue alone shows how profoundly Mozart was upset: fugue after fugue was begun and abandoned in 1782. Of the present one, he says in a letter to his sister of April 20 of that year that he composed it first and wrote it down while he was thinking out the Prelude. The subject of the Fugue recalls that of No. 1 of *The Well-Tempered Clavier.* W.G.

K. *396 *Fantasia in C minor (completed by Maxmilian Stadler) (K^6 385f)*
Origin: Vienna, early 1782
Scoring: piano

Mozart evidently intended this "fantasia" to be the first movement of a sonata for violin and pianoforte; but it suffered the same fate as twenty other works begun during 1782, and he never finished it. Indeed (so far as is known), he wrote only the exposition, and Abbé Stadler added the development and reprise, meanwhile turning the whole movement into a piece for pianoforte alone. W.G.

K. 397 *Fantasia in D minor (completed anonymously) (K^6 385g)*
Origin: Vienna, early 1782 (or 1786 to 1787?)
Scoring: piano

Mozart completed the first two sections of this fantasia, and part of a third. The central Adagio, to which the Andante and final D-major Allegretto are hardly more than introduction and coda, is a stirring piece of theater, and reminds us of an operatic *scena.* But behind this evocation of opera, with its changes of pulse and mood, its startling silences and its passionate outcries, there is a logic of construction as powerful as that of a "pure" instrumental movement. All but the final ten measures of the familiar completed version are by Mozart; the completion may be by Mozart's Leipzig admirer, August Eberhard Müller.

W.G.

K. 399 ***Suite in C major (incomplete) (K⁶ 385i)***
Origin: Vienna, early 1782
Scoring: piano

Though this is a charming imitation of a suite in early eighteenth-century style, it runs counter to the practices of Bach and Handel in two respects. First, it is quite "irregular" that the Allemande should follow the Overture without a break; and secondly, instead of every movement being in the same key, the Overture is in C major, the Allemande in C minor, the Courante in E-flat major, and the unfinished Sarabande in G minor. W.G.

K³ 453a ***Marche funèbre del Sigr Maestro Contrapuncto in C minor***
Origin: Vienna, 1784
Scoring: piano

Mozart wrote two of his piano concertos, K. 449 and K. 453, for his pupil Babette von Ployer; K. 453a is his contribution of sixteen measures of music to this young woman's autograph album, possibly in the same year as the concertos, 1784. Mozart's own title, *Funeral March By Maestro Counterpoint,* prepares us for anything, including a hair-raising progression with consecutive fifths in measure 5.

W.G.

K. 475 ***Fantasia in C minor***
Origin: Vienna, May 20, 1785
Scoring: piano

This fantasia is so complete in itself that it is difficult to think of it as a "prelude," although Mozart published it together with the C-minor Sonata, K. 457, that he had written in the previous year. It contains five sections: Adagio, Allegro, Andantino, Più Allegro, and Tempo I, in the last of which the opening Adagio returns in a relentless form to round off the whole piece. W.G.

K. 485 ***Rondo in D major***
Origin: Vienna, January 10, 1786
Scoring: piano

If you listen to this as a "rondo," you will find that, instead of the principal theme appearing always in the tonic (as for example in the rondo of the piano sonata, K. 309), it enters in any key it fancies: D, A, G, D minor, F, B flat. You will even find that there is no "principal" theme, for the simple reason that there are no episodes, no other themes at all. This Rondo is in fact a sonata movement based on a single theme, with repeat marks at the end of the exposition, a clearly defined "development," and a reprise which conducts itself with almost careless abandon. The theme of K. 485 had already appeared in the Finale of the G-minor Piano Quartet, K. 478. W.G.

K. 494 ***Rondo in F major***
Origin: Vienna, June 10, 1786
Scoring: piano

Mozart wrote this rondo in June 1786, but he published it in 1788 as the third movement of a sonata beginning with the Allegro and Andante of the piano sonata, K. 533. In the original version of

1786 the moment of dramatic culmination was the final appearance of the principal theme deep in the bass. But in preparing the rondo for publication with K. 533, Mozart inserted an exciting "cadenza" of 27 measures. W.G.

K. 511 ***Rondo in A minor***
Origin: Vienna, March 11, 1787
Scoring: piano

This rondo is a work of such harmonic daring that it prophesies aspects of Schubert and of Chopin. It unfolds on a very large scale, yet without any theatrical oppositions of rhythm or texture or outline. The principal theme and the two episodes in F and A each have a different underlying movement: eighth notes, sixteenths, triplet sixteenths. Above all, the A-minor Rondo stands close to the G-minor Quintet, K. 516, both in date of composition and in depth of meaning. W.G.

K. 540 ***Adagio in B minor***
Origin: Vienna, March 19, 1788
Scoring: piano

The design of this extraordinary Adagio is that of a movement in sonata form, but in expression it is much more like a fantasia, with many abrupt changes of dynamics, many silences (the music breaks off twenty times in three pages), and an intense quality in the outlines and harmonies. W.G.

K. 355 ***Minuet in D major (with a Trio by Maximilian Stadler) (K³ 594a, K⁶ 576b)***
Origin: Vienna, 1786 to 1787?
Scoring: piano

"K. 355" is misleading, for the D-major Minuet is of course a late work of Mozart's, as one can tell by its chromaticism, its audacious harmonies, and the extraordinary contrasts it is able to express within a single page. It stands alone, without a Trio, though Abbé Stadler added a rather remarkable one in B minor. W.G.

K. 574 ***Gigue in G major, "Eine kleine Gigue"***
Origin: Leipzig, May 16, 1789
Scoring: piano

This gigue is a masterpiece of one page into which Mozart has crowded many daring thoughts. He wrote it on May 16, 1789, for the family album of an organist in Leipzig, and evidently as a tribute to Bach. Yet it reminds us very little of Bach, except that it is a gigue in contrapuntal style; nor is it the most Mozartian piece you have ever heard. Indeed it seems to stand quite alone; a phenomenon with daring outlines, twisting rhythms, and audacious harmonies. W.G.

K. 594 ***Adagio and Allegro in F minor, "For the Organ-Works of a Clock"***
Origin: Vienna and elsewhere, October to December 1790
Scoring: mechanical organ

This work, along with two contemporaneous works for mechanical organs, K. 608 and 616, is said to have been commissioned by Count Josef Deym von Stritetz, proprietor of the Müller Wax Museum and Art Gallery in Vienna, in which were exhibited some dozens of mechanical curiosities. While in Frankfurt for the coronation of Emperor Leopold II in October 1790, Mozart wrote to Constanze:

> So I firmly resolved to write the adagio for the clock-maker then to put a few ducats in my dear little wife's hands; I have been at it, too—but it is loathsome work, I have been so unhappy that I cannot complete it—I work

on it every day—but must always lay it aside for a time because it bores me—and, of course, if it was not being done for such an important reason, I would surely abandon it entirely—so I still hope to finish it bit by bit;—well, if it were a big clock and the thing sounded like an organ, it would be nice; but instead the organ has only little pipes that sound too childish to me.

The "clock-maker" may refer to Father Primitivus Niemecz, who built organ-clocks to Haydn's music, and was custodian of the mechanical devices in the Müller Gallery. Whether the music Mozart refers to is one of the extant works is unclear, since Mozart's personal catalogue dates the earliest of them in December. If anything, it is more likely K. 616, with its range of tenor f to high f''', than to K. 594 or 608, with ranges of tenor c to high d''', or high c♯''', respectively.

Despite Mozart's ill prejudice, the three compositions are all miniature masterpieces. K. 594 is in three connected sections, fast-slow-fast. The central Allegro in F major is a sonata-form piece of heroic dimensions; it is flanked by two gravely somber Adagios in F minor, the second of which develops and resolves the material of the first.

These works have entered the public consciousness mainly in arrangements for organ and piano four-hands. Only K. 616 is known to have been actually pinned on a barrel for use in a mechanical organ.

W.C.

K. 608 ***Fantasia in F minor, "An Organ Piece for a Clock"***

Origin: Vienna, March 3, 1791
Scoring: mechanical organ

This is the second of the three works commissioned for the Müller Gallery, and is in many ways the twin of K. 594, with contrasting aspects reversed: its three sections are Allegro in F minor, Andante in A-flat major, and Allegro in F minor. The second Allegro again develops the material of the first, but this time in a fugato of considerable proportion and masterful counterpoint. It is only a step or two from this piece—especially in its four-hand version—to Franz Schubert's monumental Fantasia in F minor for piano duet.

W.C.

K. 616 ***Andante in F major, "For the Barrel of a Little Organ"***

Origin: Vienna, May 4, 1791
Scoring: mechanical organ

This is the last of Mozart's three pieces for mechanical organ. It is a rondo in **A-B-A-C-A-B-A** form of considerable proportion and elaborate filigree. While Mozart notated the previous two works on four staves (clefs: three treble, one bass) like string quartet music, he notated this piece on three staves (all treble clefs); he nonetheless retained a four-voiced texture, which gives the work a diamondlike depth in its concentrated aural space. The wealth of ornamentation and passage-work must have come off splendidly on a mechanical organ, and it would have borne the amount of repeated listening the piece must have had in the Müller Gallery.

W.C.

K. 356 ***Adagio in C major (K^6 617a)***

Origin: Vienna, 1791
Scoring: glass harmonica

Mozart presumably composed this piece for Marianne Kirchgessner, the glass harmonica virtuoso for whom he also wrote the Quintet, K. 617, at about the same time. It is a binary movement of twenty-eight measures, a memorably simple and lovely creation that breathes the aura of the ethereal, like much of the *Magic Flute* music that occupied Mozart at the time.

W.C.

EARLY SKETCHBOOKS

LIEDERSAMMLUNG

FÜR

KINDER UND KINDERFREUNDE

AM CLAVIER

FRUHLINGSLIEDER.

WIEN,

GEDRUCKT BEY IGNAZ ALBERTI, K. K. PRIV. BUCHDRUCKER. MDCCXCI.

Title page of the *Collection of Songs for Children and Their Friends at the Keyboard. Spring Songs*. Engraved by Klemens Kohl, after Johann Christian Sambach (Vienna, 1791).

This collection, published in the last year of Mozart's life, contained three of his songs, K. 596 ("Longing for Spring"), 597 ("In Early Spring"), and 598 ("Children's Games").

K. 1a–f, 2, 3, 4, 5, 5a–b *12 Pieces, "Nannerl's Music Book"*
Origin: early 1761 to summer 1763
Scoring: keyboard

The library of the Internationale Stiftung Mozarteum in Salzburg has, since 1864, owned a celebrated manuscript volume usually known as "Nannerl's Notebook." This is the music book that Leopold Mozart prepared for the use of his daughter, Maria Anna (Nannerl, born in July 1751). A label on the cover of the Notebook, inscribed by Leopold, proclaims: "Pour le / *Clavecin* / ce Livre appartient á Mademoiselle / Marie Anne / Mozartin / 1759." But what has conferred especial fame on the modest volume is the fact that soon after it came into existence, it was used by Nannerl's younger brother, Wolfgang. He not only studied and learned several of the pieces written in the book, some of them before his fifth birthday, but when a little later he began to compose, he entered his earliest compositions there in his childish hand. Leopold also entered compositions by Wolfgang, and the dates that certain pieces had been learned or composed were added by the fond father.

Thus the Notebook is at once a record of part of the music that the two Mozart children studied and assimilated and a repository of Wolfgang's earliest essays in composition. Unfortunately the book is not as complete as it once was, particularly in respect to Wolfgang's compositions. Nannerl (in whose possession the book remained until her death in 1829) is known to have given away several leaves containing pieces by her brother; and although the present location of some of these leaves is known, it is clear that others have been lost.

The Notebook originally had forty-eight leaves, or ninety-six pages; of the forty-eight leaves, only thirty-six remain. Seven additional leaves that almost certainly were removed from the Notebook survive: one each in the Museum Carolino Augusteum, Salzburg, the Universitätsbibliothek, Leipzig, and a private collection; and two leaves each in the Morgan Library, New York, and the Bibliothèque nationale, Paris. Another leaf formerly in the Mozarteum in Salzburg but now lost is preserved musically if not physically by a facsimile published in 1871. By studying the watermarks and other physical characteristics of the paper as well as the musical contents of these isolated leaves, it is possible to reconstruct where they must originally have been in the Notebook.

Thus eight of our twelve missing leaves are accounted for. And the contents of one or two others may be rescued as well, as they were published in the biography of Mozart which his widow Constanze and her second husband Georg Nikolaus Nissen published in 1828.

The surviving pieces by the infant Wolfgang presently or previously in the Notebook, with their dates of composition when known, comprise the following:

K. 1a: an Andante in C major of ten measures, bizarrely shifting between 3/4 and 2/4;
K. 1b: an Allegro in C major of twelve measures with alternating hands;
K. 1c: an Allegro in F major of twelve measures in the style of a contredanse (December 11, 1761);
K. 1d: a Minuet in F major of twenty measures (December 16, 1761);
K. 1 (1e): a Minuet in G major of sixteen measures, one of the best known of these pieces, often played by children nowadays;
K. 1 (1f): a Minuet in C major of sixteen measures, probably meant as the Trio of the previous work;
K. 2: a Minuet in F major of twenty-four

measures, also a favorite with children (January 1762);
K. 3: an Allegro in B-flat major of thirty measures, another contredanse (March 4, 1762);
K. 4: a Minuet in F major of twenty-four measures (May 11, 1762);
K. 5: a Minuet in F major of twenty-two measures (July 5, 1762);
K. 5a (9a): an Allegro in C major of forty-four measures, a tiny sonata movement;
K. 5b (9b): an Andante in B-flat major of forty-three measures, incomplete but possibly also intended as a sonata movement; and six pieces that were later reworked as movements of the violin sonatas, Opuses 1 and 2 (K. 6–9). A.T.

K[6] 15a–ss *44 Untitled Pieces, "London (Chelsea) Notebook," (K[3] Anh 109b)*

Origin: London, second half of 1764
Scoring: keyboard, or possibly also sketches for orchestra

"There is a sort of national disease here which is called a 'cold' . . . for people who are not very strong the best advice is to leave England." But if you have visited London to make your fortune by presenting your two infant phenomena to royalty, the nobility, and the gentry, you content yourself with moving to the pleasant village of Chelsea. Leopold Mozart, who wrote the rather baleful advice above in September 1764, made a complete recovery there. His eight-year-old son Wolfgang spent the seven weeks in Chelsea filling a notebook with music. After the family's return to London, he gave some concerts, composed his first symphony, dedicated a set of sonatas to the Queen, and left England forever in the following year.

The notebook, bearing the words "di Wolfgango Mozart à Londra" in the hand of Leopold, turned up again toward the end of the nineteenth century. The forty-three pieces, entirely in Wolfgang's hand, were published by Georg Schünemann in 1909. All but three of the sketches are complete, though full of blobs and small mistakes; they are unimpressive on the modern piano, but present an entirely normal texture for mid-eighteenth-century harpsichord music. Some pieces even have indications of repeated notes in the manner of a short score, and a few contain intervals not playable on the keyboard, suggesting that the little boy obviously heard this music in his mind as orchestral music.

In later years Mozart's normal practice in composing was to begin by writing out the melodic line and the bass with a few indications of accompanying figures, working at great speed in order to seize his inspiration. Later, he filled in all the other parts, a more leisurely activity. Some of these pieces are surely sketches of this kind, rather than complete keyboard works. The writing is largely in two parts with occasional chords; there is only one indication of tempo and none of dynamics. In modern times some of these sketches have been orchestrated and performed. E.S.

Appendix A

A BRIEF INTRODUCTION TO THE KÖCHEL CATALOGUE

Sir Ludwig von Köchel's *Chronological-Thematic Catalogue of the Complete Works of Wolfgang Amadé Mozart* was published in 1862 (K^1). In it were listed all of Mozart's works known to Köchel in what he understood to be their chronological order, from number 1 (infant harpsichord piece) to 626 (the Requiem). The second edition of the Catalogue, prepared by Count Paul von Waldersee in 1905, involved for the most part minor additions, corrections, and clarifications, many of them collected by Köchel himself before his death (K^2). The first thoroughgoing revision was the third edition, completed by Alfred Einstein in 1936 (K^3). Einstein adjusted the position of many works in Köchel's chronology, threw out as spurious some works Köchel had taken to be genuine, and added as authentic some works Köchel had believed spurious or not known about. He also inserted into the chronological scheme a considerable number of fragmentary and lost works, which Köchel had placed in an appendix *(Anhang)* without chronological order. Although many of Mozart's works were thus redated, Köchel's original numbers could not be dropped or reassigned, for they formed the basis for innumerable editions, concert programs, library catalogues, and reference works. Einstein therefore extended a method already established by Waldersee in K^2 for a handful of works: he inserted new numbers between old ones by adding lower-case letters. Thus, for instance, Köchel had given the date 1780 to the Six Variations in B-flat major on "Hélas, j'ai perdu mon amant" for violin and piano and assigned it the listing 360. Einstein suspected that this work was more likely to have originated in June 1781 and assigned it the new listing K. 374b, as one of a group of seven works that he inserted between K. 374 and K. 375. Now the work bears both numbers.

The third edition of the Köchel Catalogue was reprinted with an extensive supplement of corrections and additions in 1946 and is usually identified as K^{3a}. So-called fourth and fifth editions were nothing more than unchanged reprints of the 1936 edition, without the 1946 supplement. The sixth and current edition, which appeared in 1964 edited by Franz Giegling, Alexander Weinmann, and Gerd Sievers (K^6), continued Einstein's innovations by adding even more numbers with lower-case letters appended, and a few with upper-case letters as well (for instance, the Symphony in G minor, K. 183 = 173dB), when a work had to be inserted into the chronology between two of Einstein's lower-case insertions. So-called seventh and eighth editions are merely unchanged reprints at the sixth. This history of the various revisions of the Köchel Catalogue explains why many of Mozart's works bear two "K" numbers and a few three, such as the Symphony in B-flat major, K. 182 = 166c = 173dA.

In *The Compleat Mozart* Köchel listings are given, when these exist, from K^1 and from K^6. The majority of listings in K^6 have been taken over unchanged from K^3, but where changes have been made, the K^3 listing has also been added.

The chronological arrangement of Mozart's works in the Köchel Catalogue has had both beneficial and unfortunate effects on our understanding of the composer's life and works. The availability of such a detailed chronology, lacking for many other composers, has encouraged careful study of Mozart's day-to-day activities and of his month-by-month artistic development. But these seemingly concrete dates have all too often proven unreliable, as can be seen by the number of works that have been renumbered in subsequent editions of the Köchel Catalogue. Writers, taken in by the Catalogue's firm dates, have often made bold statements based upon flimsy evidence. Indeed, the very nature of the Köchel Catalogue engenders speculative behavior on the part of otherwise cautious scholars, for as the Catalogue is chronological, a work cannot be entered into it without attempting to date that work, whether or not adequate grounds for such dating exist.

One amusing advantage of Köchel's chronological scheme was certainly not anticipated by him. Because the rate at which Mozart added to his oeuvre was, despite fluctuations, remarkably constant over the long haul, Mozart's age at the time of composition of a work may be calculated with some degree of accuracy from the "K" number. (This works, however, only for numbers over one hundred.) This is accomplished by dividing the "K" number by 25 and adding 10. If one then keeps in mind that Mozart was born at the beginning of 1756, the year of a work's composition may also readily be approximated. Take a straightforward example: the Requiem on which Mozart was working when he died is K. 626. That number divided by 25 gives 25, plus ten makes 35, so Mozart was 35 when he composed the Requiem. Thirty-five added to the year 1756 gives us 1791, the year of both the Requiem and Mozart's premature death. N.Z.

Appendix B

SELECTED BIBLIOGRAPHY

The literature on Mozart is vast, amounting to tens of thousands of books, articles, reviews, and program notes in dozens of languages. The only other composers who have inspired anything like this outpouring of verbiage are Bach, Beethoven, and Wagner.

The list that follows has been selected for its usefulness to non-specialists and to fulfill two functions: the first is to identify the classics of Mozart scholarship, the books to which writers on Mozart constantly refer. In this way readers of *The Compleat Mozart* will know what is meant when the authors of our essays refer to the opinions of Abert, Deutsch, Einstein, Jahn, Köchel, Nissen, or Wyzewa and Saint-Foix, and can pursue their works further if they wish.

The second function is to provide the titles of several recent, non-technical, general books about Mozart in English that are, in the opinion of the undersigned, interesting, worthwhile, innovative, or important. By listing them I do not necessarily endorse everything in them. Rather, I hope to provide the reader with quick access to some of the latest thinking in Mozart research.

The cutting edge of research in this field, as in many others, is not primarily found in books, but in articles in specialist journals. The most important of these periodicals can be identified by referring to the extensive classified bibliography appended to the Mozart article in *The New Grove Dictionary of Music and Musicians,* edited by Stanley Sadie (London: Macmillan, 1980), which is also separately available, updated, in paperback as *The New Grove Mozart* (see below under Sadie). N.Z.

Abert

Hermann Abert, *W. A. Mozart. Neu bearbeitete und erweiterte Ausgabe von Otto Jahns "Mozart"* (Leipzig: Breitkopf & Härtel, 1919; third edition 1955; index volume by Erich Kapst, 1966)

Angermüller

Rudolf Angermüller, *Mozart's Operas* (New York: Rizzoli, 1988)

Braunbehrens

Volkmar Braunbehrens, *Mozart in Vienna, 1781–1791,* trans. by Timothy Bell (New York: Grove Weidenfeld, 1990)

Deutsch

Otto Erich Deutsch, *Mozart: A Documentary Biography,* 2nd ed., trans. by E. Blom, P. Branscombe and J. Noble (London: A. & C. Black, 1966; Stanford: Stanford University Press, 1966)

——— *Mozart and His World in Contemporary Pictures* (Kassel: Bärenreiter, 1961)

Einstein

Alfred Einstein, *Mozart: His Character, His Work* (New York: Oxford University Press, 1945, repr. 1965)

Eisen

Cliff Eisen, *New Mozart Documents: A Supplement to O. E. Deutsch's Documentary Biography* (London: Macmillan Press, 1991)

Jahn
Otto Jahn, *W. A. Mozart* (Leipzig: Breitkopf & Härtel, 1856); trans. by Pauline D. Townsend as *The Life of Mozart* (London: Novello, 1882–91, repr. Totowa, N.J.: Cooper Square, 1970)

Köchel Catalogue (K⁶)
Ludwig von Köchel, *Chronologisch-thematisches Verzeichnis sämtlicher Tonwerke Wolfgang Amadé Mozarts nebst Angabe der verlorengegangenen, angefangenen, von fremder Hand bearbeiteten, zweifelhaften und unterschobenen Kompositionen,* 6th ed. by F. Giegling, A. Weinmann and G. Sievers (Wiesbaden: Breitkopf & Härtel, 1964) (earlier editions indicated as K^1, K^2, etc.)

Landon
H. C. Robbins Landon, *1791: Mozart's Last Year* (New York: Schirmer Books, 1988)
——— *Mozart: The Golden Years* (New York, Schirmer Books, 1989)

Marshall
Robert L. Marshall, *Mozart Speaks: Views on Music, Musicians, and the World* (New York: Schirmer Books, 1991)

Mozart's Letters
Emily Anderson, *The Letters of Mozart and His Family, Chronologically Arranged, Translated and Edited with an Introduction, Notes and Indices,* 3rd ed. (New York: W. W. Norton, 1989)

Mozart's Complete Works
Wolfgang Amadeus Mozarts Werke: Kritisch durchgesehene Gesamtausgabe (Leipzig: Breitkopf & Härtel, 1877–1910, repr. Ann Arbor: Edwards Brothers, 1947) (*GA,* the old complete works)
Wolfgang Amadeus Mozart: Neue Ausgabe sämtlicher Werke (Kassel: Bärenreiter, 1955–) (*NMA,* the new complete works)

Nissen
Georg Nikolaus Nissen, *Biographie W. A. Mozarts. Nach Originalbriefen, Sammlungen alles über ihn Geschrieben, mit vielen neuen Beilagen, Steindrucken, Musikblättern und einem Faksimile,* edited by Mozart's widow, Constanze Weber Mozart Nissen (Leipzig: Breitkopf & Härtel, 1828; reprinted Hildesheim: Olms, 1964)

Sadie
Stanley Sadie, *The New Grove Mozart* (New York: W. W. Norton, 1983)

Stafford
William Stafford, *The Mozart Myths: A Critical Reassessment* (Stanford: Stanford University Press, 1991)

Wyzewa and Saint-Foix
Théodore de Wyzewa and Georges de Saint-Foix, *W.-A. Mozart: sa vie musicale et son oeuvre. Essai de biographie critique* (Paris: Desclée de Brouwer, 1912–1946; second edition 1977, reprinted with a new preface by Jan LaRue and Floyd Grave, New York: Da Capo Press, 1980)

Tyson
Alan Tyson, *Mozart: Studies of the Autograph Scores* (Cambridge: Harvard University Press, 1987)

Wolff
Christoph Wolff, *Mozart's Requiem* (Berkeley and Los Angeles: University of California Press, 1991)

Zaslaw
Neal Zaslaw, *Mozart's Symphonies: Context, Performance Practice, Reception* (Oxford: Clarendon Press, 1989)
——— (ed.), *The Classical Era from the 1740s to the End of the 18th Century* (Englewood Cliffs: Prentice-Hall, 1989)

Appendix C

BIOGRAPHIES OF THE CONTRIBUTORS

Rudolf Angermüller (R.A.), German musicologist, is professor of musicology at Salzburg University and is the academic librarian of the Internationale Stiftung Mozarteum in the same city. He is an editor of the *Neue Mozart-Ausgabe* and the author of many works about Mozart and his music.

Alfred Beaujean (A.B.), music critic in Aachen, studied sacred music as well as piano. A contributor to the West German and Bavarian Radio Broadcasting Companies, the *Frankfurter Allgemeine Zeitung,* and numerous other music and recording publications, he has published articles in Konold's *Dictionary of Orchestra Music,* among others, and has served, since 1962, on the jury of the German recording award, the Deutsche Schallplattenpreis.

Dietrich Berke (D.B.), German musicologist, serves on the editorial boards of the *Neue Mozart-Ausgabe* and the *Neue Schubert-Ausgabe* and is Director of Publications for the music publisher Bärenreiter-Verlag.

Joseph Braunstein (J.B.), Ph.D. from the University of Vienna, 1923, was a member of orchestras led by Bruno Walter, Otto Klemperer, Wilhelm Furtwängler, and Richard Strauss under whom he played *Salome, Elektra, Die Rosenkavalier, and Die Frau ohne Schatten.* He came to the U.S. in 1940 where he taught at the Mannes College of Music, the Manhattan School of Music, and The Juilliard School in New York, where he currently resides.

William Cowdery (W.C.), Assistant Professor of Music at Ithaca College, is a musicologist and keyboard player whose doctoral dissertation was on J. S. Bach's early cantatas.

Charles Cudworth (C.C.), (1908–77), curator of the Pendlebury Library at Cambridge University Music School, prepared editions of many eighteenth-century works for performance and was a prolific writer of music criticism and annotations for recordings. Mr. Cudworth was awarded an honorary doctorate by the Open University in recognition of his work on their music courses.

Sibylle Dahms (S.D.), musicologist and dance scholar, wrote her Ph.D. thesis for the University of Salzburg on Baroque theater and opera in Salzburg. Since 1978 she has been curator of the Derra de Moroda Dance Archives at the Institute for Musicology at Salzburg University. She has recently collaborated on opera productions with the Berlin Comic Opera and the Vienna State Opera.

Graham Dixon (G.D.), is a senior producer responsible for early music in the Music Department of BBC Radio 3. He has published extensively on sacred music in 17th-century Rome, applying his liturgical knowledge to problems of context in the music of other periods and places as well. He is the author of a monograph on Carissimi.

Cori Ellison (C.E.), Music Editor of *Stagebill* and Adjunct Assistant Professor of Music at New York University, is a contributor to *The New Grove Dictionary of Opera* and *Opera News.* She has served as Music Advisor for WNET's Great Performances series and is annotator for vocal programs at Lincoln Center's Mostly Mozart Festival and Great Performers series.

Karl Gustav Fellerer (K.G.F.) (1902–84), German musicologist, was until 1970 Professor of Music at the University of Cologne. The founder and editor of several musicological journals, publication series and anthologies, he is especially noted for his contribution to our knowledge of the history of music in the Catholic church.

Marius Flothuis (M.F.), Dutch composer, musicologist, and noted authority on Mozart's music was for many years artistic director of the Concertgebouw Orchestra before assuming a professorship in musicology at Utrecht University. He is a member of the Editorial Board of the *Neue Mozart-Ausgabe*.

Sir William Glock (W.G.) was for several years chief music critic for *The Observer* and later director of the Summer School of Music at Bryanston before its move to Dartington Hall. Later music critic for the *New Statesman* and Controller of Music for the BBC, he has served more recently as general editor of the Eulenberg music books published by Schott and Artistic Director of the Bath Festival.

Harry Halbreich (H.H.), Belgian musicologist and critic, has published in half-a-dozen European languages and teaches musical analysis at the Royal Conservatory in Mons.

David Hamilton (D.H.), music journalist and critic with a vast knowledge of recorded music, has for many years been music critic for *The Nation*. In addition, he is the New York music correspondent for the *Financial Times* and was a contributing editor of *High Fidelity*.

Roger Hellyer (R.H.), English bassoonist and musicologist, is an expert on European wind band music of the 18th and 19th centuries.

Wulf Konold (W.K.), German musicologist, taught musicology at the University of Kiel, was Program Director for Radio Saarland and Chief Dramaturgist for the Nuremberg Music Theater. Presently he teaches at the Hochschule für Musik und Theater in Hannover.

Uwe Kraemer (U.K.), German musicologist, lives in Hamburg where he teaches and is active as a critic and music consultant to recording companies, broadcast media, and music journals.

Alan M. Kriegsman (A.M.K.), taught musicology at Columbia University for five years. He was a music and performing arts critic on the San Diego *Union* and the Washington *Post* until his appointment as the *Post*'s dance critic in 1974. He has lectured at The Juilliard School and Harvard and Temple Universities, among others. In 1976 he was awarded the Pulitzer Prize in Criticism.

H. C. Robbins Landon (H.C.R.L.), founder of the Haydn Society, was later Special Correspondent of *The Times* writing primarily from Eastern Europe. Author of books on Haydn, Mozart and other eigthteenth-century composers, he produced many editions of the Viennese classics including the first edition of all of Haydn's symphonies and has shared in the editing of the *Neue Mozart-Ausgabe*.

Robert D. Levin (R.D.L.), American pianist and theorist teaches at the University of Freiburg. He has published completions of several Mozart fragments and cadenzas for the violin concertos as well as a noted reconstruction of the Symphonie Concertante in E-flat major for Four Winds and Orchestra, K. 297B, which has been widely performed and is the subject of a monograph published by Pendragon Press.

William S. Mann (W.S.M.), (1924–89) was for years on the music staff of the London *Times* becoming chief music critic in 1960. He was a prolific author of program and liner notes, record criticism and book reviews. In addition he broadcast regularly on musical topics. His book *The Operas of Mozart* (Oxford) appeared in 1977.

Hans-Christian Müller (H.-C.M.), studied musicology at the Universities of Berlin and Kiel. After working on the editorial staffs of the music series *Das Erbe deutscher Musik* (The German Musical Heritage) in Hamburg and of the music publisher B. Schott's Sons in Mainz, he has, since 1974, served as scholar-librarian of the Municipal and Provincial Library, Dortmund.

Wolfgang Plath (W.P.), German musicologist, was appointed in 1960 co-editor of the *Neue Mozart-Ausgabe*. His work with Mozart autographs has greatly influenced our knowledge of the chronology and authenticity of Mozart's oeuvre.

Christopher Porterfield (C.P.), is the Senior Editor in charge of the culture sections of *Time Magazine*. Formerly a music critic for *Time* and a cultural correspondent based in London, he has provided program notes for Time-Life Records and written on music for *Smithsonian Magazine* and the PBS television series "Live From Lincoln Center," among others.

Andrew Raeburn (A.R.), former Executive Director of the Van Cliburn Foundation, was born in London. Involved with music since the age of four, he has been head of Argo and New World

Records, musical administrator of the Boston and Detroit Symphony Orchestras, a writer, teacher, and radio and television commentator. Currently a consultant, he resides in Texas.

Christopher Raeburn (C.R.) has worked extensively on the first productions of Mozart operas as well as contributing over 200 hitherto unpublished documents to *Mozart: A Documentary Biography* by Otto Erich Deutsch. He has written articles for numerous periodicals including the *Mozart-Jahrbuch* and *Musical Times*. Since 1958 he has been a producer with Decca Record Company, London.

Stanley Sadie (S.S.) edited *The New Grove Dictionary of Music and Musicians* (1980) to which he contributed many articles. Formerly editor of *The Musical Times* and for many years critic for the London *Times*, he is currently preparing an extended television series on music in society which will be accompanied by an eight-volume history.

Ernst Fritz Schmid (E.F.S.) (1904–60), German musicologist, founder of the Mozartgemeinde and the German Mozartgesellschaft was, in 1954, appointed academic director of the *Neue Mozart-Ausgabe* where he worked on source materials, clarifying many details, and organized the Augsburg archives on which he had worked extensively before the Second World War.

Erik Smith (E.S.), son of conductor Hans Schmidt-Isserstedt, was brought up in England where he now lives. As recording producer for Decca London and later Philips, where he became head of A&R, he produced, among many others, the first modern recordings of *La clemenza di Tito* and *La finta giardiniera* as well as the first complete sets of Mozart's wind music, dances, and serenades.

Denis Stevens (D.S.), BBC producer for 6 years, formed and conducted the Ambrosian Singers and the Accademia Monteverdiana. Appointed to two Distinguished Professorships, he taught widely, from 1955 to 1975, in England and America where he now resides. A publisher of many editions of early music, his most recent book is *The Letters of Claudio Monteverdi* (1980).

Charles Suttoni (C.S.), a one-time advertising executive, is a free-lance writer and scholar with a Ph.D. in musicology. He has, over the years, written for *Musical America* and provided historical and program notes for Time-Life Records. His most recent publication is an annotated translation of Franz Liszt's *An Artist's Journey: Lettres d'un bachelier ès musique 1835–1841* (1989).

Alan Tyson (A.T.), British musicologist, is a senior research fellow at All Souls College, Oxford. He has worked extensively on questions of authenticity, music publishing and printing, dating, watermarks, and copying of the period 1770–1850. His seminal studies of Mozart's manuscripts have now been published in book form.

Neal Zaslaw (N.Z.), Professor of Music at Cornell University and member of the graduate faculty at The Juilliard School, is musicological adviser to The Mozart Bicentennial at Lincoln Center. He has worked extensively on music of the seventeenth and eighteenth centuries, in particular on questions of performance practice. His book *Mozart's Symphonies: Context, Performance Practice, Reception* appeared in 1989.

General Index

Index of Mozart's Works by Köchel Number

Page numbers in boldface type indicate the main entry for a particular work.

Listings K. *deest* and from Appendixes (Anh numbers) in the Köchel Catalogue

Identification List of Works by Name or Nickname

Abduction from the Seraglio, The. *See* K. 384
"Ah, lo previdi." *See* K. 272
"Alcandro lo confesso." *See* K. 294
"Andretter" Serenade. *See* K. 185
Apollo et Hyacinthus. *See* K. 38
Ascanio in Alba. *See* K. 111
"Auernhammer" Sonatas. *See* K. 296, 376–80
"Ave verum corpus." *See* K. 618

"bacio di mano, Un." *See* K. 541
Bassoon Concerto. *See* K. 191
Bastien und Bastienne. *See* K. 50
"Beginners, For." *See* K. 545, 547
Betulia liberata, La. *See* K. 118

"Cantata on Christ's Grave." *See* K. 42
"Ch'io mi scordi de te?" *See* K. 505
Clarinet Concerto. *See* K. 622
Clarinet Quintet. *See* K. 581
clemenza di Tito, La. *See* K. 621
"Coronation" Concertos. *See* K. 459, 537
"Coronation" Mass. *See* K. 317
Così fan tutte. *See* K. 588
"Credo" Mass. *See* K. 257

Davidde penitente. *See* K. 469
"Dissonance" Quartet. *See* K. 465
"Dominicus" Mass. *See* K. 66
Don Giovanni. *See* K. 527
"Dürnitz" Sonata. *See* K. 284

Entführung aus dem Serail, Die. *See* K. 384
"Exsultate, jubilate." *See* K. 165

finta giardiniera, La. *See* K. 196
finta semplice, La. *See* K. 51
Flute and Harp Concerto. *See* K. 299
Flute Concertos. *See* K. 313, 314
Flute Quartets. *See* K. 285, 285a, 285b, 298

Glass Harmonica Quintet. *See* K. 617
G-minor Quintet. *See* K. 516
G-minor Symphonies. *See* K. 183, 550

"Haffner" Serenade. *See* K. 250
"Haffner" Symphony. *See* K. 385
"Haydn" Quartets. *See* K. 387, 421, 428, 458, 464, 465
"Hoffmeister" Quartet. *See* K. 499
"Holy Trinity" Mass. *See* K. 167
Horn Concertos. *See* K. 412, 417, 447, 495
"Hunt" Quartet. *See* K. 458

Idomeneo. *See* K. 366
Impresario, The. *See* K. 486
Im Frühlingsanfang. *See* K. 597

"Jeunehomme" Concerto. *See* K. 271
"Jupiter" Symphony. *See* K. 551

"Kegelstatt" Trio. *See* K. 498
kleine Nachtmusik, Eine. *See* K. 525
Kyrie. *See* K. 33, 89, 341

"Lambach" Symphony. *See* K. 45a
"Linz" Piano Sonata. *See* K. 333
"Linz" Symphony. *See* K. 425
"Lodron" Concerto. *See* K. 242
"Lodron" Divertimentos. *See* K. 247, 287
"London Notebook." *See* K. 15a–ss
Lucio Silla. *See* K. 135

Magic Flute, The. *See* K. 620
Marriage of Figaro, The. *See* K. 492
Masonic Funeral Music. *See* K. 477
Mass in C minor. *See* K. 427
Mitridate. *See* K. 87
"moto di gioia, Un." *See* K. 579
Musical Joke, A. *See* K. 522

"Nannerl's Notebook." *See* K. 1a–f, 2–5, 5a–b
"Night Music" Serenade. *See* K. 388
Notturni. *See* K. 346, 436–439
nozze di Figaro, Le. *See* K. 492

Oboe Concertos. *See* K. 271k, 314
Oboe Quartet. *See* K. 370
oca del Cairo, L' *See* K. 422